Jewish Polity and American Civil Society

Jewish Polity and American Civil Society

Communal Agencies and Religious Movements in the American Public Sphere

EDITED BY ALAN MITTLEMAN, JONATHAN D. SARNA, AND ROBERT LICHT

ROWMAN & LITTLEFIELD PUBLISHERS, INC.
Lanham • Boulder • New York • Oxford

ROWMAN & LITTLEFIELD PUBLISHERS, INC.

Published in the United States of America
by Rowman & Littlefield Publishers, Inc.
A Member of the Rowman & Littlefield Publishing Group
4720 Boston Way, Lanham, Maryland 20706
www.rowmanlittlefield.com

12 Hid's Copse Road
Cumnor Hill, Oxford OX2 9JJ, England

Copyright © 2002 by Rowman & Littlefield Publishers, Inc.

All rights reserved. No part of this publication may be reproduced, stored in a retrieval system, or transmitted in any form or by any means, electronic, mechanical, photocopying, recording, or otherwise, without the prior permission of the publisher.

British Library Cataloguing in Publication Information Available

Library of Congress Cataloging-in-Publication Data

Jewish polity and American civil society : communal agencies and
  religious movements in the American public sphere / edited by Alan
  Mittleman, Robert Licht, and Jonathan D. Sarna.
    p. cm.
  Includes bibliographical references and index.
    ISBN 0-7425-2121-4 (alk. paper) — 0-7425-2122-2 (pbk. : alk. paper)
  1. Jews—United States—Politics and government—20th century. 2. Jews—
  United States—Societies, etc. 3. Judaism and politics—United
  States. I. Mittleman, Alan. II. Licht, Robert A. III. Sarna, Jonathan D.

E184.36.P64 J44 2002
305.892'4073—dc21   2002003364

Printed in the United States of America

∞™ The paper used in this publication meets the minimum requirements of American National Standard for Information Sciences—Permanence of Paper for Printed Library Materials, ANSI/NISO Z39.48-1992.

Managing Editor: Mark Ami-El
Typesetting: Ami-El Applications

*This volume is dedicated to the memory of
Professor Daniel J. Elazar,
founding president of the
Center for Jewish Community Studies
and the Jerusalem Center for Public Affairs,
scholar, and friend.
This project began under his inspiration and guidance.
May his memory be a blessing.*

Jews and the American Public Square is a three-year project of communal dialogue, research, and publication devoted to exploring the relationship between the faith and culture of American Jews and their civic engagement. Initiated by a major grant from the Pew Charitable Trusts, the project seeks to foster greater understanding among both Jews and non-Jews of the role of religion in American public life.

Also available:

Jews and the American Public Square: Debating Religion and Republic, edited by Alan Mittleman, Jonathan D. Sarna, and Robert Licht (2002).

Contents

Preface – *Alan Mittleman* ... ix

Acknowledgments ... xvii

Introduction – The Jewish Political Tradition and the English-Speaking World
Daniel J. Elazar ... 1

I. Communal Agencies

1. "Defenders": National Jewish Community Relations Agencies
   Steven Windmueller ... 13

2. Local Community Relations Councils and Their National Body
   Michael C. Kotzin ... 67

3. History of Israel Advocacy
   Martin J. Raffel ... 103

4. The Jewish Social Welfare Lobby in the United States
   Joel M. Carp ... 181

II. Religious Movements

5   The Conservative Movement and the
    Public Square   235
    Gordon M. Freeman

6   Reform Judaism, Minority Rights, and
    the Separation of Church and State   261
    Lance J. Sussman

7   Mainstream Orthodoxy and the American
    Public Square   283
    Lawrence Grossman

8   Haredim and the Public Square:
    The Nature of the Social Contract   311
    Samuel C. Heilman

9   Reconstructionism and the Public Square:
    A Multicultural Approach to Judaism in America   337
    David A. Teutsch

10 Jewish Renewal   363
    Allan Arkush

Afterword – *Alan Mittleman*   389

Index   391

About the Contributors   419

Preface

Alan Mittleman

Recent American social and political thought has been much concerned with civil society. Civil society is the hard-to-define realm situated between the government and the marketplace. It straddles the public and the private. It is a sphere of associations, of voluntary groups and of primordial connections without which neither democratic life nor personal life can flourish.[1] As concern over the state of American democracy has grown, many theorists look to civil society as a source of democratic renewal. Two centuries ago Alexis de Tocqueville found that a rich network of voluntary associations animated American civil society. He thought that the American tradition of voluntary association could offset the powerful centrifugal forces of unrestrained individualism, a lurking danger for the American experiment. Communal associations could channel self-interest to serve public purposes. Ever since Tocqueville, the health of associational life and the vitality of democracy have been paired.

At the dawn of the new century, there are important reasons to worry about the health of American associational life. The debate has been focused by Harvard scholar Robert Putnam, whose controversial article (and subsequent book), *Bowling Alone*, charts a precipitous decline in membership of many of the organizations that organized civil society in the twentieth century. Groups such as the PTA, service clubs such as the Lions, Elks, Kiwanis, and Masons, bowling leagues and sport clubs, religious fraternal organizations such as Knights of Columbus, and women's groups such as the League of Women Voters have lost their centrality in civic life.

Baby boomers and their children no longer look to these kind of groups, whose membership peaked in the postwar period and began to decline in the 1960s, as places to meet neighbors, serve communities, advance socially, and find satisfaction. Putnam fears a loss of "social capital," of the accrued advantages of helping networks and helpful people that flow from the culture of voluntary associations.[2]

Other observers, such as Robert Wuthnow and Nancy Ammerman, are somewhat less pessimistic. Although agreeing with Putnam that the organizations of the early and mid-twentieth century are withering, Wuthnow believes that Americans continue to join groups. The nature of these groups has changed, however. With less time for leisure, more demanding jobs, two-career households, and more loosely defined social institutions (consider how porous and untraditional the American family, for example, has become), Americans tend to join groups that ask for relatively little but seem to provide something clear and direct. Rather than work up the ladder of a comprehensive fraternal service club, someone might volunteer an hour a month at a literacy center. While a woman in the 1950s might have gathered over coffee with neighbors to share life's cares and joys, a contemporary might join a support group. Wuthnow is not entirely convinced that the new culture of associations provides the bounty of social capital that was available in the older culture, but he does not see an apocalypse of civil society on the horizon.[3]

Similarly, Nancy Ammerman observes that although some traditional religious denominations and their congregations have lost strength, other religious groups have adapted and gained. Religious communities remain robust, providing the added leverage of "moral and spiritual capital" to the social capital of other voluntary organizations.[4]

Thus all observers agree that religious groups remain an important, if not the most important, repository of social capital.[5] Religious congregations are more than places to worship: They are the most vital voluntary associations in American civil society. In addition to worship, educational, and cultural activities, religious groups are often on the front lines of social service provision in the cities. President George W. Bush's establishment of the White House Office on Faith-Based and Community Initiatives recognized this fact. The Bush White House sought to enhance the role of religious groups in civil society by removing obstacles to government funding for the welfare services that they provide. While other traditional voluntary associations have declined, religious groups continue to thrive. For some communities, such as African Americans and white Evangelicals, religious congregations are robust and central features of communal life.[6]

Religious congregations remain important for American Jews. Although Jews affiliate less with religiously based groups than do other Americans, more Jews join synagogues than other types of communal institutions. Indeed, a recent survey shows that American Jews feel increasingly remote from non-synagogue institutions.[7] The extent and quality of Jewish voluntarism is an object of increasing communal concern. Observers such as Steven Cohen and Arnold Eisen note that American Jews, like their non-Jewish neighbors, are turning to an ever more subjective, self-oriented understanding of religion. The "sovereign self," searching for spiritual meaning, rather than the ethnically identified, communally committed self is fast becoming the dominant Jewish type. This turn toward the private, the subjective, and the personal on the part of Jews mirrors the larger trend away from intensive commitment to voluntary associations and toward "loose connections." It may bode ill for the maintenance of the American Jewish communal infrastructure, let alone for international Jewish solidarity, concern for Israel, and so on.

The increasing "disconnect" between American Jews and their non-synagogue organizations may be an inadvertent by-product of the organizational realm itself. Ever since the 1990 National Jewish Population Study yielded the arresting (albeit disputed) figure of a 52 percent rate of intermarriage, the community has been thrown into profound concern about its own survival. Jewish priorities began to shift from aid to Israel and distressed or threatened Jewries abroad to "continuity" programming at home. The decade of the 1990s witnessed a new emphasis on Jewish education, culture, and religiosity. American Jews showed remarkable creativity in confronting the long developing and largely ignored "continuity crisis." Modeling the pattern observed by Wuthnow, Jews innovated new organizational structures to meet new social challenges. Older organizations also struggled to adapt to a shifting communal agenda. The new priority of enriching the religious and cultural content of Jewish identity has rendered problematic the older communal orientation toward rescue, defense, and "sacred survival." Nonetheless, for the foreseeable future both communal organizations and religious denominations will continue to be major actors on the Jewish public stage.

How to describe this organizational realm of which religious groups are parts but by no means the whole? The late Daniel J. Elazar described American Jewry as a *polity*. By polity Elazar implies that concepts such as voluntary association, religious congregation, or even community are inadequate to capture the quasi-governmental, public nature of Jewish institutions.[8] Although, since the end of the European Middle Ages Jews can no longer be said to constitute a "state within a state," a condition that was at any rate never true in the United States, their institutional infrastructure does have quasi-governmental features. A highly ramified federation of educational, philanthropic, cultural, social service, and frankly political entities complements the religious sector. The typical Jewish community has a volunteer-governed, professionally managed federation of Jewish agencies that raise charitable funds, sponsor welfare and cultural services, represent Jewish interests to local and state governments, relate to other agencies and groups in the civil society, and coordinate local Jewish public affairs. These local agencies coordinate in highly organized networks with national federations of agencies. National bodies, sometimes with local chapters, also relate Jewish interests to government and work with other ethnoreligious, public policy, educational, or civil rights groups in civil society. The Jewish public realm represents a nonsovereign, nonterritorial political system. Its essential features are not captured through the lens of religion and religious community alone, nor does voluntary association—if the primary meaning of that term conjures up the image of a club—entirely do the job. For this reason, Elazar preferred the term *polity*. The focus of this volume then is on how the Jewish polity functions in the midst of civil society, relating to both other mediating groups and to government as such.

Two types of organizational actors come together in this study: communal agencies and religious denominations. Together these groups articulate a functional American Jewish polity.[9] The pairing of communal organizations and religious movements in one study makes sense. For more than other "religious" groups in American civil society, Jewish group life is irreducibly complex. The sacred and the secular are inextricable from one another. This division of labor is not necessarily a product of modern secularization. Indeed, the historic pattern of Jewish communal life was divided into a relatively rational sphere of public governance and a relatively traditional sphere of religious obligation.[10] The thorough intermingling of sacred and secular is the classic Jewish way. In his introduction, Daniel Elazar situates the Jewish political tradition within the context of the Jewish experience in the English-speaking countries.

In Part One, the first four chapters consider the civil engagement of the communal agencies. The first chapter analyzes the twentieth-century history and recent activity of the national Jewish "defense" organizations, the American Jewish Committee, the American Jewish Congress, and the Anti-Defamation League. Steven Windmueller both narrates the institutional histories of these bodies and evaluates their relative successes and failures, as well as the current challenges that they face in the era of declining organizational membership and interest. The second chapter looks at the community relations activities of the local Jewish federations as embodied in so-called community relations councils. These agencies function as secretariats of state, relating both to other local actors in civil society and to municipal and state governments. Michael Kotzin also considers the problems of the national body, the Jewish Council for Public Affairs, which services these councils. His essay tells a cautionary tale about institutional growth, aspiration, and risk.

One of the major points at which the Jewish polity interacts with the federal government is in advocacy for foreign aid and political support for the State of Israel. This is also one of the most visible areas of American Jewish activity in the public sphere. Yet it is not only a matter of political lobbying per se; the organizations that are involved in this activity—as Martin Raffel relates—are also concerned with winning broad sympathy for Israel in the hearts and minds of Americans. Israel advocacy therefore relates both to government and to civil society. It is a high-stakes game that continually tests Jewish political acumen and competence.

The final chapter in this section explores the role of the Jewish communal sphere as a provider of welfare services. Here, as elsewhere, state and local Jewish agencies relate both to governments, as providers of funds and as licensing authorities, and to other nongovernmental service providers in civil society. As Joel Carp describes, the entire Jewish social welfare apparatus is pervasively "entangled" with government at all levels. Without public funds amounting to over $3 billion per year (if support for hospitals is included), the system could not function. In the coming era of "Charitable Choice," the significance of this mutual entanglement between the Jewish polity and American government and civil society will have to be pondered anew.

In Part Two, we consider how the more religious entities on the Jewish public map articulate their civic interests. Chapters 5 through 10 look at, for want of better terms, Jewish "denominations" or "movements." The term *denomination* is problematic insofar as it has emerged from the American Protestant religious culture. While it may well capture the self-understanding of Methodists or Presbyterians, it cannot do justice to Orthodox Jews, who see themselves as more than just another articulation of Jewish religiosity in a religiously pluralistic society. "Denomination" may convey, however, the premises of those religious groupings that have most adapted to the Protestant pattern, such as Reform or even Conservatism. "Movement," a borrowing from politics, is probably too assertive to describe the character of these groups today, although Jewish Renewal might be an exception. An alternative to both terms might be the term used for nascent religious pluralism in Israel, "stream." At any rate, for the sake of familiarity we will retain the terms *denomination* and *movement* to tag these institutional actors.

Chapters 5 through 7, as well as 9, study well-known, "mainline" religious movements. The focus in each chapter is historical. How have the core beliefs and moral orientations of members shaped their approaches to public policy? How do members conceive the responsibilities of American citizenship, of "citizenship" in the Jewish polity, and of the relationship between the two? What institutional structures have these movements created to assert themselves in the public sphere? Each of the writers is a rabbi, either ordained in or institutionally affiliated with the movement he describes. The perspective in each case is that of the critical insider.

Chapter 8 looks at a group that deviates most dramatically from the American denominational model, the ultra- or "fervently" Orthodox Jews or, as they are known in current Hebrew, the *haredim*. Unlike the Amish with which they are often, erroneously, compared, the *haredim* actively engage in political life, albeit to safeguard their segregation from civil society. While other Jewish religious groups pride themselves on their mainstream conceptions of good citizenship and Americanness, the *haredim*, though no less civically engaged, have an entirely different construction of American identity. The author, anthropologist Samuel Heilman, is a participant-observer and ethnographer of *haredi* life in Israel and the United States.

Finally, chapter 10 considers an emerging Jewish religious movement, so-called Jewish Renewal. The Renewal movement is postdenominational and institutionally porous, as is its ostensible inspiration, American new age spirituality. It has not yet articulated a comprehensive institutional structure, although the process of institution-building has begun. Allan Arkush explores the leading personalities, practitioners, and texts. It is an open question as to whether the Renewal movement, with its emphasis on subjective religious experience, will assert much of a presence in the public square or whether its very being represents a withdrawal from communal and other public concerns. However, insofar as some of the leaders of the movement were 1960s radical activists, leftist politics is no stranger to renewal spirituality. The equilibrium between subjective religiosity and public involvement has not yet been settled.

Collectively, the articles in this volume constitute a modest encyclopedic reference work on the civic and political engagement of American Jews as mediated by their institutions. If our time turns out to be one in which the voluntary associations of civil society play an increasing role in the conduct of our common life, then the stories told here may multiply in the future. If, however, ours is an age, as some fear, of civic decline then the trends of the last chapter may have the last word. Let us hope that the owl of Minerva has not yet taken flight.

Notes

1. The definition of civil society, as well as the evaluation of its significance, typically depends on a writer's normative assumptions and agenda. For a comprehensive view of the definitional problem, see Don Eberly, ed., *The Essential Civil Society Reader* (Lanham, Md.: Rowman & Littlefield, 2000), 5-8. Writers on civil society sometimes neglect the personal dimension of associational life. For an important corrective to an exclusively political perspective, see Nancy Rosenblum, *Membership and Morals: The Personal Uses of Pluralism in America* (Princeton, N.J.: Princeton University Press, 1998).

2. Robert D. Putnam, *Bowling Alone: The Collapse and Revival of American Community* (New York: Simon & Schuster, 2000), 19.

3. Robert Wuthnow, *Loose Connections: Joining Together in America's Fragmented Communities* (Cambridge, Mass.: Harvard University Press, 1998).

4. Nancy Ammerman, "Bowling Together: Congregations and the American Civic Order," Seventeenth Annual University Lecture in Religion (Tempe: Department of Religious Studies, Arizona State University, 1996), 4.

5. So Putnam: "Faith communities in which people worship together are arguably the single most important repository of social capital in America." *Bowling Alone* (New York: Simon & Schuster, 2000), 66. Americans' robust faith in the ability of churches to solve social problems and create social bonds is fully in evidence in a survey of 1,507 adults conducted in November 2000 by Public Agenda. Steve Farkas et al., *For Goodness' Sake: Why So Many Want Religion to Play a Greater Role in American Life* (New York: Public Agenda, 2001).

6. On the unique role of the black church, see Michael Corbett and Julia Corbett, *Politics and Religion in the United States* (New York: Garland Publishing, 1999), 298ff.; and Ammerman, "Bowling Together," 6.

7. Approximately 48 percent of American Jews are members of synagogues. Jewish community centers draw the next largest membership, a mere 14 percent of the Jewish community. These figures are drawn from Steven M. Cohen and Arnold Eisen, *The Jew Within: Self, Family, and Community in America* (Bloomington: Indiana University Press, 2000), 152-53.

8. Daniel J. Elazar, *Community and Polity: The Organizational Dynamics of American Jewry* (Philadelphia, Pa.: Jewish Publication Society, 1995), 5-8.

9. In Elazar's scheme, the Jewish polity has five different spheres of activity: religious-congregational, educational-cultural, community relations, communal-welfare, and Israel-overseas. For the sake of simplicity, this volume reduces these spheres of activity into two: religious movements and not explicitly religious organizations. The latter comprises, for the purpose of this study, everything except the educational-cultural sphere, which is not treated here. For the typology of spheres, see Elazar, *Community and Polity,* chap. 9.

10. Alan Mittleman, *The Politics of Torah* (Albany: State University of New York Press, 1996), 51-54.

Acknowledgments

The editors wish to thank Mark Ami-El, publications coordinator of the Jerusalem Center for Public Affairs, for his assistance in preparing the manuscript for publication. We would also like to acknowledge Sam Stein, project coordinator of the Jews and the American Public Square project, as the photographer for the cover art. The image was taken from a stained glass window at Temple Emanuel in Virginia Beach, Virginia. We gratefully acknowledge the synagogue's cooperation. This project was made possible by the Pew Charitable Trusts of Philadelphia to whom we are grateful for their substantial support. We are particularly grateful to Dr. Luis Lugo, director of Pew's religion program, for his guidance. The views expressed here are those of the authors and do not necessarily reflect the views of the Pew Charitable Trusts.

Introduction

The Jewish Political Tradition and the English-Speaking World

Daniel J. Elazar

Judaism is not simply a religion, nor is being Jewish simply being a member of an ethnic group. Rather, Judaism is a theopolitical phenomenon in which both religious and political dimensions are of enormous, even equal, importance. Not surprisingly, then, the Bible contains within it the fundamental elements of a Jewish political tradition that also speaks to Jewish religious expectations. That political tradition has, of course, developed and changed over the years, but its biblical foundations remain clearly recognizable. Not only that, but because Jews lived in their own land or in the diaspora in autonomous communities more often than not, they were able to structure much of their political life on the basis of the Jewish political tradition. This reality continued until the opening of the modern epoch in the seventeenth century when Jewish communities in Europe began to lose their autonomy because of changes in overall European society that eliminated autonomous groups within the newly emerging nation-states on that continent and in the New World, where the modern temper reigned from the first. In the course of the next 300 years the Jewish political tradition was rendered subordinate to the political traditions of the Jews' countries of residence.[1]

It is not unfair to say that in no time and place in Jewish history has there been more conflict between the Jewish political tradition and those of the countries in which Jews find themselves, than in the case of the English-speaking world from the seventeenth century to the present. This statement is based upon several factors:

1. The general acceptance of the Jews in the English-speaking countries, ranging from gradual acceptance in the United Kingdom to the situation in the United States where, in many parts of the country, Jews were among the first settlers and have both an attachment and a pedigree that gives them a place in American history as founders.

2. The pragmatic approach of the English-speaking world to issues of religious and ethnic difference led to a new and different reality for Jews, even in the United Kingdom with its established churches. Redefining and expanding this pragmatic approach was not always achieved easily, but sooner or later it always was achieved.

3. The basic openness of the civil societies in the English-speaking countries made the kinds of social and political rigidities known on the European continent or the rigidities of caste found in Asia basically unknown in the English-speaking world, as far as Jews were concerned.

Despite the foregoing generalizations, it is true that the openness of English-speaking societies to Jews has undergone considerable development since Oliver Cromwell found that he could quietly allow the Jews of England to organize for purposes of worship but could not publicly declare his intentions and secure appropriate legal status for that development, to the present when Jews in the United States are, for the most part, no longer considered a minority but part of the white European majority.

The Jewish political tradition, with which the Jews entered the modern world, was based on the assumption that diaspora Jewry was in exile and that its desired condition was one in which the Jewish community was sufficiently separate to have autonomy to live according to its own laws and to be able to enforce those laws. Here we will describe the classic dimensions of the Jewish political tradition as they were adapted in the premodern diaspora. In fact, after the mid-seventeenth century, this tradition had to be abandoned or adapted.

When the first Jews reached England in sufficient numbers to organize a community in the mid-seventeenth century, they were pleased to find that they would not be subject to the kind of structured restrictions that they had known elsewhere in Europe. Indeed, because so many of them had returned to Judaism after being *conversos* for generations, they were already prepared to live in their larger host civilization but wished to do so within their own community structure. Since they were clearly foreigners in England, that was not an outlandish expectation. The first Jewish communities in England attempted to adapt the classical tradition of the *kehillah* to this new situation. In the new situation membership was not exactly voluntary, but anybody who wanted to leave was required to drop his Judaism.[2]

However, it soon became apparent that in the more or less open societies of the English-speaking world, the Jewish communities did not have the power to compel maintenance of certain behaviors that had been the norm in the premodern *kehillah*. The *askamot* or constitutions of the seventeenth- and eighteenth-century Jewish communities in England, and even more so in British North America, are littered with provisions that turned out to be unenforceable, ranging from Sabbath observance to maintaining *kashrut*, to issues of intermarriage, and whether or not Jewish prostitutes can be accepted into the community.

By the mid-eighteenth century it had become clear that membership in the community was essentially a voluntary matter and, since voluntary, the acceptance of communal strictures was equally a matter of member choice. Still, the nascent Jewish communities in the English-speaking countries were congregational communities whereby every city with sufficient Jews had its own congregational community to which Jews in adjacent, smaller places also belonged, thus preserving a semblance of communal unity even under these voluntary conditions.

By the end of the eighteenth century or the early nineteenth century, even this measure of unity was ended. As Jews arrived from other parts of Europe, bringing their own rituals and customs with them and seeking to follow familiar paths, they established second and sometimes third or fourth congregations in the same city. The early congregations all followed the Sephardic or, more accurately, the Spanish and Portuguese rite. The new congregations followed the German, Polish, and Hungarian customs. They soon formed the majority of the local Jewish population in locality after locality. In Great Britain, some measure of Jewish unity was achieved despite multiple congregations through the Board of Deputies of British Jews, established by an Act of Parliament in 1760 to allow the Jews to develop a single representative voice in Britain. At the other extreme was the United States, where such efforts were considered unavailing since no official body could establish an official religious representative for any sect.

The Jewish situation corresponded to the general situation in Protestant countries, subject to whatever variations existed in those countries. Thus in the United Kingdom, since there was an established Anglican Church, Parliament could establish a specific representative body for the Jews. This implicitly recognized that the Jews were almost full-fledged members of British society. (To be completely full-fledged required giving Jews the right to vote and then sit in Parliament, a battle which would be fought in the nineteenth century.) In the new United States, on the other hand, the idea was that for the health of the many different churches and sects, it was important to prevent any government interference with them, so matters such as government recognition were not possible. It took the Jews at least 100 years to come to understand the full implications of this for their community.

The last major effort to establish enforceable rules came with the establishment of the abortive New York City *kehillah* in 1909. That *kehillah*, following a 2,000-year-old Jewish tradition, attempted to raise revenues by a tax on all kosher meat sold. However, in the United States not only was kosher meat sold privately, it was sold by private individuals who had no reason to accept communal discipline. Accordingly, suits were brought against the *kehillah* under the New York State Anti-Trust Act. Senior New York State officials politely informed the Jewish leadership that those suits undoubtedly would win in court and the *kehillah* would not only be stripped of its power but also severely embarrassed. The *kehillah* dropped the effort and fell into a downward spiral that led it to go out of business within the decade.

The Jews were left with a serious problem. Much of the Jewish leadership wanted to find some organizing framework that would hold the Jewish population together and enable it to provide services for its members and representation for outside the community. By the mid-nineteenth century, efforts were being made to find a way to do just that within the constraints of the American system. In fact, however, none of them worked as expected until the invention of the local Jewish federation by Boston Jewry in 1895. The federation movement was launched on the road to success precisely by disclaiming any desire to be the comprehensive communal institution in its community. Instead it claimed to be no more than a more efficient instrument for raising and distributing money for Jewish philanthropies.[3]

Although the structures of the Jewish political tradition could not be transplanted to the United States, Jewish political culture persisted. Hence, from the very first there were active efforts on the part of Jews to "take care of their own" by raising philanthropic funds for those in need. At the same time, Jews became active participants in the society, promoting liberty, equality, a social safety net, and the recognition of minorities as legitimate. In the days of the single congregational community, dues were collected in an organized manner. When that broke down, charitable appeals became widespread and diffuse. In the Civil War period efforts were made to establish organizations often named United Jewish Charities, which attempted to unify fund-raising efforts in a number of Jewish communities. All of these were later folded into the federations, in some cases keeping their identities for certain philanthropic purposes. However, the continued and growing mass immigration of Jews to the United States led to the establishment of many other charities as well, and so the process had to be repeated.

Federations, many originally called Federations of Jewish Charities and later, in the 1920s, Jewish Welfare Federations, succeeded not only because their idea was modest and sensible but also because they came in as part of the Progressive movement to introduce efficiency and economy in voluntary activity so as to deal seriously with social problems on a voluntary basis and thus eliminate the necessity for greater government intervention. By World War I, virtually every major Jewish community in the United States had a federation of this nature.

Representative organizations evolved parallel to philanthropic ones, albeit with much less unity as time went on, unlike the situation with regard to the federations.[4] The first organized effort to set up a representative body was the establishment of the Board of Deputies of American Israelites in 1859. For various reasons, the Board never became the representative body that it was intended to be. Some years later it was merged into the Union of American Hebrew Congregations where it still technically exists to this day. In the late nineteenth century B'nai B'rith began to assume these representative functions because in a period of growing anti-Semitism no one else did. As such, it reached its peak in the 1890s and in 1912 established the Anti-Defamation League as a semi-autonomous organization to undertake the fight against anti-Semitism. Today the ADL is fully autonomous and has established itself as a major public fighter against anti-Semitism in the Jewish community. Even before that, in 1906, the notables who informally led the American Jewish community came together to establish the American Jewish Committee to give some formal structure to their work. Their choice of a very modest name was designed to belie the fact that these were the most powerful Jews in the United States. For several decades the American Jewish Committee continued to play a key role in the representation of the Jews even though in 1917 the American Jewish Congress, representing the Jews of Eastern Europe, as opposed to the very German and Central European orientation of the Committee, was established as a competitor. In addition, several smaller and more specialized organizations were formed, such as the Jewish Labor Committee to represent the Jews in the labor movement or the Jewish War Veterans who represent the Jews among the veterans groups. Thus, the field of Jewish representation in the United States became rather untidy and several efforts have been made to try to tidy it up.

From the 1950s onward, the emergence of the Jewish Community Relations Councils attached to the federations established a core that, with federation backing, could not easily be ignored. These JCRCs, with the Jewish Council for Public Affairs and the federations, play the largest role in Jewish representation today, although they draw the least publicity.

In the other English-speaking countries, an early priority was the representation of the Jewish community before the non-Jewish governments. These Jewries put their efforts into organized Boards of Deputies or, in the case of Canada, the Canadian Jewish Congress. Over the course of time, however, the American model became the most interesting and successful and began to influence the others as well. With the rise of Hitler in the 1930s and the troubles that fell upon first German and then all of European Jewry, American Jewry organized the United Jewish Appeal to unify overseas relief funding. Some federations assumed responsibility for UJA fund-raising in their communities from the outset. Indeed, many of the smaller cities that did not have federations organized them for this purpose. In some of the largest cities, however, where there was still a gulf between the older ways of German and Central European Jews and the newer ways of Eastern European Jews, the federations did not accept that responsibility and separate Jewish welfare funds had to be organized. It was only in the 1950s and 1960s that the last of these were merged with the federations so that today no community has more than one federation to serve its purposes.

In the 1950s and 1960s, the federations also came to realize that part of the efficient deployment of funds involved community planning and determination of communal needs. So the federations took that task upon themselves. By the late 1960s, in effect they had become the framing institutions of local Jewish communities in the United States with their national body, the Council of Jewish Federations, as it was then known, playing a similar role on a countrywide basis. All of this remained purely voluntary, but, from the first, the community leadership had sought out the wealthiest and most prestigious people in the community to be contributors and active participants in the work of the federation. It soon became the socially acceptable thing to do to contribute to it and its work. Furthermore, the fund-raisers worked out various techniques for fund-raising that publicly pushed people to give more than they might otherwise have given, so that while remaining voluntary, contributions to the federation, at least for the upper-income members of the community, became in effect a necessary tax that had to be paid in order to remain in the good graces of one's fellows.

The Six-Day War and the federations' response to it gave their members a sense that what they were doing was not simply philanthropy but participating in the grand sweep of Jewish history. This led to the development of a new interest in achieving greater self-understanding. Early in the 1970s, efforts were made by a number of academics who were also involved in federation activities to redefine the federation's work in terms of the historic Jewish political tradition. These were readily absorbed and served to redefine the self-perception of federation leadership, especially the professional leadership who were more academically inclined. Thus matters came full circle. While the old-time *kehillah* could not be replicated in the United States, a new voluntary *kehillah* could be developed that drew upon the sources of the Jewish political tradition to shape its own work.

But history does not have an end. In the 1980s a new sense of American Jewish dissatisfaction with Israel and its peace policies, coupled with the new privatization sweeping the United States and the increasing desire of big givers to have "hands-on" contact with their beneficiaries rather than allow an impersonal organization to make such decisions, led to the beginning of the unraveling of the progressive solution. Moreover, by the mid-1990s the great tasks upon which the federations had been built—the Jewish revolt against the horrible situation in the Old World, the reconstruction of the Jewish national home, the relief of Jews in distress everywhere and their rehabilitation in new and safer places of residence—were seen as virtually concluded. This struck another blow at the federations, making their mission less clear to donors who were already looking elsewhere. Curiously enough, while all this was happening, the federations were strengthening their representational role in American Jewish life, building offices in Washington and in their state capitals to work for Jewish interests, usually in coalition with other religious and ethnic communities. While these became very significant, they remained low profile, apparently having little selling power to contributors.

Today the Jewish federations are trying to redefine themselves and especially their countrywide institutions. Consideration of such matters as the Jewish political tradition is less prominent than it was twenty-five years ago, but the fact of the matter is that the federations continue to follow the adaptations of those models as they have done for so many years, and indeed have extended them by extending their representational role in Jewish life.

Meanwhile, the other institutions of the American Jewish community were mostly built on American rather than traditional Jewish models to serve American needs. Congregations remain the exceptions. If one looks carefully at congregational structures, one sees all of the elements of the Jewish political tradition still in place, albeit with different weightings from congregation to congregation, as was always the case. When those structures were designed, the congregations *were* the communities and had communal as well as congregational roles. Today that is no longer the case in the United States or in most of the world. Congregations have formally become strictly religious institutions, and, while informally they play a major social role in Jewish life, they play almost no political role. This means that to some extent, maybe even to a great extent, the manifestations of the Jewish political tradition in the congregations have become vestigial, concerned mostly with the inner governance of the congregation in a circumscribed sphere rather than the governance of a community. That, of course, makes a great deal of sense on the American scene where church polity is important essentially in the circumscribed governance of the church rather than in a larger sphere.

In the last analysis, however, to look closely at Jewish institutions is to discover that American and other English-speaking Jews have been able to adapt to much of the classical Jewish political tradition without even realizing it. Combined with what they have adopted from the political traditions of their countries of citizenship, they have developed their own traditions of voluntary governance. This is particularly interesting in the United States because of the influence of the biblical political tradition on American structures and styles of governance, which often have served as an indirect way to bring American Jewry around to their own political tradition.[5]

Notes

[*] This manuscript was left slightly incomplete at the time of Daniel Elazar's death in 1999. Some explanatory endnotes and slight editing have been provided by Alan Mittleman.

1. Professor Elazar's basic statement on the existence and nature of the Jewish political tradition may be found in Daniel J. Elazar, ed., *Kinship and Consent: The Jewish Political Tradition and Its Contemporary Uses* (New Brunswick, N.J.: Transaction Publishers, 1997). The biblical foundations to which he refers are basically three: 1) Covenant as the basis of the Jewish political tradition; 2) a separation of power into three spheres of authority which, in the biblical setting, is represented by king, priest, and prophet; and 3) a stress on the justice of relationships rather than, as in the Greek tradition, the constitution of regimes. Elazar's basic claim is that these elements persisted across the Jewish experience of self-government, despite the loss of sovereignty in Roman times, until the threshold of the modern era.

2. A concise overview of the modern history of Jews in Britain and the process of their emancipation can be found in Geoffrey Alderman, "English Jews or Jews of the English Persuasion?" in Pierre Birnbaum and Ira Katznelson, eds., *Paths of Emancipation: Jews, States, and Citizenship* (Princeton, N.J.: Princeton University Press, 1995), 128-56.

3. For a history and contemporary appraisal of the federation movement, see Daniel J. Elazar, ed., *The Federation Movement at 100*, a special issue of *Jewish Political Studies Review*, vol. 7, nos. 3 and 4 (Jerusalem: Jerusalem Center for Public Affairs, 1995).

4. Elazar sees American Jewish organizational life divided into five spheres. They are: the religious-congregational sphere; the educational-cultural sphere; the community relations sphere; the communal-welfare sphere; and the Israel-overseas sphere. In this division of functions and authority something of the old, biblical tripartite diffusion of power persists. By "representative organizations" he means "community relations" in his standard typology. See Daniel J. Elazar, *Community and Polity: The Organizational Dynamics of American Jewry* (Philadelphia, Pa.: Jewish Publication Society, 1995), especially chap. 9.

5. For the impact of the biblical and Jewish political tradition on the institutions and political culture of the United States, see Daniel J. Elazar, *Covenant and Constitutionalism: The Great Frontier and the Matrix of Federal Democracy* (New Brunswick, N.J.: Transaction Publishers, 1998).

Part I

Communal Agencies

1

"Defenders": National Jewish Community Relations Agencies

Steven Windmueller

> Its work may be considered experimental. It has proved that the misconception in the general mind about the Jew may be corrected. An undertaking of this character is gigantic. It requires scientific analysis, careful planning and unceasing labor. Prejudice dies hard. . . . To change this stereotype of the Jew in the public mind is the great task before us. It can be done.
> —Sigmund Livingston (April 1930)

Introduction: The Emergence of the Community Relations Field

Hershel Shanks, editor of *Moment Magazine,* reflecting on the American Jewish Committee's annual meeting in 1995, noted that it was an evening filled with the "who's who" of Washington in attendance, including President Clinton, Senator Robert Dole, Israeli Ambassador Itamar Rabinovich, as well as special tributes to outgoing Committee president Alfred Moses and Sister Ann Gillan, who had been a powerful voice for Soviet Jewry and the cause of Israel. In his opinion piece, Shanks commented: "I had a strange sinking feeling. Where was reality? A frightening powerful case has been made that the American Jewish community is on its way to extinction or insignificance in a generation or two. Yet, at the Committee's closing dinner no one spoke about assimilation, intermarriage, lack of Jewish education, paucity of spiritual satisfaction, how to be Jewish in an open society. I shook my head, trying to focus."[1]

Did Shanks have it right, at least in terms of the American Jewish Committee, or was he missing something else going on in that room on that particular evening? The story of the national Jewish community relations agencies is only in part directed to the concerns of *Moment*'s editor. Was it possible he missed the significance of what was happening that night in Washington? Clearly, three central themes associated with this field were acknowledged: the affirmation of Jewish political influence; the symbolism of the Israel-diaspora relationship in a setting where this once non-Zionist agency was now deeply connected to this unique partnership; and the acknowledgement of a strong interreligious connection with the Catholic Church. In many ways the events of that evening portrayed the scope of power achieved by American Jewry and, more specifically, the positioning of the major defense agencies to address the political interests of this community.

Defining a Discipline

"Community relations" was only formally defined as a field in the 1940s. At that time it was described as "the science of advancing human dignity, cooperative intergroup relations, civil rights, and civil liberties." In 1952, Maurice Fagan provided a challenge to the field of Jewish community relations, suggesting that there were three core principles that defined this work:

1. To serve and give expression to the needs of the Jews;
2. To sensitize Jews to the needs of others in the general community; and
3. To educate and mobilize Jews for personal involvement in community activities.[2]

But even earlier Jews of America understood that they had a right as well as a responsibility to engage the public sector on matters of specific concern to their community and with reference to the general welfare of the society. The culture of civic engagement, while not new to Jews in this society, would become a significant part of their American identity, especially in the twentieth century. The engagement of Jews in the American civic culture occurs, in part, in response to the emergence of the social progressive movement, with its emphasis on mobilizing citizens around social activism. American Jews were invested in making this society operate in a just and equitable manner for others and for themselves.

More explicitly, over the course of the twentieth century, a specific Jewish civic culture would emerge built around five guiding principles:

1. The security and welfare of Jews, both in the United States and worldwide;
2. The case for the separation of church and state, as symbolic of the Jewish community's commitment to and support of America's democratic institutions and social values;
3. A commitment to civil rights, economic opportunity, and social justice concerns, developed in part through promoting intergroup relationships and coalitions;
4. The case for religious tolerance and understanding; and
5. A commitment to strengthening Israel's political standing and public affairs image.

Underlying these principles and reflected in the philosophy and actions of "the defenders" was the goal of linking Jews and their political interests with core American values and practices. By seeking to minimize differences and promote the similarities between Jews and non-Jews, these agencies could advocate on behalf of the Jewish civic agenda. The goal of insuring that Jews would feel secure within this society and be able to integrate into the American social and political experience, while advocating for their own interests, represents the underlying framework that would define the mandates for these institutions. The civic principles, cited above, would evolve over time and would be shaped by events both within Jewish communal life and outside of it.

The founding of three institutions—American Jewish Committee, Anti-Defamation League (ADL), and American Jewish Congress—was linked to the first of these principles, Jewish security. At the outset, each agency sought to respond to a specific need, whether the Committee's concern for Russian Jewry, the ADL's response to the rise of anti-Semitism in America, or the Congress's focus on building a case for Zionism.

Over time these organizations would reflect in their mission and work the other themes associated with this emerging Jewish civic culture. In reality, each of these agencies has moved through a variety of stages responding to specific Jewish considerations and reflecting the broader themes that define this civic culture.

To a great degree, the idea of a Jewish civic culture, and more specifically the Jewish community relations agenda, has been framed and managed for significant periods of time in this past century by these organizations. These agencies, more than any other group of institutions, have established the framework for defining what constitutes a "Jewish issue." Both on the national level and within the communities, the ADL and the two AJCs established the rules and defined the context and content associated with being a part of the civic culture and the discipline of community relations. Over the decades, these agencies engaged professionals who, in consultation with volunteer leadership, framed policies and initiated programs in such areas as civil rights, social and economic justice, public education, church/state relations, interreligious affairs, Israel and world Jewry, and anti-Semitism. In the course of their activities in these and other arenas, each of these organizations became increasingly identified with levels of expertise with regard to specific issues within the community relations portfolio. While each is considered a full-service human relations organization, public perception has served to label them. ADL, for instance, is viewed as fighting anti-Semitism, while the American Jewish Congress is focused on church-state concerns, and the American Jewish Committee is described as the premier human relations research agency.

While all three agencies have demonstrated a whole array of political styles and invoked a variety of community relations tools and tactics, each has been identified with possessing a particular approach to the field. Terms such as "reflective," "research-oriented," and "quiet diplomacy" have defined the American Jewish Committee's style. Correspondingly, ADL has been described as American Jewry's "protector" or "policeman" against anti-Semitism and hate, employing a more assertive or public role that has served to establish its national image. Congress, in turn, has been identified as the Jewish community's "attorney general" with its judicial focus, specifically associated with First Amendment considerations.

"A fanciful way of describing the work of these groups," wrote Paul Jacobs in his 1965 memoir *Is Curly Jewish?* "is that some guy walks into the toilet of a gin mill on Third Avenue, New York, and while he's standing at the urinal, he notices that someone has written 'Screw the Jews' on the toilet wall."[3] Jacobs reports that "an

ADL man rushes down to the bar" in order to check for fingerprints and for the purpose of placing a photo of the wall in ADL's next bulletin, demonstrating that anti-Semitism is again a problem. The American Jewish Committee, Jacobs would suggest, would then commission a study of "anti-Semitic wall-writing since Pompeii." In addition, AJC would produce a booklet proving that a Jew had created the martini. Finally, he suggests that a representative from the Congress would create a picket line outside the bar, while petitioning the Supreme Court to prohibit the sale of alcohol "to anyone making an anti-Semitic remark."

These institutional definitions, as well as the tale cited above, while clearly incomplete, represent images that have been conveyed and adopted over time as a way by which individuals define and categorize these organizations. As multifaceted agencies, each of these entities operates in a variety of arenas, carrying out diverse tasks. As a result, the public's identification with these groups, possibly with the exception of the ADL due to its high-profile role in the arena of fighting anti-Semitism, tends to be more blurred. These perceptions would stand in contrast to the work of single-issue institutions such AIPAC or specific constituency-directed agencies, such as the Jewish Labor Committee.

Reflecting on the evolution of this field in general and the roles specifically performed by these major agencies, one can see the evolution through a series of "stages" marking the growth and transformation of this discipline. How did Jews initially enter and engage the political process? Arnold Aronson commented: "Such representations generally were conducted not by the group acting openly but by some prominent or influential Jew acting unobtrusively in its behalf."[4] As this field would evolve buffeted by social and political forces, Aronson identified these transformational periods. By the 1930s, as an example, with the incidence of anti-Semitism no longer limited to sporadic episodes, these agencies began to monitor more formal networks of hate organizations, including the Christian Front, America First, and the German-American Bund. "Under the impetus of these developments, the 'fact-finding' facilities of the agencies . . . were expanded into a far-flung counter-intelligence operation."[5] Realizing that the act of simply exposing these groups would not necessarily discredit them, and in fact might even serve their ends, the ADL and the Committee, in particular, sought to introduce a program of "effective counteraction." "With this purpose in view, an educational program was launched, designed to bring about in the public mind an identification of Jews with the mainstream of American life."[6] Themes and slogans, such as "Judeo-

Christian values" and "Americans all," were designed to draw attention away from social or cultural differences. Through this process of institutional change and growth, we witness the emergence of "the defenders."

These early ideas and the accompanying strategies reflected the prevalent notion of the "melting pot," which "held that immigrant groups were to lose their identities and merge into a sort of alloy that could be cast in a standard American mold."[7] An additional concept was added to this approach, namely, that intergroup cooperation could be an effective tool in combating racial and religious bigotry. The Common Council for American Unity provided in the 1920s a mechanism for countering anti-alien movements, while the National Conference of Christians and Jews emerged as a voice against religious intolerance that found expression in the 1928 presidential campaign. These initiatives in alliance-building would mark a pattern that would be pursued and embraced by these agencies.

As this new concept of intergroup cooperation took hold, Jewish agencies would no longer view their operations in the narrow terms of fighting anti-Semitism. Their efforts were expanded to include opposition to denial of rights to any group, thereby placing these institutions in the forefront of the civil rights struggle for black Americans, in the battle against national-origin quotas, and in support of the equal treatment of other minorities.

In many ways the battleground around the church-state issue, which already had fostered Jewish institutional actions in the nineteenth century, not only would lead these agencies, in particular the American Jewish Congress, to pioneer in expanding the legal insights and social practices in defense of the principle of separation, but would come to represent a central tenet of the field of Jewish community relations. The underlying premise for these agencies, and in turn for the community relations enterprise, is represented by the desire on the part of American Jews and other minorities to be seen as full and equal participants in the American experience. The involvement, first by the Congress, and later by the other two agencies, would be a product of the post-World War II period. The range of cases would be extensive, encompassing religious symbols on public property, public and silent prayer, holiday observances, the use of school facilities by religious groups, and the teaching of "scientific creationism."

Despite the emphasis outlined above on the unique or special characteristics that served to define and separate these agencies, a common set of values has also helped to shape their collective contributions to the field and in turn have defined the Jewish civic culture. While these ideas have shifted as to emphasis and with regard to style or approach, in many ways they still resonate as essential to the operational values of these institutions. In 1957, on the occasion of the American Jewish Committee's fiftieth anniversary, in a book commemorating that event, the AJC outlined these core principles:

> To foster mutual respect among the diverse groups in America; to increase self-understanding and therefore self-respect among Jews;
> To protect and strengthen democratic institutions;
> To ensure equal opportunities for all Americans in education, employment, housing and other aspects of community life;
> To help Jews in other lands to live as equals among their countrymen; to affirm their faith and to strengthen their communal and religious institutions; to find haven for those fleeing oppression;
> To promote the sanctity of human rights throughout the world.[8]

Clearly, the field of Jewish community relations, and more directly the three major agencies, have functioned around these ideas, which serve as variations of the principles of Jewish civic culture outlined above.

An Assessment

When one reviews the respective histories of the "defenders," it is striking how consistent each of these organizations remains to its original institutional principles. The idea of an "institutional culture" is born out not only in the context of the styles employed but also in a type of reverence and regard given to past leaders or to earlier policies and actions embraced by these agencies.

In preparation for this survey, six "content" areas were examined comparing the activities of the three agencies, covering a twenty-year period from the mid-1970s through the mid-1990s. The activities and policy responses of ADL, AJCommittee, and AJCongress were explored in the following fields of interest: Anti-Semitism, Israel, Holocaust, Civil Rights, Church/State, and Inter-Religious Relations. As might be anticipated, ADL's annual reports and targeted studies focusing on trends and patterns associated with anti-Semitism dominated this particular sector. Correspondingly, Congress's judicial activism would find that agency most involved with civil rights cases and, more particularly, in matters associated with affirmative action issues, in addition to its traditional involvement with church/state considerations. The American Jewish Committee's research focus was evident in its interreligious agenda, Israel activities, and Holocaust programs. All three agencies tended to respond to the same core "trigger" issues: the Bitburg controversy (1987); the key civil rights cases (De Funes, 1974; Bakke, 1979; and Weber, 1981); church/state issues; and the Arab boycott, as well as with public manifestations associated with the issues of anti-Semitism and intergroup relations.

The world of the public square in some measure needs to be seen in the context of two prisms. The first involves the American Jewish community itself, in which the policies and practices of these agencies initially must be introduced, addressed, and confirmed. In this context the politics of consensus serves to shape and define the scope, content, and strategies that define the mission and mandate for each agency. In the second arena, the American civic culture, ADL, the Committee, and the Congress are not only conveying specific interests of their respective agencies but also seek to articulate an American Jewish presence and posture on a broad array of social, religious, and political considerations. These agencies clearly have and continue to perform within both realms. The former invites critical attention to the questions of competition and institutional standing or recognition within the Jewish world. The latter focuses on both the individualized roles and contributions made by each of these defense groups and include their shared agenda in expressing Jewish policy considerations.

More than any other set of American Jewish institutions, the "Big Three" have not only contributed to the creation of a Jewish civic culture and a set of public policy principles, they have also formulated the tools and techniques that have come to be identified as the field's "best practices." Their imprint can be seen elsewhere within the Jewish communal world and beyond. These agencies share a set of institutional characteristics that have defined their distinctive standing within the American Jewish political process. They operate through national and regional governing structures. In order to carry out their institutional missions and national agendas, they have each established regional field operations, as well as international offices. As a result of their multitiered agendas, these organizations have created complex infrastructures involving departments, commissions, task forces, and institutes designed to develop agency policy and insure its implementation. In order to promote their respective agencies, each of the three have produced and marketed extensive publications, including in-house newsletters and magazines, videos and films, and more recently websites. Their publications and programmatic contributions, which, as has been noted, are extensive and comprehensive, magnify the impact of these defense agencies, but as significant has been the research data developed by these groups in a number of areas. One can find numerous examples of the findings as well as the core data incorporated into the research of scholars and writers.

Outlined below, in summary form, are some of the core contributions made by these agencies to the field of Jewish community relations:

1. Developed strategies and approaches designed to address a whole range of political, legal, and social issues facing American society.
2. Incorporated, independently and collectively, a whole range of organizing initiatives in order to advance specific programs and policies.
3. Created research tools and measures for assessing various attitudes, behaviors, and social values in the society.
4. Produced or aided in the development of pioneering research associated with community relations concerns and a broad range of other allied issues.
5. Assisted in the development of a core set of community relations principles and practices.
6. Developed and promoted publications and other resource materials on human relations and community affairs matters.
7. Aided in creating a national discourse on a variety of social and political questions.
8. Monitored and reported on individuals, organizations, and movements whose views and actions were seen as endangering the larger society and more specifically Jews.
9. Offered critical input, policy guidelines, and significant background research data on a variety of local, regional, national, and international policy questions.
10. Trained or hired several generations of professional practitioners who have contributed their expertise to these agencies and to the broader field.

When one examines, for instance, the publication lists of these agencies, it is possible to understand the breadth and diversity of interests developed by these agencies. The AJC's seventy-fifth anniversary publications listings (1981), and those that would follow, reflect the scope of that agency's concerns, covering more than 250 items and incorporating original research and reprints of articles and studies. Carrying this notion further, the ADL has emerged as this nation's largest distributor of human relations materials. In addition, the media, including the press, television, and the film industry, have extracted from these national institutions general ideas as well as specific information for their use.

Beyond the general categories of contributions, as defined above, the three agencies have both introduced and perfected the "methodologies" so central to the discipline of community relations. Ranging from the introduction and promotion of serious academic research to the development of public relations strategies and organizing tactics, the ADL, the Committee, and the Congress have provided, not only to the American Jewish community but to the nation as a whole, a significant array of human relations concepts, programs, and resources that have shaped this professional field. These agencies have developed a shared set of community and organizational practices that they have effectively mastered and over time are reflected in their activities. These basic resources in many ways reflect the consistency and strength of these institutions. Outlined below are ten of the basic tools that serve as trademarks for these three organizations:

1. Creating and participating in coalitions both on the domestic level and with regard to the international agenda.
2. Employing diplomatic interventions and using political influence and pressure.
3. Crafting "front" groups designed to represent specific initiatives or to carry out particular programs.
4. Framing legislative proposals and policy guidelines reflective of these agencies' priorities and in response to social conditions within the society.
5. Promoting national educational and informational initiatives.
6. Developing public marketing campaigns around particular events as well as promoting the principles associated with the community relations field.
7. Drawing upon the national press and media to advance and/or interpret the policies and programs of these agencies;
8. Monitoring and infiltrating hate movements and fringe organizations;
9. Providing to government agencies and lawmakers, academic institutions, and the media background information

on public policy and legal questions, social trends, and research findings.
10. Providing programs and services designed to carry out their respective national agendas.

The goal of Jewish community relations, as understood by its founders, was to penetrate the thinking and behavior of the general society by accessing elite and principal institutions. Realizing that, as the expression of a minority community, Jewish organizations would not be in a position to reach the grassroots or general citizenry, these institutions sought to convey their specific policy concerns through four core target groups: public officials, press and media elite, the intellectual and academic sector, and the leadership of business and labor. Arguing that these constituencies often shaped public opinion and disproportionately affected policy decisions, Jewish agencies sought to penetrate these major centers of influence. It is therefore not at all surprising to note the number of occasions in which one or more of these defense agencies offers recognition to international figures and American officials or institutional leaders from each of these key influential sectors. At various times, such events are designed to honor such individuals or to recognize institutions that have fostered the same values and interests of these Jewish agencies, while on other occasions to take advantage of the name recognition provided by these leaders or groups for purposes of fund-raising. As these institutions have developed a significant marketplace within the society, they have in turn expanded their public relations presence and their fund-raising capacities. Annually, the "defenders" raise in excess of $80 million dollars (ADL $50 million; American Jewish Committee $25 million; American Jewish Congress $5 million) from donors, foundations, sales of materials and services, endowments, and memberships.

This chapter will seek to explore the core ingredients that have helped to shape the emergence of a Jewish civic culture, by examining how these agencies have operated in response to the challenges faced by the Jewish community over this past century.

Critiquing the "Big Three"

The critics of these agencies have registered five principal arguments. These concerns are outlined below:

1. Is there a need for three such institutions? The charge of duplication.
2. Why can't there be greater coordination among these agencies? The case for a national system of managed community relations.
3. Since there exists today greater political diversity within Jewish life, why don't these (or other) groups reflect these alternative viewpoints? "Who gave these organizations the right to speak for me?" The arguments for choice and representation. Do these organizations, each with its own constituencies, reflect or ought to reflect in their policy positions the consensus views of America's Jews, or more narrowly seek to incorporate the perspectives of their memberships?
4. Raising the issue of communal priorities, why is the Jewish community, or significant elements within it, investing nearly $100 million in national and local community relations activities, especially at a time of relative security and well-being?
5. Outside of the Committee's Jewish Communal Affairs Department, what defines these institutions as being uniquely or significantly "Jewish" with regard to many of their programs and some of their policy positions? The debate over the Jewish character and focus of these agencies.

Critics of these agencies specifically cite the historic and fixed position on church/state adopted years ago. Jack Wertheimer, in critiquing this policy line, argues that "the community relations field will not relent in its inflexible defense of strict separationism, even though graver challenges face the American Jewish community. The justification most frequently voiced for this inflexibility is that all historic achievements of American Jews . . . are predicated on strict separationism."[9] Wertheimer has argued that they were now "committing themselves to policies that seem tailor-made not to decrease but rather to increase the level of tension between Jews and other Americans."[10] In many ways the criticism of these agencies' lockstep position on church-state separation has been a central point of disagreement within the Jewish community, bringing together a variety of community interests, representing segments of the religious community and elements of the Jewish political right, all opposing aspects of this policy.

Another critic has suggested that if one of these agencies enters a new arena of activity, it is likely that one or both of the others will "symbolically" enter the same field. This is frequently done in order to prove to its donor base and board leadership that "it too was engaged in the enterprise." As an example of this practice, this observer cited the recent issue of *Charitable Choice* and the extensive study being undertaken by the Committee in this area, only to find the ADL convening a one-day conference on the same subject as a way to affirm its interest in this national discussion.

The charge that the competition between agencies undermines their effectiveness is nothing new. The agencies came under severe criticism for their responses, or lack thereof, during the period of the late 1930s and early 1940s. As one writer would note: "Jewish organizations did little more than engage in fratricide; they bickered, disagreed, and duplicated or undermined each other."[11] "Every committee cherishes its own committee interests, its sectarian ambitions, its exclusively wise strategy and its 'power position' in the teapot of Jewish communal competition."[12]

In some measure the failure of these agencies, separately and collectively, to respond more effectively during this critical time frame has given rise to a greater sense of involvement and attention on their part to the threats to Jewish security that would emerge in the post-World War II period. In marking their historical achievements, each of these agencies has attempted to downplay the Holocaust era. In many ways the first core civic principle, Jewish security, remained the primary standard by which these institutions would be measured by key elements within the Jewish community during the last five decades of the twentieth century. The significant engagement by each of these institutions during this period on behalf of Jewish communities in crisis and through their active support for the case for Israel reflects in part their response to the criticism directed against them during the earlier Hitler era.

It should be noted that the American Jewish Congress for years leading up to and following the founding of the State of Israel criticized the leadership of the Committee for its non-Zionist posture. This disagreement was played out on a number of institutional and public levels and was carried forth over many years.

If traditionally these agencies saw one another as competitors, then today there may be a somewhat different reality as many single-issue constituencies have emerged to challenge these agencies in a variety of arenas, both domestic and international. Some of these institutional challengers emerged, in part, as a result of the perceived failure of these groups to be effectively assertive on behalf of European Jewry during the Holocaust and with regard to the shift of Jewish influence and power into the federated system. During the

1970s and 1980s, for example, the local community relations committees, supported by federation dollars and community involvement, appeared to be successful in shifting the focus of certain activities to the communities. This pattern was particularly evident on matters related to Soviet Jewry and Israel, and with reference to certain domestic policy questions. In addition, numerous organizations outside of the Jewish community have taken up some of the core concerns of the "defenders" and, in the process, now compete for Jewish support as well. If any one institution seems to have captured some of the public spotlight, especially around the issues of anti-Semitism, the Holocaust, and to a lesser extent the Israel agenda and international concerns, it is the Simon Wiesenthal Center and its Museum of Tolerance. The capacity of the center's director, Rabbi Marvin Hier, to attract media attention and significant financial support has positioned that agency to challenge the "defenders" on several fronts. Not bound by the institutional "rules of the game" that govern the other agencies' actions and participation in such consensus-making bodies as the Jewish Council for Public Policy or the Conference of Presidents, Rabbi Hier has been less constricted in shaping the center's policies and practices.

In some measure, these and other challenges have demonstrated the vitality and openness of the Jewish community to institutional competition.

Historical Focus: Origins

While each of these organizations was established in an eleven-year time frame between 1906 and 1917, their emergence as freestanding institutions is quite distinctive. With the exception of the American Jewish Committee, which was created from the outset as an independent structure, neither the Congress nor the ADL has such a history. The Congress, as shall be examined later, was initially seen by its founders as the vehicle necessary to create a democratically elected "congress" of American Jewry, principally to address divergent class interests and, more specifically, the postwar concerns of world Jewry and the Zionist agenda. It was only later that the Congress would emerge as a multifaceted community relations agency. Similarly, the ADL emerged as a committee of B'nai B'rith but would see its role evolve over the decades as a distinct national community relations entity. The story of these national agencies can be broken down into four distinct periods: its initial attention to the image of the American Jew; its focus on Nazism and its American supporters; the postwar period and the civil rights era; and the rise of a new set of challenges both to the case for Israel and for the well-being of intergroup relations in the United States.

The early years associated especially with the American Jewish Committee and the American Jewish Congress were clearly defined and shaped by the key personalities that were identified with these agencies as their principal institutional voices. Louis Marshall, Cyrus Adler, Jacob Schiff, and Oscar Straus represented four of the Committee's most prominent leaders, while Louis Brandeis and Rabbi Stephen Wise were identified with the initial development of the Congress. These individuals and others would bring to these institutions a specific set of ideas about America and the place of American Jewry or, in the case of the Congress, the particular role that Zionism would play in framing that organization's initial purpose and focus. The input of these institution-builders would extend well beyond their own tenure of service, influencing both the style and the substance of these two organizations. These defense agencies can be seen as operating around certain core values and principles about America and Judaism that in part were articulated by their respective founding leaders. Due to the fact that the ADL functioned until more recent times as an integral part of B'nai B'rith, its unique or individualized institutional style emerged over time rather than at its inception, although Sigmund Livingston's early vision (as cited above) for an antidefamation program clearly has left its mark on that agency.

The American Jewish Committee

As Lucy Dawidowicz observed regarding the formation of the American Jewish Committee, the individuals who formed the Committee "had risen high in American society."[13] That position and their dedication to the interests of the Jews legitimated them as leaders of the American Jewish community. "They laid out an ambitious program of lobbying, research, and diplomacy, to improve Jewish conditions in Europe and combat threats at home."[14] "Indeed, precisely such men had for centuries been elevated to places of leadership in the traditional Jewish community."[15] As a result, Committee leaders could be compared to the traditional "Shtadlanim." Such players viewed their personal influence and political relationships with the society's elites as essential for pursuing Jewish interests. "But American democracy and egalitarianism had affected the outlook of many Jews in the rapidly expanding and diversifying Jewish community" of the early part of the twentieth century; as a result, these "elites" were seen as unrepresentative and acting without the consent of America's changing Jewish community.[16]

Peter Medding has suggested that Jewish politics in America was first influenced by the traditional organizational pattern, marked by these types of personal intercessions of prominent individual Jews. "These intercessors utilized their elite connections or influence to plead for the Jews."[17] In some measure, the American Jewish Committee's initial political style reflected this modality of politics.

In the early years of the twentieth century, three distinct ideas dominated Jewish institutional practice. The model represented by the Committee's early leaders, including Marshall, Schiff, and Straus, invoked the notion that Jews were joined together exclusively as a religion, devoid of the idea of peoplehood or of group rights. Wise and Brandeis, who drew their support and ideological vision from the Zionist camp, advanced this second set of beliefs. Where the Committee's leadership saw their Judaism to be a private, religious matter designed to serve the needs of the individual, the Zionist camp viewed the issues of Jewish nationalism to be a public question. A third group, weaker both in numbers and in leadership, represented the socialist and trade union elements who discounted any common bond among Jews, "arguing that the interests of the Jewish working class were incompatible with the interests of the Jewish bourgeoisie and that Jewish workers had more in common with the working classes of other peoples."[18]

AJC's influential leadership proved effective from the outset in advancing the Jewish community's interests; in 1911, using "its first full-dress demonstration of Jewish domestic clout," the Committee persuaded the Senate to abrogate the 1832 Russia-U.S. trade treaty, in response to Moscow's anti-Semitic policies.[19] "Russia's anti-Semitic laws extended not only to Russian Jews, but to American Jewish visitors as well. That violated the Russian treaty's equal protection clause, which required each country to respect the other's citizens."[20] This later point served as the necessary incentive to garner congressional action, against the objections of President Taft.

Throughout the early decades of the twentieth century, while remaining concerned about such matters as Henry Ford, the rise of the Klan, immigration restrictions, and restrictive quotas at American colleges, the American Jewish Committee would continue to focus its primary attention on the persecution of Jews in Europe, following the Bolshevik Revolution in Russia and the continuation of government-inspired discrimination and violence directed against Jews in Poland, Rumania, and Hungary. "The American Jewish Committee actively sought to meet with representatives of these countries, hoping by their efforts to alleviate the situation of the Jews. As best they could, they tried to engage American government officials and diplomats in support of their intercessions. Anti-Semitism in Europe advanced inexorably, despite the guarantees of Jewish rights, despite interventions and protests."[21]

The American Jewish Congress

The Committee had seen itself in these early years as the spokesman for American Jewry on matters of international affairs, that is, "to prevent the infraction of the civil and religious rights of Jews in any part of the world."[22] Louis Marshall opposed the idea of a "congress" of American Jews from the outset. The proponents of the "congress idea" were, of course, by all measure the political antagonists of the Committee; they represented the East European Jews, the socialist and labor factions, and the Zionist camp. The "congress" supporters argued that such an instrument was needed to advocate for America's Jews:

> To represent the Jewish people, to speak in its name, to conduct its politics, to organize it, to raise it up, to liberate and restructure its entire life cannot be done by self-appointed groups of *Shtadlanim*, by party, by faction or an organization but only by the people organized as such, working through its democratically elected representatives and through its own agencies and institutions controlled by the people.[23]

In the early stages of this contest, the Committee leadership "decided to stare down" the congress forces, believing that these elements had neither the experience, leadership, nor financial support necessary to carry forward this idea.[24] Despite early efforts to broker an agreement or "treaty," as it would come to be known, the "congress" forces led by Louis Brandeis "started a revolution in Jewish politics."[25] "The American Jewish Congress was chosen in three days of unprecedented balloting in May 1917, at polling places set up in Jewish neighborhoods across America."[26] In the end, however, it would be Marshall who would be its central figure in the 1918 Congress meetings in Philadelphia and in leading its delegation to the Paris Peace Conference, while at the same time successfully preventing any effort to establish a permanent "congress" body.

In 1922, when the Congress was "reconvened," it was in fact no "congress" at all but rather it served as Stephen Wise's "personal platform for his private blend of Jewish nationalism and militant liberalism."[27] The American Jewish Congress was reconstituted with its purposes outlined in its charter: "to safeguard Jewish rights all over the world; to fight discrimination and protect national minority rights; and to help develop Palestine."[28] The Congress's involvement with the "Palestine Question" marked the first engagement of a "defense" agency in the Zionist agenda. As it developed as a voice for American Jewry, the Congress would attract to its national leadership such prominent American rabbis, in addition to Wise, as Irving Miller, Israel Goldstein, Joachim Prinz, Arthur Hertzberg, and Arthur Lelyveld.

Anti-Defamation League

As noted above, the incorporation of the ADL within B'nai B'rith limited its earliest visibility. In many instances during the initial decades of its founding, ADL's agenda was limited and directed to specific problem areas. As early as 1908, B'nai B'rith, at the prompting of Sigmund Livingston, a Bloomington, Illinois, attorney, considered the creation of an antidefamation program "to counter the prevalent public ridicule of Jews."[29] Livingston was asked to chair an exploratory committee in order to develop a plan of action for the organization. Livingston's philosophy regarding the issue of anti-Semitism could be identified in the sentence: "The beginning to the solution to the problem must be publicity."[30]

Arnold Forster vividly recounts the ADL story: "Only a few months before the ADL's founding (1913), a young Jew named Leo Frank had been convicted of rape and murder after a trial by prejudice in which mobs choked the courthouse area screaming 'Hang the Jew.' The 'Vigilance Committee' that stormed the Georgia prison and killed Frank had been enflamed by an organized campaign of anti-Semitic propaganda directed by one of America's first political demagogues, Congressman and one-time presidential candidate, Thomas Watson."[31] The League's charter, established in October 1913, was focused on the Jewish condition in America and was directed, in part, as a response to the Frank case: "The immediate object of the League is to stop by appeals to reason and conscience, and if necessary, by appeals to law, the defamation of the Jewish people."[32] Forster, in his history of the agency, reports that the ADL was launched with a budget of $200 and two desks in a Chicago law office. Governed by an executive committee of 150 leaders who represented a "cross-section of Jewish communal life and interests," the initial activities of the League were concentrated on the "image of the Jew in the American mind."[33]

World War I brought "new and more serious problems" when, for instance, a U.S. Army manual referenced the Jew as a "malingerer," requiring President Wilson, at the ADL's insistence, to remove the document.[34] The ADL, seeking to end stereotyping and defamation, focused its energies on the press, stage, and cinema industry. It operated on the principles that "the only antidote for the poison of intolerance is understanding through education," and that "intolerance and prejudice live on ignorance."[35] Beginning with Universal Pictures in 1916, and the rest of the industry in the 1920s, ADL was able to announce that "the motion picture producers have adopted a policy that frowns upon pictures that defame racial and religious groups."[36] Between 1917 and 1920, the League spearheaded an effort involving Jewish and non-Jewish institutions to pressure schools to discontinue the teaching of *The Merchant of Venice* in America's schools. Realizing that the "issues of censorship and of artistic integrity at once take center stage, and often the problem of human relations and the evil impact of ancient canards is lost in the controversy," the League became increasingly concerned with the question of First Amendment rights.[37] "As it evolved over the years, the League's position turned upon the recognition that the medium more than the message was the critical element in dealing with the negative stereotypes of classical literature."

Collaborative Action

The rise and growth of the Klan in the 1920s as well as other manifestations of hate afforded these agencies an early opportunity to collectively mobilize their resources. Organized around the theme "Keep America American," Klan activists murdered blacks and boycotted and destroyed Jewish businesses, while leaving their trademark, the burning cross, outside synagogues. In response, ADL developed various types of hate crime legislation designed to curb Klan activities. Forster reported "a number of anti-Klan state statutes were eventually passed."[38] But this type of issue would not remain only in the purview of the ADL, as witnessed by the case outlined below.

Henry Ford and the *Dearborn Independent*

The *Dearborn Independent,* owned by Henry Ford, began to publish a series of anti-Semitic articles beginning in May 1920, which continued for ninety-one issues. The ADL described Ford's publications as the "most vicious anti-Semitic attacks ever published in the English language."[39] Drawing on the ideas of an international Jewish conspiracy as described in the infamous *Protocols of the Learned Elders of Zion,* Ford mounted the first unified, nationwide anti-Jewish drive in American history.[40] "American Jews—horrified but not intimidated—held a special conference in September 1920 to plan strategy to meet the threat."[41] Later that same year, the major defense agencies, joined by other groups, issued a pamphlet exposing *The Protocols,* which was to represent the first collaborative effort involving these agencies. "Jewish organizations, spearheaded by the American Jewish Committee, launched a counter-campaign. Over 110 of America's most distinguished leaders, including former presidents Wilson and Taft, issued a sharp protest against Ford's 'vicious propaganda.'" In 1927 following years of protest and the pressure of lawsuits, as well as the impact of public opinion, Ford agreed to end his campaign of anti-Semitism and to issue a retraction of the charges directed against the Jews. "Negotiations were concluded with the American Jewish Committee and Ford's statement of apology was drafted by Louis Marshall himself. In that statement Ford acknowledged 'the virtues of the Jewish people as a whole, of what they and their ancestors have done for civilization and for mankind and toward the development of commerce and industry, of their sobriety and diligence, their benevolence and their unselfish interest in the public welfare.'"[42]

In summarizing the impact of Henry Ford's campaign of anti-Semitism, one writer concluded that these efforts had a greater negative impact on European Jews than on American Jewry. "The restriction of immigration in accordance with the national-origins quota prevented hundreds of thousands of Jews from entering America in years to come when the difference was a difference between life and death."[43] However, within this society, Ford's propaganda "had no discernible or measurable impact on the status of the Jews in the United States."[44]

The Prewar Years

During the period 1933 through 1939, one can examine the distinctive approach and style of the American Jewish Committee, contrasting that approach and focus with the activities of the Congress, especially with regard to the crisis facing Germany's Jewish community with the emergence of Hitler. Against the backdrop of the Depression, the presence of domestic anti-Semitism, and the existence of anti-alien sentiment, the Committee faced a myriad of challenges. Invoking its strategy of "quiet diplomacy," the Committee, in contrast to the more public view adopted by the Congress, sought to use politically influential Jews and non-Jews to impact and change government policies. "The Committee adopted this policy believing it to be more effective and preferable to more public approaches which lent themselves to anti-Semitism and general public criticism of Jews and their cause."[45] Frederick Lazin, in his research of this period, cited the "extremely limited" influence that Committee representatives actually could exert. One of the approaches invoked by the Committee and B'nai B'rith in 1933 was to appeal to Secretary of State Cordell Hull to intervene with the German government over the status and treatment of its Jewish community. Again in 1935, along with the other major organizations, including on this occasion the Congress, the AJC urged that the secretary of state "speak out against the German government's anti-Jewish policies."[46]

In the end, the Committee "publicly defended its government's refusal to protest on the grounds of national interest." While some leaders of the AJC were critical of the government's inaction and of the decision of the Committee to justify such a position, the leadership of AJC continued to hold to the notion that "having information on unpublished measures that had been taken . . . the Committee felt that a majority of Americans might give credence to the anti-Semitic charges that 'the American Jews controlled the government.' Although it was increasingly aware of the limitations of its approach and the general shortcomings in State Department policy, the Committee decided to defend both. A public attack on the administration's policies would have admitted the bankruptcy of its own policies."[47]

Throughout this period, the Committee opposed Jewish-sponsored public demonstrations and protests as counterproductive with the German government and even harmful to American Jews, giving credence to the charge of an international Jewish conspiracy.

In 1933, for instance, when the Congress sponsored with Christian clergy a rally in New York against Hitler's anti-Jewish policies, AJC and B'nai B'rith sought to dissuade rabbis from endorsing or participating in such an event, and the two organizations jointly sponsored ads opposing mass protests or boycotts.[48]

Until 1935, with the promulgation of the Nuremberg Laws, the Committee argued that such public actions taken by American Jews were being discouraged as well by German Jewry. As the AJC had a close working relationship with the Central-Verein Deutscher Staatsburger Jüdischen Glaubens (CV), the umbrella framework for German Jewry, the Committee would argue that "German Jewry wanted American Jews to arouse public opinion, but not through the use of public protests and mass demonstrations."[49] But such a passive policy was increasingly challenged on both sides of the Atlantic. After 1935, when it became increasingly clear that immigration was the only option for German and later for much of European Jewry, the Committee, along with the rest of the Jewish institutional leadership, was unable to overcome public opposition and government resistance regarding a more liberal immigration policy.

The Committee engaged the support of liberal and Protestant groups to take a more direct, public approach, which it felt was not available to the Jewish community. As a result of this strategy a "united front" was created focusing on the threat of Hitler "to religion, liberalism, and democracy in Germany and in the rest of the world. . . . The Committee even supported several public protests led by non-Jews which focused on the broader issues."[50] Similarly, the Committee's Survey Committee, which had responsibility at the time to direct the agency's public relations and educational activities in the fight against anti-Semitism, proposed in 1938 a program to change the negative public image of refugees. Identified as the "refugee misconceptions campaign," the Survey Committee developed a program, much of it carried on behind the scenes, to supply resources to "interested parties" to publicly pursue this campaign. An example of this initiative was a document published by the American Friends Service Committee, *Refugee Facts*, produced and financed by the Committee.

As noted earlier, the failure of the Jewish community, and in particular the defense agencies to effectively mobilize public support in favor of expanded immigration and to successfully build a coalition of Americans opposed to Hitler would serve years later as a key incentive for Jewish political organizing around Israel-related issues and the involvement of these institutions on behalf of Jewish communities worldwide.

The War Years and Beyond

Because of the differences in membership, core philosophies, and program priorities between the Committee and the Congress during these formative years and extending beyond World War II, one can identify numerous points of organizational conflict over policies and principles of practice dividing these two institutions. The Congress leadership was especially critical of the Committee's "approach" as being counter to the principles of democracy and to the idea of institutional collaboration. The Committee's non-Zionism, as referenced earlier, particularly underscored the levels of tension between the two organizations. For instance, a Congress editorial in 1949 blasted the Committee's "belated recognition of Jewish statehood," arguing that the Committee "has never accepted and does not today accept, the concept of Jewish peoplehood or of the Jewish community."[51]

Despite the Committee's posture of non-Zionism during the prestate years, the Committee both resisted overtures by the anti-Zionist American Council for Judaism to support its efforts and joined other Jewish groups in opposing the views and actions undertaken by that institution.

In the aftermath of World War II, how were American Jews to respond to the fundamental changes taking place worldwide and within American society? Among the issues to be addressed were the security and welfare of American Jewry, the impact and fear of communism in the United States, leading to internal investigations of American citizens and their affiliations, the questions surrounding Israel and its evolving relationships with world Jewry, and the emergence of civil rights concerns in such areas as housing, education, employment, and voting. For the two AJCs and the ADL, the focus would be to confront these changing realities. While the American Jewish Committee's agenda, and to a lesser degree the ADL's, would encompass all of these arenas as well as others, including foreign affairs, interreligious activities, intergroup education, and immigration matters, the American Jewish Congress would assume a more focused field of involvement, as represented by that agency's experiments with litigation and its entry into the public policy sector. As a result, two divergent philosophies would emerge during this era. Over time it would become evident to the Committee and the ADL that the Congress's aggressive intervention in the judicial and public policy arenas represented a valid and productive approach. The original concerns held by the Committee's leadership and embraced by the ADL of an anti-Semitic backlash to the Congress's more assertive techniques would prove baseless.

The underlying idea that dominated the work of the Committee and the ADL during these years was directed to the principle that "Judaism and Americanism are mutually enriching."[52] Therefore, the notion of educating Americans about Jews was adopted as a primary community relations tool. This idea, in turn, stood in conflict with the Congress's view that only through legislative and legal interventions could one change behavior and practice and that the educational model was not a viable or effective approach to securing social acceptance for Jews or for others within American society.

John Slawson led the Committee's efforts to introduce this educational model as well as to explore the scientific basis of anti-Semitism and prejudice generally. Between 1938 and 1946, the Committee's newly formed Department of Scientific Research undertook eleven different opinion surveys assessing anti-Semitism, representing the "longest continued trend study of anti-Semitism."[53] In the 1950s, the five-volume *Studies in Prejudice* appeared, including such groundbreaking works as *The Authoritarian Personality*, *The Dynamics of Prejudice*, and *Anti-Semitism and Emotional Disorder*. This collection was described as "the first really scientific attack upon the problem of intergroup hostility."[54] These studies suggested that "the cause of prejudice lies not in the victim but in the bigot, and that the prejudiced individual dislikes not just one kind of people. He is deeply fearful; his personality is rigid; his mind is warped, abnormally dependent on authority; he is, therefore, actually or potentially anti-democratic."[55]

"During the late 1940s and into the 1950s, the American Jewish Committee became one of the nation's most important non-academic sponsors of social-science research on the roots and meaning of prejudice. The Committee helped raise the funds to support the so-called Frankfurt school, a mostly Jewish group of sociologists who had fled Germany in 1934 and settled in New York—among them Bruno Bettelheim, Theodor Adorno, Herbert Marcuse, and Max Horkheimer."[56] As J. J. Goldberg has pointed out, "the Committee's sponsorship of this research fostered a revolution in the way Americans looked at prejudice. One Committee-sponsored study by black psychologist Kenneth Clark, on the psychological impact of school segregation, became the basis for the 1954 Supreme Court decision outlawing segregated schools, *Brown v. Board of Education*."[57]

In adopting a similar framework for the Committee, ADL sponsored a project entitled the "Freedom Series" that was aimed at "the leadership group in American communities." The intent of this series was to deal with "the most pressing problem of modern times—the relations of men with their fellow men of various races, creeds and national origins." This series was introduced in order "to create a climate of opinion in which prejudice cannot take root, and to foster good human relations."[58] "Our goal is not mere freedom from scapegoating. We are striving for a society in which positive respect and active cooperation will exist among all its members," noted Dr. Gordon W. Allport, distinguished professor of psychology at Harvard University, and the author of the fourth Freedom Pamphlet, "The ABCs of Scapegoating."[59]

Beyond the use of publications, the ADL entered film production in the late 1940s, producing the film *Prejudice*, in cooperation with the Protestant Film Commission. Seeking to address the more subtle forms of anti-Semitism, the script emphasized a central theme employed by the agencies at the time, namely, that "prejudice is a disease of the mind and heart. It springs from fright, frustration, and insecurity, and finds its outlet in hostility and aggression against almost any group."[60]

The introduction of polling data and opinion surveys beginning with the prewar period, designed to study patterns of prejudice and in particular anti-Semitic views, represented another contribution made by these two human relations entities as part of their efforts to "scientifically" examine the attitudes and behaviors of American citizens. In an ADL-sponsored study conducted by the Opinion Research Center at the University of Denver, the "general factors characterizing anti-Semitism" were introduced. In that research it was determined that "a composite of the extreme anti-Semite revealed a man of 50 years or older with only grammar school education and employed as a service worker with good earnings." The study went on to suggest that this individual was inclined to be disconnected from the political process, blaming "minorities for all existing intergroup differences."[61]

In ADL's 1948 report, "How Secure These Rights?" the League laid out not only its findings regarding discrimination against Jews in "public accommodations, colleges and universities, and even in public employment" but also its commitment to pursue policies and practices that can change the state of intergroup relations. "Without such undergirding of rights by law the problem is made much more complex. Above the role of law as such also stands the responsibility of government to provide leadership in this fight."[62] Employing a variety of research tools, publications, and conferences, the ADL sought to uncover patterns of discrimination and quota practices associated with university admissions, sports organizations and athletic clubs, in addition to employment and housing concerns. Again, in this period, as it had earlier during the rise of the Klan in the 1920s, the ADL introduced model legislation directed against discrimination in education. Adopted in several states, including New York, it introduced for the first time a standard for fair educational practices.[63] Summarizing ADL's work in this arena, Arnold Forster noted: "Years of study of this complex problem lead us to the conclusion that there are three fundamental forces which can be called into effective counterplay against prejudice—law, education, and community action. . . . A secure and free people who have adequate opportunity to fulfill themselves and lead happy lives will reject those who spread hatred."[64]

The above ideas, as fashioned by the Committee and the ADL, ran counter to the approach and program to be advanced during this period by the American Jewish Congress. While not rejecting the basic core values embraced by these other agencies, the Congress would also see its agenda through the lens of Zionism. Max Nussbaum, in a 1946 essay, defined the idea of "Congressism" in the following terms: "Congress looks upon the Jews all over the world as one indivisible people."[65] "Congress ideology is Zionist ideology applied to the totality of Jewish life. . . . It takes Zionist ideology as matter-of-fact-substance and foundation of its own structure."[66]

Beyond these distinctive notions of peoplehood and Zionism, the Congress would "reinvent" itself, charting a course of action encompassing a number of initiatives and approaches not only internally directed but also outwardly focused. Under Wise's continued leadership, a cadre of new, young professionals began to redefine that agency's mission. The Congress established the Office of Jewish Information "to stimulate a positive appreciation of Jewish culture and historic identity," arguing that the destruction of European Jewry "has imposed an imperative responsibility on American Jewry for the survival of the Jewish people." Similarly, the leadership of that organization announced its support for the growth of Jewish community councils, but "demanded that these councils be created as thoroughly democratic representations of all the elements in each community and that they become instruments for integration with Jewish ideas and ways of life."[67]

Under the leadership of its assertive new national director, David Petegorsky, the Congress clearly sought to define for itself a distinctive domestic role. The core ideas for its domestic agenda were defined in a document entitled "Full Equality in a Free Society," prepared by Alexander Pekelis. The key to Pekelis's proposal was directed to monitoring and ultimately to changing the actions of those who were the enemies of pluralism. Under this model, the emphasis placed by the ADL and the Committee on the causes associated with discrimination and on the need for educational intervention as the best means for dealing with bigotry was rejected in favor of attacking those who fermented hate. "Using the law as a weapon, Pekelis argued, the Jewish community should fight discrimination whenever it occurred—and whoever were its victims. Only a society that guaranteed the rights of all could ensure the rights of anyone."[68]

David Petegorsky, addressing the future dimensions of the Congress's role in 1946, noted:

> We are convinced, in the first place, that anti-Semitism is a product not primarily of ignorance or misunderstanding but of complex political, social, and economic forces. Our attack on anti-Semitism therefore is based not on attempts to overcome ignorance through the dissemination of information or to promote good will through exhortations to tolerance. Rather, it takes the form of efforts to eliminate the causes of group tensions . . . in our social environment and to render impossible, through vigorous public action, the practice of racial and religious discrimination.[69]

Writing in *Congress Weekly* in 1949, Petegorsky further laid out his vision. Reflecting on what he described as the heightened political tensions in the United States and the new threats to civil liberties growing out of the fear of the influence of communism, he wrote: "Already the defense against subversion seriously threatens to pass over into an attack on civil liberties."[70] He noted that "where previously the extent of Jewish involvement had generally been limited to the dissemination of educational materials, that involvement today takes place in legislative campaigns, administrative intervention, test cases before the courts of the land. . . . As a result of the pioneering work of the American Jewish Congress, the level of that participation has been significantly transformed."[71]

In an effort to prove that this approach was the correct strategy for American Jewry, Wise threatened to sue Columbia University over the existence of its quota system in admissions and hiring practices, seeking to deny its tax-exempt status. In the end, Columbia elected to drop its restrictive policies. "The shock waves went out to the rest of academe: discrimination against Jews, either as students or as faculty, became a risky proposition."[72] Thus, by the early 1950s the agencies had each staked out their ideological approaches and program priorities with regard to social activism and civil rights. In turn, several of the core principles associated with the Jewish civic culture were being advanced. Intergroup understanding would be advanced by the work of the Committee and the League, while the case for the separation of church and state as well as the pursuit of a civil rights agenda would be represented through the judicial activism of the Congress.

Challenges to Collaborative Action

In a number of significant arenas, the agencies collaborated. Beginning with the challenges posed by Henry Ford's *Dearborn Independent*, as referenced earlier, the capacity to develop and promote a consultative process among the three was a major achievement, considering the institutional pressures for visibility and recognition. This success has been offset by communal criticism directed against these agencies, as noted above, which asserts the lack of differences among the three around policy and at times around practice.

One of the interesting points of tension that emerged within contemporary Jewish life relates to the question of the independence of Jewish organizations. Efforts imposed initially from the outside by the (then) Council of Jewish Federations and the (then) NJCRAC, at various times, "to seek to bring about effective coordination," have evoked strong responses from these agencies. When the issue of consolidation has been raised, these agencies uniformly have argued that each possesses a unique style or approach, serve different constituencies and interests, and offer complementary strengths and communal resources. "Mindful of the strategic and ideological differences that distinguished their organizations, they jealously guarded their autonomy and resisted calls for centralization, formal coordination, or institutionalized division of labor."[73] The Committee, more so than the other two, staunchly held to the principle that no one body or group can or ought to speak on behalf of American Jewry.

In the 1930s the pressure for Jewish unity was linked to the threat of anti-Semitism. As a result, the Joint Consultative Council involving the three agencies was created. Disagreements over tactics in dealing with the anti-Nazi struggle led to the demise of this entity. Again, in the late 1930s and 1940s, these institutions and other community relations entities would come together under various umbrella frameworks, including the General Jewish Council (1937), the American Jewish Conference (1943-1948), and the National

(Jewish) Community Relations Advisory Council (1944), and its more recent incarnation the Jewish Council on Public Affairs (JCPA). It should be noted that the American Jewish Committee withdrew from the American Jewish Conference over objections to the Conference's support of Jewish statehood. By the end of World War II, as a result, there was no institutional representation of Jewish interests, which had been the case as well at the time of World War I.[74]

The core principles that defined these national consultative and coordinating structures are best reflected in the following statement taken from the NJCRAC Program Plan (1994-1995):

> Conditions conducive to the creative continuity and well-being of the Jewish community can be best achieved only within a social framework committed to democratic pluralism; freedom of religion, thought, expression, and association; the wall of separation between church and state; equal rights; justice and opportunity; and a climate in which differences among groups are accepted and respected, and in which each is free to cultivate its own distinctive values while participating fully in the general life of the society.[75]

Naturally, these ideas resonated to the basic visions of the Committee, the Congress, and ADL. Over the years these agencies have played significant but varying roles inside this consensus-driven system. Until recently, with the creation of the JCPA, the national agencies, including the "big three," held the power of veto over policy statements and actions that might have been undertaken through this coordinating entity.

As part of an effort by the federation system to eliminate what they believed to be duplication and waste, Robert MacIver from Columbia University was engaged as a consultant in 1949 to examine the workings of NCRAC. In his 1951 report, MacIver's recommendations called for the Council to play a more centralized role in the coordination of the agencies' functions, thereby seeking to eliminate duplication of tasks. Interestingly, the report ideologically favored the substantive approaches and policies of the Committee and ADL.[76] With the release of this report, the ADL and the Committee withdrew from NCRAC, formally rejoining that body in 1965.

Partially in response to their unhappiness with these efforts over time to control their independence and with regard to proposals by the federation system to combine allocations to the defense agencies, the ADL and the Committee formed the Joint Defense Appeal

(1938) as their fund-raising arm. This collective effort remained in effect until the mid-1970s.

By the late 1980s it had become apparent, especially for the ADL and the American Jewish Committee, that their financial situations were no longer dependent on the Jewish Federation allocations process, which had been providing these agencies about 5 percent of their budgetary requirements. The current fiscal realities permitted these agencies more independence in policy and organizational matters.

Over the years these agencies have been under pressure to demonstrate their ability to coordinate their efforts around specific issues or crises. There have been a number of arenas in which such cooperation has occurred, including collective efforts in fighting the Arab boycott during the 1970s. "In an unprecedented move the three staff directors decided upon an informal and unpublished division of responsibilities in resisting the Arab boycott so as to maximize their effectiveness."[77] The ADL assumed responsibility for bringing to the public's attention individual cases of discrimination, while the Committee agreed to manage a public education campaign as to the "dangers of Arab economic warfare." The American Jewish Congress focused on federal and state legislation, in order "to formulate the legal basis for challenging boycott operations in the United States." Evaluating this framework of institutional cooperation, Will Maslow of the Congress would write: "As the organizations became accustomed to working with each other, however, the principle of joint planning and joint action was closely adhered to. The entire operation became an unparalleled instance of interorganizational cooperation in the Jewish community."[78]

If cooperation was one measure of success, then the pressure at times for these agencies to consolidate represented another consideration. Both in the 1970s and again in the early 1990s (1993), the Congress and the Committee explored merger. Economic realities represented the impetus for these discussions, but in the end, the two institutions elected not to pursue such a plan. Then presidents Alfred Moses (American Jewish Committee) and Robert Lifton (American Jewish Congress) issued the following joint statement: "After careful study by the leaders of both organizations, it is our view that the Jewish community will be better served by preserving the respective strengths, including the programmatic distinctions, of the two organizations. The effort that we have been engaged in has given us renewed appreciation and respect for the traditions and accomplishments of both organizations, something that will undoubtedly result in continued close cooperation on matters of mutual concern."[79] Institutional politics needed to take into account differences in organizational styles and the realities of distinctive constituencies, along with the concerns of staff fearing the loss of positions.

Upon reflection, a historic tension has developed for these agencies between institutional competition and the communal desire for collaborative action.

The Shared Agenda

While each of these agencies may have addressed specific aspects of the communal agenda, these institutions and the "field" of Jewish community relations focused collectively on a number of core issues during the twenty-year period immediately following World War II. These concerns included dealing with anti-Semitism, civil rights and liberties, international matters, and intergroup and interreligious cooperation. While the issue of Israel was addressed in various contexts, this policy item would emerge as the significant item following the Six-Day War in 1967.

Fighting Anti-Semitism

Of all the issues that the "defenders" have engaged, the concerns associated with anti-Semitism reflect the core missions of these entities, the protection and welfare of American Jewry. The attention to this issue has been directed to a number of diverse considerations involving overt acts of hate directed against Jews and Jewish institutions, ideas and causes that have reflected a strong anti-Jewish bias, and public images of Jews that demean or misrepresent the Jewish people and Judaism. Clearly, the ADL has been the most frequently identified with the battle against anti-Semitism, yet all three of these agencies clearly view the question of Jewish security to be the central motif of their programs.

During the interwar years, their focus centered on Henry Ford's anti-Semitic campaign and the policies of exclusion and discrimination. Assessing the presence of anti-Semitism within the country during the war years, ADL's national leadership concluded: "The mass mind of America had been prepared and conditioned by diabolical anti-Semitic genius over many years. . . . It would be unfair to assume that with the limitation of funds so long imposed and the short space of time in which we had to organize personnel and program, that we could have successfully transmuted organized minority hatreds into immediate good will."[80] Nonetheless, the League saw its expanding role to include a survey of libraries to determine the presence of anti-Semitic books, compilation of libels and canards, and compilation of material on the elimination of objectionable remarks in books and movies. Coupled with this approach toward monitoring anti-Semitic trends, the ADL attempted to build a case for Jews. This effort resulted in a " survey in important cities in the United States to determine significant contributions made to American progress by Jewish residents, past and present," and the creation of a "Jewish Roll-Call," the collection of biographical data on Jews in art, literature, science, and other fields as a "picture of contributions of Jews to the progress of civilization throughout the ages."[81] Similarly, in an effort to place prominent speakers, both Jewish and non-Jewish, before key audiences, ADL's Speakers Bureau reported that in 1943 alone over 6,000 presentations were made. "Approximately eleven million people were reached by the speakers' messages, through the added publicity achieved through radio interviews, newspaper accounts of speeches, feature stories."[82]

In the postwar years, the activities of the ADL and the Committee were directed to four areas: fringe hate groups, extremist movements (more recently, the militia movements and antigovernment factions); the presence of anti-Semitic groups and streams of thinking within minority communities; and the presence of institutions and groups who direct their energies toward specific agendas, such as the denial of the Holocaust or attacks on Israel and its right to exist. Within this arena there are a series of seminal cases or issues, marked by their high media profile or political significance. For this purpose, five such "events" have been identified. These include the fallout over Jewish student involvement in the "New Left" and the antiwar movement, when institutions such as the University of Wisconsin proposed to impose limits on out-of-state students; the 1968 Ocean Hill-Brownsville (New York) school controversy; the threatened Nazi march through Skokie (Illinois) in 1977; the 1991 Crown Heights (New York) riots; and the 1995 "Million Man March." In each case one or more of the agencies sought to deal with both the immediate problem and the crisis, as well as the longer-term implications of these events both on public opinion and policies that might be introduced to alleviate or reduce tensions in these types of situations.

Among the more difficult issues facing the Jewish community in the 1960s was the emergence of black nationalism and its rejection of Jews and Jewish participation in the civil rights struggle. As late as 1967, the ADL published a five-volume study of black anti-Semitism, asserting that "there was less such prejudice among blacks than among whites."[83] However, in 1969, Bert Gold, Executive Vice-President of the Committee at the time, argued that the Jewish community could no longer remain silent about the reality and significance of black anti-Semitism. The tensions surrounding black-Jewish relations would be manifest through a number of events covering a fifteen-year period, involving local issues, principally in the New York area, and national concerns, culminating with the Andrew Young affair in 1979 when, as UN ambassador, Young was forced to resign following his unauthorized meeting with a PLO representative.

As part of ADL's overall work in this area, that agency would develop in the 1960s a measuring system designed to assess anti-Semitic attitudes. "It asks respondents for true-false responses to a list of stock anti-Jewish stereotypes, such as that Jews are greedy, clannish, and manipulative."[84] The ADL determined at the time that individuals who agreed with five or more of these eleven items ought to be classified as "most anti-Semitic."

Dealing with the broader considerations of bigotry and extremism, these agencies, and more specifically the ADL and the American Jewish Committee, expanded their work in more recent years in countering international terrorism, monitoring militia groups, and in assisting the church community most adversely affected by arson and threats. Through its "Special Edition" and its "Frontline" series, specialized publications and catalogues, and its Audit of Anti-Semitic Incidents and Terrorism Update Reports, the ADL now provides the largest and most comprehensive set of publications reporting on the patterns of prejudice and the writings and activities of hate organizations and terrorist movements. Background materials on hate crimes and training videos for use by police departments and federal authorities are available through the ADL and its regional operations. In addition, the League serves as a major resource center assisting educators on teaching about the Holocaust. The monitoring of the Holocaust denial phenomenon remains a priority as well for that agency.

The Civil Liberties Agenda:
The Case for Church-State Separation

As Naomi Cohen writes: "The tone had been set in the war years (World War I) when the crusade for Americanization viewed ethnic (read: deviant) behavior with suspicion. Some public-spirited citizens explicitly argued that the fundamentals of Americanism included the acceptance of the Christian nation idea, and they often used the two words "Christian" and "American" interchangeably."[85] Following World War I, "under the impact of rampant anti-Semitism and Americans' insistence on conformity, Jews opted for a low-profile on church-state questions, and moderation if not passivity persisted." For example, in 1924 when the U.S. Congress enacted a strict Sunday Blue Law for the District of Columbia, there was no Jewish response. Similarly, "in 1929, the defense agencies failed to respond when a lower court in Georgia disqualified Jews from serving on juries."

The postwar period would see a fundamental shift in policy and practice with regard to church-state considerations. The focus on church-state separation would ultimately become a defining element for these agencies and for the Jewish civic agenda. In many ways this principle would be seen as the measure for defining Jewish security. A society free of religious domination and influence with standards of practice regarding the role or place of religion represented the ideal. For the American Jewish Congress this would be the centerpiece of their legislative and judicial program. Clearly, its legal team, shaped and initially led by Leo Pfeffer and currently staffed by Marc Stern, has been the primary architect for defining the positions taken not only by the Congress but frequently adopted by the community relations field. Pfeffer successfully led the charge on several fronts beginning in the late 1940s involving several seminal cases, and in the process changed the practice of the defense agencies to hold back from taking such public action, out of fear of an anti-Semitic response. The first centered on the right of a state to aid parochial schools (*Everson v. Board of Education*); a second focused on the practice of "released time," which permitted public school students the opportunity to participate in religious studies, either on or off campus (*McCollum v. Board of Education*); and the third was directed to the issue of school prayer (*Engel v. Vitale*), which involved the recitation of New York State's Regents' Prayer. This later case was initially seen by Pfeffer and the Congress as not the best case in which to enter as a friend of the Court.

In addition, the Engel case "violated the Jewish defense agencies' practice of avoiding high-profile test cases with Jewish plaintiffs, so as to minimize anti-Jewish hostility."[86] When the Engel case went to the Supreme Court on review in 1961, the three national agencies filed briefs opposing school prayer, arguing that such an act violated the "establishment of religion" clause. In a June 1962 ruling, the Court, by a six to one decision, argued that "a union of government and religion tends to destroy government and to degrade religion."[87] A year later, the Court struck down Bible readings in public schools when it reviewed a Pennsylvania case (*Abington Township School District v. Schempp*). Once again, the three national agencies, in cooperation with the Philadelphia Jewish Community Relations Council, joined in an amicus brief. "The court had formally accepted his [Pfeffer's] argument that Jews were equal partners in the American enterprise and that America could no longer conduct itself—formally or informally, nationally or locally—as a Christian nation."[88] As the American Jewish Congress would report, this represented a "social revolution for religious equality."[89]

But the relative economic strengths of these agencies would change the balance of influence. Gregg Ivers concluded that in the 1980s, "internal changes in financial resources, staff expertise, and organizational commitment to church-state issues have been among the important forces responsible for the different approach the AJCongress has taken to litigation."[90] In contrast to the Congress's need to lessen its activities in this arena, Ivers noted that the ADL, with greater resources, has expanded its legal services and involvement within the church-state field. "From the 1980 to the 1992 terms of the Supreme Court, eleven of the sixteen amicus briefs filed by the ADL in church-state cases have been solo filings, an almost complete turnaround from the organization's prior behavior."[91] Further, Ivers commented that the Committee's options in this field remained "much more constrained" than its sister agencies, electing over this same time period to be a part of interfaith coalitions on matters of church-state litigation.[92]

International Affairs

The Committee's international agenda has, since its inception, played a significant role in that agency's overall operations. This pattern would continue in dramatic fashion following World War II, as the Committee embarked upon an aggressive program of political and educational intervention in Europe and the Americas. Beginning with post-Hitler Germany, the Committee worked from the following assumption: "Convinced that a nation's attitude toward Jews was a barometer of its democratic spirit, the Committee was certain that German prejudice could only be combated through a program of general reeducation."[93] While the Committee's involvement met with limited support from American Jewry and an ambivalence from U.S. authorities in light of the rapidly developing events surrounding the Cold War, the Committee was able to convince American officials to incorporate human relations training within some of their orientation programs. In addition, the Committee, again reverting to its strategy of creating coalitional partners, helped to forge the Citizens' Council for a Democratic Germany in order to bring together liberal institutions and leaders in the United States to promote activities on behalf of German reeducation. Throughout the postwar period, the Committee remained committed to the issues of German democracy, always monitoring the patterns of neo-Nazi and anti-Semitic activities. More recently, the Committee became the first American Jewish organization to open an office in Berlin, reflecting its ties to and interest in promoting German-Jewish understanding.

With the outbreak of the Cold War, the Committee, utilizing its research findings from two major studies, *Jews in the Soviet Union* (1951) and *Jews in the Soviet Satellites* (1953), sought "to alert the United States and the UN to the Soviet treatment of minorities; to educate American and European Jewish communities about communism and the Communists in their midst; and to arouse public opinion with the hope of cutting Russia off from its allies and the neutral nations."[94] American Jewish policy toward the Russians would be based on what had been learned from the Nazi period, namely, that "counteraction could not aggravate the situation, and might even help."[95] During the postwar years, the Committee continued to employ a host of diplomatic and public relations tools, including meetings with Russian officials and State Department personnel, promoting organizational resolutions and in-house publications, and establishing third-party interventions with the Soviets, all with the intent to create pressure on Moscow with regard to this matter.

In 1964, all three of these agencies joined in the formation of the American Jewish Conference of Soviet Jewry (and later the National Conference for Soviet Jewry) that served as a national clearinghouse for policy and action.

Unlike its political activities elsewhere, however, the Committee's involvement in Latin America reflected a broader consideration for Jewish institutional needs. In Argentina, the Committee was to play a significant role both through its own office in Buenos Aires and in the creation in 1948 of the Instituto Judio Argentino de Cultura e Informacion, a Latin American counterpart to the AJC. Employing the core tools and political strategies that had defined the Committee's style, the Instituto assumed an important role in the areas of interfaith and human relations education and human rights advocacy. Identifying its work in Argentina and elsewhere in the Americas as one of "missionary diplomacy," the Committee forged institutional ties with a variety of Jewish communities in the hemisphere, while promoting its core objectives.[96] This transnational pattern of organizational connections and affiliations would become an integral part of AJC's investment in its foreign affairs program.

The ADL has more recently accelerated its international profile by opening an office in Vienna, while continuing its ongoing involvement with the issue of Nazi war criminals and in responding to issues of anti-Semitism and international terrorism on the world stage. On various occasions the League has involved itself with specific Nazi war criminal cases. In 1993, in response to a federal appeals court ruling in the John Demjanjuk case, in which the three-judge panel implied that the OSI had acted due to pressure from "various interest groups," the ADL called this ruling "fodder for anti-Semites."[97] Outraged by the events in Bosnia in 1995, the ADL joined with other agencies in seeking humanitarian assistance for civilians and in taking out an ad in the *New York Times* (August 2, 1995) calling upon the international community to provide protection and relief.

The Bitburg Controversy: A Case Study

Drawing upon the events surrounding President Reagan's 1985 visit to Bitburg, Germany, Deborah Lipstadt has provided us with an interesting case study on the roles performed by the various defense agencies leading up to the president's visit, as well as the key followup steps that resulted. On May 5 of that year, at the invitation of Chancellor Helmut Kohl, Ronald Reagan participated in a brief gravesite ceremony where German soldiers were buried. Writing in the *American Jewish Year Book* (1987), Lipstadt offers not only an account of the role played by various Jewish and public officials and the actions and statements of Jewish organizations but also the polling data surrounding this decision. Prior to the visit, a wide range of initiatives were employed designed to persuade the White House not to go ahead with this plan. The American Jewish Committee's Rabbi A. James Rudin reported, "This was not an instance where Jews had to 'solicit Christian names.' They called us."[98] Beyond an outpouring of Christian clergy reaction, veterans groups, civil rights organizations, and fraternal bodies joined with Jewish institutions in expressing criticism of this decision. As late as April 29, "through the good offices of Billy Graham," a delegation from the American Jewish Committee was invited to the White House.[99] With the Committee's significant connections in Germany, that agency's representatives helped to broker an arrangement among the various parties to add to the president's itinerary a visit to the gravesite of Konrad Adenauer as a way to minimize the negative impact of the Bitburg event.

On May 3, the American Jewish Congress held an "alternative" wreath-laying ceremony at the gravesite of two young Germans who had been engaged in the resistance movement against the Nazis. Joining the Congress officials were several prominent black officials and celebrities. This was one of several demonstrations to be sponsored by American Jewish groups. Following the events and statements surrounding Bitburg, efforts were made at "damage control," according to Abe Foxman of the ADL. Morris Abram, a past national chair of the Committee, sought to put this episode aside by suggesting that "Bitburg was the mistake of a friend—not the sin of an enemy."[100]

In part as a response to the failure of these agencies to be more proactive on the world scene during the Nazi era, the Committee, and to a lesser degree the ADL, have used their international connections to advance both specific Jewish interests and general human rights concerns. Correspondingly, through their expanding international networks these agencies have been in a position to advocate for Israel-related concerns, pursue their intergroup relations interests, and market their services and products overseas.

Intergroup Relations

One of the distinguishing features of these national agencies is represented by the scope of contributions made by these organizations to the field of intergroup relations. From the outset, these entities sought to establish standards of practice. Outlined below is a listing of some of the programmatic strategies and community relations tools initially introduced or effectively employed by one or more of these organizations. The American Jewish Committee, in great measure, pioneered in this arena, as represented by its work on white ethnic behavior in the late 1960s and 1970s; its ongoing research on intergroup relations, culminating in a 1993 national study conducted for AJC by the Gallup Organization; and its celebrated national ad campaign against hate.

The Committee's various educational ventures include "Hands across the Campus," a program designed to assist schools with the teaching of racial, religious, and ethnic diversity; and the Skirball Institute on American Values, which sponsors a number of initiatives in education for the western states, directed to clergy, teachers, and students. The introduction in 1996 of *Common Quest*, a joint publication of Howard University and the Committee, provided "an opportunity to discuss pivotal issues . . . and to explore the broader context of race, group identity, and pluralism in America."[101] In line with the Committee's interest in developing research centers and program institutes within the core areas of that agency's work, the Arthur and Rochelle Belfer Center on American Pluralism was created in 1996 "to expand AJC's vital coalitional work with racial and ethnic communities."[102] As part of its tradition as a research agency, the Committee has continued to publish background reports covering a wide range of subjects. In the arena of terrorist and militia activities alone, the Committee has produced documents on the McVeigh trial (1997), militia activities (1995), and Muslim fundamentalism (1993).

The ADL's widely acclaimed "World of Difference" program (1986) represents one of the largest intergroup educational ventures ever undertaken by a nonprofit institution. Today, this national program incorporates a number of unique segments serving school districts, colleges and universities, national organizations, municipalities, and the corporate sector, where over one hundred clients have been served. In addition to this significant investment of resources, the ADL has joined the Committee by running striking advertisements, and billboards including the "Diversity Is Our Strength" campaign in several major markets. ADL's sports posters, featuring such personalities as Nancy Lopez, Grant Hill, Eric Lindros, and Michael Chang, includes the caption: "If you really believe in America, prejudice is foul play." Similar to the Committee, the League has commissioned from time to time major national studies on racial and anti-Semitic attitudes.

Interreligious Affairs

The Committee and the League profoundly shaped the landscape in the field of interfaith relations. The civic principle associated with intergroup relations and interfaith understanding was framed out of a desire to insure the well-being of Jews and secure the status of Judaism within the society. America's acceptance of Jews in the twentieth century would be measured through the religious frame. The postwar investment by these agencies and others in the interfaith enterprise would ultimately contribute to the repositioning of the role of Judaism in the American religious constellation.

The principal focus in the early years was directed toward the goal of reducing anti-Semitism and securing the positions of Jews and Judaism within American society. Toward this end, the agencies directed their initial efforts toward educating other religious communities about Jews, seeking to deemphasize religious differences within this process. "Differences in religious ritual became a method of bringing together various denominations with the belief that knowing these differences would serve to make them less 'strange' and less menacing."[103] The Jewish community's attention at the outset was directed to the Protestant churches, which were seen as America's "ruling religion." In contrast, the Catholic Church was viewed as more hostile, in light of its embedded history of anti-Semitism.

In 1944, the ADL developed one of the most ambiguous outreach educational programs to Christian clergy. Entitled the *Christian Friends Bulletin*, this newsletter would ultimately reach 7,600 clergy or 7 percent of the total Christian clergy in the United States, providing insights and information on Jewish-Christian relations. Major seminary leaders, bishops, and church officials comprised the membership of the *Christian Friends* roster.[104] During this period, the ADL's Fact Finding and Research Departments monitored numerous Christian religious periodicals, books, and pamphlets, as well as the national religious news services.

Beginning in the 1950s, the American Jewish Committee encouraged and assisted in the financial underwriting of a series of self-studies by each of the faith communities regarding their curriculum and textbook materials, involving references and comparisons with other religious and ethnic groups. The findings from these studies, as well as a 1966 ADL-sponsored study conducted by its Survey Research Center, revealed that "Christian teachings which played 'a crucial historical role in the rise of anti-Semitism' continue to 'reinforce and foster' anti-Jewish prejudice in the United States despite an increasing spirit of good will between the faiths and a willingness on the part of many American churchmen 'to take action to combat anti-Semitism.'"[105]

During the 1960s, both agencies, along with local JCRCs, sponsored "dialogue" groups involving Jewish representatives, both volunteer and professional, in discussions with their counterparts from the Protestant and Catholic traditions. The subject matter for these sessions covered a whole array of theological, historical, and social concerns. Commenting on the value and purpose of such exercises, a prominent Jewish leader suggested: "Dialogue causes the non-Jew to view the Jew with new eyes or through new glasses. His ignorance and prejudices about us begin to fall under attack."[106]

Possibly no other interreligious event in the twentieth century was more significant than the Second Vatican Council's "Statement on the Jews," *Nostra Aetate* (1964). As a result of this document, a fundamental transformation would take place in Catholic-Jewish cooperation and involvement. Beginning in 1971, through a coalition of agencies involving the national defense agencies, the World Jewish Congress, and the Synagogue Council, a formal dialogue was established with the Vatican.[107]

Since entering this field of endeavor in 1959, the American Jewish Committee has engaged only two national directors, Rabbis Marc Tanenbaum and James Rudin, to manage its interreligious agenda. The unique relationship developed during these early years by Marc Tanenbaum with leading Catholic clergy set the tone for the accomplishments that would follow in framing new and historic church doctrine.

Upon reflecting on the accomplishments of his thirty-two year career that helped to place the Committee's interfaith work "on the map," Rabbi Rudin noted these four events: the opening of diplomatic relations by the Vatican with the State of Israel; the interreligious effort on behalf of Soviet Jewry; the perception of Jews and Judaism at all levels of Christian education and liturgy; and "the coming to the table of Christian evangelicals."[108]

The Israel Agenda

The national agencies' focus on the Israel agenda encompasses several stages. Prior to 1967 the foreign affairs programs of these organizations were directed in part to their concerns for the welfare of

Jews residing in Northern Africa and the Middle East. Despite its non-Zionist orientation, the Committee early on began to create connections to the State of Israel. The issue of Israel-diaspora relationships and the question of "dual loyalty" afforded Jacob Blaustein of the American Jewish Committee and David Ben-Gurion the occasion to formulate a framework of understanding, expressed through an exchange of letters. In 1950, Ben-Gurion would write: "The Jews of the United States, as a community and as individuals, have only one political attachment and that is to the United States of America. They owe no political allegiance to Israel. The State of Israel represents and speaks only on behalf of its own citizens and in no way presumes to represent or speak in the name of Jews or citizens in any other country." In 1970, Golda Meir reaffirmed this understanding in a letter to Blaustein, stating that "there has been no deviation from it and it is my intention that there will not be."[109]

In 1956, John Slawson, speaking at the Committee's forty-ninth annual meeting, noted: "Regardless of all the difficulties some of us may feel Israel has laid on our doorstep, the great fact remains that the creation of Israel after a spectacular struggle not only has given many American Jews a deep feeling of pride, but also helped to change the image of the Jew all over the world."[110] Realizing the significance that Israel would play in world Jewish affairs, and more specifically with regard to American policy, the Committee opened the first Israel Office among the defense agencies.

For the Committee and the ADL, during the early years of Israel's existence, the attention directed to that democracy was primarily focused around the concerns of how a Jewish state would impact on the welfare and status of American Jewry. In 1949, Benjamin Epstein, ADL's national director, speaking to the issue of "What Does Israel Mean to Democracy?," suggested that "the creation of Israel has instilled American Jewry with a new feeling of strength and confidence which enables it to contribute more effectively to the struggle for a fuller American democracy." He went on to warn that "professional anti-Semites were using the State of Israel as a springboard for a new anti-Semitic line: 'the Jews now have a place to go—send them back there.'"[111]

Lyndon Johnson in the mid-1960s urged American Jews to support the administration's Vietnam policies, if they wanted Washington to assist Israel. Jewish leaders divided along ideological lines over how best to respond, with the ADL joining with groups on the right, while Congress aligned itself with organizations in the anti-war camp. "Trying to forlornly hold the center" was the American Jewish Committee.[112]

When Israel came under attack by the mainstream media and national press during the mid-1970s and beyond, the three agencies were actively engaged in promoting a variety of responses. In three separate activities, one can explore these agencies' responses. After a 1973 CBS Radio commentary by Robert Pierpoint critical of the Jewish lobby and its power, the ADL mobilized a nationwide protest directed at CBS affiliates. One year later, American Jewish Congress mounted a campaign against *National Geographic* for an article claiming that Syria provided its Jewish citizens with full religious and political rights. Employing a national letter-writing campaign as well as orchestrating a demonstration outside of the magazine's Washington offices, the Congress helped bring the issue of Syrian Jewry to national attention. Following the 1982 invasion of Lebanon by Israel as part of its "Peace for Galilee" Campaign, the Committee undertook a major study of network coverage of these events, in light of severe media criticism of Israeli practices which served to document a "consistent anti-Israel bias."[113]

In more recent years through their Israel offices, these national agencies have expanded their roles by sponsoring dialogue groups, Israel trips, and seminars for targeted elite groups from the government, academic, media, and business sectors. The Committee, through its Institute on American Jewish-Israeli Relations, has also sponsored annual exchanges designed to build ties between American and Israeli Jews. During the debate in Israel over the "Who is a Jew?" question, the Committee arranged for the visits of Knesset members with Jewish leaders across the United States in order to provide these Israeli officials with a greater appreciation of the impact of this issue for American Jews.

The American Jewish Congress launched a major contribution to the framing of a dialogue between American Jewry and Israel in the mid-1960s when it initiated its annual "America-Israel Dialogue." Over the years this forum has addressed the difficult and complex issues impacting on this unique relationship, examining such issues as the state of the Jewish people and the prospects for peace in the Middle East. This dialogue series would introduce leading Israeli academics, writers, and political leaders to their American counterparts, creating an early and important framework for building significant connections between these two worlds. Along with the publication of the proceedings of these discussions, the Congress, as would be the case for each of the agencies, produced and/or commissioned various studies and research papers examining various aspects of the Israel-Arab conflict. During the 1980s, the Congress, under the leadership of its former executive director, Henry Siegman, sought to promote a series of peace initiatives involving Palestinians and Israelis. At the time, such an approach evoked criticism among American Jewish groups and Israeli officials.

During the period of the first Palestinian intifada, for instance, each of the national agencies sponsored public opinion studies (ADL-Penn and Schoen; American Jewish Committee-Roper; and American Jewish Congress-Martilla and Kiley). "In short, these surveys and others conducted during the year (1989) found the level of American support for Israel more unsteady than it had been for years."[114] In a response that has emulated these agencies' performance in other areas, new program and educational initiatives have been announced, designed to rebuild the case for Israel, directed at key elites. A pattern of directed giving for dealing with a specific issue or crisis has not been an uncommon practice for these institutions.

Unlike the traditional Zionist groups, the "defender's" approach to the Israel agenda can be assessed through the framework of how Americans understand and relate to the case for Israel. These agencies have approached their work in this arena through four frames:

1. Developing a crisis-response position to a particular issue or problem,
2. Promoting a public relations campaign to market the general case for Israel,
3. Targeting key influentials whose support is viewed as critical to public support in the United States for Israel, and
4. Linking the agency's Israel agenda to other institutional and community relations concerns.

Special Agendas: Jewish Continuity and the Status of Women

"By the 1960s . . . the national Jewish agencies began to re-emphasize more particularly Jewish priorities. This return to a modified form of particularism . . . reflected increasing concern over right wing extremism, the historical legacy of the Holocaust, the security of Israel, and the maintenance of Jewish group identity against the threat of assimilation."[115]

Outside of the Committee's Jewish Communal Service Department, the other agencies have been far less engaged in the issues associated with Jewish renewal, the Jewish pluralism debate, and the other past and current issues that define the internal questions associated with American Jewish life. In the 1960s, through the professional leadership and commitment of Bert Gold, the Committee carved out a significant role for itself in this area; and for over thirty years the Committee has been active within this sphere, publishing studies and offering policy pronouncements involving a variety of communal policy areas. In the 1990s the Committee launched a new advertisement series in the *New York Times* and other publications, entitled "what being Jewish means to me." The objective of this initiative was "to make compelling arguments for being Jewish in an age of choice through the often moving stories of committed Jews."[116] As part of the Committee's Jewish Literacy project, that agency sponsored a series of institutes designed to assist its members in broadening their Jewish knowledge, in addition to the publication of *Understanding Jewish History*, a self-study curriculum developed by Stephen Bayme, the Committee's current director of Jewish communal affairs.

With reference to the issues affecting the welfare of women in general, and Jewish women in particular, while the other agencies have addressed specific policy concerns, the Congress has had a historic connection to this field of interest. Activities in this arena were initiated through its Women's Division dating back to the early years of the agency and later through its Commission on Women's Equality. The former body was among the first Jewish organizations to oppose the war in Vietnam. Its women's leadership overall would play an active role in such forums as the UN World Conference on Women and the 1984 Congress-sponsored American-Israel Dialogue on "Jew as Woman, Woman as Jew," as well as through policy statements on family and women's issues. During the 1970s, the American Jewish Committee, as part of its Institute on Pluralism and Group Identity, produced a broad range of materials on women's issues and more specifically with a focus on the Jewish woman, including the publication of a newsletter entitled "Mainstream."

The specialized agendas taken up by the "defenders" tend to:

1. Re-enforce the existing core Jewish civic principles,
2. Operate within a framework of past practices and policies,
3. Respond to specific social phenomena, and
4. Occur in reaction to the marketplace and emulate the practices and initiatives of the other agencies.

Leadership

As noted earlier, the "defenders" represented institutions committed to social change and civic education. They can be seen as well through the "great men" who shaped these organizations and led them over significant periods. Stephen Wise performed that function for the Congress, while a series of distinguished volunteer leaders played this role for the Committee. These included, but are not limited to, Louis Marshall, Jacob Schiff, Oscar Straus, and later Jacob Blaustein, and Morris Abram. Their leadership visions, along with their capacities to access political elites and command broad support and communal recognition, enhanced the image and importance of their respective agencies. Over time, these agencies have groomed national leadership who would play significant roles in other Jewish communal settings and within the political framework, serving as elected officials, ambassadors, diplomats, and administrators.

In interviews with the principal players of these agencies, overwhelmingly they addressed the idea of "legacy," where each institution's leaders felt that they were carrying forward the organizational concepts developed and nurtured by their respective predecessors. Abe Foxman noted that, while each of ADL's earlier directors reflected their own "persona," a continuity of practice had been framed over the decades. These directors, including Leon Lewis (1913-1931), Richard Gutstadt (1931-1947), Benjamin Epstein (1947-1979), and Nathan Perlmutter (1979-1987), promoted, in Foxman's terms, ADL's "unique approach."[117] Indeed all three of the agencies take pride in the quality of their professional leadership, individuals who have made distinctive contributions in defining and promoting their specific institutions while in turn adding a dimension of distinction to the general field of community relations.

ADL's uniqueness has been tied to two factors: a commitment to its core objective and the leadership roles played by its executive directors. While this agency's early history is subsumed under the banner of its parent organization, B'nai B'rith, the nature of the issues it was committed to addressing and the scope and strength of the leadership that the ADL did attract led to its creating a separate institutional identity. Today, that agency sees its mandate to include its traditional role in monitoring anti-Semitism, bigotry, and racism, while expanding its focus to also include extremism, counterterrorism, and hate crimes. International affairs, religious liberty, education, and Israel encompass the other four core components on the ADL agenda.

How ADL packages and directs its core agenda, fighting anti-Semitism, represents its principal challenge. ADL's "World of Difference" education and prejudice reduction program is a prime example. Based on the essential mission and focus of the agency, this particular initiative has given ADL new market opportunities to reach broader and different constituencies. This entrepreneurial quality has to some degree separated the ADL from its fellow agencies, allowing it to expand its outreach program through educational training on the international level and within the public and private sectors. In recent years, for example, as part of its international operations, the League has incorporated the efforts launched by Rabbi Harold Schulweis to both honor and provide financial assistance to those surviving gentile rescuers who saved and protected European Jews during the Holocaust.

More recently, the ADL announced that, in cooperation with the Learning Company of Massachusetts, the agency had created and released the "ADL Hatefilter." This allows parents and others to block access to Internet sites that promote hate which is "directed at groups or individuals singled out because of their religion, race, ethnicity, gender or sexual orientation. Hatefilter redirects the user to the ADL website to get accurate, regularly updated information on organized hate groups."

In the case of the American Jewish Congress, the creativity of David Petegorski during the 1940s can be assessed in terms of the policy directions that he and his colleagues put forth. Similarly, John Slawson redefined the operational principles that drove the American Jewish Committee throughout the war years and into the postwar era. During the decade following World War II each of these agencies attracted a cadre of young professionals drawn from such areas as the law, government service, and the social policy field to design and implement an array of policies and programs. These professionals left a profound impact on their respective organizations and made a contribution to the broader discipline of community relations. Within the Congress, individuals such as Will Maslow, Leo Pfeffer, Howard Squadron, Henry Siegman, and Phil Baum provided that type of leadership and expertise.

These agencies have undergone a series of redefinitions over the course of their institutional histories. For the Congress there have been at least three such reincarnations. The initial focus of that organization reflected Stephen Wise's dream of creating a Jewish "congress," but this ceased to operate after the peace process following World War I. A different type of congress structure was formed in 1921 with its own membership base, significantly influenced and led by Wise, in order to focus on the core domestic concerns of the Jewish community, while forging ahead with its Zionist commitment. A third transformation, focusing on the Congress's judicial approach toward addressing the issues of racism and prejudice, can be seen once David Petegorsky assumed the mantle of professional leadership in the mid-1940s, and that transition was completed with the death of Stephen Wise in 1949. A Congress observer described the agency's decision-making style as one of "partnership" involving its professionals and volunteer leadership, noting the intensity and passion associated with its decision-making process. In the postwar period and beyond, while Leo Pfeffer defined the philosophy and role to be played by the Congress, many of the legal briefs filed by that agency were in fact prepared by, or had significant input from, the core of prominent and knowledgeable judges and lawyers who comprised much of the leadership of the agency.

The transitions associated with the American Jewish Committee are centered on the leadership styles and institutional priorities that were established during the tenures of their respective executive vice presidents, John Slawson, Bert Gold, Ira Silverman, David Gordis, and, currently, David Harris. While clearly organized around a volunteer and professional decision-making model, in contrast, for instance, to the ADL's dominant professional style of seeking "advice and consent" from its volunteer leadership, the Committee's institutional transformations have been more about policy than about structure or style. Moving from a non-Zionist posture to a position of engagement and support for Israel and similarly shifting from its universal perspective to a consciously engaged Jewish communal affairs agenda, the committee has repositioned itself in a number of areas but without sacrificing its core institutional image and approach.

Always committed to the notion of American Jewish pluralism, the Committee has championed its institutional independence as a means of demonstrating the political diversity within Jewish life. To its credit, despite significant criticism, the Committee has continued to sponsor *Commentary* as an independent journal devoted to neoconservative political views, incorporating articles drawn from a broad range of social and intellectual interests.

In some measure the Committee's more recent, highly publicized ventures in promoting international relief campaigns for earthquake victims in Turkey and for refugees in war-torn Yugoslavia reconnects that agency to its founding focus on world-related diplomatic considerations. Similarly, in recent years, the Committee has engaged in more publicly directed, higher-profile approaches involving ad campaigns and direct mail, designed to reach broader audiences in order to attract new members and to advance its agenda in support for Israel and in promoting Jewish continuity.

Bruce Ramer, the Committee's current national president, commenting on the agency's evolution from a volunteer leader's vantage point, observed how he has been impressed with and influenced by his predecessors, including Morris Abram, Howard Friedman, Sholom Comay, and Alfred Moses. Ramer, evaluating the Committee's diplomatic approach and reflective problem-solving style, suggested: "We would rather be there the night before, than the day after."[118] Commenting on the agency's accomplishments, Ramer offered the observation that the Committee's success was linked to maintaining its core ideological principles and to its tradition of professional excellence. When asked to define his vision for the Committee's future, he framed three principles: "increase Jewish pride, reduce Jewish fear, and enable Jewish interests openly and forcefully."[119]

In assessing the ADL's strengths and accomplishments, Abraham Foxman, its national director, described the agency as committed to the principle of "vigilance against extremism," while assisting Americans to better understand their role as knowledgeable citizens in protecting democracy. Affirming that theme, Foxman noted that six months before the Oklahoma City bombing, the ADL had identified fourteen "armed and dangerous" militia groups. He saw the agency's role in promoting hate crimes legislation, for example, as symbolizing its position as the "watchdog on anti-Semitism." With regard to the issues of competition and the oft-repeated charges of duplication, Foxman affirmed the principle of "letting the marketplace speak" and of the respective "styles" of these agencies, adding that he would prefer that the president of the United States "get more than one letter" from American Jewry.[120]

Phil Baum, the national director of the Congress, defined his agency's uniqueness through two perspectives, that of Stephen Wise's imprint and early vision and in the organizational genius of Alexander Pekelis. Wise helped to define the "character" of the Congress, while Pekelis established the principle of advocating for civil rights and liberties through legislation and the courts. "We were the ones in the court," noted Baum. Responding as well to the issue of duplication, Baum suggested that these agencies had developed different "markets, approaches, and priorities."[121]

The story of "the defenders" is in many respects the tale of the twentieth-century American Jew. These agencies, at their founding, reflected Jewish fears and concerns of a community endeavoring to "make it in America." Seeking through their respective missions and programs to respond to these considerations, "the defenders" sought to represent the Jewish community at all the centers of power that would ultimately shape the society and have an impact on the welfare of world Jewry. In the process of these representations, they have helped to shape a discipline that incorporated the strategies and tools of analysis and advocacy. Through their expertise and insights over eight decades, a unique body of knowledge about social behaviors and the civic culture has been developed. As pioneers of judicial intervention, intergroup practice, and interest group politics, these agencies have established a framework for communal activism. Their institutional stories reflect the American Jewish saga of this past century and, in turn, they have contributed to the texture of American life and culture.

These agencies framed their work around both a set of civic principles and a code of best practices. As a result, in the earlier years, the conduct of community relations as practiced by these institutions was seen as creative and resourceful. There has emerged in more recent years a type of uniformity of practice that has drawn criticism around the lock-step performance of the "defenders." Critics have suggested that these agencies are pursuing an agenda devoid of substance and uniqueness, where current institutional practice is designed to be more self-serving than cutting edge. Others have raised questions as to the nature of their being representative today of Jewish viewpoints and the diversity of interests that comprise American Jewry. Will the economies of operation and the narrowing of the consensus around a communal agenda force the closure or merger of these entities? This may depend in part on economic factors, new policy, and community challenges that may face American Jewry, and the possible repositioning of one or more of these agencies on the political spectrum.

Notes

1. Hershel Shanks, "No Galvanizing Issue?" *Moment* (August 1995): 4.
2. Maurice Fagan, "Trends in Jewish Community Relations Work," *A Reader in Jewish Community Relations*, A. G. Wolfe, ed. (New York: Ktav Publishing House, 1975), 2.
3. Paul Jacobs, *Is Curly Jewish? A Political Self-Portrait Illuminating Three Turbulent Decades of Social Revolt* (New York: Atheneum, 1965), 32.

4. Arnold Aronson, "The Origins of the Community Relations Field," *Journal of Intergroup Relations* 1(2) (Spring 1960): 45.
5. Aronson, "Origins," 44.
6. Aronson, "Origins," 45.
7. Aronson, "Origins," 45.
8. American Jewish Committee, *The Pursuit of Equality: A Half Century with the American Jewish Committee* (New York: Crown, 1957), 91.
9. Jack Wertheimer, "A Jewish Contract with America," *Commentary* (May 1995): 35.
10. Wertheimer, "Jewish Contract," 35.
11. Roberta Feuerlicht, *The Fate of the Jews* (New York: Times Books, 1983), 133.
12. William Orbach, *The American Movement to Aid Soviet Jews* (Amherst: University of Massachusetts Press, 1979), 192-93.
13. Lucy Dawidowicz, "A Century of Jewish History, 1881-1981," *American Jewish Year Book* (Philadelphia: American Jewish Committee and Jewish Publication Society, 1982), 4.
14. J. J. Goldberg, *Jewish Power: Inside the American Jewish Establishment* (New York: Addison-Wesley, 1996), 102.
15. Dawidowicz, "A Century of Jewish History," 4.
16. Dawidowicz, "A Century of Jewish History," 4.
17. Peter J. Medding, "The New Jewish Politics in America," *Terms of Survival,* Robert S. Wistrich, ed. (London: Routledge, 1995), 84.
18. Dawidowicz, "Century," 43-44.
19. Goldberg, *Jewish Power,* 102.
20. Goldberg, *Jewish Power,* 103.
21. Goldberg, *Jewish Power,* 103.
22. American Jewish Committee, *Act of Incorporation—Laws of New York in the Fifth Annual Report* (New York: American Jewish Committee, 1912), 24.
23. Jonathan Frankel, *Prophecy and Politics: Socialism, Nationalism, and the Russian Jews, 1862-1917* (Cambridge: Cambridge University Press, 1981), 515.
24. Frankel, *Prophecy,* 325.
25. Frankel, *Prophecy,* 325.
26. Goldberg, *Jewish Power,* 103.
27. Goldberg, *Jewish Power,* 63.
28. Fagan, "Trends," 9.
29. Nathan Belth, *A Promise to Keep: A Narrative of the American Encounter with Anti-Semitism* (New York: Times Books, 1979), 38.
30. Belth, *Promise,* 39.
31. Arnold Forster, *The Anti-Defamation League,* vol. 28, nos. 33 and 34 (1975): 53.
32. Belth, *Promise,* 42.
33. Belth, *Promise,* 42.
34. Belth, *Promise,* 42.

35. "Light in the Dark of Prejudice," *B'nai B'rith Monthly* 40, no. 5 (1926): 144.
36. "Light in the Dark," 144.
37. Belth, *Promise,* 51-52.
38. Forster, *Anti-Defamation League,* 53.
39. Forster, *Anti-Defamation League,* 54.
40. Forster, *Anti-Defamation League,* 54.
41. Belth, *Promise,* 78.
42. Belth, *Promise,* 56.
43. Belth, *Promise,* 57.
44. Belth, *Promise,* 57.
45. Frederick Lazin, "The Response of the American Jewish Committee to the Crisis of German Jewry," *American Jewish History,* 68 (1978-1979): 287.
46. Lazin, "Response," 287.
47. Lazin, "Response," 287.
48. Lazin, "Response," 291.
49. Lazin, "Response," 293.
50. Lazin, "Response," 293.
51. American Jewish Congress, "Timely Topics," *Congress Weekly,* February 7, 1949, 16(6): 4.
52. American Jewish Committee, *Pursuit of Equality,* 80.
53. Arnold Forster, *A Measure of Freedom* (Garden City, N.Y.: Doubleday, 1950), 112.
54. American Jewish Committee, *Pursuit of Equality,* 63.
55. American Jewish Committee, *Pursuit of Equality,* 64.
56. Goldberg, *Jewish Power,* 131.
57. Goldberg, *Jewish Power,* 131.
58. *B'nai B'rith Monthly* (1949): 191.
59. *B'nai B'rith Monthly* (1949): 191.
60. *B'nai B'rith Monthly* (1949): 191.
61. *B'nai B'rith Monthly* (1949): 191.
62. *B'nai B'rith Monthly* (1949): 312.
63. Forster, *Measure of Freedom,* 211.
64. Forster, *Measure of Freedom,* 212.
65. "Congress Ideology Redefined," *Congress Weekly,* February 24, 1946, 6.
66. "Congress Ideology Redefined," 8.
67. "The Congress Convention," *Congress Weekly,* June 4, 1946, 4.
68. Goldberg, *Jewish Power,* 121.
69. David Petegorsky, "Congress in Action," *Congress Weekly,* June 4, 1946, 8.
70. David Petegorsky, "Frontiers of Jewish Activity," *Congress Weekly,* November 28, 1949, 5.
71. Petegorsky, "Frontiers," 7.
72. Arthur Hertzberg, *The Jews in America* (New York: Simon and Schuster, 1989), 311.

73. Stuart Svonkin, *Jews against Prejudice: American Jews and the Fight for Civil Liberties* (New York: Columbia University Press, 1997), 4.
74. Oscar Janowsky, *The American Jew* (Philadelphia: Jewish Publication Society, 1972), 335-36.
75. NJCRAC, *Program Plan: 1994-1995* (New York: NJCRAC, 1995), 12.
76. Janowsky, *The American Jew*, 335-36.
77. Will Maslow, "The Struggle against the Arab Boycott," *Midstream* 23(7) (August/September 1977): 12.
78. Maslow, "Struggle," 12.
79. Joe Dimow, "Inside the Jewish Community," *Jewish Currents* (July/August 1994): 33.
80. Anti-Defamation League, *Annual Report* (New York: ADL, 1943), 4.
81. Anti-Defamation League, *Annual Report*, 7.
82. Anti-Defamation League, *Annual Report*, 8.
83. Hertzberg, *Jews in America*, 366.
84. Goldberg, *Jewish Power*, 330.
85. Naomi Cohen, "The Faces of American Jewish Defense in the 1920s," in *An Inventory of Promises*, Jeffrey Gurock and Marc Lee Raphael, eds. (New York: Carlson Publishers, 1995), 15.
86. Goldberg, *Jewish Power*, 123.
87. Goldberg, *Jewish Power*, 124.
88. Goldberg, *Jewish Power*, 124.
89. Goldberg, *Jewish Power*, 124.
90. Gregg Ivers, *To Build a Wall* (Charlottesville: University of Virginia Press, 1995), 197.
91. Ivers, *To Build a Wall*, 198.
92. Ivers, *To Build a Wall*, 199.
93. Naomi Cohen, *Not Free to Desist: The American Jewish Committee, 1906-1966* (Philadelphia: Jewish Publication Society, 1972), 481.
94. Cohen, *Not Free to Desist*, 499.
95. Cohen, *Not Free to Desist*, 500.
96. Cohen, *Not Free to Desist*, 530.
97. Goldberg, *Jewish Power*, 190.
98. Deborah Lipstadt, "The Bitburg Controversy," *American Jewish Year Book* (New York: American Jewish Committee and Jewish Publication Society, 1987), 32.
99. Lipstadt, "Bitburg Controversy," 34.
100. Lipstadt, "Bitburg Controversy," 37.
101. American Jewish Committee, *Annual Report* (New York: American Jewish Committee, 1996), 8.
102. American Jewish Committee, *Annual Report*, 8.
103. Fagan, "Trends," 143.
104. R. E. Gutstadt, "To the Executive Committee of the Supreme Lodge of B'nai B'rith" (Washington, D.C.: B'nai B'rith, 1945), 5.
105. Fagan, "Trends," 156.

106. Fagan, "Trends," 166-67.
107. Goldberg, *Jewish Power*, 6.
108. Steven F. Windmueller, Interview with Rabbi A. James Rudin, 2000.
109. Fagan, "Trends," 256-57.
110. Fagan, "Trends," 248-49.
111. *B'nai B'rith Monthly* (1949), 304.
112. Goldberg, *Jewish Power*, 207.
113. Goldberg, *Jewish Power*, 296.
114. Douglas Kahn and Earl Raab, eds., *Civil and Political Intergroup Relations,* vol. 90 (New York: American Jewish Committee and Jewish Publication Society, 1990), 213.
115. Svonkin, *Jews against Prejudice,* 7.
116. American Jewish Committee, *Annual Report,* 14.
117. Steven F. Windmueller, Interview with Abraham Foxman, 1999.
118. Steven F. Windmueller, Interview with Bruce Ramer, 1999.
119. Windmueller, Interview with Bruce Ramer, 1999.
120. Windmueller, Interview with Abraham Foxman, 1999.
121. Steven F. Windmueller, Interview with Phil Baum, 1999.

2

Local Community Relations Councils and Their National Body

Michael C. Kotzin

Introduction

Well over 100 Jewish Community Relations Councils (JCRCs) (some of them with different names) are found in American cities throughout the country. Some are committees of federations, some are federation departments, and some are freestanding organizations. For some of them, the constituents are individuals from the community serving on a Board of Directors; for some of them, the constituents are representatives of local organizations or of the local chapters of national organizations; and for some of them the constituency is a hybrid. Though in the past some of these bodies served jointly as CRCs and regional offices of national organizations, today that is rare. The key to the uniqueness of the JCRCs is that they are locally based bodies. While benefiting from the possibility of drawing upon the expertise of national organizations, they frame positions expressive of the perspectives of their constituents and they carry out action agendas on behalf of and in the name of the local Jewish communities.

The importance of the CRCs is emphasized by Daniel Elazar: "From the 1950s onward, the emergence of the Jewish Community

Relations Councils attached to the federations established a core that, with federation backing, could not easily be ignored. These JCRCs, with the Jewish Council for Public Affairs and the federations, play the largest role in Jewish representation today, although they draw the least publicity."[1] With many of the issues revolving around the subject of Jews and the American public square being carried out in the local arena, Jewish Community Relations Councils are indeed significant players, and their importance has increased over recent years as Jewish organizational life, along with national life in general, has become more and more decentralized.

Community Relations Councils began to come into being in the 1930s. According to Jerome Chanes, their purpose was "to provide a means for coordination of defense activity within a community" since "communities were no longer content to leave activity entirely to national organizations who rarely consulted with one another or with local leadership." They were also meant "to serve as forums for the discussion of varied views."[2] Like the three community relations "defense" organizations—the American Jewish Committee, the American Jewish Congress, and the Anti-Defamation League of B'nai B'rith—CRCs primarily focused on combating anti-Semitism.

Chanes questions the generally received view that at their inception CRCs were a product of the federations in the various communities. But he acknowledges that even if that was not the case originally, after the Council of Jewish Federations brought fourteen CRCs and four national agencies (the aforementioned defense organizations plus the Jewish Labor Committee) together to form the National Community Relations Advisory Council (NCRAC) in 1944, the federation world became the prime mover for the establishment of CRCs throughout the country.

By 1950, when Professor R. M. MacIver was engaged by the NCRAC system to prepare a *Report on the Jewish Community Relations Agencies*, the numbers of CRCs had grown considerably. In his report, published in 1951, MacIver declared that "one of the healthier developments in the complicated skein of Jewish organizational activity has been the formation of integrative community councils and particularly, from our present viewpoint, of community relations committees. . . . These bodies have gradually been taking hold, increasing in number and status and setting an example of unified action that furnishes a significant contrast to the operation of the jealously separatist national agencies."[3]

While preparing his study, MacIver was able to observe a shift in the agenda of the community relations world from the time the earliest CRCs were created. Though the need to protect Jewish security and maintain Jewish rights had remained central to the community relations agenda, in the post-World War II environment anti-discrimination efforts had broadened. Anti-Semitism was made less legitimate in America by the impact of the Holocaust and by efforts to counter anti-Jewish bigotry, though discrimination lingered in areas such as employment, housing, and educational opportunity. At that point, the community relations field enunciated as a cornerstone of its activities the premise that the security and well-being of the American Jewish community was directly tied up with guarantees of equality for all Americans. In so doing, the field became an active player in the nation's civil rights movement, working in coalition with like-minded bodies.

While Abraham Joshua Heschel and local rabbis may have brought religion-based convictions into the civil rights struggle, community relations activities at this time were generally less tied to an overt expression of Jewish concepts than was to become the case later. Insofar as the community relations organizations were operating with a self-conscious sense of Jewish principles and with the aim of projecting Jewish values into the public square, their sources and vision for the most part derived from what is commonly referred to as the "prophetic tradition."[4] Their initial goals, to a great extent, were universalistic. That was to change in the coming years.

A turning point came in the late 1960s and early 1970s, in the context of several other developments. It was at that time that identity politics began pitting one group against another in America, and many Jews were made to feel less at home in the civil rights movement. At the same time, like others, Jews developed their own intensifying sense of group identity. Especially significant for the Jewish community was the impact of the Six-Day War, which occurred in June 1967, when Israel had to defend itself against Arab neighbors in a military conflict preceded by a period of great tension.

In a recent book which takes an acerbic approach to the organized Jewish community, Peter Novick asserts that Israel was not really in serious danger at that time, and he implies that Jewish leaders deliberately exaggerated the threat and stoked people's fears of the coming of another Holocaust in order to promote sympathy and support for Israel.[5] A more accurate and fair-minded accounting of that period would assert that however strong Israel's military may have been, the prewar fears were based on a realistic understanding of what was at stake. Though most American Jews may have believed that Jewish security had been assured after 1948, they suddenly faced the shocking recognition that the very place which they had regarded as safeguarding Jewish lives and guaranteeing that the horrors of a new Holocaust could not occur was itself at risk. Israel's swift and decisive military victory did not erase the realization that Jewish survival was more tenuous than had been believed, and many Jewish organizations became far more focused on efforts to strengthen American support for Israel's security than they had been. At the same time, the victory also evoked a sense of pride, dignity, and assertiveness from American Jews.

Thus, at a time when the American intergroup relations landscape was itself being transformed, American Jews more than ever before linked their identity and their destiny to the State of Israel and to their brothers and sisters there. Israel and other explicitly "Jewish" subjects increasingly came to the fore on the community relations agenda, with ties to Jewish tradition becoming increasingly more pronounced, and a more assertive, stand-up-for-yourself style began to be demonstrated in the public arena on behalf of these priorities.

Stimulated in great part by the same historic event, many Jews in the Soviet Union were inspired by the Six-Day War to return to their Jewish roots with pride and to pursue the right to practice their religion and the right to emigrate to Israel. Activity on behalf of Soviet Jewry, which was already underway, received an added boost, and the American Jewish community relations world had another top priority added to its agenda in these years. At the same time, with consciousness of the Holocaust coming to the fore and with survivors more and more willing to speak about their experiences, that catastrophic event, seen increasingly in a "Jewish" way, also began to form a greater part of the transformed communal agenda.

Different as this more particularist agenda was from the more universalistic one which preceded it, it was not as though the old priorities were altogether replaced, but more like these new ones were layered on top of them. The old civil rights and civil liberties agenda was maintained in the framework of what often became spoken about as a social justice agenda, while the new priorities clearly began to dominate community relations activities. This continued for over two decades, when a modulating process began which is still unfolding.

Focusing on a single community relations council to illustrate these trends, the next part of this chapter traces the past thirty years of work by the Jewish Community Relations Council of the Jewish United Fund of Metropolitan Chicago, which offers a paradigmatic illustration of the activity characteristic of that period. The chapter then looks at the fashion in which the national body which was established in 1944 as the National Community Relations Advisory Council has itself evolved, a body which is attempting to define the role it will play in the public square today and in the years ahead.

I

The establishment of Chicago's JCRC may be traced to the February 28, 1970, visit to Chicago by French President Georges Pompidou. His country had just refused to sell supersonic jets to Israel after supplying over 100 of them to Libya, an implacable enemy of the Jewish state. In an incident reported prominently by the local media, some 15,000 members of Chicago's Jewish community demonstrated against that policy, disrupting the calm of Pompidou's visit to the city. The protest was organized by what was called the Ad Hoc Committee on International Affairs, made up of grassroots leadership as well as leaders of the Jewish Federation and Jewish Welfare Fund of Metropolitan Chicago. One result of the protest was an impetus for establishing something more permanent in the federation framework. In 1971, the Welfare Fund thus formed an exploratory Public Affairs Committee (PAC). In January 1972, after it was determined where in the federation family the new entity would best fit, that committee was reorganized under the Jewish United Fund and began to function.

Observing the anomaly presented by the fact that neither Chicago nor New York had a JCRC in 1951, R. M. MacIver had said then: "While we are reluctant to suggest any addition to the already overelaborate structure of Jewish community relations agencies, we nevertheless believe that, were effective steps taken to establish a CRC for each of the two greatest metropolitan areas, the effect would be salutary." He suggested that the reason these cities lacked CRCs may have resulted from the "presence in these areas of headquarters of national agencies."[6] Local observers recall that the objections of the branch offices of the national organizations (one of which, the ADL, had even had its national headquarters in the city until the late 1940s) had indeed played a part in preventing a CRC from being established any sooner in Chicago. Particularly instrumental in getting such an entity formed in Chicago was Philip Klutznick.

A former U.S. ambassador to the United Nations and future secretary of commerce, Klutznick was a major force in national Jewish communal life as well, having served as national president of B'nai

B'rith and having been a key player in the Conference of Presidents of Major Jewish Organizations during its early years. Locally, he had helped bring the federation's fund-raising efforts together after the Six-Day War. Once he applied his powers of persuasion in this area, the Chicago offices of the national agencies were ready to join a number of local organizations within the framework of a federation-sponsored community relations council called the Public Affairs Committee, with Klutznick as its first chairman.

Constituents of this body, in addition to the local offices of the national defense organizations and the federation itself, comprised a broad range of religious, Zionist, and social action groups, each of which had veto power in the decision-making process. As laid out in a "statement of purpose, interest and function" issued in June 1972, the "areas of concern" of the Public Affairs Committee consisted of "events and issues affecting Jews in Israel, in the Middle East, in the USSR, and wherever the status and welfare of Jews may be affected." In dealing with "the creative survival of American Jewry as a flourishing community dedicated to the preservation of Jewish values and the traditions of American democracy," the committee addressed a range of topics grouped under "individual liberty and Jewish security; . . . church-state relations; . . . and urban problems as they affect Jews living in an urban society." As it moved forward, the PAC was guided by Klutznick's assertion at its first meeting that "the committee was not expected to be just a debating society but rather a means for common planning and action."[7]

From that first meeting in March 1972, which greatly focused on participation in a National Solidarity Day for Soviet Jewry on April 30, the issue of Soviet Jewry continued to be one of the dominant subjects for Chicago's Public Affairs Committee. The group's agenda revolved around demonstrations, meetings with elected officials, petition campaigns, interfaith prayer efforts, involvement in national planning, and more.

Israel was also a staple of the agenda. Almost immediately after the PAC was founded it began conversations about communitywide planning for Israel's twenty-fifth anniversary year. The group also quickly became involved in monitoring the treatment of Israel in the media and in local museum exhibits, as well as reacting to terrorist incidents directed against Israel. Attention then leaped forward following the Yom Kippur War in October 1973, with concerns expressed regarding the treatment of Israelis held prisoner in Syria, continuing U.S. aid to Israel, and related matters. At the time, the PAC's Committee on Scope, Structure, Planning, and Membership urged the federation to add an additional staff slot to the PAC to deal with these matters. A report from that committee specifically said: "The overriding priority is and must be the Middle East," with committee meetings scheduled to take place weekly—but, at the same time, with Soviet Jewry not to be neglected.

Various pro-Israel steps were taken through the 1970s. These included opposition to the Arab boycott; measures to counter anti-Israeli activities, often seen on local campuses; confrontation with U.S. senator Charles Percy as his activities regarding the Middle East took a troubling turn; and coordination of communitywide Israel Independence Day observances on an annual basis. When the third chairman of the PAC was installed in 1977, the PAC's executive was quoted in the organization's minutes stressing that, like Chicago's, "most CRCs' priorities have been Israel and Soviet Jewry." When Egypt's Anwar Sadat came to Israel that year and set in motion an intensified peace process involving Israel and Egypt, the PAC's attention to Israel-related matters intensified even more. Meanwhile, in 1982 the Chicago Conference on Soviet Jewry was established within the PAC framework to coordinate and advance ongoing local efforts in that area.

Some domestic issues also attracted the attention of the PAC in the early years. According to PAC minutes, following a report by a spokesman of the ADL at its December 1974 meeting, "the feeling was expressed that the Public Affairs Committee is not devoting enough time to effectively deal with domestic affairs." The report had focused on the way that General George Brown had used disparaging stereotypes about Jews when speaking at Duke Law School. Thus, the effort to combat anti-Semitism and the wish to participate in intergroup activities to assist in that effort and promote other communal interests, a goal of other CRCs from their establishment in the 1930s, can also be seen as forming the core of the domestic agenda of Chicago's PAC.

At the PAC's early meetings there was talk about taking action against vandalism and swastika smearings that had occurred at the time in the community. At one of the meetings, a speaker from the American Jewish Congress addressed the question: "What are we doing about discrimination against Jews?" As the decade of the 1970s moved forward, increasing attention was given to an upsurge in local neo-Nazi activity, mostly revealed in public demonstrations.

By 1977 and 1978, neo-Nazi activity had increased dramatically in Chicago, and one particular sequence of events, which the PAC played a key role in addressing, virtually put a Chicago suburb on the national map. Well aware of the advantages which could accrue to them from publicity and of their power to inflict psychic damage,

Chicago's band of neo-Nazis, headed by Frank Collin, announced that they were taking their show out of Chicago's southwest side and into the northern suburb of Skokie, with its large Holocaust survivor population. They got the reaction they sought. As limited as their ability to do physical damage may have been, by reminding Skokie's citizens and Chicago's Jewish community of the horrors wrought by Hitler and his swastika-wearing henchmen, Chicago's neo-Nazis set in motion a strong communal response intended first and foremost to keep them out of Skokie.

The community's reaction, involving several organizations, was coordinated by the PAC, with Sol Goldstein, a survivor leader and member of the federation board who chaired the PAC's Committee on Individual Liberty, spearheading the effort. (When Hollywood later made a movie about this episode called "Skokie," the Sol Goldstein part was played by the movie's leading actor, Danny Kaye.) Though the courts which heard the case rejected the legal attempts to stop the Nazis from marching in Skokie, in the end Collin and his followers chose to demonstrate in Chicago's Marquette Park instead, where they were met by a PAC-organized counterdemonstration.

Among the results of this episode was the discovery by many members of the Jewish community that there were limits to their support of the tenets of the American Civil Liberties Union; for them, when emotions were high and the perceived interests of the Jewish community were at stake, these interests would hold sway. In a way, then, this episode can thus be seen as a marker demonstrating a shift from the organized Jewish community's behavior in the public square in the 1960s, when it was largely driven by a universalistic civil rights/civil liberties agenda, to the way it acted in the 1970s and beyond, when a more particularist approach began to take hold. Furthermore, the episode occurred concurrent with—and locally contributed to—the addition of another "Jewish" priority to the communal agenda: the Holocaust.

On the national scene, the late 1970s saw the screening of the television mini-series *The Holocaust*; the rise of the Holocaust denial movement—which had an early and highly visible local proponent in the person of Arthur Butz, a professor of electrical engineering at Northwestern University who authored *The Hoax of the 20th Century*; the establishment of an Office of Special Investigations in the Justice Department to pursue war criminals who had illegally made their way into the United States; and an increased readiness by survivors themselves to talk about their experiences. In the Chicago area, the Skokie episode was followed by the establishment of a survivors group, which pushed for the nation's first statewide legislation mandating the teaching of the Holocaust in the classroom, and by the efforts of another group, which led to the construction of a memorial in Skokie. With Goldstein staying involved, the PAC itself continued focusing on Holocaust-related matters.

Israel, Soviet Jewry, anti-Semitism, and Holocaust-related matters formed the core of the PAC agenda at the time. A special meeting held in October 1979 demonstrated how far matters had evolved from the 1960s when much of the nation's community relations attention was devoted to civil rights. The issue of concern at the meeting centered around tensions that had surfaced in black-Jewish relations in part as a result of Andrew Young's having to resign from his post as ambassador to the United Nations for holding an unauthorized meeting with the PLO. The issue had a local dimension due to the Chicago presence of black community leader Jesse Jackson. Discussion revolved around anti-Israel and anti-Semitic attitudes expressed in segments of the black community, and the PAC director urged the "beginning" of a dialogue to address such matters locally. The close coalitional partnership that had prevailed between Jews and blacks in the previous decade had become a thing of the past. Now, threats to the Jewish community and its interests were seen to reside within the ranks of that erstwhile partner in the fight against discrimination—a factor that was to intensify in the 1980s, particularly in Chicago, home of Louis Farrakhan and the Nation of Islam.

The community relations agenda forged in the late 1960s and maintained in Chicago as well as elsewhere in the 1970s remained largely intact throughout the 1980s. Church-state issues also received increasing attention, and strict separation was supported locally as well as nationally. Revealingly, in December 1987, the Chicago organization (which a year previously had been renamed the Jewish Community Relations Council) opposed the erection of both a crèche and a Hanukkah menorah at the Daley Plaza in Chicago, even though it was a Jewish organization (albeit not a member of the JCRC) which had erected the menorah. In other areas, support for Israel became complicated by the incursion into Lebanon and discomfort with Israel's settlement policy in some quarters; changes were obviously afoot in the Soviet Union; the community was doing more to memorialize the victims of the Holocaust; but, by and large, the trends established earlier remained intact.

At the end of the 1980s, a new period in community relations affairs began to reveal itself. One of the propellants of change was a "religious revival" which could be seen impacting on American life in general during this period. In the Jewish community, the trend toward increasing attachment to religious activities and values was compounded by developments highlighted in a population study issued by the Council of Jewish Federations in 1991. Tracking statistics regarding assimilation and intermarriage, this study awakened the view that the greatest threat to the future of the American Jewish community was not from enemies outside but from community members' lack of connection with their own roots. The result of this confluence of influences was a greater overall emphasis on what became known as "continuity." This included a more self-conscious turning to Jewish traditions, texts, and modes of behavior. In some cities, activity in the JCRC began to be promoted as offering a point of entry into overall Jewish communal life. In Chicago, the deepening attachment to tradition was demonstrated by the introduction of a *d'var Torah* at the beginning of each JCRC meeting, in which delegates to the JCRC, rabbinic and lay alike, take turns in offering reflections on the Torah portion of the week, frequently finding rationale in these Jewish sources for community relations activity practiced by the JCRC.

A particularly striking way in which the "continuity" agenda has impacted on community relations affairs is seen in the changing attitudes to public funding for religious day school education in the form of vouchers. In Chicago, given the divisions within the JCRC membership, a majority of whom hold firm in opposition—largely for church-state reasons—but a minority of whom would favor making vouchers available—mostly because of the assistance which might be provided to parents of day school students—the JCRC has remained without a position on this issue.

As significant as the "continuity" thrust of the 1990s may have been in effecting changes in the agendas of some CRCs, developments set in motion by the collapse of the Soviet Union and the end of the Cold War have had at least as great an impact on the overall community relations agenda. At the time following the end of that international engagement, when much of America began turning inward, the Jewish community followed suit to an extent, but the community's involvement in and concern about international matters remained greater than that of Americans in general. Still, though the community stayed involved, there were significant differences in the nature of its involvement, given the dramatic changes which were taking place in the world.

For one thing, the fall of the Soviet Union, which opened the gates to free emigration and allowed Jews who remained in that region of the world to reconnect with their origins and traditions, greatly transformed the Soviet Jewry agenda. Beyond that, the disappearance of the support which the Soviet Union had provided to its Arab allies and the end of the flow of arms to them enhanced Israel's security and made possible the breakthroughs in the peace process that came early in the 1990s, so the community did not sense as great a need as it did before to act to ensure Israel's safety. At the same time, internal issues which were turned loose in Israel during the decade led some members of the American Jewish community to get involved in those matters, and some others to feel less connected. Finally, with information involving the Holocaust era, which previously was inaccessible behind the Iron Curtain, suddenly available and triggering various responses, Holocaust-related affairs became even more central to the community's agenda.

It is not so much that the community relations field moved on to other areas of concern as that it transformed the fashion in which it deals with its longstanding agenda items. With less need for external advocacy in these areas, many Community Relations Councils began to become more and more involved in activities within and for the Jewish community itself, albeit with an occasional or partial outward thrust.

Thus, since there are still realistic concerns about the fashion in which instability and economic difficulty can put Jews at risk in a traditionally anti-Semitic and increasingly nationalistic Russia, and since there is lingering nervousness about free emigration, activity to address those kinds of problems has continued. But this goes on at a reduced level, and it has been joined by a more "hands-on," project-centered type of activity. So Chicago's JCRC spearheaded a local "Cans for Kiev" project and, in a framework being established by the federation, organized a "*kehilla*" type relationship with that Ukrainian community involving various forms of partnering. Other JCRCs, such as those in Baltimore, Boston, and Cincinnati, have also moved forward significantly with such twinning relationships with communities in the former Soviet Union.

As far as Israel is concerned, the institutionalization of communitywide Israel Independence Day programming, introduced some years ago, continued as a central part of the local agenda in Chicago, with the large-scale celebration of Israel's fiftieth anniversary replicated in different ways around the country having highlighted that activity. In addition, the JCRC and federation were able, within a day, to bring 5,000 members of Chicago's Jewish community together following the tragic assassination of Prime Minister Rabin. In dealing with Israel in the 1990s, JCRCs continue to carry out some of the "old-style" activity—still advocating for a strong American-

Israel relationship; still working with the media to ensure fair and accurate treatment of Israel; still reaching out to the non-Jewish community to enhance understanding of Israel; still taking steps to blunt the efforts of Israel's proclaimed enemies, steps which began to include opposing terrorist activity of a new sort, tied not as much to states or ideology as to extremist religious impulses. (Chicago's JCRC drafted and advocated statewide legislation to outlaw the raising of funds intended to support international terrorist activity. The first of its kind in the country when it became law in 1996, the legislation served as a model for other JCRCs.) At the same time, there began to be a new dimension to this activity, which in great part focused on helping the Jewish community itself to better understand what was going on in the peace process as the Israel government demonstrated a willingness to talk to one-time mortal enemies and to take risks in an attempt to bring about peace. That new kind of activity also involved working along with federations to help American Jews and Israelis develop enhanced understanding of each other and to prevent the religious diversity issue in Israel from causing a breach between the two communities. With the collapse of the Oslo process in the fall of 2000, JCRCs found themselves both returning to their "old style" advocacy in some ways and working within the community to enhance solidarity with Israel.

In the 1990s, JCRCs such as Chicago's found themselves becoming more and more involved with Holocaust-related matters—promoting Holocaust education; having more of a role to play at Holocaust memorials as the survivors themselves increasingly disappear from the scene; and providing support to the Office of Special Investigations, whose efforts accelerated with the availability of previously inaccessible data. Most of all, JCRC offices in Chicago and several other cities have found that a major addition to their work beginning in the 1990s has been providing assistance to survivors and their families in exploring their rights and pursuing the possibility of retrieving some of those Holocaust-era assets which have been shaken loose through various steps taken during recent years. In Chicago this has included offering extensive person-to-person assistance; organizing day-long information sessions with the state's Department of Insurance; putting together a day-long conference with Northwestern Law School; and serving as the advocacy arm in a multiagency support structure for survivors.

The JCRC's domestic agenda also changed in the 1990s, here, too, in part, because of changes on the world scene. No longer driven by fear of a communist threat, domestic hate groups now have their paranoia stimulated by imagined plans for a "new world order" driven by an international conspiracy aimed at undermining America. As usual when conspiracies come into play, it is the Jew who is demonized as the primary villain. So, while anti-Semitic attitudes have lessened on the national scene, those which prevail can have the power to drive members of extremist groups who are inclined to violence over the edge. That happened during the weekend of July 4, 1999, when Benjamin Smith, a disciple of an extremist group leader, went on a shooting rampage which was first directed at Jews on their way home from synagogue in Chicago, and which ultimately took the lives of a well-known African-American figure in nearby Evanston and an Asian student in Indiana. In a contemporary way, the need to combat anti-Semitism and its effects thus remains high on the community relations agenda.

In the decade of the 1990s, the nature of relations between the Jewish community and other communities underwent certain changes. Relations with Poles and members of other Eastern European ethnic groups were strained as Holocaust-related issues increasingly came to the fore. Louis Farrakhan's ascendance created a hurdle to be overcome before dialogue and relationships could go forward with the African-American community, though there were ways in which positive relationships between blacks and Jews were maintained during the decade. The Jewish community also saw itself forging new relations with America's growing ethnic minorities, particularly Asian Americans and Latino Americans. (The possibility of forming closer relations with Muslims, something which might have seemed to be enhanced by the steps taken to resolve the conflict between Israel and its Arab neighbors earlier in the decade, faced handicaps. For one thing, Jews and Muslims had limited shared history in the United States, and for another, numbers of Muslim activists in America separated themselves from Yasser Arafat's moves toward reconciliation with Israel and maintained ties with the Palestinian rejectionist camp.)

In today's transformed community relations world, the Jewish community is, in general, less tied to long-term coalition partners with whom it shared a multifaceted, ongoing agenda than it once was. Instead, partnerships are formed mostly on a situational basis, depending on the subject. If the issue is hate crimes, then there are partners to be found in various minority communities. If the issue involves religious rights, then other kinds of partnerships may be forged. Thus, the JCRC and other Jewish organizations in Illinois have found themselves standing behind the barricades with members of the Evangelical community in promoting a statewide religious freedom restoration act. Meanwhile, drawing upon their longer-standing experience in the public arena, JCRCs have also provided advice and assistance to newer groups as they organize themselves to promote communal interests and to reach out to the media and the public in general.

The intergroup climate in which these activities have taken place is one in which the watchword is diversity. In a world where balkanization has become not just a metaphor but a description of the bloody and awful direction in which intergroup conflict and hatred can go, America has had its own problems in dealing with intergroup issues. At times that has meant seeing various groups following the path of a negative multiculturalism by circling the wagons, regarding others only as enemies, and being driven by a psychology of victimization. Certain racial and ethnic groups have acted out this form of multiculturalism in a fashion detrimental to the Jewish community—segments of which have even themselves at times been drawn to such a mode of behavior. But as destructive as such domestic tribalism can be, full-scale implementation of the old-time notion of a melting pot would endanger the traditions and values which give positive identity and meaning to the lives of members of many religious, ethnic, and racial groups, Jews included. The challenge is to build a society where pluralism and diversity can flourish, a society made up of groups which maintain their own specialness, understand and respect others' differences, and join together with shared belief in the common humanity of all people and a shared commitment to basic American principles. In Chicago, a city greatly defined by its ethnic, racial, and religious mix, a model for this kind of positive intergroup relationship has been established in the relationship between Jews and Catholics, in which the JCRC has played a significant role.

One of the institutional frameworks in which leaders of the two religious communities come together in Chicago is a structure called the Catholic-Jewish Scholars Dialogue. It was organized at the initiative of the late Joseph Cardinal Bernardin shortly after he came to Chicago in the early 1980s, and its partners are the Archdiocese of Chicago, on the one hand, and the Jewish federation and Chicago Board of Rabbis, on the other, with the JCRC office serving as facilitator. Over the years, the dialogue has regularly brought its members together every other month for presentations and discussions that have given members of each group deepened understanding and appreciation of the traditions and beliefs of the other community, and a framework for dealing together with particularly sensitive issues of the day. A statement that the dialogue issued regarding the convent at Auschwitz, endorsed by Cardinal Bernardin, was said to have had a direct impact on the decision of the Vatican to intervene in the crisis which had surrounded that issue. Another statement, which gained national attention, acknowledged differences in the way each of the groups' traditions deal with abortion and called for dealing with the subject with civility and respect for alternative points of view.

A climactic moment for the dialogue, which its efforts helped make possible, was a 1995 mission to Israel led by Cardinal Bernardin during which he gave a groundbreaking speech on "Antisemitism: The Historical Legacy and the Continuing Challenge for Christians." The trip was described as the first-ever interfaith mission to Israel led by a cardinal, and, through virtually nonstop local media coverage, it brought to Chicagoans of all backgrounds a powerful image of meaningful intergroup relations in action. Bernardin's successor, Francis Cardinal George, has made clear his own commitment to sustaining this relationship, which continues to flourish in Chicago.

Significantly, this prototype for successful contemporary intergroup relations functions in a religious framework, with the participants seeing themselves as representing two "faith communities." As the members of the dialogue study scriptural texts and discuss subjects like repentance, prayer, implications of the new millennium, and such staples of the Jewish community relations agenda as Israel and the Holocaust, they do so with specific reference to their religious identities and religious traditions. In its nature, this kind of intergroup framework can be seen as symbolic for the current era.

Overall, then, in ways both profound and simple, as the Jewish community has forged its agenda in the public square over the past three decades, it has done so in a fashion increasingly tied to its past, its sense of peoplehood, and its traditions. The annual calendar of the organized community's programming has far more to do with observances and anniversaries derived from Jewish experience than it once did, and respect for Shabbat and various holidays during the year is also more manifest than it once was. More principles of action are linked to concepts enunciated in the traditional religious sources. More words in the working vocabulary are taken from Hebrew, the ancient language of scripture and prayer and the living language of the modern State of Israel. Increasing use of the term "Shoah" instead of Holocaust may annoy a critic of the organized community such as Peter Novick,[8] but it is exemplary of this trend, as is reference to Israel's Independence Day as Yom Ha'Atzmaut. The fact that the Vatican, in issuing its statement on the Holocaust in 1998, used the word "Shoah" and described its own movement toward repentance with the Hebrew term *"t'shuvah"* demonstrates the impact of the Jewish community's use of this language. Even those most tied to a universalistic social justice agenda have taken to basing their behavior on a concept represented by the Hebrew phrase *tikkun olam* (repair of the world). Although, as Mordecai Lee, a former CRC director, has observed, this term makes few appearances in the sources and the way it is being used today may be questionable on a traditional basis, the impulse for using it is consistent with current trends.[9]

As in the use of terminology, one can see a shift to ever more self-consciously promoting what are defined as Jewish communal interests in various aspects of the community relations universe. At a time of burgeoning social service demands, for some JCRCs that has meant using techniques and contacts garnered from advocating on behalf of Israel, Soviet Jewry, and other issues to advocate on behalf of communal needs addressed by federations and their agencies. (In Chicago, that role is handled by the federation's Government Affairs Program; conversely, the federation's Government Affairs Offices in Washington, D.C., and at the state capital in Springfield serve as arms of the JCRC on community relations issues, as does the federation's Israel office.) At the same time, the "continuity" agenda and world events have caused JCRCs, the ambassadors of their communities to the outer world, and the state departments of the federations in their cities to become increasingly involved with the relations between members of their own community. In the current environment, that form of activity has taken on special significance. With denominational, political, and other differences between segments of the community becoming ever more strident, the JCRC has emerged as a rare entity which offers a table where all groups in the community can come together to find common denominators and pursue common interests. Whereas Philip Klutznick had told Chicago's Public Affairs Committee, meeting in May 1972, that "at no time have there been fewer issues of controversy in the Jewish community than today," that is not something which could be so easily asserted today. Now, the JCRCs serve the crucial role of promoting communal unity, thereby preserving ties of Jewish peoplehood while continuing to represent the community in the public square.

Besides functioning in their individual communities, today 122 community relations councils join together along with thirteen national organizations in a national body. The following section reviews the history of that body and examines issues surrounding its current status.

II

What is now called the Jewish Council for Public Affairs (JCPA) was formed by the Council of Jewish Federations and Welfare Funds in 1944 as the National Community Relations Advisory Council (NCRAC). It initially brought together fourteen community relations councils from around the country and four national organizations: the American Jewish Committee, the American Jewish Congress, B'nai B'rith's Anti-Defamation League, and the Jewish Labor Committee.

Those four national bodies had previously joined in an entity called the General Jewish Council, but the notion of bringing them together with CRCs in an attempt to coordinate community relations activity nationwide was something new. The triggering impetus was a desire to forge a unified front against anti-Semitism. In an analysis of the early years, Walter A. Lurie has noted the importance attached to combating discrimination in war industries, and he has observed that employment discrimination in general quickly became a top priority for the organization.[10]

In 1952, two major defense organizations, the ADL and the AJCommittee, withdrew from NCRAC in reaction to the report issued by Professor R. M. MacIver the year before, unhappy by what they saw as a threat to their autonomy in the report's call for a realignment of the national defense agencies and other recommendations in it. They were not to rejoin the national body until 1965. Nevertheless, with a structure augmented by other national organizations and additional CRCs, NCRAC continued to deal with security, discrimination, and other such issues on its early agenda. But then, with the social climate in America transformed following the war, the role played in the public square by the organized Jewish community, both locally and nationally, underwent significant changes.

Introducing a 1981 collection of papers on "Jewish Communal Services in America 1958-78," Earl Raab spoke of "three 'periods'" in the field of Jewish Community Relations. The First Period was dominated by the grim fight against overt anti-Semitism, here and abroad, plain and simple. The Second Period was marked by the post-World War II surge in American prosperity and idealism, and in American-Jewish integration; it was dominated by activity on behalf of a democratic and pluralistic America, the by-words being civil rights and civil liberties. The theme was also relatively plain and simple: the security of the Jew depended on such an American society."[11]

NCRAC, which was born at the very end of Raab's first period, came of age during the postwar period. Led by its first executive director, Isaiah Minkoff, NCRAC distinguished itself in the civil rights struggle that was taking shape at the time. With the organization's deputy director, Arnold Aronson, staffing what became the Leadership Conference on Civil Rights, NCRAC assumed a significant national profile on this issue. At the same time, it provided an early forum for the community to debate efforts to advance the separation of church and state. As tracked by Gregg Ivers in *To Build A Wall: American Jews and the Separation of Church and State*, those debates pitted the more aggressive and litigious AJCongress, represented and led in this area by Leo Pfeffer, against the AJCommittee and ADL. With the former group ultimately carrying the day despite the others' greater caution about the impact on intergroup relations and local concerns, the community relations field became a strong supporter of the principle of strict separation.[12]

As Raab and others emphasize, priorities changed beginning in the late 1960s. In describing the Six-Day War of 1967, the impact of which he called a "watershed," Raab wrote in his 1981 piece: "The public defense of Israel, which had been a negligible part of the Jewish community relations agenda in the Second Period, has come to dominate that agenda in the Third Period." Looking at other events of the time, Raab went on to say: "One of the results of these developments was a burgeoning of the Jewish community relations field. At the beginning of this period about three dozen local community relations councils or committees were affiliated with the National Jewish Community Relations Council. At the end of the period, about a hundred such local agencies were affiliated. . . . By the same token, as a result of these developments, the American Jewish public affairs agenda seemed to 'turn inwards,' as some put it, away from the Second Period preoccupation with the internal nature of the American society."[13]

It was in 1969, in the increasingly more self-consciously "Jewish" environment of the times and, as Walter Lurie has put it, "as a response to shifts since 1944 in Jewish and general acceptance of public group identification,"[14] that NCRAC added a word and changed its name to the National Jewish Community Relations Advisory Council (NJCRAC). With Israel and the cause of Soviet Jewry coming to dominate the field's agenda, NJCRAC played an important coordinating role. In November 1973, three weeks after the Yom Kippur War, the General Assembly of the Council of Jewish Federations voted to fund the activities of a special task force on Israel to be operated out of the NJCRAC offices. As early as 1964, NCRAC had taken a turn in coordinating the recently created American Jewish Council for Soviet Jewry, a role taken over shortly after that on a permanent basis by NCRAC staffers, first Albert Chernin, then Abraham Bayer, until 1971, when the AJCSJ became the National Conference on Soviet Jewry.[15]

Despite NJCRAC's involvement and the focus of some of its staff members and organizational constituents on the more specifically "Jewish" communal agenda, during the 1970s and 1980s and into the 1990s segments of NJCRAC's leadership and constituency remained committed to the kind of universalistic emphasis on civil rights and civil liberties which had held sway during the earlier era. Exemplifying an emerging debate as it was to take shape in the last decade of the century were two 1991 articles in the *Journal of Jewish Communal Service*, in a forum on "The Jewish Agenda and Public Policy: Directions for the 1990s." In one article, Murray Friedman, executive director of the American Jewish Committee's Philadelphia office, expressed his concern for what he saw as "the difficulties that our Jewish communal agencies have had in dealing with . . . the transformation of the civil rights movement, the breakdown of traditional norms, and the erosion of support for Israel." Arguing that "it is no contribution to inter-group relations if our involvement means we back away from guarding direct Jewish interests and concerns," he called for "a redefinition of an older liberalism about which we can be very proud and the conversion of it to a more realistic understanding of Jewish and American interests and public policies as we move into the 1990s."[16] In contrast, in the same issue of that publication, Albert Chernin, by then executive vice chairman emeritus of NJCRAC, harkened back to the era when "the premise underlying the community relations field's activities was that the security of American Jews was directly linked to the strength of the American democratic society." Addressing the present moment, he proclaimed that "the same assumptions that guided the development of our policies and goals in 1945 still should continue to guide us in 1990."[17]

The tension between these two organizational trends can be examined from a structural perspective. Not only were the ADL and the AJCommittee absent from the National Community Relations Advisory Council lineup from 1952 until 1965 but so were such major communities as New York and Chicago. As MacIver noted with chagrin in his report, neither of those cities yet had a CRC. When they did form such bodies and join NJCRAC in the 1970s, it was with strong support for the Israel-connected aspects of the communal agenda. Furthermore, in representing what, until Los Angeles passed Chicago in population, were the country's two largest cities, they significantly affected the balance of power within NJCRAC. (New York was and has remained, by far, home to the largest Jewish community in the country. Though Chicago lost its status as number two some time ago, the strength of its community continues to manifest itself through a very successful annual federation campaign, second largest in the country, in addition to the production of key national leadership and other means.)

For many of the old guard who had long been active in NJCRAC, along with others who entered Jewish communal life later but had begun their personal involvement in the public square in the early 1960s, the civil rights era was seen as a "golden age" which provided a defining context for the organization. With the bloom somewhat off the Israel rose following the incursion into Lebanon in the early 1980s, and with the hard-line policies of Israel's Likud government seeming to some to hold back progress on peace, segments within NJCRAC were ready to break ranks with those who maintained the traditional position of the organized community that decisions about peace and security were to be made by the democratically elected government of Israel, with diaspora Jewry having no public role in that process. Urging the organization to publicly criticize the government's settlements policy, this grouping within NJCRAC was headed by activists associated with the AJCongress, a charter member of NCRAC, and the Union of American Hebrew Congregations, which had joined the national body almost immediately after NCRAC's founding. The other side, which carried the day in national debates, was led by the New York and Chicago JCRCs and the ADL, none of which were part of NCRAC during the civil rights era, along with other communities and national organizations.

Israel-linked activity continued to be coordinated by NJCRAC's Israel Task Force, and one of the organization's finest hours came in 1991 when NJCRAC helped organize the national day of advocacy in Washington on behalf of loan guarantees for Israel, which provoked President George Bush's notorious outburst against "some powerful political forces" represented by "something like a thousand lobbyists on the Hill." Still, following the breakthrough in the Middle East peace process in the early 1990s which was touched off by the Oslo agreement, there was an increased tendency in some NJCRAC circles to talk of reducing significant involvement with Israel-related issues. (Complicating matters further, by now there were rightist segments of the community outside of the NJCRAC orbit ready to publicly demonstrate and to take to Capitol Hill in direct opposition to the peace policies of the Israeli government—but that is another story.) Similarly, while NJCRAC had played a key role in bringing the communities together for a massive Soviet Jewry rally in Washington in December 1987, by the 1990s core activity regarding Jews in the Soviet Union—direction for which in any event had long been passed on to the National Conference on Soviet Jewry by NJCRAC—was reduced further. Since it could be claimed that less attention would need to be directed to overall overseas concerns in the new global environment, the notion of returning to a predominantly domestic agenda was encouraged by some NJCRAC leaders.

Still, as much as these circles within NJCRAC may have wished the organization to act in the 1990s as it had during the civil rights era, the milieu was a different one. Not only was the particularistic Jewish agenda still around, but for many the need for taking that kind of approach had intensified as a result of their fear that increasing assimilation, as measured by the national population study conducted by the Council of Jewish Federations, was the true emerging threat to the future of the American Jewish community. Furthermore, though the Middle East peace process and the fall of the Soviet Union had created new realities, that did not mean that the Jewish community's interests in those areas of involvement had evaporated. Indeed, rather than clearing the decks for a return to the agenda of Raab's second period, developments which took place at the turn of the decade set in motion what may be seen as a fourth period in community relations affairs. The institutional tension which became heightened at this moment of transition was aggravated by the fact that some NJCRAC activists, failing to recognize that a changed context for community relations activity was beginning which called for an appropriately altered kind of behavior from the Jewish community, were instead driven by the urge to return to a posture more suitable to an earlier era.

As it happens, at the very time that this tension prevailed between those who would respond to the current conditions by stressing the social justice attitudes of the 1960s and those looking for ways to adapt to the emerging realities of the early 1990s, NJCRAC undertook a strategic planning process to examine the mission, structure, and function of the agency. Ironically enough, while the national agencies had had problems with recommendations in the MacIver Report that had been issued over four decades earlier which had aimed at limiting organizational duplication, now it was they who had a problem with duplication, objecting to the possibility that NJCRAC might become more like them. Indeed, this time around, while there was no threat to their autonomy, the restructuring took away from these national bodies the veto power which gave them particular clout in NJCRAC. It also established a NJCRAC presence in Washington, which, charging that it would make NJCRAC a functional agency like them, they had long opposed, and it gave the organization a new name and other trappings of its own autonomy, including an executive committee renamed a board of directors. Still, except for those denominational movements which successfully insisted on the retention of a veto on religious issues, the national organizations ultimately held their fire for the most part, tempering their criticism and going along with the changes. On the other hand, this time it was from the ranks of the communities, to which NJCRAC would presumably be thought to be the closest, led by Chicago and New York, that the greatest expressions of concern with the restructuring came. These concerns especially revolved around issues of governance and the organization's role in serving its communal constituents.

As the strategic plan was debated, voices were raised in certain communities arguing for the need for NJCRAC's procedures to reflect its constituency-driven nature. To advance that goal, it was asserted, there needed to be a way that the communities would be represented in a fashion more or less commensurate with their size. In response to language proposed for the new by-laws, which talked of members of the board of directors acting in an *"ad personum"* fashion, it was stressed that delegates to the annual plenum and to the board of directors meetings should be representatives of their communities and organizations, to which they would be accountable.

While the final language of the plan was modified to take these objections into account, concerns continued as the strategic plan began to be implemented. A key concern dealt with the focus of the organization, as implied by its name. A large number of constituents had expressed a preference for calling the group the National Jewish Community Relations Council—to maintain recognizable continuity, to point to the "national" component of the body, and to emphasize its community relations function. In the end, though, the choice was to rename NJCRAC the Jewish Council for Public Affairs. Not only was the name new but it also suggested a subtle but significant priority shift from involvement in community relations activities to attempting to impact on public policy—a shift which revealed itself in other ways as well.

In the days of NJCRAC, the organization annually produced something called a "Joint Program Plan for Community Relations," which was further described as a "Guide to Program Planning of the Constituent Organizations." Its propositions were reviewed in draft form by the member organizations and then refined and voted on at the annual plenums. Besides summarizing the consensus positions of the communities and the national organizations, these propositions recommended practical steps for action. In its new form, that product was renamed the "JCPA Agenda for Public Affairs." Though it still contained a series of propositions, the action principles were removed from them; instead, beginning with the publication for 1998-1999, a statement opening with such phrases as "The JCPA supports" and enunciating policy positions was inserted to highlight the presentation of each proposition. Meanwhile, the JCPA began spending more time than it previously did on preparing resolutions to be issued to the general public.

In practice, the resolutions process denied communities and national organizations much opportunity to review proposed statements before the organization's annual plenum (let alone before the twice-annual meetings of the board of directors, for which no specific resolutions procedures were established). What was brought before the plenum, rather than being a statement drafted in an attempt to lay the groundwork for a consensus position, often originated with a national organization or a community which was likely to be partisan on one end of the spectrum or another. This was hardly the kind of system one would expect to see adopted by an organization aiming to bring communities together to ratify bottom-line points of shared concern. And indeed, in the first years in which the new procedures were in place, plenary meetings were at times marked by acrimonious difficulty in coming to agreement and by the tabling of resolutions when the majority felt it was inappropriate for the organization to even be looking at a given subject.

A graphic demonstration of the way the priorities of the organization shifted is provided by a comparison of its key publication over a twenty-year span. Though the sizes of the pages were no longer the same, their proportionality is revealing. The Joint Program Plan for 1979-1980 devoted eleven pages to "Israel and the Middle East" and "Arab Economic Warfare," and another four to "Energy," which was then closely tied to U.S.-Middle East Policy. It added six pages on "Soviet Jewry," two pages on "Jews in Other Lands," and one page on "International Human Rights," for a total of twenty-four pages devoted to overseas issues. The JCPA Agenda for Public Affairs 1999-2000 grouped all of these matters (except for energy, which was then part of a section called "The Environment and Jewish Life") together under the heading "Israel and Other International Concerns," which altogether filled only fourteen pages. In the domestic areas the contrast is similarly striking. In 1979-1980, three pages were devoted to "Individual Freedom and Jewish Security," four to "Church-State Relationships," two to "Jewish-Christian Relationships," and eight to "Social and Economic Justice," for a total of seventeen pages focused on the domestic agenda, plus two more on Holocaust-related matters. By 1999-2000, the section called "Jewish Security and the Bill of Rights," which absorbed church-state issues and interreligious relations as well as the Holocaust, had alone grown to thirteen pages. Meanwhile, the section then called "Equal Opportunity and Social Justice" had grown to fourteen pages and, accentuating its new significance, it had by then moved up to be at the top of the domestic topics. At the same time, the whole new section on "the Environment and Jewish Life" was added, with nine pages altogether.

If, to be consistent, one were to place energy concerns in the international area for both publications and the Holocaust were to be seen as a domestic concern in both cases, the numbers would line up as follows: 1979-1980, twenty-four pages for overseas matters and nineteen for domestic; 1999-2000, eighteen pages for overseas issues and thirty-two for domestic. To an extent this agenda shift reflects a change in world conditions, on the one hand, and in the priorities of the contemporary American Jewish community, on the other. But it could also be argued that the changes are too drastic to accurately reflect a widespread assessment of the needs and priorities of the overall community, certainly as maintained in a good many local JCRCs. Instead, this shift can be taken as a reflection of the sort of issues which certain forces within the JCPA wished to see the organization focus on in asserting itself as a policy-setting body.

Statements made in the late 1990s by the group's executive vice chairman, Lawrence Rubin, illustrate the attempt by elements within the JCPA to remake the organization primarily as a policy-making body focusing on a wide-ranging universalistic domestic agenda. Rather than seeing consensus-respecting inclusion as the organization's greatest strength, Rubin declared to the annual plenum of 1999 that "controversy is not always bad, and consensus is not always desirable." Rather than reflecting on ways that a refined pro-Israel action and advocacy program might be part of the organization's current agenda, he limited his discussion of Israel to arguing that the JCPA had a "responsibility" to help Israelis better understand that American-style separation of church and state provides a desirable model for them. Elaborating on the "important issues" to which he felt the JCPA should be directing its attention in the coming years, he predicted that "questions related to the need for an independent counsel, or the importance of real campaign finance reform, or private behavior and public responsibility will rise to the top of the public policy agenda." Besides referring to "Freedom of Speech on the Internet," he went on to say: "Filling with civic values the naked public square, the matter of assisted suicide, expanded civil liberties for gays and lesbians, even cloning, present interesting and pressing public policy questions."[18] At that same plenum, while the organization listed hate crimes and the Middle East peace process among four "priority public affairs concerns of the organized Jewish community" when preparing delegates for meetings with their congressional representatives, the other two issues it named, at a time when Soviet Jewry and other particularistic concerns still prevailed for others in the community, were public education and the "clean air problem of vehicle emissions."

The emphasis of the JCPA on policy issues, and the kinds of issues which it was choosing to act upon (and those it was not choosing) attracted criticism. On June 30, 1999, the president and executive vice president of the UJA-Federation of New York sent the chairman and executive vice chairman of the JCPA a letter saying that their volunteer leaders "increasingly view JCPA as 'out of touch' with the New York Jewish community." Shortly thereafter, the president of the Jewish Federation of Metropolitan Chicago wrote the same recipients, noting differences between the New York and Chicago federations regarding some of the specific policy issues on the JCPA's agenda but reiterating an ongoing concern in Chicago with the fact that "in taking public positions on policy issues, the JCPA does not always adequately reflect the range of attitudes held in Jewish communities around the country today, nor does it always function as a consensus-driven, bottom-up structure." That letter went on to say: "In our view the JCPA would fulfill its role better if, instead of focusing so much on the formulation of policy on an extended list of issues, it would do more to present itself as a community relations entity, functioning more extensively and effectively as the national resource and coordinating body for community relations councils and federations around the country."

Though these communications were sent privately, the issue became public when they were published by the *Forward*, a weekly paper known for playing up conflicts in Jewish organizational affairs, complete with a banner-headlined front-page story. Focusing on the New York letter, the *Forward* dealt with the subject in a political context which reflected its own ideological predilections, declaring: "A sea change in the political stance of American Jewry is being heralded by a newly disclosed letter written by the leaders of the community's largest charity, challenging the prevailing liberal orthodoxy that has obtained in the community since the 1960s and 1970s."[19]

While the New York letter expressed concerns "that JCPA's domestic legislative agenda ignores views held by many in our community about important issues," it itself did not lay this matter out in specific conservative versus liberal terms—and the Chicago letter did not even suggest that that was the framework of its concerns. Nevertheless, once the *Forward*'s interpretation was put forth, the battle lines seemed to be drawn. In subsequent issues of that paper, columnists and writers of letters to the editor followed suit. For example, Leonard Fein (a regular columnist but also an official of the Union of American Hebrew Congregations and a long-time advocate for "liberal" activity within the JCPA) wrote a piece the headline of which proclaimed: "That 1960s Consensus Is Not Dead Yet." He disputed views which he portrayed as proposing "that JCPA turn from its historically broad range of interests and its definitively liberal stance."[20]

A somewhat related reading of the letters was offered by J. J. Goldberg, journalist and author of *Jewish Power: Inside the American-Jewish Establishment*, who put his own spin on the topic. One story by Goldberg in the *New York Jewish Week*, with the headline "Family Feud," had a subheading which said: "Two big Jewish federations seek to rein in an outspoken Jewish advocacy group." A followup piece in the same publication asserted that what was driving Jewish community leaders nationwide was the desire to have "the community's resources focused on Jewish needs. They don't think that includes the environment or abortion rights. They want to maintain essential community services, like elder care and Jewish rescue. Everything else should go to ensure Jewish identity in the next generation."[21]

Though many community leaders may indeed have been concerned that traditional areas of communal social welfare activity were at risk of damage through reduced funding and may have believed that Jewish identity should be a priority for the entire community, that did not necessarily make them advocates of wholesale abandonment of the community relations agenda. Furthermore, though those leaders may indeed have questioned whether the overall organized community must support abortion rights or make the environment one of the community's top priorities, members of the Jewish community with strong personal interests in these issues could readily associate themselves with any of a number of Jewish community organizations which advocate for them, without turning their backs on the unified community relations enterprise. In fact, for most of the critics of the JCPA, the problem was not, as some others chose to frame it, that the organization was too "liberal" per se in its choice of agenda items and in the positions it took on them, but that it often seemed to be going off the track as the unique coordinating body for the entire organized community in deciding how it should be spending its time, which issues it should be taking on, and how it arrived at positions regarding those issues.

The subject of public funding for parochial schools is illustrative. In an article in the December 1999 issue of *Commentary* magazine entitled "Who's Afraid of Jewish Day Schools?" Jack Wertheimer, provost of the Jewish Theological Seminary, was critical of the JCPA for resisting "every plan that might in some way bring government assistance to support the general-studies education offered by religious schools, including, as is often proposed today, in the form of direct subsidies to parents." In looking at a 1998 report prepared by the JCPA, Wertheimer referred to "its datedness, as if preserved in amber from the 1950s."[22]

That JCPA report was published after a year-long study from which one JCPA organization, the Orthodox Union, had dissented. Though the report itself said that "the JCPA received feedback from communities across the country, large, medium and small, that had examined the voucher issue locally within the last two years," it did not point out, as an earlier draft had, that of its 122 community members, only 28 had indicated that they had "examined the voucher issue within the last two years." Such results were hardly an overwhelming sign that the communities shared the JCPA's interest in treating this kind of topic in this fashion, nor that they had strong consensus-based feelings on it which they wished to have heard. While Chicago's JCRC, following the lead of the national body, did examine this topic, it reported that since there was no consensus on the vouchers issue in its community, it itself did not take a position. Instead of supporting either side in the debate, the Chicago JCRC forwarded the JCPA statements prepared by each of its constituent members who wished to provide a summary of their stands on the subject.

The kinds of positions taken by those on either side of the voucher question are instructive. On the one hand are members of the Jewish community who hold to the long-standing view that any softening whatsoever on church-state questions might endanger the wall of separation which has protected the religious freedom of American Jews. In a universalistic fashion, many of those who hold this position fear that the creation of state-sponsored vouchers which could be used for parochial schools would weaken public school education. On the other side of the debate are those who claim that the constitutional dimensions of this issue are not all that clear and the Supreme Court has yet to offer a definitive ruling on the matter. Some of these advocates of vouchers say that with regard to education in inner-city communities, some members of those very communities favor vouchers as a device for improving educational opportunities. Above all, for the proponents of vouchers and those ready to take a new look at the subject, as for Wertheimer, there is a significant communal interest at stake in assisting parents to send their children to Jewish day schools.

Critics of the JCPA were thus suggesting that a national organization which is meant to embrace the entire community would be doing its job best if, instead of insisting on coming down on one side or the other of a controversial issue of this kind and rejecting the view of one section of the community or the other, it created a study which described the alternative positions held in the community, fairly reporting on the proportions of the community on each side but also acknowledging and exploring the developing trends in the area.

For many of its critics, the JCPA was seen as an organization which paid insufficient attention to Jewish communal self-interest of the times and which was too locked in to the civil liberties, universalistic approach of an earlier era. Though some observers may have talked of this as a battle between liberals and conservatives, most of the critics of the JCPA themselves said that they would be uncomfortable if such an organization seemed predominantly linked to any partisan agenda; for them, the point was that the organization seemed insufficiently open to the range of positions taken within the community on certain issues, and to the reasons why those positions were taken.

For most of its critics, a body like the JCPA, which they said was neither conceived of by its founders nor regarded by its constituents as an autonomous organization with independent members who come together to take positions on an open-ended number of issues of the day, should not approach all issues from any particular ideological point of view. For them, the JCPA is an organization of organizations which, when it deals with public policy issues, should focus on those in which the community has particular matters at stake and on which consensus exists or can be found. It is, they held, a body which should follow a process whereby representatives accountable to organizations and communities forge positions on those issues in the name of the overall community. The critics stressed that such an organization has the primary purpose of serving as a coordinating body which assists its constituents in programming to advance those communal interests, and they expressed the view that in recent years the action-centered aspect of the JCPA's role, though not entirely overlooked, had been slighted.

While JCRCs from communities like New York and Chicago actively played out their unhappiness with the JCPA (New York's by not attending plenums), two of the most powerful national agencies, the ADL and AJCommittee, mostly followed a passive route reflective of their perception that the JCPA is less of a force than it once was, increasingly marginalizing their involvement in JCPA affairs. The federation system, the original parent body, which continued to provide the bulk of the organization's funding, might have been expected to play a role significantly impacting on the choice of direction for the JCPA. Instead, however, it was greatly preoccupied with organizational restructuring of its own, as the Council of Jewish Federations underwent an extended and complicated merger period with the United Jewish Appeal and United Israel Appeal to form the United Jewish Communities. Still, in the summer and fall of 1999, disfavor with the JCPA also began to be seen coming from the federation world, witness the letter from the New York Federation, adding to pressure being put on the JCPA to modify its way of doing business.

In a post-ideological age, when the Jewish community was striving to steer its course in a changing world and a changing community relations environment, the JCPA appeared to its critics to be out of step. While JCPA leadership began engaging in dialogue with some of the organization's critics and talking about making moves to respond to them as the 1990s drew to a close, that did not occur sufficiently to quell all of the concerns of those critics. But if the JCPA was slow in responding to new realities and in playing the kind of role of coordinator of communal activity which was being looked for, communities in the field increasingly pushed the organization in those directions.

An example of this trend can be seen in the way that treatment of the issue scheduled for year-long study in 1998 and 1999 played out. The original plan was to take a look at "Race, Public Policy, and Affirmative Action." Several CRCs then objected that there was little to be gained from entering into an extensive debate aimed at reasserting or modifying a position on affirmative action. A much more useful endeavor, they urged, would be to look at issues surrounding race relations in America today and to see what was being done around the country through action aimed at addressing these problems in a pragmatic way. Furthermore, said several of the communities, race relations today involves more than black and white relations. So the study, renamed "Race, Ethnicity, and Public Policy," became a two-year project with on-the-ground considerations noted and with the complex racial mix in America today taken into account.

Somewhat similarly, the JCPA office was at first virtually oblivious to what quickly became a major agenda item in many JCRC offices in the 1990s: the need to assist survivors and to deal with other aspects of the swirl of issues surrounding Holocaust-era assets. With the subject achieving primacy in Chicago, New Jersey, Miami, and Los Angeles, JCRCs from those areas pushed the JCPA to give it appropriate attention, which the organization began to do. Although this attention thus came somewhat belatedly, once the JCPA did assume the role of coordinator, the organization was able to demonstrate the kind of resource function which it is in a position to play for the national community.

With the JCPA's difficulties having become public, a number of the issues at hand crystallized during the JCPA's annual plenum in February 2000. Delivering an address called "The Ghetto and the Globe," Larry Rubin described the Internet as a worldwide phenomenon and complained that "even as worlds are opening around us, the organized Jewish world is turning inward." After noting that the priorities of the agency which he led had at first been "largely domestic" and then, after the Six-Day War, had become "increasingly international," Rubin asked: "What about now?" His answer was: "I believe that there continues to be a justice agenda in America." Though he later added that "the justice agenda demands our efforts to extend democracy to all corners of the world, for now that is where we live," the domestic thrust of his argument was clear.[23]

For Rubin and those in JCPA circles who shared his perspective, priority setting which begins by considering the community's particularist needs is a form of "ghettoization" which deserves to be regarded in a disparaging way. Ironically, though, in playing down international concerns and calling for a returned focus to the domestic social justice agenda, they, in a way, were the ones who were turning inward. Ignored by them was the fact that the Jewish community, even when coming at things from a subjective point of view, has provided wide-ranging leadership to the nation as a whole on a host of issues. Concern about the terrorist violence directed against Israel and Jews in Argentina and elsewhere around the world, for example, enabled the community to have useful insights as America itself became a direct target of the scourge of international terrorism in the early and mid-1990s. Similarly, communal responses to hate crimes, initially conceived of primarily because such acts were often being directed against Jews, have provided useful general models for addressing that problem as the country has increasingly focused on it. Furthermore, the Jewish community's still-resonating memories of the Holocaust enabled it to provide moral underpinning for international action when the ethnic cleansing in Kosovo, different but in a way reminiscent, unfolded. Indeed, the American Jewish community's interest in Israel and Jewish communities around the world has made it the primary backer of foreign aid overall and of the principle of foreign engagement for this nation, as government spokesmen have acknowledged. What begins with a particularist impulse may thus end up with universal impact.

When Rubin closed his plenum speech he announced that at the end of the year 2000 he would be leaving the JCPA. Though he was hardly the only one to take the kinds of positions that he espoused, the declaration of his departure was seen by many as providing the occasion for the organization to take a fresh look at itself at a significant moment. In assuming the chairmanship of the organization at that time, Leonard Cole gave strong indication that he was prepared to lead it in doing just that. An article of his which appeared in *The Jewish Week* shortly thereafter further demonstrated sensitivity to the concerns of those calling for the setting of institutional priorities on the basis of a determination of communal interests.[24] At the same time, the United Jewish Communities initiated its own new look at its relationship with the JCPA.

In the year that has followed, a good deal has happened, but while the tensions between the JCPA and its critics have become less acute, the issues surrounding those tensions have not yet been fully resolved. The Palestinians' turn to violence and their accompanying public opinion campaign have made Israel-related activities an unquestionable priority on the agenda for the community relations field, and the JCPA has played an important role in coordinating nationwide activities in that area. In that and other ways, under Cole's chairmanship and with a new executive, Hannah Rosenthal, the JCPA has become less wedded to a policy-centered, domestic-focused agenda than it had been under its previous leadership. Furthermore, the terrorist attacks on America of September 11, 2001, introduced new realities with an undefined but likely long-term impact on America's Jewish community and the community relations field. Still, as this chapter was being completed (in October 2001), the precise nature of the role to be played by the Jewish Council for Public Affairs in the years ahead and its relationship with its constituents and with the federation system remained uncertain.

Conclusion

At the turn of the new century, the fashion in which the Jewish community represented itself in the public square through its organizational entities was undergoing redefinition. On the one hand, community relations councils around the country continued to fulfill their historic role of combating anti-Semitism and related threats to the security of the Jewish community and to join coalition partners in advancing contemporary aspects of the traditional civil rights and civil liberties agendas. On the other hand, they also found themselves focusing on priorities which reflected the evolution of the more particularistic sort of agenda that first achieved prominence in the late 1960s, and they increasingly were framing and carrying out projects within the Jewish community itself. More and more, many of them were serving as the advocacy arm of the federations in their communities by helping to strengthen governmental support for those agencies' social welfare activities.

At a time when American Jewry had greatly "made it" into the mainstream of American life, finding greater acceptance and opportunity, the community relations enterprise maintained a longstanding role by striving to protect the rights of all Americans and to expand overall tolerance. At the same time, however, with the movement into the mainstream having come to be regarded in part as potentially threatening the future of the community, with many individuals increasingly seeing their identities tied up with their religious background and communal ties, and with religion-based principles, in general, becoming a more public matter in the country, the community relations field also found its role in advancing communal interests taking it into new territory.

In this context, the dialectical nature of Jewish communal affairs came to the surface in the national arena. The body newly named the Jewish Council for Public Affairs had increasingly assumed the shape of an entity tied to an earlier era's universalistic approach while greatly focusing on the pronouncement of policy positions on a broad range of public affairs issues of the day. Meanwhile, a countervailing approach called for that body to be more committed to an evolving particularistic agenda that more clearly identified itself as the vehicle of its collective constituent members, whom it represents and assists in carrying out their action-centered roles. The controversy surrounding the JCPA which emerged was an expression of differences between these answers to the question of what kind of community relations body the national Jewish community should have and how the community should be represented in the public square at that moment in its and the nation's history.

While this author's own perspective on these matters admittedly owes much to his experience with the federation-linked Chicago CRC as described in the initial section of this chapter, the conclusions drawn from an analysis of that operation offer useful insight into these broader issues. That experience suggests that the most effective and appropriate national body for the day would be one which serves as the community relations arm of the overall federation-linked system while maintaining its ties with its national member organizations. Focusing on community relations action and facilitating and coordinating such action as carried out by its constituents around the country, it would address significant needs by providing leadership, resources, models, and ideas to the national community relations enterprise in those priority areas which have been of concern since CRCs began to be established and those which have emerged over the following decades. When it did take public policy positions, they would be on "bottom-line" matters where the community had a prevailing consensus and where the organization's constituents felt that there was a clear-cut communal interest. Thanks to the broad communal base of such an entity, its pronouncements on these issues would have strength and credibility. Individual CRCs, while empowering such an entity, would benefit from this kind of national structure while modifying their own agendas in tune with local circumstances.

A solution of this kind would blend organizational elements from an earlier time with current realities. Synthesizing aspects of the universalistic approach to community relations issues of the past with the more particularistic approach which emerged subsequently and which has continued to take shape, it would position the Jewish community relations field to meet the problems of the present and future in a fashion in line with the organized community's assessment of its prevailing and emerging interests.

Given the various factors involved in dealing with institutional matters, one cannot be certain how these issues will indeed be resolved. But while the precise answer to the question of the structural way in which Jews will be represented in the American public square in the twenty-first century by the bodies which are the subjects of this essay remains open, it is clear that, to a great extent, the trend toward increasing emphasis on the "Jewishness" of Jewish community relations will remain intact.

Notes

1. Daniel J. Elazar, "The Jewish Political Tradition in the English-Speaking World," unpublished manuscript.
2. Jerome A. Chanes, "The Voices of the American Jewish Community," *Survey of Jewish Affairs 1989*, William Frankel, ed. (Oxford: Basil Blackwell, 1989), 125.
3. R. M. MacIver, *Report on the Jewish Community Relations Agencies* (New York: National Community Relations Advisory Council, 1951), 99.
4. Jerold S. Auerbach is harshly critical of those segments of the Jewish community which, in his view, elevated and distorted the prophetic tradition in an attempt to be accepted by Christian Americans. "Severed from the Jewish covenantal tradition and grafted to Christian theology (and then to liberal politics), prophecy came to define enlightened Judaism." *Rabbis and Lawyers: The Journey from Torah to Constitution* (Bloomington: Indiana University Press, 1990), 99.
5. Peter Novick, *The Holocaust in American Life* (Boston: Houghton Mifflin, 1999), 148-51, and ff.
6. MacIver, *Report,* 101.
7. This and subsequent references to early Public Affairs Committee deliberations are taken from PAC minutes and related documents.
8. Novick, *Holocaust,* 133.
9. Mordecai Lee, "A Jewish 'March of Dimes'? Organization Theory and the Future of Jewish Community Relations Councils," *Jewish Political Studies Review*, 12:1-2 (Spring 2000).
10. Walter A. Lurie, entry on "NJCRAC" in *Jewish American Voluntary Organizations*, Michael N. Dobkowski, ed. (New York: Greenwood Press, 1986), 347-55.
11. Earl Raab in *The Turbulent Decades; Jewish Communal Services in America 1958-78*, Graenum Berger, ed., vol. I (New York: Conference of Jewish Communal Service, 1981), 537.
12. Gregg Ivers, *To Build a Wall: American Jews and the Separation of Church and State* (Charlottesville: University Press of Virginia, 1995), esp. chap. 4, "Separation to the Fore," 100-45. See also J. J. Goldberg, *Jewish Power: Inside the American Jewish Establishment* (Reading, Mass.:

Perseus Press, 1996), 122-5. Goldberg covers several other developments reviewed in this chapter as well.

13. Raab, *Turbulent Decades*, 537-38.

14. Lurie, "NJCRAC," 348.

15. Albert D. Chernin, "Making Soviet Jews an Issue: A History," in *A Second Exodus: The American Movement to Free Soviet Jews*, Murray Friedman and Albert D. Chernin, eds. (Hanover, N.H.: Brandeis University Press, 1999), esp. 44-45 and 62-63.

16. Murray Friedman, "Jewish Public Policy: Its Unexamined Premises," *Journal of Jewish Service*, vol. 67, no. 3 (Spring 1991): 175, 177-78.

17. Albert D. Chernin, "The Liberal Agenda: Is It Good or Bad for the Jews?" *Journal of Jewish Service*, vol. 67, no. 3 (Spring 1991): 166, 173.

18. Lawrence Rubin, "Y2B in Y2K: And If Not Now, When?" speech delivered February 21, 1999.

19. Ira Stoll, "End of Liberal Consensus Is Bruited by UJA-Federation," *Forward*, October 29, 1999, 1. The letters are reprinted on 9.

20. Leonard Fein, "That 1960s Consensus Is Not Dead Yet," *Forward*, November 5, 1999, 9.

21. J. J. Goldberg, *The Jewish Week*, November 5, 1999, and November 12, 1999.

22. Jack Wertheimer, "Who's Afraid of Jewish Day Schools?" *Commentary* (December 1999), 52.

23. Lawrence Rubin, "The Ghetto and the Globe," speech delivered February 27, 2000.

24. Leonard Cole, "Quick, Name a Jewish Issue," *The Jewish Week*, May 5, 2000.

3

History of Israel Advocacy

Martin J. Raffel

Introduction

This analysis is not about the complex relationship between American Jews and Israel, the positions of Israeli governments over the years, or U.S. policy in the Middle East, although all three provide necessary context for understanding the topic. Rather, this is intended to be an examination of the organized American Jewish community's (hereinafter referred to in most places as the community) advocacy on behalf of Zionism and Israel in the American public square. Historically, the purpose of this advocacy has been to "sustain a U.S. foreign policy that supports the security and survival of Israel within the framework of U.S. national interests. This includes U.S. military and economic support at levels needed to assure Israel's means of self-defense and economic viability."[1] The community's efforts to influence the U.S. government's involvement in the Middle East peace process will be examined, as will the substance of and process for determining the community's policy positions, the principal organizations that convey those positions in the public square, and their strategies and tactics. The Israel advocacy agenda has been promoted both directly, through various channels of communication with administration officials and members of

Congress, and indirectly, via the mobilization of pro-Israel sentiment in key sectors of American society, along with efforts to counter those forces seen as hostile.[2]

The history of Israel advocacy in America can be divided roughly into four periods. The first is from 1897, the date of the first Zionist Congress in Basel, Switzerland, until World War II and the years leading up to statehood. During that period there was a vigorous debate about whether or not to support Jewish nationalism. Following the Holocaust, Jewish leadership, with the Zionist movement in the vanguard, generally turned to the task of helping the State of Israel come into existence and winning early recognition and material support from the United States. Many of the national and grass roots organizations that would propel the advocacy effort from 1948 on were established during the pre-state era. Thereafter, from the founding of Israel until 1967, the community—still on a relatively modest scale—endeavored to create a solid foundation for ongoing U.S. governmental and public support. The 1950s witnessed the establishment of two organizations, the American Israel Public Affairs Committee (AIPAC) and the Conference of Presidents of Major American Jewish Organizations (Presidents Conference), which were intended specifically to serve as vehicles for influencing U.S. policy on Israel and the Middle East.

It was the 1967 Six-Day War that transformed Israel advocacy into a dominant preoccupation of organized American Jewish life. The post-1967 period—which saw changing Israeli governments and policies, the Jewish state's struggle for security and international acceptance, as well as the beginning of a peace process with the Arab world—was the most active in terms of Israel advocacy. Finally, in the early 1990s, new Jewish communal priorities emerged as the peace process accelerated dramatically in the wake of the Soviet Union's collapse and the Persian Gulf War. These factors and others led to considerable erosion in Israel activism as an issue that galvanized and mobilized the Jewish community's grassroots. A lively internal Jewish community debate, reflecting sharp differences over issues in the peace process, spilled into the public arena. At the start of the twenty-first century, such differences appeared to be giving way to an emerging political consensus. The failure of the Camp David Summit in July 2000, followed by Palestinian-initiated violence in the so-called al-Aksa *intifada*, have returned Israel to a prominent place on the community's public affairs agenda. Whether this will be relatively transitory or a long-term phenomenon depends primarily on the situation in the region. This analysis also will touch briefly on ways the community has sought to enhance ties between the United States and Israel on the basis of "nonpolitical" initiatives.

Since this is an historical overview, most if not all of the events dealt with here have received much more extensive treatment elsewhere. But this abbreviated retrospective is an essential ingredient for reflection on the causes and meaning of recent trends in Israel advocacy and their implications for the community's involvement in the American public square generally.

The American Jewish Community's Embrace of Jewish Statehood (1898-1948)[3]

Early Zionist Stirrings

In contrast to European Jewry, which was heavily influenced by the early Zionist movement, American Jews at the end of the nineteenth century generally viewed Zionism as a marginal issue. Important segments of the community, particularly the German Jews who already had achieved considerable financial and social success in their new land—the so-called uptown Jews—believed that Zionism was inimical to their interests. A profound commitment to Americanism, they believed, left no room for allegiance to another nationality.

Theodor Herzl published his visionary *Der Judenstaat* (The Jewish State) in 1896 and the First Zionist Congress, which convened in Basel in 1897, called for Jewish settlement in Palestine, "the organization and binding together of the whole of Jewry," and the strengthening of "Jewish national sentiment and consciousness." These developments led to the founding convention in New York City in July 1898 of the Federation of American Zionists (FAZ), which affiliated with the World Zionist Organization (WZO) and endorsed the Basel program. The Reform movement's Central Conference of American Rabbis (CCAR) and its synagogue body, the Union of American Hebrew Congregations (UAHC), roundly denounced the Basel Congress. Such major American Jewish leaders as Jacob Schiff and Louis Marshall, who later would be among the founders of the American Jewish Committee in 1906, also repudiated it.[4]

The Orthodox community generally remained distant from Zionism largely on religious grounds, believing that the restoration of Jewish sovereignty in Eretz Israel (Land of Israel) should await divine intervention, although a small pro-Zionist group of Orthodox leaders founded the Mizrachi Organization of America in 1911. On the other hand, leaders of the Conservative movement, particularly Solomon Schechter, the revered president of the Jewish Theological Seminary, were strongly supportive of Zionism. As the Conservative movement grew, its synagogues would become an important source of support for the Zionist cause in America at the local level. At the turn of the twentieth century, however, this was the weakest of the three religious movements. The relatively small Reconstructionist movement, an offshoot of Conservative Judaism, also took a strong pro-Zionist line, reflecting the concept of "Jewish peoplehood" advocated by its leader Rabbi Mordecai Kaplan. The first Labor Zionist organization, Po'alai Zion, was founded in March 1903 in New York City, and it succeeded in attracting a small number of adherents from the ranks of Jewish socialist and labor movement circles. Other, more powerful, pro-Zionist forces, including B'nai B'rith and the American Jewish Congress, would emerge in the early part of the century as well.

Louis Brandeis Joins the Movement

The FAZ remained weak in the early years of the twentieth century due to a lack of strong leadership and direction, a dearth of funds, and constant squabbling among the many autonomous local Zionist societies. A dramatic shift in fortunes occurred in 1914 when Louis Brandeis, the prominent Boston attorney and confidante of President Woodrow Wilson, agreed to assume the chairmanship of the Zionist movement in America. Other influential figures joined him, including Judge Julian Mack, Rabbi Stephen Wise, and Henrietta Szold. These new leaders succeeded in shaping an understanding of Zionism that was compatible with the cultural pluralism and "Americanism" espoused by the philosopher Horace Callen. In his famous 1915 speech to an assembly of Reform rabbis, Brandeis asserted, "Let no American imagine that Zionism is inconsistent with patriotism. Multiple loyalties are objectionable only if they are inconsistent. Indeed, loyalty to America demands rather that each American Jew become a Zionist."[5] Under the stewardship of Brandeis and his colleagues—reinforced by events during and following World War I described below—membership in the FAZ grew from some 12,000 in 1914 to over 176,000 in 1919.

The Balfour Declaration

Zionist aspirations received a significant boost on November 2, 1917, in the form of the Balfour Declaration, a letter from British secretary of state for foreign affairs Arthur Balfour to Lord Rothschild calling for the establishment of a national home for the Jewish people in Palestine. The Zionist movement immediately and enthusiastically welcomed it. On the other hand, the American Jewish Committee, the most powerful Jewish public affairs body in the first half of the twentieth century, waited a full six months to respond. A number of staunch anti-Zionists in the organization lobbied unsuccessfully for a clear-cut condemnation of the Balfour Declaration. In the end, the American Jewish Committee's statement conveyed support for the establishment in Palestine of "a center for Judaism for the stimulation of our faith, for the pursuit and development of literature, science and art in a Jewish environment, and for the rehabilitation of the land." Lest there be any misunderstanding, the statement also stressed that "the Jews of the United States have here established a permanent home for themselves and their children . . . and recognize their unqualified allegiance to this country, which they love and cherish and of whose people they constitute an integral part." The objective of securing a sovereign Jewish nation in Palestine clearly was not yet a cause championed by non-Zionist groups.

President Wilson, against the advice of his State Department, which had expressed concern over the Arab reaction, endorsed the Balfour Declaration ten months after it was issued—in part as a result of intensive lobbying by Zionist leaders, especially Rabbi Stephen Wise. A Reform rabbi with close ties to the Democratic Party and substantial oratorical talent, Wise would assume leadership of the American Zionist movement in the mid-1930s.

Other Advocacy Organizations Formed

Meanwhile, Brandeis and other Zionist officials—working with Rabbi Stephen Wise and the so-called downtown Jews of Eastern European origin who resented what they regarded as the elitist approach of the American Jewish Committee—convened an American Jewish Congress in December 1918. The purpose was to produce a democratic and broadly representative Jewish body that would be able to advocate Jewish interests at the Paris Peace Conference. This congress went on to adopt an unequivocal pro-Balfour Declaration resolution on behalf of the entire American Jewish community. Zionist leaders, recognizing that the "Congress movement" represented a structural concept of American Jewish life that differed dramatically from that of the American Jewish Committee, transformed the American Jewish Congress into a permanent institution several years later. B'nai B'rith, the Jewish community's oldest service organization, would be an important actor on behalf of Zionism and Israel. The agency not only provided direct support, but its leadership also played instrumental roles in establishing national coordinating organizations (e.g., American Jewish Conference and Presidents Conference). In addition, B'nai B'rith founded the Anti-Defamation League (ADL) in 1913 for the purpose of fighting anti-Semitism and bigotry. While this was and remains ADL's principal mandate, the organization also became an important instrument for Israel advocacy in the post-1967 era.

Schism in the Movement

The Zionist Organization of America (ZOA), the successor organization to the FAZ, was established in 1918, the same year the American Jewish Congress convened. The ZOA, reflecting the orientation of Brandeis and most other American Zionist leaders, focused on the economic development of the Yishuv (Jewish community) in Palestine. In contrast to the American Zionist movement, Dr. Chaim Weizmann, president of the World Zionist Organization and later the first president of Israel, and the European Zionists placed heavy emphasis on ideological issues, including Jewish cultural and spiritual revival in the ancient homeland. This tension matured into a full-blown schism, which resulted in Brandeis being voted out of office by the ZOA at its 1921 convention in Cleveland. At that point, Attorney Louis Lipsky assumed leadership of the movement. Brandeis and his circle of supporters then formed the Palestine Development Council to concentrate on economic development in Palestine. American Zionism, weakened substantially by the Weizmann-Brandeis rupture, only managed to regain a measure of cohesion in the 1930s with the appearance of Nazism in Europe and the return of Brandeis to leadership of the movement. Hadassah, the women's Zionist organization of America founded by Henrietta Szold, was the exception. It steadily grew in membership and influence throughout the 1920s and became a major force within the Zionist establishment. Weizmann himself came to see that the ideological thrust of European Zionism was not well suited to American Jewry. Consequently, the United Jewish Agency, which was formed by Weizmann in cooperation with the Council of Jewish Federations, American Jewish Committee, and other non-Zionist groups to collect funds for overseas needs, was intentionally kept apolitical.

The Reform movement's initial opposition to Zionism gradually eroded during the 1920s and 1930s. In 1935, the CCAR permitted the movement's rabbis to adopt their own personal positions on the issue. Two years later both the CCAR and the UAHC pledged to work for the rebuilding of the Jewish homeland. However, with the exception of the hard-core ideological American Zionists and despite growing pro-statehood sentiment at the grass roots, most national American Jewish leaders throughout the 1930s still viewed Palestine not as a potential Jewish state but in humanitarian terms as a safe haven for Jews fleeing Hitler's persecution. Dr. Abba Hillel Silver, a pro-statehood Reform rabbi and one of the few Jewish leaders of his time associated with the Republican Party, derided this approach to Zionist activity as nothing more than "refugeeism."

Biltmore Platform

The British White Paper in 1939, which dramatically curtailed the number of Jewish refugees permitted to immigrate to Palestine, led the philanthropically oriented American Zionists and even the non-Zionists to reassess their priorities. With the outbreak of World War II, the ZOA created the American Emergency Committee for Zionist Affairs, which later became the American Zionist Emergency Council (Emergency Council). This body, which served as spokesman for the movement, convened a convention with representatives of most of the Zionist and non-Zionist groups—with the notable exception of the American Jewish Committee—at New York's Biltmore Hotel in May 1942. The "Biltmore platform" identified the establishment of a Jewish commonwealth in Palestine as the Zionists' highest postwar priority. Later that year, the American Council for Judaism was formed under the leadership of Lessing Rosenwald and Rabbi Elmer Berger, a group that remained vigorously opposed to Jewish nationalism even after the Holocaust. Led by Dr. Silver, the Emergency Council over time succeeded in persuading the American Jewish Committee and other mainstream non-Zionist groups to join in the struggle for statehood. Despite the overwhelming support

American Jews gave the Democratic Party and its candidates for office, Silver insisted on maintaining a nonpartisan approach to the community's pro-statehood activism. Both the Democratic and Republican national conventions in 1944 adopted resolutions consistent with the Biltmore program. By the end of World War II, the notion that American Jewry had an obligation to promote Jewish statehood—rather than focusing its efforts almost exclusively on humanitarian concerns in Palestine—had become an established principle.

Umbrella Bodies Established

The 1940s also witnessed the creation of two additional "umbrella" bodies. The American Jewish Conference was set up in 1943 at the behest of B'nai B'rith to advocate the community's post-World War II interests, particularly on the issues of Palestine and the Holocaust. This was similar to the role envisioned for the American Jewish Congress during the period of World War I. The conference, which included virtually all the Zionist and non-Zionist groups, pressed a strong pro-statehood position with national and international bodies. However, following withdrawal of the American Jewish Committee and Jewish Labor Committee, it gradually lost influence following World War II and ceased to function altogether after 1948. But the concept of a central communal voice on Israel-related concerns resurfaced in the following decade in the form of the Conference of Presidents of Major American Jewish Organizations (Presidents Conference). Meanwhile, the National Community Relations Advisory Council (NCRAC) was established by the Council of Jewish Federations in 1944. (The word "Jewish" was added in 1969 and the full name of the agency was changed in 1998 to the Jewish Council for Public Affairs. It will be cited hereinafter as the JCPA.) Comprised at that time of four national agencies—the three defense agencies and the Jewish Labor Committee—and fourteen community relations councils or committees (CRCs), the JCPA was intended to bring cohesion to national and local public affairs efforts and to give a voice to communities at the national level. While its agenda was dominated by domestic concerns well into the 1950s—particularly the struggle to remove legal barriers facing Jews and other minorities in employment, education, and housing—it would come to play an important role in coordinating and stimulating broad grassroots Israel advocacy following the Six-Day and Yom

Kippur Wars. Indeed, it would apply the same principle employed in the 1940s and 1950s to advance the community's domestic agenda, establishing coalitions with like-minded groups in the general community in order to build public support for Israel.[6]

UN Partition Plan

The United States strongly supported the United Nations Partition Plan of November 29, 1947, which provided the international legal foundation for the establishment of the State of Israel. This posture was by no means assured in light of the vigorous opposition to Zionism from senior U.S. officials, including Secretary of State George C. Marshall, a World War II hero, and Secretary of Defense James V. Forrestal. Other powerful forces were lining up against Jewish statehood, including members of the OSS (predecessor of the CIA), some liberal Protestant groups, oil company executives, Arab embassies in Washington, and major newspapers and journals. Opposition came from within the Jewish community as well, primarily the American Council for Judaism and a number of influential leaders of the American Jewish Committee. (AJC itself supported partition.) President Truman's record was mixed. As a U.S. senator from Missouri, he had criticized the British White Paper of 1939 limiting Jewish immigration into Palestine, but he refused to endorse a pro-Zionist congressional resolution in 1944, fearing that it might undermine the war effort.

The Emergency Council had been working for years to line up support for statehood among members of Congress, the labor movement, media, non-Jewish clergy, and others. In addition, they found allies within the White House, particularly two Roosevelt aides retained by Truman, Judge Samuel I. Rosenman and David K. Niles, assistant for minority affairs, who had built a close relationship with Rabbi Stephen Wise. A key weapon in the Zionists' arsenal was Eddie Jacobson, Truman's close friend and former partner in a Kansas City haberdashery, who used his personal relationship to influence the president. With the UN partition vote nearing, the State Department's strategy was to endorse the proposal officially but to bring about its demise by refusing to actively lobby other countries on its behalf. After some vacillation, Truman ordered U.S. diplomats to undertake an intensive campaign on behalf of partition, a decision that proved decisive in its eventual adoption. The community frequently would be challenged to find ways of securing presidential support for Israel against contradictory advice from an "Arabist" State Department. Ironically, many years later during the George H. W. Bush and Clinton administrations, when the peace process entered its most dynamic phase, Jews would come to occupy key positions in the State Department's Middle East policymaking apparatus.[7]

U.S. Recognition of Israel

The violent Arab response to UN partition of Palestine encouraged anti-Zionist forces in the Truman administration to seek an American retreat from its earlier position. Indeed, on March 19, 1948, the chief American representative at the United Nations, without Truman's knowledge or sanction, recommended that a temporary UN trusteeship replace the partition plan. However, the day before, Truman, at the urging of his old friend Eddie Jacobson, had agreed to meet with Chaim Weizmann to reassure him of U.S. support for Jewish statehood. With the 1948 election approaching, and third-party candidate Henry Wallace making inroads in New York State, there clearly was a political component to Truman's pro-statehood posture as well.[8] A confrontation between the State Department and the president took place on May 12, 1948, during which Secretary Marshall insisted that the United States refrain from recognizing Israel. During the next two days, Truman's assistant, Clark Clifford, managed to blunt the force of State Department opposition. Eleven minutes after David Ben-Gurion declared statehood, the White House announced its recognition of the provisional government as de facto authority of the new commonwealth. The Soviet Union, primarily to assure the termination of British control over Palestine, was the first country to offer Israel de jure recognition.

Building the Foundation of a U.S.-Israel Partnership (1948-1967)[9]

AIPAC and Presidents Conference Established

Now that Herzl's vision had been realized, the community's immediate objective was to create the foundation for ongoing U.S. military, economic, and diplomatic support of the fledgling Jewish state.

Not only were there obvious defense requirements, Israel also was in desperate need of assistance to help with the absorption of hundreds of thousands of Jewish refugees fleeing persecution in the countries of North Africa and the Middle East. The United States already had provided a substantial Export-Import Bank loan, but what the Israelis really desired was a grant. They looked for someone to lead a lobbying campaign in Congress and settled on I. L. (Si) Kenen, who already was working closely with Israel's ambassador to the United Nations, Abba Eban.[10] Eban soon would serve as Israel's ambassador in Washington as well. Kenen previously held the position of information director at the Emergency Council, which after the war was renamed the American Zionist Council (AZC). It was not a foregone conclusion that Kenen would act independently of the Israeli government. A senior official at the Israeli embassy argued that he, an Israeli diplomat, should serve as overall coordinator of the lobbying campaign. With the backing of AZC leader Louis Lipsky, Kenen successfully resisted Israeli government efforts to seize control of the operation. Thus, instead of serving as a foreign agent, he was able to register as a domestic lobbyist.

Working in coordination with the Washington representatives of national Jewish organizations, the expanding grassroots network of CRCs, as well as supportive members of Congress, Kenen led a concerted campaign that resulted in $65 million in U.S. economic assistance to Israel in 1951. The following year, Kenen and his allies persuaded Congress to increase the package to $73 million. In addition, Kenen succeeded in getting both political parties to adopt pro-Israel planks in their 1952 platforms. On the Republican side, Kenen sought and obtained the assistance of Senator Richard Nixon of California, whom he astutely identified as Eisenhower's probable running mate.

From 1951 to 1953, Kenen carried out his activity as the Washington representative of the AZC, a nonprofit organization subject to strict limitations on the amount of time its employees were permitted to lobby members of Congress. Consequently, in 1954, in order to unshackle himself from these restrictions, Kenen registered his operation as the American Zionist Council of Public Affairs (AZCPA) and began soliciting funds that were not tax-deductible. It took considerable effort to come up with the modest sum of $50,000 required to support the new organization. The AZCPA was renamed the American Israel Public Affairs Committee (AIPAC) in 1959, in order to encourage participation in the organization's governing bodies of Jewish leaders who identified themselves as non-Zionists, a move that prompted the ZOA to temporarily distance itself from AIPAC.[11]

As concern over the Eisenhower administration's posture toward Israel grew, the community came to recognize that executive branch advocacy was no less important than Kenen's congressional activity. At the same time, one of Secretary of State John Foster Dulles's aides, Henry Byroade, recommended to Dr. Nahum Goldmann, then head of the World Jewish Congress, that all the major Jewish organizations should coalesce so that the White House and State Department could be addressed by one Jewish voice. Goldmann, working with Abba Eban and Philip Klutznick, newly elected leader of B'nai B'rith, convened an informal gathering in March 1954 of a Conference of Presidents of Major American Jewish Organizations. Sporadic meetings quickly evolved into a formal organizational structure. Klutznick was selected to serve as the group's first volunteer chair and Yehuda Hellman, a colleague of Goldmann's from Israel, was hired as its staff director. The Presidents Conference, it was agreed, would be viewed as the spokesman of the Jewish community to the U.S. administration on Israel-related issues. The central vehicles that would be utilized by the organized Jewish community to pursue its Israel advocacy agenda were now in place.

The Suez Campaign and Strains with the Eisenhower Administration

The Eisenhower era saw modest advances in the U.S.-Israel relationship, particularly between the countries' respective intelligence communities. However, it also was characterized by periods of strain that challenged the community's advocacy prowess. Aid to Israel was suspended temporarily in 1953 to protest an Israeli commando raid into the Jordanian town of Kibya led by Ariel Sharon. Intended as an attack against fleeing terrorists, the Israeli military action caused the death of some sixty-nine men, women, and children. This tragic incident came shortly after Israel attempted to develop a water diversion project in the northern sector of the Jordan River, which elicited strenuous protests from Jordan and Syria. Reluctantly, Israeli prime minister David Ben-Gurion relented to U.S. economic pressure and halted the Jordan River irrigation project. Increasingly, Israeli reliance on American economic, military, and diplomatic support would give future U.S. administrations similarly strong leverage over decision making in Jerusalem.

The Eisenhower administration started arming Iraq as part of its "containment" strategy against the Soviet Union. AIPAC's Kenen immediately, and in the end unsuccessfully, sought to build opposition to the transfer of weapons to one of Israel's sworn enemies. Prior to the 1954 elections, Kenen circulated a survey to congressional candidates asking them to condition U.S. arms sales to Arab states on their willingness to pledge to defend the Free World from communist aggression, sign a peace treaty with Israel, and end the direct and indirect boycott of Israel.[12] The community, to this day, has refrained from expressing opposition to any U.S. arms sale to an Arab country at peace with Israel.[13] Czechoslovakia announced a major weapons sale to Egypt in 1955, which marked the beginning of a massive transfer of sophisticated military hardware from the Soviet bloc to the Arab world that continued for several decades. The community, fearing that the sale would alter the strategic balance of power in the region, enlisted the support of former president Truman, Eleanor Roosevelt, labor leaders, congressional friends, and prominent Jewish Republicans, such as Detroit philanthropist Max Fisher, to press the administration to end its arms boycott of Israel. While Eisenhower and Dulles stood firm, they privately encouraged Britain, France, and Canada to supply military equipment to Israel.

But the most serious challenge to U.S.-Israel relations came in 1956 when Israel, in alliance with France and Britain, captured the Sinai Peninsula. This operation followed Egyptian president Nasser's decision to nationalize the Suez Canal and limit access to the international waterway that afforded Israel access to its southern port at Eilat. Although the Soviet Union had just crushed a popular revolt in Hungary, an outraged Eisenhower chose to deliver a major address condemning Israeli aggression and insisting that the invading forces pull back. Once again, the possible suspension of U.S. aid to Israel was used as a means of achieving this objective.

In addition, recognizing that American Jewry was transferring substantial sums of money to Israel, some administration officials hinted that U.S. tax laws might be revised to eliminate the deduction for contributions to foreign states. Sanctions against Israel by the UN Security Council were threatened as well. In order to counter the administration's pressure, Abba Eban enlisted the help of the pro-Republican Rabbi Abba Hillel Silver as well as high-ranking labor union officials with influence on Capitol Hill, including the AFL-CIO's Walter Reuther and George Meany and their legal adviser Arthur Goldberg.[14] Senate majority leader Lyndon Johnson, who was a major political force, also agreed to weigh in strongly against anti-Israel sanctions. In the end, however, Ben-Gurion agreed to withdraw from the Sinai, but he secured a U.S. pledge—which would go unfulfilled ten years later—to assure free passage of ships through the Straits of Tiran.

Jewish groups also began to confront some of the "community relations" aspects of the Middle East. During the 1950s, the community's activity was framed largely as a response to the virulent anti-Semitism of Arab propagandists in the United States and abroad, as well as to the patterns of discrimination against American Jews. Among the chief concerns at that time were the refusal of Arab governments to permit Jews to travel and do business in Arab countries and their denial of entry permits to Jewish service personnel assigned to American military bases in the Middle East.

Toward a Shared Strategic Vision: The Kennedy and Johnson Years

Despite these examples of strained relations, through the 1950s American policy makers, especially in the defense establishment, gradually came to see Israel and its increasingly potent army as a valuable asset in the Cold War struggle with the Soviet Union. Israel's status as a U.S. ally also advanced significantly under the Kennedy and Johnson administrations. This can be explained in part by the Jewish community's influence within the Democratic Party, but, more important, a strong Israel fit into the American strategic vision of defending Western interests against Soviet expansionism. This perspective would reach its fullest realization during the Nixon and Reagan administrations. In 1962, Kennedy became the first president to openly sell arms to Israel, five batteries of Hawk anti-aircraft missiles. The level of economic aid to Israel grew as well. In 1964, Israel received $40 million; only two years later the amount was $130 million. President Johnson, unlike his predecessors, also agreed to sell Israel offensive military weapons such as M-48 tanks and Skyhawk bombers, and he encouraged Israel to use American aid funds to purchase them. These steps paved the way for the United States to replace France as Israel's principal arms supplier.

From the Six-Day War to Madrid and Oslo (1967-1991)

Israel Becomes the Focus of American Jewry

For American Jews born after 1960, whose views of the Middle East were shaped during the 1980s and 1990s, it is very difficult to imagine an existentially vulnerable Israel. The generation who lived through the tension-filled weeks leading up to the 1967 Six-Day War, when fears of a "second Holocaust" were being expressed openly, and the trauma of the surprise 1973 Egyptian and Syrian attack against Israel on Yom Kippur, was shaped by a very different reality. In June 1967, seemingly threatened with annihilation and then with its lightning victory over three Arab armies and the capture of the Old City of Jerusalem, Israel was transformed into the central focus of the organized American Jewish community. While the prevailing emotion prior to the war was one of concern for Israel's safety, American Jews reacted to the outcome of the conflict with tremendous pride and exultation. That emotional wave led the community to manifest enhanced commitment to Israel in a variety of ways. An emergency fund-raising campaign organized by the United Jewish Appeal (UJA) produced extraordinary results; allocations to the UJA rose from $64.5 million in 1966 to $240 million in 1967. Israeli missions in the United States were flooded with calls by American Jews offering to go to Israel as volunteers. In fact, several thousand young American Jews did travel to Israel in the wake of the war to spend extended periods of time, and a small percentage of them remained to settle in the country. Such responses reoccurred in the wake of the Yom Kippur War. Again, volunteers streamed to Israel and the UJA campaign in 1974 reached $511.2 million, twice the amount collected the previous year.[15]

As the community intensified its activity in the spheres of philanthropy and volunteerism, it also recognized the central role that the United States had played in both conflicts by providing Israel with crucial political and military support. The massive airlift of weapons and ammunition ordered by President Nixon during the difficult days of the Yom Kippur War proved essential not only in Israel's war effort against the Egyptian and Syrian armies but in boosting morale among the Israeli population as well. Thus, advocacy for the strongest possible U.S.-Israel strategic relationship rapidly became the community's primary public affairs enterprise. This shift in priorities had a dramatic impact on the funding and focus of Jewish advocacy organizations. "In May 1967, AIPAC had been broke. Its director Si Kenen had to pay for letters, telephone calls, and telegrams to public officials, politicians and commentators out of his own pocket. But by the time the Israeli forces were in command of the entire Sinai, the West Bank of the Jordan, all of Jerusalem and the Golan Heights, AIPAC's bank accounts were suddenly healthy and would never again be in the red."[16] In 1968, the ADL, an agency long involved with domestic anti-Semitism and racism, established a Middle East Affairs Department and named Abraham Foxman—today the agency's national director and one of the community's most influential leaders—as its first director.[17]

Following the Yom Kippur War, the Council of Jewish Federations provided $965,000 over three years to the newly created Israel Task Force of the National Jewish Community Relations Advisory Council (NJCRAC; later the Jewish Council for Public Affairs—JCPA) for the purpose of influencing key sectors of American society. Proposals were submitted by the body's national member agencies with a view toward developing programs that would strengthen local Israel-related community relations activities. The approved projects included public opinion surveys, television and radio programs, information services to the African-American press, and outreach efforts to trade unionists in areas of the country with small Jewish populations. Additional funding was provided to the task force in 1980. The national defense agencies, which had long pursued a multi-issue agenda, began to devote a greater share of their resources to Israel advocacy.

National and local Jewish advocacy organizations developed a comprehensive approach and a coordinated campaign of public interpretation in order to respond to new challenges created by the Yom Kippur War. This included preparation of background materials geared to different audiences, the establishment of speakers' bureaus and Israel information centers, as well as rallies, demonstrations, and prayer meetings. The budgets and staffing of the three defense agencies and NJCRAC began to reflect the shift in priorities. In dramatically building up the advocacy function, the Jewish community was "moving away from the reliance on the wealthy *shtadlan* (individual intercessor) and entering into the modern era of full participation in group politics characteristic of 1970s America."[18] Israel and Zionist advocacy prior to 1967 in many ways is a story of how prominent individual Jewish and non-Jewish leaders utilized their personal influence with decision makers in Washington. Following the Six-Day and Yom Kippur Wars, the national and grassroots organizations themselves became the instruments through which American Jews, who felt increasingly at home in America, sought to achieve their policy objectives.

Public Messages: The Search for Consensus

The Six-Day War also marked a turning point in terms of the community's effort to project agreed-upon public messages (not that there were monolithic responses to events prior to 1967). Indeed, as previously noted, it took the tragedy of the Holocaust to end community divisions over the very principle of Jewish statehood. Even after the Holocaust, significant Jewish leaders continued to resist the Zionist idea for many years. Questions were raised as well regarding the wisdom of Israel's Suez campaign in 1956. However, in general, the community unhesitatingly defended Israel against pressures coming from the Eisenhower administration. From the period of the state's establishment until 1967, the message was simple. The United States should support Israel militarily, politically, and economically because a strong Israel served vital American national interests. While Israel had always hoped to establish normal relations with its neighbors, there was no movement in that direction during this period. Thus, the specifics of Israeli and American peace policies were not seen as particularly relevant.

However, the effort to identify and nurture community consensus has been a significant part of the Israel advocacy narrative since 1967. First, it must be understood that not all of the Jewish organizations operate on the basis of community consensus. Indeed, most do not. There are at least three kinds of Jewish agencies that function in the public affairs arena. Some represent a particular political or religious ideology. For example, the Union of Orthodox Jewish Congregations of America (UOJCA) will take certain public policy positions based on interpretation of *halakhah* (Jewish law). American Friends of Likud, a constituent organization of the Presidents Conference, clearly has a particular political orientation, as does the Labor Zionist Alliance. Americans for Peace Now (APN), while maintaining an independent policy-making structure, closely coordinates and draws purpose and direction from the movement in Israel. Others are membership bodies whose constituency may include a wide diversity of political and religious perspectives. The three defense agencies, B'nai B'rith, Hadassah, and National Council of Jewish Women fall into this category. While the positions they espouse may represent a consensus of their members or leadership councils, they do not claim to speak for the community as a whole. Lastly, there are "umbrella bodies" which operate on the basis of broad community consensus. They involve representatives of other organizations, with varying degrees of inclusiveness, in their decision-making processes. The three principal consensus organizations at the national level are AIPAC, the Presidents Conference, and the JCPA. The JCPA, in contrast to the Israel focus of both AIPAC and the Presidents Conference, maintains a multi-issue agenda that includes both international and domestic concerns. The community relations councils or committees (CRCs), which function on a local level somewhat similarly to the way the JCPA functions on a national level, also serve as consensus instruments for Israel advocacy.

The term "consensus" is often used, but it is seldom if ever defined. The author has attended numerous meetings in which participants have asserted (paraphrasing Supreme Court Justice Potter Stewart's often quoted comment about pornography) that while they may not be able to define consensus, they know it when they see it. In 1999, the Presidents Conference grappled with this issue in the drafting of a new document on Processes and Procedures, and opted not to define the term. The conference seeks to avoid formal votes; its chairman and professional executive typically are authorized to formulate the agency's public positions based on discussion among representatives of the constituent organizations. At the JCPA, where voting routinely takes place at meetings of its board of directors and at the agency's annual plenary session, it is understood that consensus lies somewhere between a simple majority and unanimity. An issue of special importance or sensitivity generally will require a higher standard of agreement. AIPAC has an executive committee, comprised of its own volunteer leaders and organizational representatives, which develops an annual policy statement. In addition, it also embraces positions adopted by the Presidents Conference, and often sends senior officials to participate in and inform the debate at the conference's policy-making sessions.

In reality, more attention has been given over the years to the process of determining consensus than to its definition. "The achievement of consensus . . . requires an ongoing exchange of views and information. . . . This process requires free debate in an atmosphere of mutual respect and civility. . . . The achievement of consensus inevitably requires a willingness to seek to accommodate conflicting points of view and a readiness to seek formulations that whenever possible will bridge differences among the various agencies. . . . The reality that American Jews disagree on certain issues cannot be ignored. In the end, the way to achieve a genuine consensus in umbrella bodies is to enable the disparate views . . . to be aired in a thoughtful process."[19]

The Significance of Consensus

Decision makers in Washington—whether at the White House, the State Department, or the Congress—do not determine their positions in a vacuum. American national interests are paramount in policy making, but clearly public officials also take into account domestic political considerations. The Jewish community, with its considerable influence, undoubtedly is an important factor in regard to Israel-related issues. Therefore, it is not surprising that policy-makers are eager to know where the "red lines" are drawn—that is, whether a position will be welcomed or condemned by most American Jews. The existence of sharp differences on a particular issue generally has the effect of neutralizing the community's ability to influence U.S. policy on that issue. This is especially true in terms of the executive branch. Members of Congress may be inclined to follow the lead of influential Jewish constituents in their districts or states whether or not those constituents are conveying consensus positions. Most members of Congress are sophisticated enough to recognize the community's red lines. Jewish dissent from Israeli government policies, whether from the left or the right, merely tends to give them political cover for positions they already were inclined to take anyway. American Jews are far from monolithic when it comes to Middle East issues—or any issue for that matter—but Israel has benefited over the years from the community's ability to deliver clearly defined messages to the nation's policy makers. This ability to unify around shared positions contributes to the community's political potency.

The Impact of Israeli Government Policies

Many Jews and non-Jews mistakenly believe that Jewish advocacy organizations reflexively support the policies of whichever Israeli government happens to be in power. The views of Israel's government, whether led by Labor or Likud (and sometimes both), always are weighed heavily. However, while generally avoiding public disagreements with Israel's government, the community never served as a mere rubber stamp for decisions made in Jerusalem. Indeed, according to U.S. law, American Jewish leaders and organizations cannot receive funds from or operate under the control of the Israeli government without registering as foreign agents. Simply put, the American Jewish community is not and does not act as an extension of the Israeli embassy and consulates in the United States.

AIPAC, as previously noted, was registered as a domestic lobby to work on legislation and public policy that enhance the U.S.-Israel relationship. As such, it may engage in an unlimited amount of congressional lobbying and is free to exchange information with Israeli leadership in carrying out that function. At the same time, it retains full autonomy in deciding when and how to act. Other national advocacy organizations, for example, the three defense agencies, the JCPA, and the Presidents Conference, are "educational" entities [501(c)(3) status in the Internal Revenue Service Code]. Since the amount of time they can devote to lobbying is strictly limited by law, contributions to such groups are tax deductible. They, too, meet with Israeli officials on a regular basis as a means of informing their decision-making deliberations, but not to take "marching orders." At times, the community and Israel differed on important policy questions. For example, the Israeli government sharply condemned the decision by the United States to initiate a dialogue with the PLO during the last days of the Reagan administration. Jerusalem viewed this step as damaging to Israel's interests, and clearly would have welcomed American Jewish support of that position. However, following consultations that included AIPAC, the Presidents Conference, and the three defense agencies, a statement was issued on December 15, 1988, expressing "understanding" of Secretary of State Shultz's decision to commence the dialogue. The community believed that the administration was acting responsibly in light of statements Arafat had made in Geneva rejecting terrorism and accepting UN Security Council Resolutions 242 and 338. It should be noted, however, that such public differences are the exception, not the rule.

There are a number of self-imposed restraints that cause the community to be extremely cautious about openly disagreeing with Israeli policies. On matters defined as security-related, American Jews, who do not bear the direct consequences of such life and death decisions, are reluctant to second-guess democratically elected Israeli governments. In addition, many Jews expressed concern that Israel's detractors might use criticism of specific policies to bolster their anti-Israel efforts. Thus, rather than disagreeing publicly, the community often chose to remain silent, neither endorsing nor criticizing unpopular Israeli policies.

The community faced a particularly complex situation during much of the 1980s, when Israel had a "unity government" comprised of both Labor and Likud. While both sides of the government managed to agree on many issues, there were significant policy differences as well. Those disagreements sometimes erupted in plain view. In one extraordinary exchange of correspondence, Prime Minister Shamir wrote on October 1, 1987, to Morris Abram, then chairman of the Presidents Conference, complaining about remarks made by Foreign Minister Shimon Peres in New York in support of an international peace conference. "In a democracy it is the duty and privilege of a political party and its leaders to try to persuade the electorate to support their position. To circumvent this process by appealing to friends abroad who do not vote in Israel would deal a blow to our sovereignty and democratic tradition." Several days later Peres shot back in a letter to the prime minister, "I did not, nor do I have any intention to invite the Presidents Conference to adopt a decision on this issue. But neither did I, nor do I have any intention of placing a muzzle over their mouths. . . . [F]or the sake of unity, we must respect different opinions, while defending the right to express them and listening to them with tolerance."

Areas of Broad Agreement

Israel-related messages delivered by the community in the public square must constantly be adapted to changing conditions. But there are many broad areas of agreement that have been consistent for the last fifty years, especially support for strengthening the U.S.-Israel strategic alliance. National interests at the heart of this alliance are not only geopolitical and strategic. The identity of the U.S and Israeli value systems has produced extraordinarily close ties between the peoples of both nations. The special relationship has taken many concrete forms, including a robust annual military and economic assistance package for Israel, the sale of sophisticated U.S. weapons to Israel—including preservation of Israel's "qualitative military edge" first articulated by the Nixon administration—and sharing of intelligence. AIPAC played a pivotal role in providing the conceptual framework for the exceptionally close U.S.-Israel strategic partnership during the early 1980s when the Reagan administration wished to move in this direction. There also has been a broad consensus in opposition to the transfer of U.S. arms to Arab states, unless and until they conclude peace agreements with Israel. Campaigns against such arms sales, however, normally were undertaken only if they were viewed as potentially damaging to Israel's security interests. In recent years, the United States has demonstrated a commitment to work with Israel in the struggle against the scourge of terrorism. On the diplomatic front, the community has pressed the United States to spearhead an effort to normalize Israel's relationships with the international community, including Israel's status and treatment at the United Nations, and to block efforts by the Arab world to weaken the Jewish state through an economic boycott.

With regard to the peace process and the U.S. role in it, the community has consistently stressed the need for direct, face-to-face negotiations between Israel and its neighbors as the preferred vehicle for resolving the conflict. Outside pressure has been resisted vigorously. In 1969, the Rogers Plan, named after President Richard Nixon's secretary of state, called upon Israel to return to its pre-1967 borders in return for security guarantees and enhanced access to Jewish sites in Jerusalem. The community successfully mobilized to block this initiative. In 1982, President Ronald Reagan offered a set of principles to guide negotiations between Israel, Jordan, and the Palestinians. They included rejection of Palestinian statehood and recognition of Israel's need for defensible borders. While Prime Minister Begin strongly condemned the proposal, a number of Jewish leaders, including the then AIPAC director Tom Dine, reacted more favorably. As a rule, peace "plans" (as opposed to ideas and bridging proposals) presented by third parties—even by Israel's best friend, the United States—have been strongly resisted.[20]

On the other hand, the United States always has been encouraged to facilitate negotiations between the parties and to offer incentives for flexibility. Exactly how active a role the United States should play is a question that has surfaced repeatedly, and was the focus of much discussion during Benjamin Netanyahu's period as prime minister (1996-1999).

The consensus has been consistent on some issues and has shifted ground on others. Since 1967, the community had been united on maintaining Jerusalem under Israeli sovereignty as its "undivided and eternal capital." This mantra-like position is being reassessed in the wake of the July 2000 Camp David summit, a subject discussed below. For many years there was broad Jewish communal consensus opposing Yasser Arafat as a negotiating partner, as well as establishment of an independent Palestinian state. This changed dramatically in 1993 with the signing of the first Oslo Accord by Israel and the PLO. The community has never adopted a formal position on Israel's possible withdrawal from the Golan Heights as part of a peace agreement with Syria, although statements consistently stressed the critical strategic value of this territory.

Differences over Peace Process Issues/Settlements

The Six-Day War, which resulted in Israel's acquisition of large territories on three fronts, as well as administrative and military control over major Palestinian population centers in the West Bank and Gaza Strip, fundamentally altered Israel's existential reality. The question of what to do with the territories and the Arab population in them would dominate Israeli politics for more than a generation, and would embroil the American Jewish community as well. The issue actually goes back much further, to the period of the British Mandate when Jews in Palestine and around the world debated how to respond to proposed divisions of Palestine. Just as Israelis lined up on different political sides, so too did American Jews, at least in terms of their private opinions. But for American Jews—whose distinctive role was to assure American support for Israel and who would not directly experience the consequences of Israeli governmental decisions—the question of how to express their views became a matter of great sensitivity. Another issue relates to the responsibility of individual organizations whose positions differ from community consensus. Among the "antiestablishment" organizations that in the 1970s and 1980s posed a challenge from the left were Breira (Choice) and the New Jewish Agenda. The question at that time was whether such groups should feel free to publicly express their dissent or should accept the constraints of communal consensus.[21]

In the wake of the 1967 War, the Arab world reaffirmed its rejection of Israel's legitimacy with the three negatives of the Khartoum Resolution: no peace, no recognition, and no negotiation with Israel. Thus, the fact that different approaches existed in Israel with respect to the issue of territorial compromise—broadly represented by the Labor and Likud Parties—was of little consequence in the absence of an Arab interlocutor. The community pursued its advocacy agenda confident that Israel's government, any Israeli government, would be prepared to reach a reasonable accommodation with Arab leaders willing to come forward to negotiate directly and without preconditions.

At the same time, centrist elements in the community, not just ideological groups on the left, viewed certain Israeli actions as unhelpful to the cause of peace. An issue that divided the Jewish community early on, and which continues to be a source of vigorous debate to this day, was the movement by Israeli Jews to establish civilian settlements in the West Bank and Gaza Strip. It is widely and mistakenly perceived that these divisions date from 1977, when Likud leader Menachem Begin—who was a strong advocate of massive Jewish settlement in these areas—wrested governmental control away from the Labor Party for the first time in Israel's history. The first settlers actually came from the ranks of the Labor Party and national religious circles (Gush Emunim). Some established communities for security reasons soon after the Six-Day War, particularly in the strategically important Jordan Valley. Others were motivated by religious fervor to resettle all of the ancient Land of Israel. Active American Jewish support for Israeli settlement activity generally has been limited to parts of the Orthodox community and those groups associated with Israel's Likud Party. Through the years U.S. administrations have condemned such activity either as illegal or harmful to peace, or both.

For many years after the Six-Day War, most American Jewish groups focused on continuing Arab hostility to Israel and the need to maintain Israel's strength. But public reactions by mainstream leaders critical of Israeli behavior began to appear in the early and mid-1970s, well before Begin's victory in 1977. The Social Action Commission of Reform Judaism condemned Israel's "irresponsible practices" and "provocative actions," citing, among other concerns, settlements in the territories.[22] Rabbi Henry Siegman, then executive director of the Synagogue Council of America, published an article in the January 1976 issue of *Moment* magazine in which he criticized Israel for failing to appropriately come to grips with its control of the administered territories and their Palestinian population.[23] Siegman would later become the executive director of the American Jewish Congress, where he would continue to express strong public reservations about Israeli settlement activity. The American Jewish Committee at times also expressed concern about the impact of settlements on the peace process. A cautious readiness even within consensus bodies to allow for some expression of dissent from Israeli policies and actions was reflected in comments by Reform Rabbi Alexander Schindler upon assuming the chairmanship of the Presidents Conference in 1976. "I am not for one moment suggesting that there will be a public posture of opposition. I am merely suggesting, for the time being at least, that we owe one another [Israel and American Jewry] the truth."[24] Schindler subsequently developed a warm working relationship with Begin, despite their political differences, and he became an exemplar of self-discipline in his role as chairman of the Presidents Conference. Critics of Israeli government policy voiced concern about both the moral and the security ramifications of the military occupation. Philadelphia attorney Ted Mann, past chair of the Presidents Conference, the JCPA, and the American Jewish Congress, often said that he could support Israel's occupation of the territories if it was out of necessity, but "not as a matter of choice."

Respecting the absence of consensus on this issue, the three umbrella bodies and many national advocacy groups chose not to endorse or condemn settlements, preferring instead to interpret Israel's policy as not inconsistent with the pursuit of peace. If and when Arab partners come forward to negotiate, these groups stressed, Jewish settlements need not be a barrier to achieving political agreements. In fact, some argued that settlements served as an inducement to peace-making by encouraging the Arabs to see that demographics and time were not on their side. The successful Israeli and Egyptian negotiation at Camp David, despite the existence of Yamit and other Jewish communities in the Sinai, tended to reinforce this argument.

One reasonably can ask whether all the heated debates about the appropriateness of expressing community differences with Israel "outside the tent" were superfluous. The fact is that those who follow such issues closely, the decision makers in Washington and influential figures around the country, generally knew when such differences existed. Ironically, the so-called internal discussions often received more media attention than the carefully crafted consensus statements issued for public consumption.

The Rise of Likud and Camp David

The community's unease with Israeli policy increased significantly after the 1977 Israeli election, when American Jews were expected to support an Israeli government that accelerated settlement activity and opposed—for security, religious, and historical reasons—the idea of territorial compromise. This dilemma grew when Egyptian president Anwar Sadat boldly traveled to Jerusalem in November 1977 to initiate, for the first time, a genuine peace process with Israel. In early 1978, with American Jews expressing concern about the degree of Israel's responsiveness to Sadat's initiative, the volunteer and professional leadership of the JCPA and three defense agencies went to Israel to meet with Prime Minister Begin. According to the then professional head of the JCPA, Albert Chernin, "[We] had always taken the position that our function was not to issue public pronunciamentos on Israeli government policy. We felt we had ample opportunities to express our differences through discreet channels."[25] In fact, the group had prepared a well-documented brief outlining in detail how Begin's policies were undermining support for Israel in the Congress, the media, and other key sectors of American society. At the same time, the community also fought to prevent President Carter from pressuring Prime Minister Begin into accepting Sadat's peace terms. If there was to be a treaty, it would have to emerge from an agreement freely entered into by both Israel and Egypt, not a formula imposed from the outside. The ultimate success of the U.S.-brokered negotiations between Begin and Sadat at Camp David relieved whatever dissatisfaction had been building within the Jewish community toward Israeli policies. In addition, a huge psychological barrier had been breached. For the first time since the beginning of the Zionist movement, the prospect of Israel's ultimate acceptance by the Arab world became a distinct possibility.

AWACS: AIPAC Assumes Primacy

Long before Israel was established, Jewish leadership understood that Congress could serve as a key ally in influencing American policy in the Middle East. While the U.S. Constitution gave the executive branch responsibility for conducting foreign affairs, Congress possesses the "power of the purse" and can make its views felt in other ways as well, including the authority to block arms sales to other countries. Although they do not have legal teeth, "Sense of the Congress" resolutions can help create a political climate that may influence foreign policy decisions as well. Over the years, policy differences between an administration and the Jewish community often played out in Congress. Two such episodes stand out, the attempt in 1981 to block the sale of AWACS (airborne warning and command system) reconnaissance planes to Saudi Arabia and the campaign in 1990-1991 to persuade the George H. W. Bush administration to approve absorption loan guarantees for Israel.

Following formal notification by the administration that it intends to sell military equipment to another country, Congress has thirty days to express disapproval. A majority vote in both the

House and Senate against the sale prevents it from taking place. While the community's effort to stop the AWACS sale failed (the House voted against it by a margin of 301-111, but the Senate voted in favor 52-48), the ability of the Jewish advocacy network to mobilize an effective national and grassroots campaign left a deep impression in Washington. It sent an unmistakable message to the White House that confrontation with the Jewish community would come at a price.[26]

Institutionally, AIPAC had evolved significantly following the Six-Day and Yom Kippur Wars under the stewardship of Si Kenen. Its growth accelerated from 1975-1980 when Morris Amitay served as the organization's executive. But many observers believe that it was the AWACS campaign, which marked the coming of age of a Washington-centered legislative process and the beginning of a shift in dominance from the defense agencies to AIPAC. In reality, the AWACS effort was far from being AIPAC's alone. The JCPA, Presidents Conference, and defense agencies all played pivotal roles as well. Indeed, the AWACS campaign was a dramatic illustration of interagency cooperation. Yet as a result of AWACS, AIPAC came to be seen as much more than merely a specialized instrument to be wielded by other Jewish organizations. It would serve as the vehicle through which community leadership would exert its influence and power. AIPAC's reach quickly spread well beyond the Washington Beltway; initially, the organization expanded its institutional presence around the country primarily for fund-raising purposes. But as the Arab-American community and its allies undertook a concerted effort to influence the Democratic Party platforms in 1988, AIPAC decided to augment its work in Washington with intensified community-based activism as well. The goal, largely realized in ensuing years, was to create political caucuses comprised of "key contacts" in all 435 congressional districts.[27]

The Lebanon War: A Time of Soul-Searching

The 1967 Six-Day and 1973 Yom Kippur Wars were seen in Israel and among American Jews as necessary struggles for self-preservation. In contrast, Israel's 1982 incursion into Lebanon, which followed years of attacks by the PLO against towns and kibbutzim (collective farms) in the north, was Israel's first "elective" war. Operation Peace for Galilee received strong support from U.S. leaders and American Jewry in its early stages when the stated goal was to establish a secure buffer zone in southern Lebanon. The advance to Beirut and the shelling of PLO fighters hiding within the city's civilian neighborhoods, however, elicited widespread condemnation in the international community and mass media. Toward the end of the conflict, the massacre of Palestinians in the Sabra and Shatila refugee camps by Israel's Christian allies—allegedly under the watch of Israeli military units—caused an outpouring of criticism by Israelis and segments of the American Jewish community as well. This was the most difficult time for pro-Israel advocacy since the founding of the state, testing the ability of the consensus-driven agencies to maintain unity and discipline.

The mixed response of the community was reflected in the 1983/84 JCPA Joint Program Plan. "Despite *concerns* triggered by the Lebanon campaign, the American Jewish community maintained a strong consensus in support of Israel's *basic* action" (emphasis added).[28] At a time of strain on the communal consensus, it was important to recall that basic U.S. and Israeli policies were consistent: restoration of Lebanese sovereignty, withdrawal of all foreign forces, and creation of conditions that would guarantee a secure Israel-Lebanon border. While most Jewish organizations focused on preserving U.S. support for Israel's objectives in Lebanon, many in the Jewish community were deeply agitated by perceived bias in the mass media. Controversy surrounding media coverage of Israel and Middle East events has continued to this day.

The Case of Jonathan Pollard

In 1985, Jonathan Jay Pollard, an American Jew serving as a U.S. Navy intelligence analyst, was arrested on charges of passing classified information to Israel. He received a life sentence, despite having agreed to a guilty plea in exchange for the prosecution's recommendation of leniency. Pollard's actions and Israel's use of an American Jew to spy against the United States were almost universally condemned in the organized Jewish community. Several years later, responding to appeals by Pollard family members and supporters, the JCPA established an ad hoc committee to examine allegations that the judicial process—including the submission to the court of a special memorandum by Caspar Weinberger—had been tainted with anti-Semitism or hostility toward Israel. The committee, which was chaired by Phil Baum of the American Jewish Congress, concluded that there was no persuasive evidence supporting the charge that the prosecution or the court had acted improperly. By the mid-1990s, many in the Jewish community had come to believe that Pollard—having already served a lengthy sentence, a portion of which was in solitary confinement—should be released as a matter of compassion. Because the evidentiary material is sealed, it is impossible to know exactly what information Pollard passed to the Israelis or the consequences of his actions. However, the fact that other spies convicted of similar charges received lighter sentences helped galvanize community sentiment in favor of his release. The JCPA sent two letters on Pollard's behalf. In 1994, when President Clinton had taken up Pollard's commutation request, the umbrella body asked that a sentence modification be considered if the review uncovered anything inappropriate in the judicial process. The following year, several months before Pollard completed his minimum sentence, the JCPA called upon authorities to act favorably on a parole request should one be forthcoming. Thus far Pollard has not exercised his prerogative to seek parole. By 1998, the Presidents Conference had set up its own committee, and sent a letter to President Clinton asking for Pollard's release "as a humanitarian plea to allow Mr. Pollard to rebuild his life." Many other Jewish organizations, including some that in earlier years had avoided this issue, communicated on Pollard's behalf as well. It is worth noting that at no time during the last fifteen years has the Jewish community contemplated restraining its involvement in the public square because of the Pollard fiasco, reflecting a strong sense of security in America and deep commitment to Israel advocacy.

The *Intifada* and Human Rights

The outbreak of a massive civilian rebellion in the West Bank and Gaza Strip in December 1987, known as the *intifada*, would test the Jewish community's advocacy skill as never before. Night after night, scenes of Israeli soldiers firing on stone-throwing women and youth led the national news broadcasts. Implementation of Defense Minister Yitzhak Rabin's orders to "break their bones," dramatically caught on camera, sent shock waves through the entire country, and profoundly touched the Jewish community. Some in the media began drawing comparisons between Israeli military occupation of the Palestinians and white apartheid rule in South Africa. The community's natural inclination was to spring to Israel's defense. Yet many American Jews, most of them privately and some prominent leaders publicly, expressed concern about Israeli policy. The result was paralysis. Normally, in such situations, national and local community relations agencies would be meeting with newspaper editors, religious and civic leaders, and elected officials to discuss these events. Many were expressing reluctance to do so. As in 1978, when the community expressed malaise in connection with floundering Israel-Egypt negotiations, the JCPA, the three defense agencies, and AIPAC organized regional consultations to allow members of the Jewish community to air their concerns and to seek to develop agreed-upon responses. A background paper emerged from these gatherings that provided consensus messages for use in public interpretation.[29]

First, the paper sought to identify broad areas of agreement on fundamental issues. Consensus-building often requires a return to the basics.[30] For example, the paper identified as consensus positions opposition to an independent Palestinian state west of the Jordan River and to the PLO as a legitimate negotiating partner. Without taking sides, it provided lengthy analysis of the differences between the Labor and Likud Parties, which at the time were joined together in a government of "national unity." The community, the document went on to assert, need not exaggerate the importance of these differences because at that time Israel lacked a suitable Palestinian partner with whom to negotiate a political settlement. The other aspect of the *intifada*, which required some explanation to Jews and non-Jews, involved the raw violence. Israel, the document stressed, was not dealing with mere civil disobedience, but rather rioting on a mass scale. Bricks and large chunks of concrete were being thrown at Israeli soldiers with intent to kill and maim. It also was clear, however, that something would have to be said about the behavior of Israeli soldiers. The paper denounced the use of "excessive force in some situations," while pointing out that senior military officials had expressed their concern and were moving to "correct departures from Israel's longstanding policy of restraint in the use of force."

Despite the ongoing violence in the administered territories, Prime Minister Shamir and his housing minister, Ariel Sharon, sought to establish "facts on the ground" by intensifying Israeli settlement activity. Individual organizations, identified with the political left, had publicly criticized such policies. The umbrella bodies refrained from doing likewise. Several national agencies, including the American Jewish Congress and the Union of American Hebrew Congregations, attempted unsuccessfully to pass an antisettlement resolution at the 1991 JCPA plenary session. The following year a special nonvoting session on settlements was held at the annual gathering of community relations leaders. While some at that conference sharply condemned the Israeli government, a clear majority opposed any public expression of criticism, particularly in light of the fact that just four months before, at the Madrid peace conference, the parties themselves had agreed to address this issue in their negotiations.

Israel has employed a variety of techniques over the years to maintain order in the West Bank and Gaza Strip, including deportation, demolition of terrorists' homes, administrative arrest, and, more recently, targeted killing of terrorist ringleaders. Human rights organizations, such as Amnesty International and Human Rights Watch, harshly condemned such policies. While many American Jews felt discomfort with some of Israel's security measures, Jewish advocacy groups sought to explain the rationale for their use and to provide legal and contextual background. They also accused the human rights organizations of ignoring the provocations which led to Israel's responses in the first place, and of focusing disproportionate attention on Israel in comparison with much more severe human rights violations occurring elsewhere in the world.

The Persian Gulf Crisis

Iraq's invasion of Kuwait and its threatening posture toward Saudi Arabia deflected public attention away from the *intifada* and served as a dramatic reminder that instability in the Middle East does not stem solely from the Arab-Israeli conflict. It also underscored retrospectively the wisdom of Israel's bombing of the Iraqi nuclear reactor at Osirak in 1981, an act that was severely criticized by the media and the international community at the time. While the Palestinian issue was still viewed as important, the Persian Gulf crisis focused Americans on broader strategic questions. The Jewish community's concern was twofold; as all Americans, there was uncertainty about the role the United States would be called upon to play in any military action and, of course, fear that Saddam Hussein would fulfill his threat to attack Israel with ballistic missiles. Jewish organizations generally sought to maintain a low public profile during this period to avoid enmeshing Israel in the debate over how the United States and the international community ought to respond. They did, however, react assertively to any attempt to draw comparisons between Iraq's occupation of Kuwait and Israel's occupation of the West Bank and Gaza Strip. At the grassroots level, CRCs established special ad hoc task forces to coordinate information dissemination and programming in the communities.

As prospects for a diplomatic solution to the crisis faded through the fall and early winter, the community decided that it must express its views to a deeply divided Congress. The JCPA Task Force on Israel met on December 2, 1990, as debate raged on Capitol Hill over whether to support a Bush-endorsed UN resolution authorizing the use "of all means necessary" to turn back Iraq's aggression, a phrase commonly understood to mean military intervention. With popular opposition to the war growing, and some of it taking on distinctly anti-Israel overtones, the task force voted to back the UN resolution. Many members of Congress began to urge that military action be delayed in order to give sanctions more time to take effect. The JCPA statement asserted that, while it supported ongoing efforts to resolve the crisis peacefully, it was unwise for Congress to tie the administration's hands. "The threat of military force," it read, "actually serves to reinforce the effectiveness of sanctions and diplomatic efforts." On January 9, 1991, just one week before the deadline for Iraqi withdrawal, the Presidents Conference also weighed in by urging the administration to take "the necessary steps—including the use of military force—to achieve the goals of the international community." AIPAC became deeply involved as well, particularly lobbying Democratic members of Congress when, at the eleventh hour, it appeared that the administration's position might be in jeopardy.

The months leading up to the January 15, 1991, deadline for Iraqi withdrawal were extremely tense ones for the American Jewish community, and much more so for the Israeli people who had to live under the shadow of a possible missile attack. Would the attack come and, if it did, would the missiles be armed with chemical or biological weapons? Even a nuclear attack could not be ruled out altogether. It also was a difficult time for Israel-diaspora relations, as Jewish groups from the United States and other parts of the world canceled plans to visit the country. Israelis bitterly expressed their sense of abandonment. Some organizations, however, including the Presidents Conference, joined Israelis in donning gas masks and sitting in sealed rooms after the Scuds started falling. When Israel reluctantly agreed, at the insistence of the U.S. administration, not to strike back at Iraq, the community sought to convey the extent of sacrifice entailed by Israel's self-restraint. This would be one of the rare occasions in which Prime Minister Shamir elicited praise from President Bush, Secretary of State Baker, and the American media.

Absorption Loan Guarantees

The Soviet Union's collapse and opening of the gates to emigration in the early 1990s resulted in a wave of Jewish immigration to Israel. In order to provide necessary absorption services to these newcomers, Israel required an immediate influx of capital. Prime Minister Shamir requested $10 billion in U.S. loan guarantees over a five-year period so that Israel could borrow funds in the world financial markets at favorable rates. This request, which the Jewish community viewed as an urgent humanitarian need, required the approval of both Congress and the Bush administration. Most members of Congress were inclined to provide the guarantees, particularly since no large expenditure of U.S. funds was involved. But Bush said he would oppose them unless Shamir agreed to stop settlement activity in the territories. The stage was set for a monumental confrontation between the administration and the Jewish community.

A significant segment of the Jewish community shared the administration's displeasure with Israeli policy. Nevertheless, a broad consensus existed for the proposition that there should be no linkage between this humanitarian program and settlements. Whether during the Suez Crisis or the loan guarantee episode, the Jewish community always stood firm against the use of American economic assistance to pressure Israeli governments. At the 1992 JCPA Plenum, Michael Pelavin, past chair of the organization and a leading political dove, told Bush adviser Richard Haass that, while he personally deplored the settlements, there was a moral obligation to assist in absorbing the Russian immigrants. When over 500 delegates burst into spontaneous and prolonged applause, Haass turned to those seated on the dais and said, in Hebrew, "I hear you."

The community, operating through a special task force under the auspices of the Presidents Conference, mounted a massive campaign in support of the guarantees. To drive the point home, a national advocacy day was organized in Washington for September 12, 1991. Over 1,000 Jewish leaders representing federations, CRCs, synagogues, and national groups responded to the call by the national coalition to participate in this event. With his dramatic press conference that day attacking the "powerful political forces" arrayed against "one little lonely guy in the White House," Bush managed to deflate congressional support for quick action on the loan guarantee request. He also infuriated many American Jews, who saw in his remarks a thinly veiled attempt to challenge the community's right to participate fully in the political process. White House officials expressed shock when they received an outpouring of anti-Semitic calls and letters supporting the president. Bush sent a letter to Presidents Conference chair Shoshana Cardin sharing his concern that some of the press conference statements "caused apprehension within the Jewish community." The references to powerful political forces, he asserted, "were never meant to be a pejorative in any sense." Advocacy for the loan guarantees, albeit on a more modest scale, continued through the remainder of Shamir's term of office, but it took the election of Yitzhak Rabin as prime minister in 1992 and a freeze on new settlements to finally win approval for the guarantees. In the end, a strong Jewish consensus and broad congressional support were not enough to overcome Bush's firm resistance. This and other experiences have shown that it is extraordinarily difficult to circumvent a president on foreign policy; difficult but not impossible, as demonstrated by passage of the Jackson-Vanik legislation, which linked human rights in the Soviet Union with U.S. trade benefits, over the objections of Henry Kissinger and presidents Nixon and Ford.

Pro-Israel PACs—Another Vehicle for Direct Influence

In addition to advocacy, American Jews wanted to secure more direct influence on who gets elected to Congress, and, like many other interest groups, they turned to PACs (political action committees). PACs are organizations established by businesses, trade unions, and other interest groups to channel financial contributions into political campaigns. They solicit contributions, pool funds, and make donations to the campaigns of candidates for national, state, and local offices. While individuals may donate no more than $1,000 to a candidate, a PAC may donate up to $5,000, and related PACs may coordinate their contributions, resulting in a much larger amount for a congressional candidate coming from the same set of interests or individuals. As mentioned previously, AIPAC is a nonpartisan domestic lobby, not a PAC. Pro-Israel PACs made their appearance in the 1980 congressional elections, and they have been a significant feature of the political landscape ever since. The struggle in 1981 to defeat the sale of AWACS planes to Saudi Arabia ignited intense interest among American Jews in the PAC system. In 1982, pro-Israel PAC money was instrumental in bringing about the defeat of Representative Paul Findley, one of Israel's harshest critics in the

House. Two years later, funds were directed successfully against an even bigger target, Senator Charles Percy of Illinois, who at the time chaired the Senate Foreign Relations Committee. In the 1984 elections, over seventy Jewish PACs contributed $3.6 million to congressional candidates.[31]

While scores of local PACs were springing up, Marvin Josephson established Nat PAC as a Washington-based, national pro-Israel PAC in 1982. Former AIPAC director Morris Amitay, who was instrumental in facilitating the creation of local PACs, had some reservations about a national body that would serve as a lightning rod for anti-Israel sentiment. Indeed, over the years, Arab-American groups and others filed complaints with the Federal Election Commission charging AIPAC and pro-Israel PACS with illegal collusion. Such allegations were never substantiated.[32]

Most PAC money is directed not to defeat members of Congress deemed hostile but rather to elect or keep Israel's supporters in office. Incumbents with senior committee positions are usually the principal beneficiaries. Not surprisingly, University of Michigan political scientist A. F. K. Organski found a high correlation between favorable voting records of U.S. senators on Israel-related issues and the amount of financial support they received from Jewish donors. He concluded, however, that lawmakers were not pro-Israel because of these contributions. They were motivated primarily by their perception of Israel's value to American national interests. Financial support merely served to reinforce their preexisting inclinations.[33]

Mobilizing Friends and Countering Foes

Christians

American Jewish organizations from the very beginning sought to recruit friends for Israel from among the leadership of the general community and attempted to minimize the impact on public opinion and policy of those perceived as unfriendly. The Christian religious community can be divided into three broad categories, even though each segment is internally complex. There are liberal Protestant denominations, evangelical and fundamentalist Protestants, and Catholics. Especially after the Six-Day War, liberal Protestants were seen as the most hostile to Israel.[34] In 1970, the American Friends Service Committee (AFSC), a politically active Quaker organization based in Philadelphia, published a report entitled "Search for Peace in the Middle East." The ADL and the American Jewish Congress vigorously criticized the work as biased, distorted, and one-sided. Other denominations, including the Presbyterian Church (USA), encouraged Congress to condition U.S. foreign aid on Israel's agreement to stop settlement activity in the administered territories and to desist from alleged human rights violations.

The National Council of Churches of Christ in the USA (NCC), the umbrella group comprising mainline Protestant denominations and Orthodox communions, defined its basic policy toward the Middle East conflict in a statement adopted in November 6, 1983. The statement recognized the PLO and called upon Israel to accept the Palestinians' right to establish their own political entity, including a sovereign state. Churches for Middle East Peace (CMEP), the Washington, D.C., advocacy arm of the NCC and mainline Protestant denominations, over the years has encouraged U.S. policy makers to take a more "balanced" position on the Middle East. While the NCC's stances appear moderate today from the perspective of the Oslo process, it is necessary to view them in an historical context. At that time, the PLO was still engaged in terror and much of the Arab world was involved in a campaign of economic and diplomatic warfare against Israel. Therefore, the NCC statement was seen as pro-Palestinian.

In an effort to influence the positions of mainline Protestant groups, national and local Jewish organizations encouraged Protestant friends to participate in their church bodies' deliberations. The American Jewish Committee, in particular, was deeply involved in interreligious affairs. Jewish-Protestant dialogues in the 1970s and 1980s often focused on the Middle East as the principal irritant in relations between the two religious groups. Ultimately, the mainline Protestant bodies proved ineffective in swaying members of Congress and even their own adherents, who, according to opinion surveys, continued to side more with Israel than the Palestinians. The NCC, perhaps partly because its Middle East initiatives were souring relations with the Jewish community, placed less emphasis on this issue in subsequent years. Despite their disagreements, the Jewish and mainline Protestant communities managed to cooperate on a range of other international and domestic concerns.

The Catholic Church in America, represented through the U.S. Conference of Catholic Bishops (Bishops Conference), has tended to take a lower profile in regard to the Middle East. While the Bishops Conference in its 1989 statement affirmed the Palestinians' right to self-determination (widely understood as meaning statehood), it also noted that Israel's security "requires strict limits to the exercise of Palestinian sovereignty." The Jewish community appreciated the Bishops Conference's willingness to engage in a process of consultation leading up to the adoption of its statement. American Catholic leaders quietly encouraged the Vatican to establish diplomatic relations with Israel, which finally took place in 1994. As they did with the Protestants, Jewish groups routinely reached out to local and national Catholic leaders in order to sensitize them to the community's Israel-related concerns.

The evangelical community, for obvious theological reasons, has taken a keen interest in Israel.[35] (It is worth noting that many evangelicals are not associated with the so-called Christian right and they too have been among Israel's supporters over the years.) Christian right leaders have expressed strong rhetorical support for Israel, and encouraged fund-raising to aid Israel in resettling Jews from the former Soviet Union, Ethiopia, and elsewhere. Many American Jews were ambivalent about such support, not only because the theological rationale for assisting the Jewish ingathering was to hasten the "second coming" but also because the community and the Christian right have disagreed fundamentally over important church-state and social issues.

At the same time, given Israel's constant struggle for physical security and international acceptance, support from this community was welcomed cautiously by Jewish leaders who stressed that this support would not influence their positions on domestic policy. After Menachem Begin's election in 1977, a closer relationship developed with Christian right leaders who were quite willing to endorse the Likud-led government's rejection of territorial compromise in "Judea and Samaria" (West Bank), part of ancient Eretz Yisrael. On the other hand, the Christian right chose not to participate in the fight against the sale of AWACS planes to Saudi Arabia in 1981, at a time when that constituency certainly possessed considerable influence with President Reagan. Moreover, there has been very limited advocacy on behalf of Israel's military and economic assistance packages over the years and virtually no support for a robust U.S. foreign aid program generally. The Christian right could have been expected to strongly support the campaign for absorption loan guarantees. While some leaders did endorse the program, little effort was expended to mobilize the evangelical grassroots.

The Anti-Israel Lobby

Arab-American advocacy organizations emerged following the Six-Day War (e.g., the National Association of Arab Americans [NAAA] was founded in 1972), but they only began to manifest some political clout in the 1980s. Their stated objective was to break the Jewish community's "stranglehold" over U.S. decision makers and American public opinion. Among the issues they utilized over the years in an attempt to drive a wedge between the two countries was Israel's mistaken attack on the U.S.S. *Liberty*, an American naval intelligence ship located off the coast of Israel during the Six-Day War, which resulted in the deaths of thirty-four Americans. Their principal target has been U.S. military and economic assistance to Israel, arguing that such support is unjustified in light of Israel's alleged violation of Palestinian human rights and intransigence. While they harbored no illusions that government policy and public opinion could be turned against Israel altogether, these groups believed that an aggressive campaign might result in a more "even-handed" approach.

While the *intifada* raged, their campaign took off in 1988. That summer, the Arab-American Anti-Discrimination Committee (ADC) placed ads in the Washington Metro and other subway stations with a photograph of several Palestinian women apparently cowering in fear before Israeli soldiers. The caption read, "Israel Putting Your Tax Dollars to Work . . . Only Congress Can Stop the Madness."[36] The ADC opened up another front in June 1988 by filing a petition with the office of the U.S. Trade Representative (USTR) requesting an inquiry into Israeli labor practices in the West Bank and Gaza Strip. Leading the community's response, the Jewish Labor Committee (JLC) provided background materials to and testified before the USTR, and mobilized the support of organized labor. The U.S. Trade Representative, Carla Hills, ultimately found Israel in full compliance with internationally recognized standards for workers' rights. This episode prompted the JLC to prepare a series of in-depth papers describing massive violations of workers' rights taking place throughout the Arab world.

Throughout 1988, Arab American groups, led by American Arab Institute president Jim Zogby, launched a grassroots campaign to influence the Middle East platform of the Democratic Party. Local political activists were recruited to press for planks in state platforms calling for recognition of Palestinian self-determination, with the hope that such a position ultimately would be adopted at the national party convention. For its part, the organized Jewish community, which had become accustomed to flexing its political muscle primarily inside the Beltway, responded by ratcheting up its already extensive engagement at the local level. The national agencies and the CRCs joined in an intensive and systematic effort to block "pro-Palestinian" initiatives in states all across the country. Organized labor, yet again, served as one of the Jewish community's key allies. At the same time, Arab groups had made some inroads with local union leaders, who were influenced by the *intifada*'s violence and had little or no historical experience of the movement's close connections to Zionism and Israel. Supporters of presidential candidate Reverend Jesse Jackson and a number of Christian groups backed the campaign as well. The result was that Democrats voted to endorse Palestinian independence in at least seven state party conventions.[37] Zogby then proposed that the national Democratic Party platform should include support for "Israel's security within internationally recognized borders and the Palestinian people's right to self-determination." After a spirited debate on the floor of the party's convention in Atlanta, the proposal was defeated. Sobered by the experience, those present for the discussion reported that Zogby's proposal was defeated not on the merits, but primarily out of the Democratic Party's desire to prevent a split with the Jewish community, one of its most important constituent groups.

On another front in 1988, the Arab-American organizations and their allies launched local pro-Palestinian statehood initiatives in San Francisco, as well as in Newton, Cambridge, and Somerville, Massachusetts. In Berkeley, a proposal to create a sister city relationship with the Jabalya Palestinian refugee camp was on the ballot. Recognizing that it had no chance to compete with the Jewish community at the national level, the Arab groups clearly had made a conscious decision to employ a grassroots strategy. While most of these efforts eventually were blocked, they served as a wake-up call. AIPAC launched a project to establish pro-Israel "caucuses," or clusters of influential people, in all 435 congressional districts. It particularly sought to identify and recruit advocates in places where there was no strong and effective local community organization. Workshops were held around the country to guide activists in becoming more involved politically at the local level. Having operated in Washington so effectively, in terms of directly influencing administration officials and members of Congress, the community recognized the need to reinvigorate its grassroots activism.

While national Arab and Jewish groups tended to view each other in adversarial terms, there were sporadic efforts, especially after the

Oslo Accords, to build bridges based on shared interests. The JCPA and NAAA succeeded in developing a joint statement of principles in 1995, which conveyed opposition to terrorism in all its forms, abhorrence of ethnic stereotyping, and support for the Middle East peace process. The American Jewish Congress had a record of cooperation with the NAAA as well, particularly on domestic concerns. When the former Yugoslavia erupted in violence, Jewish organizations and the religious movements worked with Arab and Muslim groups to advocate for a stronger U.S. and international response to the atrocities committed in Bosnia. In 1999 the NAAA merged with the ADC, an organization that is widely viewed by the community as hostile to Israel. CRCs gradually were forming relationships with local Arab and Muslim leaders as well, particularly in the context of broad intergroup coalitions working on concerns unrelated to the Middle East.

In recent years, the defense agencies have expressed concern that a number of the Arab and Muslim American organizations, including some with which they had worked together in the past, are providing indirect or direct support to extremist groups in the Middle East. Representatives of such groups, including the American Muslim Council (AMC) and the Committee on American Islamic Relations (CAIR), have been invited to White House and State Department functions. The defense agencies and the Presidents Conference opposed the nomination by Representative Richard Gephardt of Salam al-Marayati, head of the Los Angeles-based Muslim Public Affairs Council (MPAC), to a national commission dealing with terrorism. Further, they urged Jewish organizations to refrain from meeting with him. Al-Marayati's public statements, they argued, showed sympathy for Middle East terrorist groups such as Hamas. Other agencies raised questions about this "quarantine" approach. Despite objections by the defense agencies, the San Francisco Jewish Community Relations Council invited al-Marayati to address its board of directors.

It also must be stressed that these high profile Arab and Muslim American leaders represent only a small segment of the anti-Israel lobby in America. There is a long history of former U.S. officials and members of Congress joining together in organizations with innocuous sounding names (e.g., Council for the National Interest, Americans for Middle East Understanding) to attack Israeli policies. An early manifestation of this phenomenon was the American Friends of the Middle East (AFME), founded in 1951, which even received a subvention from the Central Intelligence Agency via the "Dearborn Foundation" located in Chicago.[38] In addition, American corporations, particularly oil companies with obvious economic self-interest in the Arab world, have been involved in anti-Israel efforts.

African Americans

Despite the strong pro-Israel leanings of early civil rights leaders, such as Martin Luther King, Jr., Bayard Rustin, and A. Philip Randolph, African Americans were seen as potential allies in these anti-Israel efforts for a number of reasons. The economic and military relationship between Israel and the apartheid regime in South Africa was one source of tension between African Americans and the Jewish state. While strongly opposing apartheid, Jewish groups sought to explain Israel's relationship with South Africa in terms of the struggle for survival. When most of the world had isolated Israel diplomatically and economically, including the countries in sub-Saharan Africa with whom Israel had close ties in the 1950s and 1960s, there was no choice, these Jewish groups argued, but "to do business with the devil." At the same time, Jewish leaders privately told Israeli officials that Israel's military relationship with South Africa was not only hurting Israel in public opinion, it was offensive to Jewish values. Eventually, possibly in part due to the community's influence, Israel discontinued its military ties with South Africa and conformed with the Western European approach to Pretoria, which permitted carrying on civilian commerce only.

Some African-American leaders expressed resentment over the generous American foreign assistance to Israel when important urban programs were being cut or eliminated altogether. In addition, domestic policy strains between Jews and African Americans, such as differences between the two groups on quotas and affirmative action, may have produced a Middle East spillover effect.

The Andrew Young affair in 1979, when the first African-American ambassador to the United Nations was forced to resign after his unauthorized meeting with a PLO representative at the world body, became a major source of tension. The resignation was widely, but mistakenly, viewed as the result of Jewish pressure on Washington. Pro-Palestinian statements and friendly meetings with PLO chairman Yasser Arafat by a number of prominent African Americans through the 1980s, including the Rev. Jesse Jackson, also soured the environment. Another factor affecting the black community's relationship with Israel was the perception after the Six-Day War—widespread in the 1960s and 1970s among those with a Third

World orientation in international affairs—that Israel was a colonialist power oppressing an indigenous population. Some of Israel's detractors took great satisfaction in portraying Israel as the Middle East's Goliath and the Palestinians as little David. America's "underdogs," some black leaders urged, should side with the Middle East's "underdogs."

Despite these problems, African-American members of Congress have been among Israel's strongest and most consistent supporters, including casting votes for foreign aid. These African-American members recognized the importance of Israel to U.S. national interests, but they also took into account the Jewish community's advocacy on behalf of social and economic justice and its support for American aid to the developing nations of sub-Saharan Africa. While the activities of pro-Palestinian African-American leaders grabbed headlines (the media seemed to relish black-Jewish confrontations), many others at both the national and the local levels identified with Israel's cause. Jewish community relations agencies and the religious movements, particularly the Reform movement's leader Rabbi David Saperstein, have devoted much time and resources in cultivating friends among the leaders of various ethnic communities. No group received more attention than African Americans, although in the late 1980s and through the 1990s, efforts increasingly were directed at other fast-growing groups, particularly Asians and Hispanics.

Labor Movement

In 1917, the American Federation of Labor declared support for "the legitimate claims of the Jewish people for the establishment of a national homeland in Palestine on the basis of self-government."[39] Labor's affinity with Zionism and Israel is rooted in many factors, among them the fact that Jews were in the forefront of the union movement in the United States and held positions of leadership for many years. In addition, there has been a close and long-standing relationship with the Histadrut, Israel's national trade union federation. Since the Six-Day War, the Jewish Labor Committee also sought to build pro-Israel sentiment within the major unions, focusing on those areas of the country with politically weak Jewish communities.

Labor's political support for Israel has been manifest in areas that, at least on the surface, appear to contradict its own self-interest. For example, the movement has vigorously opposed the transfer of U.S. military hardware to the Arab states, including the 1981 AWACS sale to Saudi Arabia. Administrations often justified these arms sales by underscoring their positive economic impact, particularly in creating defense industry jobs. Union leaders also have consistently endorsed generous foreign aid packages for Israel. AIPAC and others have tried very hard to persuade the public that foreign aid is good for the domestic economy. But most Americans, including union workers, still view the program as a drain on the nation's resources. In 1991, labor unhesitatingly joined the campaign for absorption loan guarantees.

Although in the last ten to fifteen years labor support for Israel has remained strong, it is not as uniform and unequivocal as in the past, probably due in large measure to the growing scarcity of Jews in union leadership positions. The United Autoworkers, with many Arab-American members in the Detroit area, has projected a more "balanced" approach to Middle East issues. Nevertheless, the Jewish community continues to rely on labor as an important ally in the public square.

Leadership Missions

One of the most effective tools used by Jewish advocacy groups over the years is the leadership mission—a partially or fully subsidized trip to Israel of relatively short duration designed to expose the participant to the political, military, social, and economic challenges facing Israel. Most leadership missions are locally initiated, usually by CRCs. Over the years, thousands of political figures, business and civic leaders, university presidents, and other influential people in the general community have been taken on trips to Israel. In its missions program, AIPAC has focused on members of Congress and key Capitol Hill aides. The American Jewish Committee runs a very active program through its Project Interchange, which at one time was a branch of the America-Israel Friendship League. The league sponsors trips to Israel for state attorneys general, and the American Jewish Congress maintains a regular program for mayors of American cities. The Jewish Institute for National Security Affairs (JINSA) has brought American military brass to Israel, and the ADL also was active in this arena as well, particularly in the 1980s. Pro-Arab groups have tried to emulate the Jewish community's extensive missions program, but lacking the community's resources and the local connections fostered through years of intergroup activity, the results of such initiatives seem meager by comparison.

Public Opinion

The community generally does not direct its advocacy efforts to the general public. Principal targets are decision makers, administration officials, and members of Congress, as well as opinion-molders—leaders of industry, ethnic and religious groups, and the media—who influence the decision makers. Most Americans, particularly since the end of the Cold War, have tended not to be interested in foreign affairs, unless it is an issue that is seen as directly and substantially affecting national security. This trend has strengthened. Unless the United States is directly involved in military conflict, domestic concerns dominate presidential and congressional elections.

Nevertheless, considerable resources have been devoted to tracking and seeking to influence public opinion. The U.S.-Israel alliance, while primarily shaped by governments, is anchored in the American public's positive attitudes toward the Jewish state. "General American feelings for Israel have remained consistently favorable since the inception of the Jewish state in 1948. Various polls, utilizing different methods and measurements, have revealed relatively high percentages of national samples stating that Israel is a close, strong and reliable ally of the United States. This pattern has remained constant even in times of tension and disagreement between the two governments and during controversial events."[40]

When the Arabs placed an embargo on oil supplies to the United States following the 1973 Yom Kippur War, and prices at the pump skyrocketed, polls showed that the American people blamed oil companies, the federal government, wasteful energy consumption, and the Arab states. Less than one percent held Israel responsible.[41] The controversial 1982 Lebanon War did not change fundamental American attitudes toward Israel, although there was a substantial but temporary dip during the "siege" of Beirut and the massacres at Sabra and Shatila. In addition, although Americans continued to dislike the PLO, a greater percentage expressed sympathy for their situation and endorsed an intensified effort to find a political solution to the Middle East conflict. Despite consistently reassuring polls, many rank-and-file members of the Jewish community harbored concerns that the Lebanon War might erode American support for Israel in the long term.[42] The community's concern about the status of public opinion rose even more sharply during the early phase of the *intifada*. Yet polls indicated that support for Israel had "hardly eroded at all. . . . Furthermore, even with the emotionally charged media coverage of Israeli soldiers beating Palestinian civilians, the American public still placed blame for the riots on the PLO, not on Israel."[43] No doubt there are many reasons for the resilience of the American public's positive attitudes toward Israel. The ongoing and intensive efforts of national and grassroots Jewish agencies, which shifted into high gear during periods of stress in the U.S.-Israel relationship, may be a significant factor.

The Mass Media

There is a relatively entrenched perception among American Jews that the media have not dealt fairly with Israel over the years, especially since the rise of Likud to power in 1977. When violence erupted in the region, particularly the Lebanon War and the *intifada*, many Jews thought that the media devoted disproportionate attention to Israel's military responses compared with Arab violence that precipitated the conflict. What was missing from much of the coverage, they felt, was necessary context and historical perspective. Of course, absence of context and perspective is not automatically the result of journalistic bias. Other factors, such as the reporter's limited knowledge of the subject as well as time and space constraints, came into play as well.

There has been a particularly strong response to perceived bias in programming at the Public Broadcasting System (PBS) and National Public Radio (NPR) since they are partially funded by American tax dollars. In 1989, the community mounted a major campaign against the showing of "Days of Rage: The Young Palestinians," a one-sided, stridently anti-Israeli documentary on the *intifada* aired by PBS. In New York, WNYC, the city's public station, refused to air what it deemed to be "a pure propaganda piece." The other public station, WNET, decided to run the program with a panel discussion "wraparound." Several months after the "Days of Rage" was seen on PBS, a thirty-minute program entitled "Search for Solid Ground: The *Intifada* through Israeli Eyes," funded by Jewish philanthropists, was aired by WNET and many local PBS affiliates. CNN, widely seen in the community as biased, has been a special concern, particularly as many in the United States and around the world use it as their principal source of news.

As previously mentioned, American public support for Israel has not wavered. Therefore, even assuming that the charge of media bias is partially correct, such bias has not resulted in erosion of support for Israel. The community has sought to influence journalists by taking them on fact-finding trips to Israel, providing interpretive materials and access to Israeli officials and Middle East experts. In addition, there were face-to-face exchanges, mostly in the 1980s, with such high-profile television journalists as John Chancellor, Mike Wallace, and Don Hewitt.

Some Jewish organizations have sought to counteract perceived anti-Israel reporting and commentary by placing information ads in major newspapers. Dueling ads between Jewish groups with differing political positions also have become commonplace, with Likud-led governments attacked from the left and Labor-led governments from the right. Experts generally dismiss the effectiveness of ads in shaping public opinion. They can be useful if directed toward mobilizing letters of support for a particular bill pending in Congress or some other specific purpose, but not for "educating" the general public. Letters welcoming or criticizing Israeli prime ministers have been placed in major publications primarily for their cathartic effect, and are directed primarily at the Jewish community.[44]

The Arab Economic Boycott

The community strove to counteract the Arab economic boycott against Israel.[45] Begun by the Arab League in 1946 as a boycott against the Jewish population in Mandatory Palestine, by 1952 the policy included not only a refusal to deal directly with Israel but also a secondary boycott against anyone doing business in or with Israel. A tertiary boycott against anyone doing business with companies blacklisted for trading with Israel was instituted as well. Companies were asked by the Arab League to certify that they were not conducting business with Israel in order to avoid being placed on the blacklist. Throughout the 1950s and 1960s, Jewish organizations sought to persuade American firms to voluntarily refrain from complying with boycott requests. Attempts to enact legislation in 1964 and 1965 to require such behavior failed.

The meteoric rise in oil prices following the 1973 Yom Kippur War and the growing influence of Arab petrodollar wealth on American corporate behavior prompted the renewal of legislative efforts. The political climate improved with the election in 1976 of President Jimmy Carter, who was not as resistant as President Gerald Ford to legislation that would impose sanctions against American corporations found complying with the boycott. A working group comprised of the three defense agencies, AIPAC, and the JCPA, and prominent volunteer leaders with influence in Washington including Al Moses and Morris Abram, was formed to address this issue. At the grass roots, CRCs, using model bills prepared by experts in the three defense agencies, especially the ADL and American Jewish Congress, mounted a campaign to adopt state antiboycott laws. There were other forms of pressure, including the use of shareholders suits by the American Jewish Congress. Members of the organization would buy stock and then show up at the company's annual meeting to challenge its boycott policies. Recognizing that these pressure tactics would likely increase, the corporate and banking communities expressed a preference for federal legislation that at least would standardize the antiboycott regulations. At the climax of the legislative campaign, ADL leader Burt Joseph led discussions with the powerful Business Roundtable. An agreement between that group and the Jewish community cleared the way for comprehensive antiboycott legislation (as amendments to the Export Administration Act), which President Carter signed into law on June 22, 1977. The law's provisions prohibit compliance with or participation in the secondary and tertiary boycotts. The office in the U.S. Commerce Department charged with implementation of this law has levied millions of dollars in fines over the years and received commitments by the offending companies that their boycott-related activity would not be repeated.

Efforts to get Western European countries and other major industrialized nations to adopt similar antiboycott legislation were largely unsuccessful. An antiboycott committee, informally staffed by the ADL and chaired by New York businessman Walter Stern, worked on this issue throughout the 1980s and well into the 1990s.[46] Breakthroughs in the peace process, coupled with lower oil prices and weakening Arab economies, resulted in substantial erosion in the boycott as a weapon against Israel. On September 30, 1994, the countries of the Gulf Cooperation Council, including Saudi Arabia, announced that they were discontinuing the secondary and tertiary boycotts; shortly thereafter, the antiboycott committee disbanded. The Commerce Department continues to monitor American corporate behavior and to implement the 1977 legislation.

In 1999, the American Committee on Jerusalem and American Muslims for Jerusalem formed a coalition of fourteen Arab and Muslim American groups for the purpose of leading a boycott of American companies that do business with Jews living in the West

Bank, Gaza Strip, or Golan Heights. This coalition managed to get Burger King to withdraw its permission for a franchise in a West Bank settlement and the Vermont-based Ben and Jerry's ice cream chain discontinued its use of mineral water from the Golan Heights. The Disney Corporation, on the other hand, resisted pressures to close down Israel's millennium exhibit at Epcot Center, which had Jerusalem as its central theme. Furthermore, Nasdaq Stock Market executives were pressured not to open a "sister exchange" in Jerusalem, as Prime Minister Barak had suggested during a visit to the American market in November 1999. Ironically, this renewed boycott activity by Arab and Muslim Americans came during a period in which prospects for commerce between Israel and the Arab world had improved in the wake of progress in the peace process.

Middle East Education

The community long has been concerned about the way the Arab-Israeli conflict has been taught in universities and in secondary schools. Since World War II, programs focusing on the contemporary Middle East proliferated at American universities as the United States emerged as the dominant power in the region. Middle East studies programs and centers often became nothing more than platforms for the dissemination of Arab propaganda. The Middle East Studies Association (MESA), the established professional association of Middle East scholars, also had a well-founded anti-Israel reputation. The Israel Studies Association was formed to provide an alternative forum for Middle Eastern scholars. American Professors for Peace in the Middle East (APPME), a pro-Israel interfaith group of academicians representing multiple academic disciplines, was active in the 1970s and 1980s and published the *Middle East Review*.

Anti-Israel bias in educational settings was compounded by the activities of major foundations and the federal government, which under the Higher Education Act (HEA), Title VI, supported university-based Middle East studies. The law mandated that a portion of this government assistance be used for "outreach," resulting in dissemination of materials and development of teacher-training and other types of programs designed to educate the community as a whole about issues affecting the region. Consequently, a number of secondary school textbooks produced by some of the largest publishing houses were found to contain significant bias. The Anti-Defamation League and Hadassah were active in this area, not only in reviewing textbooks and recommending appropriate changes but also in developing new Middle East materials suitable for use in secondary schools. A number of CRCs, particularly in Los Angeles and San Francisco, also sought to develop responses to this problem. In the 1970s and 1980s, the Arab world, particularly Saudi Arabia and other Persian Gulf states, used petrodollar wealth to create and expand Middle East studies programs at major American universities. The American Jewish Congress led a successful campaign to adopt federal and state "disclosure laws," which required universities to report any conditions attached to major gifts received from foreign entities.

United Nations

The Jewish community has long recognized the importance of the United Nations in relation to Israel and the Middle East. Thus, it has encouraged the United States to support Israel there, particularly in the Security Council where American vetoes at times were needed to protect Israel from the imposition of sanctions. On numerous occasions, nonbinding anti-Israel resolutions in the General Assembly often were opposed only by Israel and two other states, the United States and Micronesia. The most egregious example of anti-Israel (indeed anti-Semitic) behavior at the UN was adoption by the General Assembly in 1975 of a resolution equating Zionism with racism. Following an intensive diplomatic campaign led by Israel and the United States, with the support of Jewish communities in the United States and around the world, this resolution was rescinded in December 1991.

Throughout the 1990s, the community mobilized support for Israel's admission into one of the UN's regional groups. Such membership is a precondition for participating in the Security Council and other important UN bodies. Having been denied entry into the Asian Group, its natural geographic home, Israel was accepted in 2000 by the Western European and Others Group (WEOG). However, this positive step was conditioned on a number of important restrictions, including denial of Israel's participation in UN bodies outside of New York City. The community pledged to support Israeli and American efforts to remove these restrictions.

1991-Present: The Peace Process Accelerates

Impact of Madrid and Oslo on Pro-Israel Advocacy

Saddam Hussein's invasion of Kuwait in August 1990 set in motion a chain of events that altered the region's landscape, as well as the Israel advocacy role played by the Jewish community. Iraq's decisive defeat at the hands of the American-led international coalition, coupled with the demise of the Soviet empire, left the United States in a position to exercise enormous influence in Middle East affairs. The Bush administration, drawing upon its heightened international status in the wake of the conflict, succeeded in bringing together Israeli, Palestinian, Jordanian, Syrian, and Lebanese leaders at an international peace conference in Madrid. While the late Israeli prime minister Menachem Begin recognized the "legitimate rights" of the Palestinian people at Camp David, in Madrid Prime Minister Shamir commenced direct negotiations with a "non-PLO" Palestinian delegation, which was only loosely affiliated with the Jordanian participants. By doing so, an Israeli government, for the first time, implicitly accepted the logic that a separate non-Jordanian solution would have to be found for the Palestinian people. Very little progress, however, was made in the months following Madrid. Shamir, some observers argued, may have been reluctant to pursue negotiations he knew would inevitably require territorial concessions.[47] At the same time, the Israeli government greatly accelerated its settlement activity in the West Bank. With the *intifada* continuing, and the Bush administration and media routinely criticizing Israeli policies, there was growing malaise within the Jewish community.

The election of Yitzhak Rabin as Israel's prime minister in 1992 paved the way for back-channel discussions that led to the political equivalent of an earthquake—the signing of the first Oslo Accord on the White House lawn on September 13, 1993. The taboo against negotiating directly with Yasser Arafat and the PLO, which had been a bedrock consensus position in Israel and among American Jews since the 1960s, was shattered with one historic handshake. American Jews were stunned. A genuine Israeli military hero stood face to face, albeit uncomfortably, with a personality long regarded as one of the world's arch-terrorists. Overnight, Jewish groups faced a radically altered landscape. Meanwhile, Israeli opponents of Oslo and their American Jewish counterparts geared up to oppose a process they believed would seriously undermine Israel's vital security interests.

In the wake of Oslo, some Jewish leaders expressed concern that AIPAC and the Presidents Conference were too closely associated with Likud policies and, as a result, might fail to adequately reflect the community's pro-peace sentiments. In fact, Prime Minister Rabin, misunderstanding how the Jewish community functions, reportedly called for the resignation of the heads of AIPAC and the Presidents Conference, an appeal that was repudiated immediately by all mainstream organizations. (Rabin quickly developed a healthy respect for and close working relationship with Jewish advocacy groups.) In reality, the Presidents Conference, by its very nature, was incapable of openly criticizing the Oslo Accords. At the same time, the conference was constrained by a significant constituency that opposed the Israeli government's initiative. It is also worth noting that, in contrast to the multi-issue JCPA and CRCs, AIPAC and the Presidents Conference tend to attract leaders whose principal or exclusive public policy concern is Israel. Surveys have shown that American Jews with the closest emotional attachment to Israel—the ones most likely to be drawn to these "single issue" organizations—generally hold more hard-line views on peace process issues.[48]

From 1993 on, pro-Oslo and anti-Oslo elements tried to push the community's "consensus" in one direction or the other. During the Rabin and Peres years, opponents of Oslo generally refrained from attacking Israeli policy directly. Instead, they sought to discredit the Palestinians as peace partners by highlighting PLO violations of previously agreed upon commitments. Oslo supporters, on the other hand, argued that while Arafat was a flawed peace partner, he and other Palestinian officials finally had made a "strategic decision" for peace. With United States and international encouragement, they asserted, the Palestinians eventually would move toward genuine reconciliation with Israel.

In the wake of Oslo, new actors emerged on the scene arguing that they represented a more authentic expression of community sentiment, often buttressing their claim on opinion polls they and other like-minded groups commissioned. On the right, the ZOA, under the vigorous leadership of Morton Klein, mounted a campaign against U.S. financial support of the Palestinian Authority. This effort was reinforced by several former Israeli officials—including one who had held a senior post at the embassy just a couple of years before—who regularly visited Republican leaders on Capitol Hill in an effort to undermine the policies of the Israeli government. This certainly was not the first time Israelis, either on the left or right, had come to the United States bearing messages contradicting official policy in Jerusalem. But the intensive and systematic way in which these officials conducted their campaign caused discomfort in the Jewish community, including among some who agreed with their political positions. On the left, the Israel Policy Forum (IPF)— led by veteran "doves" like Ted Mann and its professional Jonathan Jacoby—and a reconstituted Americans for Peace Now (APN) came forward to project enthusiastic support for Oslo.

Members of Congress expressed confusion about where the Jewish community stood with respect to the peace process. In response, the JCPA, AIPAC, and the Presidents Conference joined forces to convene a National Peace Process Advocacy Day in Washington on December 12, 1995. After hearing presentations by Prime Minister Shimon Peres, chief U.S. negotiator Dennis Ross, U.S. ambassador to Israel Martin Indyk, House Speaker Newt Gingrich, and other congressional leaders, hundreds of Jewish activists from around the country fanned out on Capitol Hill to convey support for the Israeli-Palestinian negotiations and for an active U.S. role as facilitator.

The community continued to engage in traditional forms of advocacy directed at non-Jewish leaders. However, with the media and world leaders generally praising prime ministers Rabin and Peres for their bold peace initiatives, there no longer seemed to be as much need to defend Israeli policies in the general community, as had been the case in previous periods. Rather more effort was expended in shoring up support for the peace process within the Jewish community. One Israeli diplomat quipped that, in light of changes taking place in the Middle East, American Jews were the ones requiring "reeducation."

Jerusalem and the U.S. Embassy

Alongside the Oslo process, an effort to persuade the United States to relocate its embassy in Israel from Tel Aviv to Jerusalem gathered momentum. With his presidential bid looming, former Kansas senator Robert Dole announced at the 1995 AIPAC Policy Conference that he intended to introduce a bill in the Republican-controlled Congress requiring the United States to relocate its embassy to Jerusalem. While many at the conference recognized his political motivation, Dole's initiative enjoyed an enthusiastic response. The Clinton administration was determined to fight the measure, which it regarded as a serious threat to the integrity of the peace process. Thus, the community found itself uncomfortably squeezed between congressional Republicans and a Democratic administration, with each side legitimately arguing that it was acting in Israel's best interests.

Some urged Republican congressional leaders to stand firm for the immediate relocation of the embassy, but most Jewish groups called on Congress and the administration to negotiate a compromise that would avoid turning Jerusalem into a partisan political issue. There was and there remains community consensus in favor of moving the U.S. embassy; differences exist only in regard to the timing. Following a prolonged and sometimes acrimonious process, a law was passed deferring relocation until May 1999—the target date under Oslo for concluding the permanent status negotiations—and granting the president authority to delay the move for intervals of six months if warranted by national security. Citing concern for the peace process and American security, President Clinton exercised that authority consistently until the end of his administration. Jewish groups on the right were critical, while others expressed an understanding of the president's actions.

During the 2000 election campaign, candidate George W. Bush declared his commitment to move the embassy. Early in his administration it remains unclear if and when he intends to act on this pledge, since he moved to delay relocation in June 2001.

Erosion in Grassroots Activism

Throughout the 1990s high-profile activity "inside the Beltway" and lively policy debates left the impression that Israel advocacy continued to be among American Jewry's highest priorities. For many national bodies, particularly those created specifically to deal with Israel-related issues, that was the case, but at the grass roots the situation was different. Reflecting a major shift in communal priorities, federations and synagogues were redirecting resources toward an internal challenge, initially termed Jewish "continuity," now popularly referred to as "renewal" or "renaissance." At the Reform movement's December 1999 convention, workshops on social action and Israel drew relatively few participants. The most popular sessions focused on issues such as "God and Theology," "Reform Worship in the 21st Century," and "Torah and Observance in the Principles of Reform Judaism."[49]

This internal focus was triggered in part by the 1990 National Jewish Population Survey, which for the first time documented an intermarriage rate in excess of fifty percent. Reservations about the survey's accuracy were expressed in ensuing years, but perception often is as important as reality. There was palpable concern that assimilation and intermarriage were leading to the dissolution of the American Jewish community. In addition, sharp differences over the peace process resulted in heated debate and made the task of forging consensus difficult. Many CRCs chose to avoid local discussion of these issues, preferring to participate in policy formulation and action within a national context. It was easier to mobilize the community to defend an embattled Israel, or an Israel facing international condemnation. The challenge of assisting Israel in its peace-making efforts simply did not seem to motivate the grass roots the way the "survival agenda" did in earlier eras.

Iran and Weapons of Mass Destruction—New Focus of National Jewish Activism

The Rabin government's Oslo initiative was based largely on the premise that Israel's real existential threats emanated not from its proximate neighbors but from a rogue Iranian regime armed with weapons of mass destruction. Peace with Jordan, Syria, Lebanon, and the Palestinians, it was argued, would enable Israel to confront this challenge from a position of strength. At the same time, Israel encouraged the United States and the international community to do everything possible to prevent, or at least slow, Iran's acquisition of such weapons. AIPAC took the lead in working with Congress to develop legislation authorizing the president to impose sanctions against foreign companies investing in Iran's oil industry or transferring potentially dangerous technology and "dual use" products. The United States also warned Moscow that U.S. assistance might be jeopardized if Russian companies and institutions engaged in such transfers to Iran. The Clinton administration was uncomfortable with legislative initiatives, and it preferred to try to find diplomatic solutions to this problem.

Israel also viewed Iraq as a potential strategic threat, but the placement of a UN force (UNSCOM) in that country following the Persian Gulf War, with the mandate to dismantle Saddam Hussein's missile and weapons of mass destruction programs, initially mitigated its concerns there. However, because of the collapse of this regime and its replacement in January 2000 by the ineffective United Nations Monitoring, Verification and Inspection Commission under the leadership of Swedish lawyer Rolf Blix, UN inspectors have been prevented from entering Iraq. The community has been encouraged by initial efforts of the George W. Bush administration to win international support for continued nonhumanitarian sanctions against Iraq.

The Rabin Assassination

The anti-Arafat/PLO consensus came to an abrupt end with a September 1993 handshake on the White House lawn, but the deep-seated hostility to an individual who had spent decades engaged in terrorism and efforts to delegitimize Israel did not and could not reasonably be expected to abate overnight. In the minds of many Israelis and American Jews on the political right, Prime Minister Rabin's act was an enormous strategic blunder. To the radical right, acceptance of Arafat as a negotiating partner was tantamount to treason. The clash between Oslo supporters and the opposition in Israel was ugly and at times violent. Harsh confrontations took place on American shores as well. Itamar Rabinovich, Israel's ambassador to the United States, was pelted with an egg when speaking at a New York area synagogue, and New York consul general Colette Avital was jostled during a local Israeli Independence Day event. The language of discourse within the Jewish community became increasingly strident. When the JCPA's board of directors hosted Arafat at New York's B'nai Zion House in October 1995, Jewish demonstrators outside shouted epithets at the leaders as they departed the meeting.

The unthinkable occurred on November 4, 1995, when Jewish extremist Yigal Amir gunned down Israel's prime minister following a peace rally in Tel Aviv. While the intensity of the political debate had been clear for all to see, Israelis and American Jews were shocked that antagonism to Rabin's policies could result in such an act. Not surprisingly, the tenor of discussions about Oslo moderated in the months following the assassination, although the Israeli and American Jewish left bitterly accused opposition figures, including the charismatic Benjamin Netanyahu, of fomenting a "poisonous" atmosphere that encouraged the assassin. Just over six months later, in the wake of horrific suicide bombings in Jerusalem and Tel Aviv that claimed the lives of over sixty Israelis, Netanyahu narrowly defeated Shimon Peres to become Israel's first directly elected prime minister.

Prime Minister Netanyahu: The Israeli and Jewish Right Reluctantly Join Oslo

Although he had vigorously criticized the Oslo Accords, Benjamin Netanyahu entered office in 1996 vowing to fix the peace process, not end it. He insisted on "reciprocity," that is, that Israel should be expected to fulfill its obligations only if the Palestinians adhered to their commitments. From the very beginning, the relationship was strained between Netanyahu and Clinton, who was anxious to see rapid movement toward a permanent Israeli-Palestinian agreement and had clearly preferred Peres in the 1996 election. Despite his considerable political and oratorical skills, Netanyahu enjoyed little support in the mass media and among world leaders. Thus, the Jewish community found itself caught between a natural impulse to defend Israel's government and a close relationship with what was regarded as perhaps the most pro-Israel administration ever. While Netanyahu's supporters and detractors escalated their efforts, many Jewish leaders chose to resolve this dilemma by remaining silent.

When the peace process stagnated, both parties asked Clinton administration officials not just to facilitate negotiations but also to mediate and at times arbitrate. This more intensive involvement occasionally took on the appearance of pressure, even as administration officials constantly affirmed that only the parties could make the "hard decisions" required to achieve peace. In 1998 the parties were having difficulty reaching an interim agreement on the amount of territory Israel was required to transfer to the Palestinians under Oslo—a step that could pave the way for permanent status talks. The administration informed Netanyahu that a withdrawal of thirteen percent in the West Bank would be needed to break the deadlock. Was this an ultimatum or simply a constructive bridging proposal that Israel was free to accept or reject? AIPAC responded by organizing a Senate letter with over eighty signatories warning the administration against using pressure tactics, while other Jewish organizations expressed support for the administration's efforts. Netanyahu eventually accepted the U.S. recommendation, which resulted in the Wye River agreement. As during the Rabin-Peres years, Jewish activism in Netanyahu's era played out primarily at the national level, with groups on the left and right of the political spectrum, such as the ZOA, APN and IPF becoming even more assertive and visible. Debate over the peace process continued to stir passions in Israel and among American Jews. But Netanyahu's signing of the Hebron and Wye River agreements meant that Israel's moderate right, albeit reluctantly, had finally joined the Oslo process.

Prime Minster Barak: High Expectations and Dashed Hopes for Peace

Many analysts observed that Ehud Barak's 1999 landslide victory over Benjamin Netanyahu was not about the candidates' differing approaches to the peace process. The Israeli public had come to believe that it was not a question of whether there would be agreements with the Palestinians, Syria, and Lebanon. It was just a matter of when they would be reached. Barak understood his victory as a mandate to expeditiously conclude the peace negotiations so that he could move on to address the serious domestic challenges facing Israel in the economic, social, and religious spheres. The prime minister immediately launched a peace campaign directed at both the Palestinians and the Syrians, although progress with Damascus clearly was his first choice.

Barak appeared to have learned from the bitter experiences of his long-time mentor, Yitzhak Rabin. Instead of seeking to remove his political opposition to the margins, particularly Jewish settlers in the West Bank and Gaza Strip, he sought to include them within his governing coalition. The tranquil political environment that characterized his first months in office, which sharply contrasted with the turbulence of previous years, earned Barak the moniker "national anesthesiologist." This new mood in Israel seemed to have a calming effect on American Jewry as well.

American Jews reacted favorably to the new Israeli government. AIPAC's spokesman declared shortly after the Israeli election that the new prime minister was "like a breath of fresh air."[50] The community was ready to support Israel's accelerated peace efforts. When a $1.9 billion U.S. aid package associated with the Wye River agreement stalled on Capitol Hill because of lingering tensions between congressional Republicans and President Clinton, AIPAC led a concerted campaign to win its approval. At least one of the Likud operatives who had lobbied against Oslo during the 1993-1996 period appeared on the Hill again, this time to oppose the Wye River aid. But he quickly discovered that, as in Israel, much of the opposition to Oslo had collapsed. Criticism of the aid package came only from groups outside the mainstream, such as Americans for a Safe

Israel (AFSI) and evangelical Christians, particularly Richard Hellman of the Christians' Israel Public Action Campaign (CIPAC).

The calm mood would be short lived. Many Israelis and American Jews grew agitated in late 1999 when it appeared that a deal with Syria might be in the offing that would involve Israel relinquishing all of the Golan Heights. In January 2000, the Jewish Institute for National Security Affairs (JINSA) reported on a "landmark poll" that revealed "dissatisfaction among registered American voters with proposals that the United States fund an Israeli withdrawal from the Golan Heights and possibly commit troops to monitor both Israel and Syria even under the most favorable circumstances." A short time before his death, President Assad decided not to finalize an agreement with Israel. Syria's new leader, Assad's son Bashar, thus far has shown no inclination to engage Israel in a serious peace effort.

Israel and the United States then turned their attention to the Palestinian track. In July 2000, President Clinton convened an intense fifteen-day summit at Camp David with Barak and Arafat, which ended without agreement. However, for the first time in an official framework, Israeli and Palestinian representatives discussed their competing positions on the politically explosive issues of Jerusalem, Palestinian refugees, and the status of Jewish settlements. Barak was ready to consider transferring over ninety percent of the West Bank and accepting Palestinian sovereignty over Arab areas inside Jerusalem's municipal boundaries, including the Old City. The Temple Mount, holy to Jews and Muslims, would not be under either exclusive Israeli or Palestinian sovereignty. Barak's departure from the historical consensus position of maintaining Israeli sovereignty over all of Jerusalem stirred considerable controversy in Israel and among American Jews. Anticipating his positions, Barak's key coalition partners, the Shas Party and Natan Sharansky's Yisrael B'Aliyah Party, left the government prior to Camp David. A number of past chairs of AIPAC and the Presidents Conference and other prominent Jewish leaders signed an ad in the *New York Times* criticizing the prime minister. However, most mainstream groups continued to back Barak's efforts. The Reform movement, which had not been particularly active during the Rabin-Peres years, decided to demonstrate its strong support for the peace process. Teens attending Reform summer camps were bussed to Camp David during the talks as a tangible demonstration of solidarity.

The Al-Aksa *Intifada*: Israel Returns to Center Stage

Following Camp David, President Clinton left little doubt that he blamed Arafat for the summit's failure. In an effort to bolster his sagging international status, the Palestinian leader embarked on an extensive diplomatic mission but discovered that many world leaders shared Clinton's assessment. Then in late September, Ariel Sharon, to dramatically demonstrate his opposition to Barak's policy on Jerusalem, visited the Temple Mount in the Old City, present day site of the Dome of the Rock shrine and the Al-Aksa mosque. The next day, massive violence erupted in Jerusalem and Palestinian-controlled areas in the West Bank and Gaza Strip. Calling this *intifada* II, or the al-Aksa *intifada*, Palestinian leaders sought to place blame for the violence on Sharon's "provocation." Israel's government responded that Sharon's Temple Mount visit was merely a convenient excuse, and that the violence was not spontaneous but rather planned and orchestrated by the Palestinian Authority. Comments made by Palestinian leaders months later tended to confirm Israel's version of these events.[51]

The 2000 U.S. presidential race and the tortuous postelection process to determine Florida's final vote count were the focus of public attention through the fall months. But the viciousness of Palestinian violence and anti-Israel rhetoric from Arab capitals shocked American Jews, especially in light of the flexibility Barak had shown at Camp David and the subsequent talks at Taba. Although most of the casualties were Palestinian, the community grew deeply apprehensive about Israel's predicament. After an extended period of diminishing pro-Israel activism, the grass roots swiftly launched a multifaceted response to the crisis. Local groups, especially CRCs, convened Jewish and interfaith solidarity gatherings in scores of cities across the country and sent regular leadership missions to Israel under the auspices of the United Jewish Communities (UJC). UJC is the organization that grew out of the merger of the Council of Jewish Federations, the United Jewish Appeal, and the United Israel Appeal. In addition to conveying solidarity with Israel's beleaguered population, such missions also made a modest contribution to Israel's devastated tourism industry. The community's national advocacy organizations intensified their efforts as well.

As in past Middle East conflicts, particularly the Lebanon War and the *intifada* of the late 1980s, many American Jews accused the media of anti-Israel bias. The dramatic video of the shooting death of a twelve-year-old boy in the Gaza Strip and other images of young victims were disturbing to all. The brutal lynching of two Israelis in Ramallah by a frenzied Palestinian mob also was caught on tape. A battle of images was being waged parallel to Israeli-Palestinian warfare in the streets. Apprehension grew that these pictures, broadcast without perspective and context, might turn American public opinion against Israel and ultimately lead to erosion in American government support.

Meanwhile, despite the mounting Palestinian casualties and the vigorous efforts of anti-Israel groups, public opinion surveys revealed continuing strong American public support for Israel.[52] As discussed previously, this consistent support for Israel does not appear to be significantly influenced by events in the region or media coverage of them. In reality, most editorial writers and a number of authoritative columnists, particularly Tom Friedman of the *New York Times*, placed blame for the crisis on Arafat and the Palestinians.[53] Concern about Israel's image lingered, however, and with the help of public relations experts, a committee comprised of senior Jewish professionals worked to prepare a sophisticated pro-Israel advocacy campaign. Major Jewish philanthropists weighed in as well by establishing a new Israel advocacy think-tank called Emet, headquartered at Tel Aviv University with offices in the United States.[54]

Ariel Sharon in a Landslide and the George W. Bush Administration

Israel and the Palestinians continued to negotiate over Jerusalem and other permanent status issues despite the violence and after Barak announced his resignation, which triggered the scheduling of an early prime ministerial election. Opinion surveys showed that Barak's popular support had slipped badly. Israeli attorney general Elyakim Rubinstein observed that while Barak retained the authority of prime minister, it was inappropriate for him to conduct negotiations following his resignation. A number of American Jewish leaders agreed.[55] Meanwhile, President Clinton pledged to assist the effort to reach an agreement until his last day in office. Indeed, special U.S. Middle East envoy Dennis Ross was in the region striving unsuccessfully to bridge the gaps during the administration's final week.

Fearing an eleventh hour deal, Natan Sharansky and other Israeli opposition leaders beseeched world Jewry to pressure Barak against making any concessions on Jerusalem. Presidents Conference chairman Ronald Lauder responded by attending a January 8, 2001, rally in Jerusalem widely seen as a protest against the government's policies. Lauder had sought but failed to receive the umbrella body's endorsement. Although he identified himself at the event as an "individual Jew," a significant number of the Presidents Conference's constituents strongly objected to Lauder's actions. In the wake of this controversy, the organization adopted a rule allowing its chairman to speak officially only on the basis of consensus. In addition, all future chairmen will be expected to relinquish their "right" to speak as individuals during their two-year term of office.[56]

As predicted by the pollsters, on February 6, 2001, Ariel Sharon was elected prime minster by a landslide. At that point, the interesting question of how the community might have reacted to an Israeli-Palestinian agreement reached after Barak's resignation became moot. A controversial figure in Israel and the Middle East, and historically one of the most unpopular Israeli leaders with U.S. and other Western policy makers, Sharon's emergence caused some anxiety in the community about how he would be received by the international community and media. The formation of a national unity government with Nobel Peace laureate Shimon Peres as foreign minister served to allay those concerns considerably. With the exception of widespread vilification in the Arab world, most seemed prepared to give the new prime minister a chance to develop his own policies and approaches.

Meanwhile, the United States witnessed its own changing of the guard. George W. Bush became the nation's forty-third president and General Colin Powell was appointed as secretary of state. The new administration's Middle East policy remains unclear, although it appears that there will be less emphasis on Palestinian-Israeli negotiations and greater attention paid to the challenges posed by Iraq and Iran. This approach is suited to the current mood in Israel and the Jewish community. Many supporters of Oslo had become disillusioned with Arafat and believed that productive negotiations would not be possible anyway unless the Palestinians halted the violence and ceased anti-Israel incitement.[57] Congress continued to demonstrate that it is a bulwark of support for Israel when the new House of Representatives adopted a resolution 410-1 congratulating Sharon on his victory and urging Arafat to end the Palestinian-initiated violence. Pressed by allies in Europe and pro-Western Arab states to play a greater role, the Bush administration backed a commission led by former senator George Mitchell to examine the situation in Israel and the Palestinian areas and to make recommendations on how to get the peace process back on track. CIA chief George Tenet also was dispatched to the region and managed to broker a "cease-fire" agreement between the two parties. As of the time of this writing, the violence continues. Israel and the community, while expressing some reservations about the Mitchell report, welcomed it as a basis for restoring calm to the area and providing a roadmap to guide future political discussions.

Implications of Israel-Based Jewish Power

The community's reputation as the most politically potent religious/ethnic group in America, despite comprising less than two percent of the total population, is integrally linked to its impressive Israel advocacy network. The community's influence is magnified through the coordination of national and local efforts. Washington-based "lobbyists" are more effective when members of Congress receive the same messages from Jewish activists back in their home districts. AIPAC has been cited by *Fortune* magazine as among the most influential lobbies in the nation's capital. Many world leaders seeking assistance from Washington have come to believe that the road to the White House and Capitol Hill runs through the American Jewish community. That is why presidents and prime ministers visiting this country often find time in their busy schedules to meet with the Presidents Conference, ADL, the American Jewish Committee, and other groups. A number of foreign embassies in Washington even assign political officers to develop relationships with officials in key Jewish agencies. This also is why certain countries with minimal clout in the United States have turned to the Jewish community to represent their interests here. For example, at Azerbaijan's request, a number of Jewish organizations have been trying to persuade Congress to repeal sanctions imposed because of that country's violation of human rights and boycott against Armenia.

Because it represents such an influential segment of the sole remaining superpower, the community bears great responsibility for the safety and well-being of Jews in other parts of the world. Jewish groups working together under the auspices of the Presidents Conference mobilized international support in an effort to secure the release of thirteen Iranian Jews imprisoned and convicted of groundless spying charges. The administration and Congress were enlisted in the cause and played an important role in the campaign, even though direct American influence in Teheran is extremely limited. In the 1990s, terrorist bombings of the Israeli embassy and the

AMIA Jewish Community Center in Buenos Aires traumatized Argentinean Jewry. The community enlisted the administration and Congress to press the Argentinean government to bring the perpetrators to justice. Previously, U.S. influence was brought to bear on behalf of Jewish communities in Syria, Yemen, Ethiopia, and elsewhere. Erosion of the community's influence in Washington, or even the perception of such erosion by leaders in other nations, might compromise its ability to protect the interests of fellow Jews in other places.

The extraordinary success of the community's Israel advocacy has enabled it to project greater influence in the domestic arena as well, from church-state issues to social and economic justice. Yet Israel had become so dominant a Jewish concern that politicians often expressed surprise when Jewish audiences raised other issues. Cleveland Jewish communal leader Bennett Yanowitz asserted, "our visible and forceful presence in fighting for better schools, better housing, full employment, in short, a strong, democratic, humane America, will convey . . . the perception and reality of the American Jewish community's concern about the best interests of the United States. Regrettably, we have not played this role as actively as we did in earlier years. Our failure to do so may be more responsible for our being seen as a one-issue community than any other factor. The fact that the Jewish community relations field is concerned with the total American agenda makes it the effective advocate of Israel. Sole preoccupation with issues related to Israel undermines our ability to interpret Israel to our friends."[58] With the possible exception of the civil rights struggle of the 1960s, the Jewish community never came close to generating the kind of passion and grassroots activism that existed for Israel advocacy in the post-1967 period.

Promoting "Nonpolitical" U.S.-Israel Relationships

While the Jewish community's Israel advocacy has received much attention, extensive and largely unpublicized efforts have been underway to build mutually beneficial "nonpolitical" relations between Israel and the United States. For example, when Israel's economy prospered in the 1980s and 1990s, initiatives to expand trade between the two nations proliferated. Some states set up permanent operations to facilitate expansion of joint initiatives and export/import opportunities. Trade missions, often led by the governors themselves and organized in cooperation with CRCs and federations, have become routine programs.

Economic development is only one facet of this relationship. The American-Israeli Cooperative Enterprise has documented an elaborate set of contacts, often promoted by the Jewish community, in education, medicine, science and technology, agriculture, energy and the environment, and many other arenas. A number of organizations have sought to "import" programs and expertise from Israel to address challenges facing American society. For example, a think-tank at Hebrew University in Jerusalem, supported by the National Council of Jewish Women (NCJW), has been developing innovative programs to address critical educational challenges facing Israeli society. Among these programs is the Home Instruction Program for Pre-School Mothers (HIPPY), which trains mothers from low socio-economic backgrounds in ways of enriching their children's pre-school experience. Former president Clinton, while governor of Arkansas, was one of the first U.S. officials to adopt the program. Today it is operating in over fifteen states. From 1984 until the mid-1990s the Washington Action Office of the Council of Jewish Federations administered a Memorandum of Understanding between the U.S. Department of Health and Human Services and the Israel Ministry of Labor and Social Affairs. This MOU encouraged the exchange of research and experience by social service organizations, state and local government agencies, universities, hospitals, government officials, and others. These initiatives promote the kind of people-to-people contact that leads to long-term relationships. It is hoped that Americans over time increasingly will come to view Israel not only in terms of shared strategic and geopolitical interests but also as a nation with similar values and societal concerns.

American Jewry's Israel Agenda: A Paradigm Shift

A central proposition of this analysis is that until the outbreak of violence in the fall of 2000, the community's Israel advocacy had been in significant decline. A number of factors drove this trend, which was most sharply felt at the grass roots. These included the perception of a more secure and economically prosperous Israel moving toward peace with its Arab neighbors, the community's turning inward to address the so-called continuity challenge, and diminished emotional attachment that young Jews feel toward Israel.

This apparent distancing from Israel also may be partially explained by the differing conceptions of Judaism held by these two communities. Sociologists Steven M. Cohen and Charles Liebman argue that "even among the more traditionally inclined Orthodox [not to mention Reform, Conservative, and Reconstructionist], the distinguishing characteristics of the religious life of American Jews can be summarized . . . as personalism, volunteerism, moralism and universalism. . . . Religion in Israel is very much a public affair."[59] A "post-Zionist" Israel that severs its relationship with Judaism and the diaspora, and becomes simply a state for its citizens, is still far from becoming a reality. Yet warnings increasingly are heard that certain Israeli intellectuals and cultural elites, together with Israel's large non-Jewish population (almost twenty percent), are pressing in that direction. Some argue that with the passage of time Israel is evolving into a "post-Zionist" society in practice, if not in ideological or legal terms.[60] If such a trend continues, the gap between Israel and American Jewry could grow wider.

A reduced commitment to Israel advocacy was being felt not so much in those organizations such as AIPAC and the Presidents Conference whose raison d'être is to represent Israel in the public square. Rather, its impact was greatest on those multi-issue Jewish agencies—the defense agencies, the JCPA, and the CRCs. In most places, the CRC is a committee of the federation assigned responsibility for the community's public affairs agenda. The handful of "independent" Jewish community relations councils receive most of their funding from federations and, thus, are generally more responsive to emerging communal priorities. Following the Six-Day and Yom Kippur Wars until the early 1990s, when the defense of Israel was at the top of the Jewish agenda, CRCs were given a clear mandate to emphasize traditional forms of advocacy. Prior to the Al-Aksa *intifada,* this no longer was the case. Community-building activities were favored over consensus policy formulation and advocacy. In the three defense agencies, fewer staff members were dedicated to Israel than before, even though the budgets of the ADL and American Jewish Committee were healthier than ever. Also experiencing the impact of reduced commitment to Israel activism, pro-Israel PACs reported substantially reduced funding levels.

What then had begun to replace traditional forms of Israel advocacy? The community was beginning to focus more on policy made in Jerusalem than in Washington. American Jewry had become accustomed to, if not comfortable with, the "religious status quo" worked out by Prime Minister David Ben-Gurion and the Orthodox establishment in the early period of Israel's statehood. Under this arrangement, the Chief Rabbinate was given exclusive control over issues of personal status for Jews in Israel, including marriage and divorce. Marriages and conversions conducted outside of Israel were to be recognized for civil purposes even if the rabbinate did not accept their validity under Jewish law. In the 1980s, the Orthodox parties sought to use their political leverage to amend the Law of Return—the law granting Jews and their close relatives automatic citizenship—in order to exclude from its reach any convert to Judaism whose procedure had not been conducted according to *halakhah*. The American Jewish community mounted a vigorous and ultimately successful campaign to dissuade the leaders of Labor and Likud from agreeing to such a change. The battle cry of "maintain the status quo" prevailed. Of course, this was a status quo that had enshrined Orthodoxy as Israel's only officially recognized form of Judaism in important areas of the nation's religious and social life.

Driven by the increased assertiveness of Reform and Conservative Jews in Israel, American Jewry seemed ready to challenge the old Ben-Gurion formulation. "Religious pluralism" in Israel was beginning to replace Israel advocacy as the dominant international concern of the grass roots. This came at a time when discussion of the reexamination of the status quo in Israel had never been greater. While American Jewish influence played a modest role, a much more important factor was the massive influx of hundreds of thousands of non-Jewish immigrants from the former Soviet Union. These are the non-Jewish relatives of Jews who came to Israel under the expansive terms of the Law of Return. Who will have the authority to supervise their conversions? How will they be married? Where will they be buried? These were questions that aroused debate in Israel, and many American Jews felt they had a stake in this discussion as well. The Jewish character of Israel and the rights of the non-Orthodox streams, they argued, have enormous implications for diaspora Jews and their relationship with Israel. Will Israel grant equal status to non-Orthodox rabbis? Should Israel embrace some form of separation between religion and state? While the American form of separation is deemed unacceptable by most, many asked whether a unique Israeli/Jewish model could be designed. Ultimately, Israel's government and the Knesset will decide whether, or in what ways, to change the existing legal framework. But American Jews and Israeli leaders began to grapple with the question of how to construct a new compact that would satisfy Israelis, diaspora communities, and the religious movements.

The community had been seeking to interact with Israel and Israelis in other ways as well. In recent years, many looked for ways to become meaningfully involved in addressing quality of life issues in Israel. Federations increasingly channeled funds directly to programs and institutions in Israel that contributed to a healthier, more just Israeli society. The United Jewish Communities (UJC) is positioned to help the federation system determine how to pursue this agenda. The UJC has established three "pillars" of ongoing activity, including one that deals with Israel and overseas concerns. In addition, it has set up an Overseas Needs Assessment and Distribution (ONAD) committee to work with communities and the principal international social and human service delivery bodies, the Jewish Agency for Israel (JAFI), and the JDC in identifying the community's "collective" priorities in Israel and around the world. The federations presumably also will build on the geographically based Partnership 2000 program, initiated by the UJA prior to the merger, which sought to create mutually beneficial linkages between American Jewish communities and Israeli regions and cities.

Another model of American Jewish-Israeli engagement is based on shared interest rather than geography. For example, in response to growing concerns over absorption problems facing Ethiopian Jews in Israel, a Jerusalem-based Coalition on Ethiopian Education was formed to develop a comprehensive plan to enhance educational opportunities for Ethiopian children at all levels. The Israeli coalition is comprised of Ethiopian educators and activists, representatives of concerned Israeli and American Jewish groups, and government officials. A North American coalition, led by the Joint Distribution Committee, Jewish philanthropists, national organizations, and a number of federations, was set up to provide the Israeli group with financial and political support. The ADL led efforts to encourage greater Israeli government responsiveness. Joint strategy meetings involving participants in both coalitions have taken place via videoconferencing. Such a framework could be adapted to many other shared concerns, including the environment, women's issues, ethnic and religious tensions in Israel, and human rights.

Israelis and American Jews are building relationships based on professional affiliations as well, which often result in joint initiatives. Israeli and American Jewish doctors have joined to respond to medical emergencies around the world. The New York UJA-Federation is considering a proposal to develop an international Jewish peace corps. Birthright Israel, a project supported by major Jewish philanthropists, the federations, and the Israeli government, is founded on the premise that every young American Jew is entitled to at least one expense-free experience in Israel. The underlying rationale here, based on a number of studies examining the link between life experiences and personal commitments, is that a trip to Israel at an early age is perhaps the most important building block to Jewish identity. These are just some of the programs and activities that appeared to be filling the vacuum left by a withdrawal from traditional grassroots Israel advocacy. At least until the outbreak of the al-Aksa *intifada*, major Jewish donors, who in an earlier era might have directed resources into Israel advocacy, began to focus on other communal priorities such as synagogue transformation and Jewish education.

Return to Grassroots Activism: But For How Long?

In the first half of 2001, the situation in the Middle East was grim. Palestinian violence continued, including from Arafat's own Fatah wing of the PLO. Terrorism took more Israeli lives and the number of Palestinians killed in street confrontations grew. Leaders in the Arab world made bellicose statements, sought to isolate Israel diplomatically, and began to raise the old "Zionism equals racism" canard. At a UN-sponsored World Conference against Racism, Racial Discrimination, Xenophobia, and Related Intolerance (WCAR)— held in September 2001 in Durban, South Africa—Arab and Islamic nations led a concerted campaign to label Israel a racist/apartheid state. As a result, Israel and the United States reluctantly withdrew from the conference. Under pressure from the European Union nations, including threats that they too might leave the conference, participants agreed to a final resolution that simply called attention to the plight of the Palestinian people under "foreign occupation." The NGOs' conference, which preceded the governmental gathering, did adopt a resolution accusing Israel of being a "racist, apartheid state" that engaged in "ethnic cleansing." Jewish organizational representatives reported that the atmosphere at the NGOs' conference was palpably anti-Semitic. A number of important American NGOs, including the Leadership Conference for Civil Rights, repudiated the extreme resolution. But many Jewish officials expressed disappointment that their response came so late.

However unlikely it appears at the time of this writing (October 2001), it is yet possible that over time the Israeli government and Palestinian leadership will resume serious negotiations toward a settlement. It also is possible that the situation will deteriorate further, and lead to wider conflict. Knowing very well how to respond in times of crisis, the community is attempting to dust off its advocacy apparatus. Whether it will be able to sustain a high level of activity over time remains to be seen. It also is too soon to tell whether significant communal resources will be shifted again toward Israel advocacy. Particular concern is being expressed over advocacy needs on the campuses where Jewish students appear to be ill-equipped to respond to sophisticated anti-Israel initiatives. A national "divestiture" campaign has been planned for the 2001/2002 academic year. Drawing upon the anti-apartheid model of the 1980s, the aim is to encourage universities to divest holdings in companies that do business in Israel. Hillel has instituted a number of steps to address this situation, including, for the first time, hiring an Israeli *shaliach* (emissary) who will be responsible for coordinating and enriching Israel-related activity on the campuses.

Even under the most optimistic scenario—the violence stops and the parties reach peace agreements—there still will be a need for continued activism. The role of the community, the challenge it must meet, is to assure that the United States continues to provide the kind of leadership that will solidify and give real long-term meaning on the ground to any arrangements between the parties. As in the case of the Wye River agreement, this will include willingness by both the administration and Congress to support substantial economic and security assistance packages for Israel and its negotiating partners. Such American leadership also would be necessary in order to win support from other wealthy nations, particularly in Western Europe and the Far East. A future agreement with Syria involving territorial compromise on the Golan Heights and a final status deal with the Palestinians would generate the need for a very large congressional appropriation well in excess of the $1.9 billion Wye River package. Given the mood of Congress in recent years, the public's antipathy to foreign aid, and uncertainty about the depth of commitment to Middle East peace-making by the current or future administrations, this is likely to be a formidable challenge.

What has made the community's advocacy machinery so effective is the mutually reinforcing synergy of its "inside the Beltway" efforts and coordinated local activity. A weak grassroots response would undercut any final push for Middle East peace. Even after formal treaties might be signed, U.S. leadership would be required to facilitate genuine Arab-Israeli reconciliation involving normal relations among the peoples of the region. This more complex process would take generations to complete.

Beyond the Palestinians, Syria and Lebanon, and the moderate Arab states of North Africa and the Persian Gulf, there remains the problem of rogue regimes, especially Iran, Iraq, and terrorist groups. The proliferation of nonconventional weapons poses new dangers to Israel as well as to other regional and international interests. Long-term stability in the Middle East ultimately will depend on the establishment of democratic institutions and economic reform in the

Arab world. Today these nations are ill-equipped to compete in the global marketplace, and the specter of radical Islamic fundamentalism continues to hang over much of the region. The United States is the only power that could possibly lead an international effort to encourage modernization in the Arab/Muslim world, recognizing that the impetus must come from the region itself. The ability of the community to mobilize effectively at the national and grassroots levels will assure the greatest impact on the American government and public opinion. Local organizations, particularly CRCs, will have to be persuaded that, even if the current crisis is resolved, they still have a continuing stake in and responsibility for influencing American foreign policy in the Middle East.

In terms of the impact on Jewish political influence more broadly, no doubt the community's status as a key player on the public affairs scene in recent years derives in large measure from its Israel activism as well as advocacy on behalf of Soviet Jewry. A community that increasingly turns its resources inward to address the problems of Jewish intermarriage and assimilation may be seen as less potent in the American public square. Thus, diminished Israel advocacy may reduce Jewish influence on a range of other international and domestic concerns. This is not to suggest that additional attention to the internal vitality of the organized Jewish community is unwarranted. On the contrary, an enhanced focus on Jewish education, the quality of synagogue life, and programs designed to engage young people is long overdue. But if these priorities are addressed at the expense of the advocacy function, the community, Israel, and Jews throughout the world, particularly those living in politically insecure conditions, may end up paying a heavy price.

E-Mail Advocacy

New technology—the Internet and e-mail—has begun to have a profound impact on the nature of grassroots advocacy. Information about virtually all the issues on the Jewish community's public affairs agenda now can be accessed at the touch of a button. Furthermore, e-mail provides the capacity to send requests for action almost instantaneously to thousands of armchair advocates around the world. Communications can be sent to members of Congress, editors of newspapers, and others from the comfort of one's computer room. An increase in the volume of communications to decision makers, however, may not necessarily result in greater influence.

Historically, congressional offices have given more weight to a small number of handwritten letters than to hundreds of postcards sent through an organized campaign. In today's world, e-mails are regarded as the equivalent of postcards. While the Internet enables information to be conveyed quickly to large numbers of people, it also has the same potential to spread misinformation. Once set loose, e-mail myths are not easily corrected. Increasingly, Jewish advocacy groups find themselves serving as e-mail filters, determining what is true and what is not. Anti-Israel groups also have recognized the potential benefits of this new technology, creating such web sites as Intifada.com and the ElectronicIntifada with action alerts directed at their supporters.

Final Thoughts

It is difficult not to be pessimistic about prospects for peace in the Middle East in light of recent events. Indeed, some observers compare the current status of Israeli-Arab relations to the situation that preceded Anwar Sadat's historic journey to Jerusalem in 1977. But Egypt and Jordan have signed and continue to respect peace treaties with Israel, and some Palestinians questioned Arafat's decision not to accept the Barak-Clinton proposals at Camp David. If potential for progress still exists, it is due in no small measure to the role the community has played in helping construct a rock solid U.S.-Israel alliance. After almost a century of implacable hostility to Zionism and Israel, a segment of Arab leadership grudgingly recognized that the United States could not be persuaded to abandon Israel. Strengthened by American support, Israel could not be defeated militarily or isolated politically and economically. The Jewish state was a reality that had to be accommodated.

American support for Israel was rooted in the conviction, which crossed party and ideological lines, that a strong and secure Israel served vital U.S. national interests. Yet, as discussed at length in this analysis, other influential forces in America sought with great determination to undermine the special U.S.-Israel relationship. In the "battle for Washington," American Jews were hardly secondary players. Working nationally and locally, the community poured enormous financial and human resources into mobilizing an army of generals and ground troops whose mission was to sustain American support for Israel. This was not merely an expressive exercise. The instrumental impact these efforts had, particularly in the post-1967 era, should not be underestimated.[61] While media often focused on differences that at times divided Israelis and American Jews, or on competition among the various Jewish organizations, the real story is one of extraordinary cooperation in this common cause.

As a military and economic superpower, the United States will continue to play a dominant role on the world stage well into the twenty-first century. Future American administrations and Congresses will be challenged to nurture the hopes for peace, encourage the growth of democratic institutions and market economies in the Arab world, and lead the international community in addressing the challenges of radical Islamic fundamentalism. As the community properly focuses on ways of reinventing its institutions, in an attempt to stave off the debilitating impact of assimilation and intermarriage, American Jews do not have the luxury of disengaging from Israel advocacy. A long-term commitment, regardless of how the current crisis plays out, is not only vital for Israel's well-being but also will help preserve the Jewish community's influence as it pursues a broad set of interests in the American public square.

The writing of this chapter was begun in 1999, well before the eruption in 2000 of Palestinian violence known as the "Al Aksa *intifada*" and the resulting collapse of the Oslo peace process. A central theme of the chapter is the erosion of grassroots activism in an era of relative calm and an increased focus on internal Jewish community issues, a theme which had to be revised to take these new developments into account. As the project moved toward publication, Afghanistan-based terrorist leader Osama Bin Laden and his Al Qaeda network struck the United States on September 11, 2001, with devastating suicide attacks in New York City, Washington, D.C., and western Pennsylvania, which claimed some 3,000 lives. It is premature to examine in depth the implications for U.S Middle East policy and the community's Israel advocacy. Indeed, events of this magnitude, widely described as this generation's equivalent of Pearl Harbor, can transform international affairs in profound ways. In the short term, there is likely to be an enhanced American identification with Israel as it too has suffered at the hands of Islamic extremists. Indeed, early public opinion polls reflected a spike in support for Israel. A CNN/USA Today/Gallup poll taken on September 14-15, 2001, found that 55 percent of Americans said their sympathies were more with the Israelis in the Middle East situation, while 7 percent said they are with the Palestinians.

On the other hand, there are geopolitical considerations to factor in as well. The "war on terrorism," declared by President George W. Bush on behalf of the civilized world, necessarily has brought into play U.S. relations with the Islamic world. America's Arab allies, particularly Egypt and Saudi Arabia, were courted to join an international antiterrorism coalition. They, in turn, pressed the United States to move more urgently to resolve the Palestinian issue. President Bush subsequently declared that his administration's vision of the Middle East includes an independent Palestinian state alongside a secure Israel, perhaps the first dividend of such pressures. The administration also asked Congress to delay passage of the Middle East Peace Commitments Act (MEPCA), legislation intended to punish the Palestinian Authority for failing to fulfill its obligations to Israel. Prime Minister Sharon publicly rebuked the Bush administration, asserting that Israel would not be sacrificed as Czechoslovakia had been sacrificed to appease Hitler on the eve of World War II. He subsequently apologized for the outburst. Many American Jews shared Sharon's concerns, and the principal advocacy organizations discreetly urged the administration to reassure Israel. Overall, however, American Jews were strongly supportive of President Bush and his commitment to seek the eradication of international terrorism, including dealing with countries that harbor and provide support to extremist groups. The community also expressed the expectation that Hamas, Islamic Jihad, and Hezbollah terrorist groups, operating primarily against Israel, eventually would be targeted along with bin Laden and Al Qaeda.

In addition, some Arab leaders, as well as anti-Israel advocacy groups in the United States, argued that Israeli policies were the principal cause of hostility toward the United States in the Islamic world. In response, the community stressed that terrorism against the United States is fundamentally grounded in a disdain for democracy, secular society, pluralism, and Western culture—illuminated by the choice of the World Trade Center and Pentagon as bin Laden's targets. Building the broadest possible support for a sustained and comprehensive assault on terrorism became the community's central advocacy agenda. At the same time, it continued to encourage the United States to press the Palestinian Authority to end the violence and to return to a productive negotiating process.

Notes

1. Executive Committee Statement, Jewish Council for Public Affairs (JCPA), June 11, 1990.
2. "Pro-Israel" is defined here as any policy position or action that is viewed by community consensus as advancing Israel's interests.

3. Material in this section was drawn primarily from the following sources: *The Jewish People in America*, Henry L. Feingold, general ed., vol. III, *A Time for Building—The Third Migration 1880-1920*, Gerald Sorin, chap. 8, "Cultural Pluralism and Zionism," and vol. IV, *A Time for Searching—Entering the Mainstream 1920-1945*, Henry L. Feingold, chap. 6, "Zionism and the Restructuring of Jewish Political Life" (Baltimore, Md.: Johns Hopkins University Press, 1992); Melvin I. Urofsky, *American Zionism from Herzl to the Holocaust* (Garden City, N.Y.: Anchor Press/Doubleday, 1975); Naomi W. Cohen, *Not Free to Desist* (Philadelphia, Pa.: Jewish Publication Society of America, 1972), chap. 6, 103-10; David Shapiro, *From Philanthropy to Activism: The Political Transformation of American Zionism in the Holocaust Years 1933-45* (New York: Pergamon Press, 1994); Allen Weinstein and Moshe Ma'oz, ed., *Truman and the American Commitment to Israel* (Jerusalem: Magnes Press, 1981).

4. For much of the first half of the twentieth century, the American Jewish Committee, the first of the community's national public affairs organizations, was a committee of prominent and wealthy German Jewish men. They believed that the preferred way to influence American public policy was through discreet intervention with key government officials.

5. Arthur Hertzberg, ed., *The Zionist Idea* (Garden City, N.Y: Doubleday, 1959), 518-19.

6. The system of JCPA national and local member agencies often is referred to as the field of Jewish community relations. The federations had tried to set up an umbrella body in 1938 called the General Jewish Council (GJC), which would have been comprised only of national agencies. This experiment failed primarily because the communities were not included and there were very few rules of procedure agreed upon at the outset. But the concept of a national coordinating instrument was conceived and laid the groundwork for the CJF's establishment of the JCPA six years later. Isaiah Minkoff was appointed to head the GJC and later became the founding executive of the JCPA.

7. Dennis Ross served as head of the "peace team" and Aaron Miller as his deputy. Martin Indyk served both as ambassador to Israel and assistant secretary of state for Near Eastern affairs.

8. Alonzo L. Hamby, *A Life of Harry S Truman: Man of the People* (New York: Oxford University Press, 1995), 435-36.

9. See Abraham Ben-Zvi, *Decade of Transition: Eisenhower, Kennedy, and the Origins of the American-Israeli Alliance* (New York: Columbia University Press, 1998).

10. I. L. Kenen, *Israel's Defense Line* (Buffalo, N.Y.: Prometheus Books, 1981).

11. Kenen, *Israel's Defense Line,* 110. See also David Howard Goldberg, *Foreign Policy and Ethnic Interest Groups: American and Canadian Jews Lobby for Israel* (New York: Greenwood Press, 1990).

12. Goldberg, *Foreign Policy,* 124.

13. At this time, Egypt, Jordan, and Mauritania are the only Arab states that maintain full diplomatic relations with Israel, but a number of states

in North Africa and the Persian Gulf have initiated partial diplomatic and economic ties.

14. Goldberg, of course, later would serve as U.S. ambassador to the UN at the time of the Six-Day War and as a Supreme Court justice.

15. Philip Bernstein, *To Dwell in Unity* (Philadelphia: Jewish Publication Society of America, 1983), 338.

16. Yossi Melman and Dan Raviv, *Friends in Deed: Inside the U.S.-Israel Alliance* (New York: Hyperion, 1994), 132.

17. *ADL and Israel: 50 Years of Israel Advocacy* (New York: ADL, 1998).

18. Dr. Gary Schiff, "American Jews and Israel—A Study in Political Conduct," *Forum,* no. 24, 1976.

19. Executive Committee Statement, Jewish Council for Public Affairs, June 11, 1990.

20. See Steven Spiegel, *The Other Arab-Israeli Conflict* (Chicago: University of Chicago Press, 1985), 181-92 (Rogers Plan) and 418-25 (Reagan Plan).

21. In the case of the JCPA, the right of dissent is respected. Any of its member organizations is entitled to publish dissenting views, alongside the consensus positions, in the JCPA Public Affairs Agenda.

22. *Washington Post,* May 5, 1976.

23. *Washington Post,* May 5, 1976.

24. *New Outlook,* April/May 1976, 53.

25. J. J. Goldberg, *Jewish Power: Inside the American Jewish Establishment* (Reading, Mass.: Addison-Wesley, 1996), 212.

26. For a description of the lobbyists and corporate forces arrayed in support of the AWACS sale to Saudi Arabia, see Steven Emerson, *The American House of Saud* (New York: Franklin Watts, 1985), chaps. 10 and 11.

27. In his book *Jewish Power,* journalist J. J. Goldberg attributes AIPAC's ascendance in the 1980s to three factors: Reagan's decision to make Israel a key part of his strategy against the Soviet Union; the recognition by Likud-led governments that they needed a strong organization defending their interests in Washington; and internal structural changes that took power out of the hands of the New York-based national Jewish organizations and gave it to a politically powerful and affluent AIPAC volunteer leadership. See also Wolf Blitzer, *Between Washington and Jerusalem* (New York: Oxford University Press, 1985), chap. 6, "American Jews and Politics," 119-40; and Melman and Raviv, *Friends in Deed,* chap. 16, "The AIPAC Decade," 306-27.

28. At the agency's 1983 plenum, its annual policy-making conference, JCPA chair Bennett Yanowitz reflected the turbulence below the surface in his address to the delegates. "This vision of Israel as a light unto the nations, our deep affection for the country, our historic ties to the land of Zion, all of these, as well as other considerations may give rise to feelings of uncertainty or unhappiness with specific Israeli actions from time to time." 1983/84 JCPA Joint Program Plan, 23.

29. JCPA memo and position paper, April 22, 1988.

30. While a number of these "fundamental" elements remain in place—such as support for an undivided Jerusalem as Israel's capital and recognition that Israeli security requirements will not permit the return to pre-1967 borders—there have been significant changes as well.

31. *Wall Street Journal*, February 26, 1985.

32. Interview with Morris Amitay, September 30, 1999.

33. A. F. K Organski, *The $36 Billion Bargain: Strategy and Politics in U.S. Assistance to Israel* (New York: Columbia University Press, 1990).

34. See the monograph by Judith Hershcopf Banki and Gary Wolf, "Israel at Risk: The Campaign to Erode Christian Support," *American Jewish Committee*, 1990.

35. See the monograph by Rabbi A. James Rudin, "Evangelical-Jewish Relations in the 1990s," *American Jewish Committee*, February 1990.

36. *Washington Post*, July 29, 1988.

37. *New York Times*, June 23, 1988, 1.

38. Kenen, *Israel's Defense Line,* 115.

39. "Issue Summary: The AFL-CIO and Israel," Jewish Labor Committee pamphlet.

40. Eytan Gilboa, *American Public Opinion toward Israel and the Arab-Israeli Conflict* (Toronto: Lexington Books, 1987), 305-13.

41. Dr. George Gruen, "Arab Petropower and American Public Opinion," *Middle East Review* (Winter 1975/76): 34.

42. Eytan Gilboa, "Effects of the War in Lebanon on American Attitudes toward Israel and the Arab-Israeli Conflict," *Middle East Review* (Fall 1985): 30-42.

43. Mark J. Penn and Douglas Schoen, "American Attitudes toward the Middle East," *Public Opinion* (May-June 1988): 45-48.

44. See "The Mass Media, the Image of Israel, U.S. Foreign Policy: A Reassessment Report," *Jewish Council for Public Affairs*, June 1980.

45. "Blacklisting Israel: A Current Perspective on the Arab Boycott," *ADL Special Report* (Spring 1989). See also Dr. George Gruen, "The United States, Israel and the Middle East," *American Jewish Yearbook* (New York: Jewish Publication Society of America, 1978), 111-20.

46. The group placed special emphasis on pressing the Japanese and South Korean business sectors to avoid compliance with the boycott.

47. According to journalist Tom Friedman, Shamir was asked by A. M. Rosenthal in an interview in 1986 what the prime minister hoped people would say about him when his term was up in two years. He responded, "I want them to say that I kept things quiet." *From Beirut to Jerusalem* (New York: Farrar, Strauss, and Giroux, 1989), 283.

48. See, for example, the two surveys sponsored by the American Jewish Committee after the signing of the Oslo Accords: "The Palestinian Autonomy Agreement and Israel-PLO Recognition" by Renae Cohen (January 1994), and "The Israeli Peace Initiative and the Israel-PLO Accord" by Renae Cohen and Jennifer Golub (February 1995).

49. *Jewish Telegraphic Agency Bulletin*, December 21, 1999.

50. *Jerusalem Post*, May 23, 1999.

51. In *Newsday*, April 4, 2001, Palestinian minister of communications Imad el-Falouji was quoted as saying that the uprising "had been planned since Chairman Arafat's return from Camp David, when he . . . rejected American pressure for Palestinian concessions as part of a peace deal."

52. In a survey of American opinion conducted between January 25 and February 17 by Penn, Schoen & Berland, Inc. and First International Resources, Inc., more than two-thirds of the general public and three-quarters of elites (high income and educational levels) say they are favorable toward Israel. By a margin of 3 to 1, Americans are more likely to blame the Palestinians and not the Israelis for the current violence. The survey was commissioned by the United Jewish Communities, the Presidents Conference, the Anti-Defamation League, and the American Jewish Committee.

53. According to Tom Friedman, "when Prime Minister Ehud Barak of Israel and the U.S. president put forth a peace plan that, while not entirely acceptable to the Palestinians, contains for the first time all of the elements of a deal they were seeking . . . and the Palestinian leadership rejects this offer and the Palestinian street reacts to Ariel Sharon's silly provocation on the Temple Mount rather than to the Barak-Clinton proposals on the table, then you have to admit that another paradigm is at work today." *New York Times*, March 6, 2001.

54. *New York Jewish Week*, March 9, 2001.

55. Abe Foxman, "Barak Is Stretching His Mandate," op-ed in *New York Jewish Week*, January 5, 2001.

56. *Jewish Telegraphic Agency Bulletin*, February 2, 2001.

57. Resolution adopted February 26, 2001, at the JCPA's annual plenary session: "Chairman Yasser Arafat and other leaders of the Palestinian Authority have much to do to restore a sense of hope in the peace process. They must stop the Palestinian-initiated violence, cease anti-Israel incitement, eliminate hatred toward Israel and Jews being taught in Palestinian schools, and fulfill all of their obligations under the Oslo Accords."

58. Yanowitz's speech as JCPA chair at the organization's 1983 plenum is found in 1983/84 JCPA Joint Program Plan, 21.

59. Charles S. Liebman and Steven M. Cohen, *Two Worlds of Judaism: The Israeli and American Experiences* (New Haven, Conn.: Yale University Press, 1990), 158.

60. See Bernard Susser and Charles S. Liebman, *Choosing Survival* (London: Oxford University Press, 1999), chap. 7.

61. See Nimrod Novik, *The United States and Israel: Domestic Determinants of a Changing U.S. Commitment* (Boulder, Colo.: Westview Press, 1986); Abraham Ben-Zvi, *The United States and Israel: The Limits of the Special Relationship* (New York: Columbia University Press, 1993).

4

The Jewish Social Welfare Lobby in the United States

Joel M. Carp

Introduction

This chapter documents the importance and scope of the social welfare lobbying efforts of the American Jewish community. It describes the state of the art as it is presently practiced, provides some national and state-level examples of our community's lobby at work, discusses the extent and significance of the massive growth in the public funding of services provided by the organized American Jewish community, describes its near-term social welfare agenda, and considers what needs to be done to enhance the community's level of skill in this arena. All of this must be viewed within the Jewish community's historic political perspective, and the Jewish traditions and values of *tikkun olam* and *tzedakah*.

In a speech to the 2000 Plenum of the Jewish Council on Public Affairs, Arnold Eisen provided an important insight into the Jewish community's interest in politics when he observed: "Jews have always cared inordinately about politics. We have had no choice but to care about it, for reasons rooted both in normalcy and in covenant. The interests of a perpetual minority . . . demand constant vigilance. What has kept the Jews alive for two millennia against all odds is the prophetic demand that justice sit at the very top of the Jewish communal agenda. A right social order—the goal of covenant—is not simply one among many things Jews are meant to strive for but the essential thing, the completion of creation for which God "elected" Israel in the first place.[1]

Although it is certainly true that the organized Jewish community's interest in the financial consequences of domestic public policy for the Jewish human services is self-evident, it would not only be too simplistic but also too cynical to assume that money alone drives the process. While funding is a major motivating force for our federated communities' involvement in the domestic agenda, there is a direct link from our Jewish tradition to the present-day issues that we engage at the state and federal levels. Again Eisen's comments are enlightening: "Jewish commitment of whatever sort begins with the command to take care of other people's bodies, and only then permits us to proceed with the improvement of our own souls."[2]

If the Jewish context and tradition from which the roots of most of the present-day social activism in the Jewish community still derive are often not known or consciously understood by many Jews, it is still important to consider their significance because of the distinctive manner in which those roots set our community apart. The Jewish community continues to function largely from within Jewish legal and historical perspective that made both individual and communal responses to human tragedy a requirement, in fact a commandment, rather than a voluntary option.

But one must also acknowledge and consider the change, and perhaps the erosion as well, that has taken place in that tradition because of the increasing importance of the role of public funding for the Jewish community's health and social services. This central *halakhic* principle—that responsibility for those in need is a Jewish requirement that is rooted at the very foundation of our communal processes—creates a social framework that marks us uniquely as a people. Solomon Schechter remarked on this in his lectures on Jewish philanthropy, delivered to rabbinical students as part of their training between 1913 and 1915: "There are some who think that charity is a product of Christianity. It is true that we have no orders such as Brother of Mercy or Sisters of Mercy. We have no foundations or hospitals dating from the Middle Ages, for we were not allowed to obtain any landed property."[3] He goes on to describe how Christian writers portray Jewish charity, as part of their effort to depict Christian charitable endeavors: [The Christian writer] "contends that Jewish charity, while superior to that of pagans, was inferior to that of Christians. For it is the outcome of the Law, and is lacking in love. It is not *in* the Jew but *outside* of him. It is wanting in tenderness and delicacy, in ennobling and equalizing the poor, etc. But the Christians never understood the spirit of the Law."[4] Schechter taught that the Jewish people have always understood that caring for the poor and the sick was too important to be a matter of individual conscience alone.[5]

The leadership of the American Jewish community no longer has the communal authority or ability to sanction nonparticipation in *tzedakah*. The communal practice of tithing 10 percent per household disappeared many decades ago. However, the linear descendents of this powerful communal idea, the UJA annual and special campaigns, and the more recent nationwide, major endowment development efforts, remain alive and well and, in fact, continue to grow and raise huge amounts of funds annually. Truth be told, even in the face of all the problems that those of us in Jewish communal service confront daily, our communal enterprise is envied by all our colleagues in the nonprofit sector.

Historical Background

It would be a serious error to assume that concern about public social policy and its impact upon the Jewish community has been a communal priority only during the last forty to fifty years. In fact, there is dramatic evidence to the contrary in the literature of the American Jewish community dating back 100 years. In June 1900, the First National Conference of Jewish Charities was held in Chicago, Illinois. Forty-five delegates, representing twenty-six constituent societies, as the federations were then referred to, heard papers from the volunteer and professional experts from various communities, debated the issues of the time for three days, and made site visits to local service agencies. If the description of the conference sounds familiar, that is because it was, in essence, the first "General Assembly" of an organization that later evolved into the Council of Jewish Federations and the United Jewish Appeal, which more recently has been transformed into the new United Jewish Communities. Prominent on the agenda at that meeting in 1900 was a discussion of the effects of state laws governing the provision of public assistance to the poor, and how to deal with the phenomenon of what was then called desertion. An important session at the conference was devoted to a major paper concerning the relationship between the public and private sectors. Another paper dealt with how Jewish values determined how Jewish charities dealt with poor Jews in a framework that tried to insure dignity and independence, while the public charities were perceived as both badly administered and destructive in their attitudes toward the poor.[6] One cannot help but observe that 100 years later many of the same issues of concern continue to dominate our communal agenda.

Public policy and lobbying was also on the agenda of local federations in the 1900s. As an example, one can cite the successful efforts of the Associated Jewish Charities in Chicago, as the Jewish Federation of Metropolitan Chicago was then known, to persuade the state of Illinois to enact what became the first foster care law in the United States. One hundred years later, as will be described later on, the Chicago Jewish Federation continues to be a high-profile, aggressive, and effective advocate in the public social policy arena.

Although much of the public attention during recent years has focused on the efforts of the Jewish community's effective lobbying on Israel's behalf in Washington, D.C., the fact is that state and local governments have had more power and control over the scope and fate of human services since 1980. It is true that the Reagan administration's policies accelerated that trend by light years, but the shift of power to the states in determining the core policies and expenditures for health and human services was already well underway before then. In response to this, in most states where the largest numbers of Jewish Americans reside, Jewish federations established state-level lobbying programs in the 1980s. Resources allocated for domestic social policy lobbying in Washington, D.C., by the Council of Jewish Federations, and subsequently by the United Jewish Communities, have been increased dramatically. This was a watershed development, as a consequence of which the federation system became the central force in social welfare lobbying on behalf of the Jewish community. What this change reflects really deserves a full and separate analysis, but the effect of that decision was also to shift the primary responsibility for political work on behalf of the Jewish community to those outside the Jewish community relations field, which had been historically responsible for this work. The primary reason for that decision was that local Jewish Community Relations Councils ("JCRC") had, with a few outstanding local community exceptions, abandoned the domestic social welfare agenda decades earlier. Where the local JCRC is an instrumentality of the Jewish federation, its political role on behalf of the community continues to be important.

This was also a period in which a large number of major developments in public and nonprofit social welfare policy and employment and training (e.g., welfare, health care, social security programs, the development of the Title XX Social Services program, education for social work as a profession, the role of the voluntary sector, and child welfare services) in the United States were shaped and influenced in major ways by a number of Jewish professionals whose formative experiences took place in Jewish communal service. Philip Bernstein, who was for a long period the executive of the Council of Jewish Federations, was instrumental in creating a national organization called the Independent Sector ("IS"). He gave major leadership to it for many years, and was among the handful of professionals who singularly nurtured that organization during its critical, early years. For the first time in the history of nonprofit work, IS brought together all the major organizations in a permanent coalition, dedicated to protect and further the interests of the voluntary sector in the United States.

The importance of this development is shown in data from the early 1990s about the voluntary or nonprofit sector. The data reveals an interesting set of facts: There were about 1.6 million nonprofit organizations in the United States, including 655,000 human service providers, 140,000 action agencies, and 352,000 religious institutions. These organizations had annual revenues of $670.3 billion, representing 8.8 percent of the gross domestic product. The nonprofit sector employs more than 10.9 million people, representing 7 percent of all employed persons. The sector also uses the skills and talents of 6.3 million volunteers annually.[7] By 1995, the sector's revenues grew to $899 billion. According to the Internal Revenue Service, total assets of the nonprofit organizations were $1.9 trillion, and the sector accounted for 12.4 percent of the U.S. economy in 1995.[8]

The Jewish community's involvement in public social policy is an area that continues to be fraught with contradictions. A primary, ongoing motivation for the federations' engagement in public social policy advocacy derives from the fact that public funds became available to support services provided to the Jewish and non-Jewish communities. It should also be noted that once at the table, community's leaders quickly perceived the vast potential of this funding source, well beyond the long-standing needs of hospitals and long-term care facilities. Once community leaders understood that they had the ability to protect public policies that served the community, and that they often had the ability to control the development of policies that could hurt the community, they realized that there was no choice except to become involved in a significant manner. This was especially so at the state government level. An evaluation of the success of similar efforts by Catholics and Lutherans also convinced the community of the wisdom of its investment.

Furthermore, because of the strength of the community's core funding from the annual campaign, it might be able to avoid some of the consequences experienced by other groups for whom public funding became the very core of their programs. Nonprofit agencies that are overly dependent upon government for funding are also likely to have significantly less ultimate freedom to fight bad policy proposals. Money, and not *tikkun olam*, was the driving force that initially pushed most federations into state government advocacy during the past two decades. Despite the community's growing use of public funds, in most of the community's core human service programs it has been rather successful at preserving the primary mission of serving the Jewish community. Not surprisingly, however, the volunteer and professional people who supervised and guided the advocacy efforts, as well as the people hired to represent the community, more often than not came with strong commitments to progressive public social policy. Their personal belief systems were typically based upon identification with Jewish tradition and values.[9]

The Jewish community's interest in obtaining funding for its services sometimes separated the community institutionally from many of the broader social policy battles. At the same time, however, the Jewish progressive tradition and the values of the community's volunteer and professional representatives have just as often drawn the community into the fray of many mainstream social policy debates. Then, too, the case can be made that in recent years the environment in the Jewish community has shifted, with some limited exceptions. There is more interest now in matters of public social policy because issues like health care, social security, funding for education, the needs of the elderly, welfare reform and its impact upon refugees and legal immigrants, and services for children at risk have become preoccupations of most American citizens, Jews included. They have become mainstream concerns for all communities.

Demographic changes, some of which have major implications for the Jewish community (e.g., the growth in the number of frail elderly, the anticipated growth in the number of Jewish elderly overall, the continuing significant number of single parent families, and the dispersion of Jews to ever-larger geographic circles around metropolitan areas), also serve to dramatically heighten interest in governmental policies that affect the community's ability to do its job. Thus, whether Republican or Democrat, Jewish community leaders appear to be more concerned about public policy and its direct impact upon the community.

Paradoxically, despite the phenomenal growth of social welfare lobbying efforts by Jewish federations throughout the United States during the past two decades, there has been little systematic attention paid to it. Practice is not documented, policy is not debated with any degree of regularity in the pages of the literature of the field of Jewish communal service, curricula for teaching the skills required do not exist, the national system does not offer training programs for volunteer leaders or professionals, and none of the Jewish community's sponsored or affiliated graduate degree programs preparing new professionals deal with the subject in more than a cursory manner.

Public Social Policy: The Literature of the Field

During the early 1960s the growing extent of government funding for Jewish communal services, the impact of government contracts and grants on intake policies, the primary mission of Jewish agencies to care for Jews, and other service delivery policies became the subject of an intensive debate. The National Conference of Jewish Communal Service established a Committee on Public Issues chaired by Martha Selig, who prepared an extensive report analyzing the issues from a funding perspective. The report's findings were the focus of extensive and animated discussion at the annual meeting of the conference in 1962.[10] The conversation, however, was focused solely upon the challenges to Jewish agencies using government money while trying to be true to their institutional mission. In 1966, when *Trends and Issues in Jewish Social Welfare in the United States, 1899-1958* was published,[11] government funding and public social policy in general could not be characterized as even marginal issues. Indeed, the topic does not appear as a matter of significant concern and not one of the chapters in the book directly addresses the subject. Some leaders in the Jewish community also recognized that the 1960s were a period in which there was a great increase in interest in social policy. In 1970, a group of Jewish Community Center ("JCC") and Jewish federation professionals came together under the auspices of the National Jewish Welfare Board to frame and field a survey of the views of center and federation executives about the role and responsibility of JCCs in dealing with Jewish communal problems, including such social problems as drug abuse, poverty, juvenile delinquency, family dysfunction, and the like. But here, too, the focus was upon the center's role in working on social problems *internal* to the Jewish community. There was no examination of the role of the center in the wider community, the consequences of public policies, or what the Jewish community could or should do about them.[12] In 1976, when Daniel Elazar first published his now famous work, *Community and Polity*, he, too, paid scant attention to the sleeping giant that government would shortly become in the Jewish community. His only reference to the role of government was a very brief description of the consequence of government funding replacing the Jewish community's earlier support of Jewish medical and health care institutions.[13] What is even more curious about this is that Elazar was deeply involved in the U.S. government's commission on federalism and the states, of which he was an appointed member for many years. Federalism was his second major area of expertise and academic involvement, about which he also wrote widely.

In 1976 the Council of Jewish Federations convened thirty-five of the most prominent leaders from the federation field and the field of social welfare for two days of intensive discussion on the subject of "Government and Voluntary Responsibility: The Changing Relationship in Meeting Welfare Needs." The colloquium participants were provided with background data and a series of papers prepared by experts. Over several days they discussed the importance of advocacy as a personal and communal obligation, the need to improve the federation's ability and skill as an advocate, the nature of the voluntary agency-government partnership, the need to modify service models, the impact of government funding on service delivery, and the need for the council to immediately expand its capacity to support federation involvement in the dramatically expanding role that government was playing in supporting services delivered by voluntary agencies.[14] Despite this event, there is little evidence of a long-term federation strategy to deal with the juggernaut that government funding had become. By 1981, when *The Turbulent Decades—Jewish Communal Services in America 1958-1978* appeared,[15] four separate chapters addressed the subject. Most instructive is Graenum Berger's comment in the opening chapter:

> The headlong shift to seek government support for sectarian agencies was marked by some of these factors: (1) Agencies, unhappy with the modest increases received annually from Jewish Federa-

tions, saw an opportunity for dramatically enriching and widening their services. (2) Federations unable to meet the demands of their societies encouraged their affiliates to seek such help. In New York, the Federation created a department of government relations to exploit every avenue of government aid. (3) Agencies had become enamored of "big" business attitudes: planning, expansion, computerization, executive suites, use of government consultants, and so forth. There was a definite power shift towards the professional with expertise in government contracts. (4) There was a widespread acceptance of the rationalized social welfare principle which mixed public and private welfare as a boon to experimentation, efficiency, economy and expansion. (5) New services in mental health, in work with the retarded, the aged, those in need of rehabilitation, in drug addiction, in research, and, of course, service to the poor, could now be funded in a way undreamed of by private Jewish philanthropy.[16]

In 1981 when the Council of Jewish Federations published *An Index of Community Organization Articles Published 1924-1980*,[17] less than a dozen articles could be found over a fifty-six-year period concerning this topic. This pattern continued in 1991 when a survey volume, *Changing Jewish Life—Service Delivery and Planning in the 1990's*, contained no references to the advocacy efforts of the Jewish community.[18] Indeed, the words public policy, advocacy, and government do not appear in the index. Finally, in 1998, in *A Portrait of the American Jewish Community*,[19] there are two references. One recounts the comments by Graenum Berger, cited earlier. The second appears in an article surveying the first 100 years of the Jewish federation: "Public policy and advocacy (tax-deductible groups avoid the word "lobbying") have become increasingly important to the federations and CJF. At this time fifteen states maintain associations of federations that focus on public-policy issues being debated in the respective state capitals."[20]

The fact that the literature of the field contains little substantial work describing Jewish communal practice in public policy derives from several sources. Historically it has been extremely difficult to get Jewish communal professionals to document their work, and unlike colleagues in academic settings, they are neither expected to write nor are they supported institutionally in such endeavors. Then, too, this is the stuff of "politics," personalities, lobbying, and "backroom deals." The often necessary cloak of secrecy and the desire for a purposefully maintained low profile, surrounding much of the work in public social policy lobbying, often works against the rigorous collection of information required to support the development of written descriptions of the successes and failures in advocacy work. It is likely that due to the increasing ranks of the professionals working in this field, that the next five to ten years will see both greater recognition of their contribution to the community as well as professionalization of their work. At the end of 2000 a professional association of government affairs professionals was formed. One hopes that as a result of this development, there will be a serious effort to build a literature in this field.

The Scope of Public Funding in Jewish Community Services

Data elaborating the extent of public funding in the domestic services resource mix of Jewish communal agencies is relatively sparse, and it is not compiled or updated with any degree of consistency or regularity.[21] Nevertheless, we are able to develop a picture contrasting the late 1950s with the 1990s. In 1958, although the data is very incomplete, the picture looked like this:

- Of fifty-nine Jewish hospitals reporting, public funding supported between 3 and 50 percent of the operating budgets of forty-eight.
- Of sixty homes for the elderly reporting, seventeen reported receiving public funds.
- Twelve out of seventeen child welfare agencies received 33 percent of their operating funds from government.
- Out of seventy-four family service agencies reporting, only ten reported receiving any government funding. Such funding amounted to less than 5 percent of their revenues.
- Jewish community centers and camps reported no use of public funds in 1958.
- 50 percent of vocational service agencies reported receiving public funds.

The 1958 survey revealed that only 100 federation agencies in the United States received public funds, and half of those were hospitals.[22] Although we are afforded only a partial picture of that period, it is clear that by the late 1950s government support for the services of the organized Jewish community was still in its infancy, as compared to the 1990s. At that point in time there were few analysts who focused on the question of social welfare policy in Jewish communal services. Those who did were more concerned with the nature of the impact of public funding on the Jewishness of the agencies, and their ability to serve Jews in need in light of government restrictions concerning the populations eligible for service.

By 1976 an extensive analysis prepared for a national colloquium by the Council of Jewish Federations and Welfare Funds provided the following picture:

- Government funding of Jewish agencies, including Jewish hospitals, increased from $27 million in 1962 to $561 million in 1973, a twenty-fold increase.
- If hospital funding were excluded, the total would be $108 million in 1973 compared to only $8 million in 1962, a twelve-fold increase.
- Among the nearly sixty-five Jewish family service agencies surveyed, although government funds increased fivefold over a ten-year period, they still represented only a minor portion (10 percent) of their resources.
- For Jewish child welfare agencies government funds represented 48 percent of all their income in 1962, and by 1973 rose to 63 percent, an increase of almost one-third. Most child welfare agencies received government funds.
- Homes for the elderly, the service area of greatest increase, went from $2 million in 1962 to $86 million in 1973, from 7 percent to 66 percent. By 1973, government funding for homes had increased by forty times over 1962. In 1962 only one-third of the sixty Jewish homes for the elderly received government funding, but by 1973 all received such support.
- Less than 20 percent of all Jewish community centers received any government funding in 1974. In 1971 government funds accounted for 1.5 percent of their resources, and rose to only 1.9 percent of an estimated total income of $100 million in 1974.
- Jewish vocational services reported that over a five-year period—1968-1973—government payments increased by 77 percent, from $7 million to $12.7 million.
- The thirty-five Jewish hospitals surveyed experienced a twenty-four-fold increase in government support. By 1973 this amounted to $453 million, an increase over an eleven-year period from 10 percent to 49 percent of their revenues.[23]

In 1995, when the Council of Jewish Federations conducted the first major national survey devoted exclusively to the public funding of Jewish communal services,[24] it was discovered that in every community where significant numbers of Jews resided, public funding played an even greater role in the community's ability to provide human services than most informed community leaders realized. Data for the year 1994 revealed that, excluding public funds to hospitals, more than 59 percent of the total resources available to Jewish agencies for the provision of human services came from government.

By 1995, although those that remained were included in the survey, the era of Jewish hospitals that primarily served the Jewish community's needs had already passed. An interesting outcome of that development is the conversion of Jewish hospitals to Jewish health care foundations (i.e., Cleveland, Cincinnati, Pittsburgh, Denver, Kansas, and Chicago). These foundations are the repository of many hundreds of millions of dollars, most of which was contributed by donors from the Jewish community. This could have significant implications for the Jewish community's role in public policy development, as well as the potential for increased experimentation and expansion of services, Jewish community agencies, including the remaining hospitals, received more than $3.6 billion in government funding in 1994. Excluding hospitals, more than $1 billion in public funds are part of the resources Jewish agencies use annually and, as noted, these dollars represent more than 59 percent of the operating funds (41 percent without New York City) used to provide services to the people served by Jewish federation agencies.

The impact of public funding in various specific fields of service ranges from about 55 percent in some, to more than 75 percent in others, as shown in table 4.1. In every single important field of human service to the community, government funding plays an essential role and without it, much of what we are able to do as a community would not exist.

In 1996, Independent Sector, a national coalition of nonprofit organizations, also conducted a national survey of a sample of 100 agencies and found that, by comparison, 37 percent of the budgets of social service agencies nationwide came from public funds.[25] The possible explanation for the differences in the findings of the two studies is that Jewish agencies have become very skillful at competing for public funds, are less concerned with the downsides of public funding in their budgets, and have become very creative at developing methods to insure that they can continue to serve our primary constituency. In addition, while the requirements imposed by public funding continue to be a mixed bag, Jewish agencies have become less concerned about them than they were in the late 1950s. Perhaps, unlike several decades ago, the Jewish community may also see its human services mission as broader and more embracing than it once did. Despite the organized Jewish community's continuing ability to raise hundreds of millions annually, the dollars needed to sustain the Jewish community's domestic human services are not increasing at the rate the agencies require, and thus the community has had no choice but to take more public money, as well as to expand other resource development efforts. Unlike the 1950s, today no hospital and none of the Jewish community's long-term care facilities could operate without public funding. Few Jewish child welfare, family services, or vocational services could either. No Jewish community-sponsored housing for the elderly or disabled could. The same would be true for many of the other Jewish social services were not funds available from Title XX Social Services, Older Americans Act resources, or HUD money for the homeless.

Table 4.1

Government Funding for Jewish Agency Service by Field, 1994

Field of Service	*Total Government Funding*	*Percent of Annual Budget of Jewish Agencies*
Jewish Hospitals	$2.580 billion	55
Jewish Nursing Homes	$550 million	76
Jewish Family Services	$134 million	61
Jewish Vocational Services	$135 million	77
Jewish Community Centers	$13 million	5
Other Services *	$245 million	63
Total—Excluding Health Care	$1.077 billion	59.4
Total—All Funds	$3.657 billion	55.7

* "Other Services" includes such programs as housing for the elderly and disabled, funds to day schools, services for the elderly, substance abuse and prevention services for adolescents, and arts and humanities.

The Jewish Social Welfare Lobby

During the past four decades, the organized Jewish community has gone through a number of cycles of debate, withdrawal, engagement, disillusionment, and partnership with respect to the place of government funding in Jewish communal services. One objective of this discussion is to examine the dramatic growth of the Jewish community's involvement in lobbying in the public social policy arena in the last two decades, in particular, and to try to identify the factors that underpin the incredible success of these efforts. Much attention has been and continues to be paid to the so-called Jewish lobby in Washington, but virtually none to the magnitude of state-level lobbying operations of the Jewish community. There are two significant exceptions to this: the Center for Jewish Community Studies organized a two-day conference on the Jewish community's state lobbying efforts in February 1997. In preparation for the conference on the "Jewish Community and the States," Daniel Elazar developed a survey of the eighteen states then active in lobbying efforts. The project was conducted in collaboration with the National Association of Jewish State Legislators, some of whose members also participated in the survey. Afterward, a special report on the conference and the survey was written by Elazar and published by the Jerusalem Center for Public Affairs.[26] Some of the information from that survey of the concerns and work issues dominant in 1996 will be discussed below, and compared to the dominant themes of today. Yet some twelve years earlier, the looming significance of these efforts in Chicago was described in a report commissioned by Elazar, who clearly recognized the potential and importance of federation involvement in the political process.[27]

However, we must first consider two facts:

1. It is well known among most federation leaders that these offices, sometimes with the direct assistance of the Washington Action Office of the United Jewish Communities (UJC), are singularly responsible for assuring that more than $1 billion annually in public funding ($3.6 billion annually if funds for health care are included) is available to federations and their agencies to care for people in need.

2. Even assuming a modest annual growth rate of 3 percent per year since the 1994 survey, it can be estimated that government funds in Jewish communal services by 2000

amounted to about $1.286 billion. Thus, the public funds supporting the Jewish community's entire array of social services provide nearly a third of a billion dollars *more* annually than all the combined UJA campaign efforts. The UJA campaign raised $820 million in 2000, a $25 million increase over 1999, for all local services, national agencies, and overseas needs.[28]

Although the annual UJA campaign continues to be a magnificent representation of the strength and values of the Jewish community, the fact is that public funding dwarfs the 30-40 percent of those funds allocated annually by federations that are used to support all domestic local services. Thus, in 1996-1997 (the latest year for which data were available) while public funding provided more than $1 billion to support local human services in the Jewish community, federation allocations by comparison provided about $306 million for *all* local services, including Jewish education. In 1996-1997, federation allocations to human services totaled about $246 million, while Jewish education received allocations of $60 million. These allocations included funds from local federation endowments and other sources, as well as the annual local campaign, but do not include agency-generated income from fees or other nongovernmental sources. This does, indeed, suggest the need for thoughtful consideration of the implications of the increasingly significant role that government funding plays in the Jewish community.[29]

It is also interesting to note that many Jewish communities are extremely reluctant to speak publicly about the amount of government funds they receive. There is a fear that contributors to the annual campaign will be deterred should they learn of the vast sums of money government provides in support of services. However, it is instructive that in both New York and Chicago, the two Jewish communities that annually receive the largest amounts of government funding, one also finds the largest annual local campaigns that continue to grow significantly despite widespread public discussion of the role that public funds play in those communities. Both communities have also experienced enormous growth in endowment and other types of donor-advised funds. For many years in Chicago, the widely distributed annual report of the federation has contained a detailed list of every government and foundation grant to the federation and all of its partner agencies. Over a six-year period (1995–2000), the federation allocated between $25 and $28 million per year for all local services, or under $160 million. Government funding during the same period amounted to $227.8 million (excluding

Medicare and Medicaid funds to hospitals). In every one of those same years, the Jewish United Fund campaign in Chicago raised $1-2 million in additional funds over the prior year, with the 2000 campaign closing at $65.2 million. It appears that, if information about the role of government is properly communicated, there is no risk to a community's core resource development efforts, including growing endowment funds.

Every state in the United States where there is a significant Jewish population now has a formal program in place supported by the Jewish federations in the area, led by a professional, who is backed up by politically engaged volunteer leaders. Forty-five Jewish communities across the country now have resources dedicated to work in the domestic social policy arena. These communities range from small to large metropolitan, and include some JCRCs, as well as state government affairs offices dedicated solely to domestic social policy. Several of the larger states also include in their mandate the responsibility to work in the municipal, county, state, and federal arenas. Table 4.2 looks at the chronological development and level of financial investment by the Jewish community among the state government offices that have been in existence for the longest period of time.

Selected colleagues from those Jewish communities that have been working at this task the longest, and who are among the Jewish community's most effective social welfare lobbyists, were invited to share their thoughts about their work. They were asked to comment about:

- Their perceptions of their mission.
- Their thoughts about the role of volunteer leaders and other Jewish communal professionals in their work.
- Identification of the critical issues on their agenda.
- Where they had succeeded and where they had failed.
- How they are perceived in their own local communities.

The Jewish community is represented by an outstanding and talented group of government affairs professionals who are dedicated to meeting the needs of the community and to the task of *tikkun olam* (repairing the world). For comparative purposes, the data from the survey conducted by the Center for Jewish Community Studies in 1996 are illuminating. Respondents were asked to reflect on what they thought their greatest successes were, what their greatest needs were, and they were asked to provide a description of the issues on their agenda. Greatest successes included: making the Jewish com-

Table 4.2

Data on Selected Jewish Federation State Government Offices[30]

Year Established	State	1999 Budget	Staffing Pattern	Est. Government Funds
1970s	FL	- NA -	Part-time (Contract Lobbyist)	$41.0 mil. – 1999 **
1980	NY	$500,000 *	Full-time (4 fte)	$3 billion – 2000 **
1981	IL	$350,000 *	Full-time (2.75 fte)	$161.6 mil. – 2000 **
1982	OH	$175,000	Full-time (1 fte)	$71.1 mil. – 2000 **
1982	NJ	$165,000	Full-time (1 fte)	$25.6 mil. -- 1994 **
1987	PA	$130,000	Full-time (1.5 fte)	$277.1 – 1994 **
1987	WI	$55,000	Part-time (Contract Lobbyist)	NA
1988	MO	$70,000	Part-time (Contract Lobbyist)	$3.0 million – 1998
1989	MA	$116,000	Full-time (1.5 fte)	$268.7 mil. – 1998 **
1993	CT	$142,000	Full-time (2.0 fte)	$70.3 mil. – 2000 **

* Includes the cost of lobbying and advocacy activities in Washington, D.C.
** Figure includes Medicaid and/or Medicare.

munity aware of the importance of state issues, the growing involvement of Jews in both major parties, building a unified coalition among federations in their state, becoming the central focus of state government efforts, fostering openness in state legislatures to Jewish community voices, and building strong relationships with government officials. The greatest needs included: more staff and more adequate budgets, more participation by top volunteer and professional leaders, and increasing the awareness of the importance of the stake of the Jewish community in state government issues.[31]

Data from the more recent informal inquiry conducted among ten selected state government offices revealed that the issues on the community's agenda in 1996 were not much different from the list in 2000. The list of priority needs has also not changed significantly, except that in recent years Medicaid and Medicare funding has become more of a priority for state government offices. That most state offices continue to be seriously underfunded by their federations is surely puzzling in view of the continuously increasing annual financial contribution these efforts make to the Jewish community. The range of issues that state government lobbyists address today includes: Holocaust education; rates for long-term care facilities; managed care policies; assisted living services; immigration and refugee services; domestic violence; state-Israel economic exchange programs; welfare reform; state efforts to eliminate nonprofit tax exemption; capital grants for Jewish agencies' facilities; state policies supporting elderly residents' right to return to their original nursing home after hospitalization; Holocaust reparations; ensuring Jewish community representation on state advisory and policy bodies; policies governing state "charitable choice" programs and monitoring their operation; Jewish cemetery problems; hate crimes/antiterrorism legislation; licensing programs affecting Jewish refugees in the professions; health care; social services for children, families, and the elderly; day care; housing for the elderly and disabled; mental health services; home health care; job training; and privacy and genetic testing.

The primary mission assigned to these offices is to secure government funding, and to generally represent the interests of the Jewish community. All state government offices surveyed reported strong reliance upon coalitional involvement as a major strategy to accomplish their lobbying goals. Similarly, all emphasized the importance of the role of volunteer leaders and agency representatives as keys to success. While some programs are adequately funded, others are so poorly supported that their representatives cannot always attend the annual conference sponsored by the UJC's Washington office at the annual General Assembly. In most states there is great respect for the Jewish community's lobbyists, and despite expressions of concern about inadequate budgets, most of the surveyed lobbyists report that they feel highly valued by their federation.

The Jewish Federation of Metropolitan Chicago Government Affairs Program—An Example of a Comprehensive Approach

Recognizing the importance of the role that states were going to play as a result of the policies of the Reagan administration, the Jewish Federation of Metropolitan Chicago opened an office in its state capital, Springfield, in 1981. This followed the development of a program proposal, review of all legal considerations by their legal counsel, and adoption of the plan and budget by the federation board of directors. Five years later, in 1986, the federation opened its Washington, D.C., office. The Chicago Federation's Washington office is located in the United Jewish Communities' Washington Action Office. The YMCA, and the Catholic and Lutheran communities, had already been working the state capital for decades. In fact, for many years, several Jewish state legislators had been urging the Jewish federation to become active in the state capital to represent Jewish interests. Jewish federation leaders realized that although the Reagan administration formalized the concept of shifting more money and power to the states, in fact a major shift had already taken place, albeit with less fanfare and drama. This major change, along with the overall decline in government funding for human services during the Reagan years, accelerated the need for the federation to protect the interests and needs of the tens of thousands of Jews and non-Jews its agencies served.

The federation's Government Affairs Program had several key goals: to develop relationships with key legislators, provide testimony on matters of importance to the Jewish community as a means of influencing policy, secure additional government funds for programs, and develop and enact legislation important to the Jewish community. From the very beginning, it was strategically determined to include many social welfare issues of broad concern that might have only limited and sometimes no direct benefit to the Jewish community because of concern for the needs of the total community. This helped to develop the excellent reputation enjoyed by the Chicago Jewish community among government officials. There is a clear understanding that, although the Jewish community protects its interests, it is also often a leader on issues of wide concern affecting all of the state's residents. Operating in and through coalitions has also been a hallmark of the Jewish federation since the inception of its lobbying program. Coalitions also provide singular advantages because operating through these structures permits institutional/organizational involvement in an issue, without the necessity of being the only entity taking on the visible lead role in lobbying for an issue.

Federations, as do other social welfare lobbying organizations, make a range of decisions about which lobbying strategy to use, depending upon the issues and who the coalition partners may be. Recently, for example, in deciding how the Jewish federation ought to lobby to retain the Illinois state gasoline tax, which contributes $300-400 million annually to state revenues, the federation decided not to join a high-profile coalition that included many organizations it often works with. Instead, based on a discussion at a Government

Affairs Committee meeting, which included many Jewish elected officials, a recommendation was made to keep a low profile but to support continuation of the tax. The Jewish federation board of directors approved the committee's recommendation. Federation contacted the governor and the state House of Representatives majority leader privately to express its position that the tax should be retained. The federation's state capital office director also let the other advocacy organizations know of the federation's position and the support of the federation board to retain the tax.

To accomplish the aims of the program, a statewide network of all the federated/UJA Jewish communities in Illinois was created, with the expectation that they would contribute annually according to their means toward the budget. Similarly, the agencies of the Jewish Federation of Metropolitan Chicago also contribute significant "dues" of up to $16,000 each annually, depending upon the size of their gross operating budget, to support the program. A committee of the federation's board of directors is responsible for oversight of the program. In addition, the committee includes volunteer and professional representatives of all federation agencies and of all the Jewish federations statewide. Important, too, is the fact that many of the committee members are Jewish staff from the offices of city, county, state, and federal elected and appointed officials, former staffers of elected officials, professional lobbyists, and former Jewish elected officials. All sitting Jewish elected and appointed officials who reside in the Chicago area are also invited to participate in the work of the committee. Many of the volunteer members of the committee are among the most politically active and influential Jewish community members locally and nationally in both Republican and Democratic circles. This mix is incredibly useful because it provides the federation with a wide array of insights and advice. The discussion at committee meetings is also an educational forum where elected officials and staffers learn about social welfare issues and the position and interests of the Jewish community. This information is often translated into the day-to-day work of these individuals. Jewish state legislators hold leadership positions in the Illinois General Assembly and chair key committees dealing with human services.

The federation also has access to a significant number of annual local campaign contributors and other Jewish community leaders who can be brought into the political process as needed. The Jewish community in Chicago is extremely politically active, and is also the home to a number of independent political action committees. A substantial number of those activists have made their nationwide political relationships available to the Jewish federation. Thus, on the national level when issues require it, the reach of the Chicago Jewish Federation can extend well beyond the Illinois delegation and includes members of the leadership in both houses of Congress. Annually, unrelated to any special problem or crisis of the moment, the federation takes a delegation of about thirty to forty volunteer and professional leaders from the federation board, the Government Affairs Committee, and its partner agencies to Springfield, and separately to Washington, D.C., to lobby on a wide range of issues of interest to the community.

Including these two- to three-day trips, the Government Affairs Committee meets about six to eight times annually. Each fall the committee spends time developing its policy agenda for the year, with the intention of selecting three or four major issues that represent long-term policy concerns for the Chicago Jewish community. These constitute the committee's agenda, in addition to the annual budget cycle and other social welfare policy and appropriations crises that develop at various levels of government. Work on selected long-term issues is done through a series of subcommittees or working groups that function for as long as necessary until the committee feels it has achieved its objectives, or has lost the battle.

Trips to Israel have long been a means of building life-long relationships with elected officials. The federation has taken dozens of state and federal elected officials to Israel during the past two decades as its guest. In 2001 a trip was planned for congressional office chiefs of staff and legislative directors. These visits are funded through a special annual allocation from a donor who left a major unrestricted bequest to support the work of the federation, and not through donors' contributions to the annual campaign. A week or ten days traveling together is a truly special opportunity to get to know elected officials and their interests. In the case of Illinois, with only a few exceptions, every person who has been elected to Congress over the past two decades came out of the Illinois General Assembly, and every individual was well known to the Jewish community long before they became a candidate for federal office. Thus, the investment in a state government operation also has significant long-term payoffs for the community.

Major emphasis and energy is put into developing staff-to-staff relationships with the people who "make things happen" at City Hall and in county government, in all the various departments of state government, the governor's office, both houses of the state legislature, the administration, and every congressional office of interest to the Chicago Jewish community in Washington, D.C.

The very first issue in which the federation became engaged at the state level set the tone for the future of the federation's state government office. Literally, just as the Jewish federation opened its state capital office, then governor Jim Thompson vetoed legislation that would have continued to fund several important budget lines, thereby eliminating a special matching program known as the "Donated Funds Initiative," which was part of the state's Title XX social services program. The Title XX Social Services Block Grant is a major federal program providing social services from cradle (day care) to grave (senior transportation and home delivered meals) throughout Illinois, and involves major programs in all of the state's human services agencies. The initiative is also significant because, unlike many government-funded programs, its services are not restricted only to people with low incomes. The program is structured so that the United Ways throughout the state fund 25 percent of the voluntary agencies' match, or 25 cents of every $1 they contribute. In total the voluntary agencies and the United Ways fund 25 percent of all dollars in the program. On the same day in March 1981 when the Jewish federation chartered a plane and flew forty-four top volunteer leaders to the capital to dedicate its new state office, federation staff participated in the formation of the first successfully organized Statewide Coalition on Human Services. The YMCA of Metropolitan Chicago, the United Ways of Illinois, the Jewish Federation, the United Way of Metropolitan Chicago, the Juvenile Justice Task Force, Marrilac House (a Catholic settlement house on the west side of Chicago operated by an order of nuns), and the Day Care Action Council formed the core of the coalition and its leadership.

After a couple of weeks of intense, nasty, aggressive, high-stakes political battle, the coalition won. The Illinois House of Representatives was convinced to unanimously override the governor's veto. The coalition gained the support and the votes of all 128 Republican and Democratic members. The defeat astounded both the governor and his lobbyist. Thus, when the bill came to the state senate, the Republican leadership (many of whom supported the coalition's position) was forced to advise the governor to accept the compromise the coalition proposed for the remainder of that fiscal year, with the understanding that the program would be fully funded in the following year. The governor accepted the deal, and a new era was born.

The tradition in Illinois is that on the day the governor announces his budget, a special Education Budget and Program Initiatives briefing is held afterward with the leaders of the education establishment of the entire state. At the briefing, the attendees are provided with specially prepared materials, and have an opportunity to engage in in-depth conversation with the governor's staff and the state government's top education leadership. In the year following "The Year of the Veto Override," the governor's office announced that there would be a Human Services Budget briefing following his budget address, and various groups including the Jewish federation were invited. That, too, has become a tradition in Illinois, and there has been such a briefing annually ever since, continuing through the terms of the two governors who have since succeeded him.

A few weeks after the legislative session was over, the chairman of the federation's Government Affairs Committee, who was also a close personal friend of the governor, arranged a meeting between the governor and the federation's top leadership. At the meeting, the governor apologized for "listening to the wrong voices" and he told the Chicago Federation leaders that such a mistake would never happen again. The governor said that whenever the Jewish community needed to communicate with him, he wanted to hear it. He advised the small leadership gathering that the federation could reach him through the deputy governor (a Jewish woman who was standing at his left), or through the federation's government affairs chairman (who was at his right), and that his top staff had been advised that if the Jewish federation called, they were to answer. He told the assembled group that he wanted to know what the Jewish community's concerns were. The federation took him at his word and began to send him a letter annually, prior to the date when he announced his proposed budget for the coming year in which the Jewish community's priorities were spelled out. In addition, a new pattern began to emerge. Every year several of the federation's stated priorities made it into the governor's budget, either as a new initiative or with additional funds added to an existing budget line. This pattern continued until the conclusion of the governor's sixteen years of service. The practice of sending the governor a letter with the Jewish community's priorities, and sending periodic letters "To the Friends of the Jewish Federation" in the legislature, has now become a regular occurrence. Over the years it has turned out to be one effective way of communicating positions on issues, priorities, and concerns when the community feels a need to do so in a more formal public fashion.

No governor in Illinois has dared to tamper with the funding for that program since, with one exception. In the end, the program was continued and the governor came to regret his position because of the unrelenting statewide pressure brought to bear on his office and leaders and members of the legislature.

Another means of affecting state policy, programs, and finances is through service on advisory bodies, task forces, commissions, and planning groups attached to the governor's office and various state departments. Federation volunteer leaders, staff, and federation agency representatives have been named to a great number of those groups over the years. The Jewish community's service on these bodies is valued because it is perceived as an honest broker and as an upfront advocate for what is truly in the best interests of all Illinois residents.

Other examples of the range of problems and issues that Chicago's lobbying efforts have addressed in Chicago, Illinois, and Washington, D.C., include:

- Legislation to exempt day and resident camps from paying unemployment insurance for summer staff.
- A committee member intervening with a large public school system to break through an entrenched bureaucracy to secure a significant rate increase for students enrolled in the special education school operated by the Jewish Children's Bureau.
- Participation in city, county, and state task forces on homeless services.
- In the community relations area: Secured the passage of legislation to permit intensive surveillance of paramilitary groups, hate-crimes legislation, a state religious freedom restoration act, and legislation criminalizing the collection of funds for terrorist organizations.
- Participation in local suburban municipal senior advisory bodies to work on problems associated with a lack of adequate transportation for the elderly.
- City and state task forces and advisory bodies concerned with welfare reform and assistance to families.
- Modification of the formula governing how funds from the federal Older Americans Act would be distributed to the states.
- Wrote the language in the Older Americans Act that defines the role that social service agencies that provide services can play, if they so choose, in also assessing an individual's need for community care services.
- Proposed the creation of a state-funded "endowment fund" to provide capital grants to nonprofits to enable them to acquire, build, or renovate facilities in which human services are provided.

- Prevented the state from capping and thereby closing enrollment in a home health program for persons with HIV/AIDS at a cost of about $800 per month per person, which would have resulted in many going into a hospital for nine days at a cost of more than $8,000 per person. Proposed as a budget austerity measure by one department, it turned out that half of that money would have come from state revenues, with the other half coming from the federal Medicaid program administered by another state agency.
- Worked to get the state to continue its program of providing mammograms and glasses to public aid recipients, after state bureaucrats proposed the elimination of these benefits.
- Federation staff chaired the Task Force on Hunger for the mayor's office of the city of Chicago.
- Arranged for the mayor of the city of Chicago to create a Task Force on Homelessness, that resulted in the legalization of all shelters in Chicago and the subsequent provision of tens of millions of dollars in funding for services and facility renovation.
- Federation was instrumental in establishing a state-level Emergency Food and Shelter Board and program, and was one of three advocates that wrote the language for the state of Illinois statute that provides the legal authority for the state to operate and fund a program of services for the homeless. That program began with a token appropriation of $300,000 that the Jewish federation and several coalition partners put into the budget of the Department of Public Aid, which now annually provides $8.6 million for services for the homeless.
- At the federation's request, the city of Chicago and Cook County agreed to operate a joint FEMA Emergency Food and Shelter Board program.
- Opposition to inappropriate, bureaucratic regulation and support for reasonable accountability by state-funded, non-profit service providers.
- With the public support of the state AFL-CIO, and some cemetery owners behind the scenes, enacted legislation prohibiting cemetery labor-management agreements from banning Sunday burials.
- Enacted state legislation prohibiting state contactors from participation in an Arab boycott of Israel.

- Creation of state-funded replacement programs for legal immigrants and refugees barred from federal programs under welfare reform.
- Enacted state legislation exempting Holocaust reparations payments from state income taxes and from being counted as income/assets in programs where a means test is used to determine applicant eligibility.
- Played an important role in rescuing Sinai Health Systems, a federation affiliate, several times, and assured its being on the comptroller's priority weekly payment list.
- Protection of the Jewish community's interests in election law amendments to assure that primary and general election days do not fall on Jewish holidays.

The Jewish federation also plays other significant roles in Illinois. For the past twenty-five years the federation has been the prime contractor for the state in managing its statewide refugee resettlement program. To assure continuity of core services for newcomers in the face of ever-changing federal appropriations for state refugee programs, for the last several years the federation has been responsible for assuring that $2 million annually in state general revenue funds is provided for the state's refugee services program. More recently, the federation has taken on a somewhat similar role in helping the state plan for and implement the state-funded program to encourage and prepare legal immigrants and refugees for naturalization as U.S. citizens, an expansion of the program created at the request of the Jewish federation several years ago. These programs and contracts with the Jewish federation involved more than $10 million in FY 2001. All the agencies throughout Illinois that provide these services do so under contracts with the Jewish Federation of Metropolitan Chicago.

Some years ago Congress enacted the State Legalization Impact Assistance Grant program that provided funds to the states to provide a range of services leading to the legalization of aliens illegally residing in the United States under a federal amnesty. It was estimated that about 185,000 such persons were in residence in Illinois, mostly Latinos and a smaller but significant number of people from Poland. The Jewish federation was strongly encouraged to apply to implement and manage the statewide education, skills training, and preparation for citizenship programs. In collaboration with a Latino community partner, the federation ran this $36 million program for four and a half years with a diverse, statewide group of more than eighty subcontracting social agencies, school districts, community colleges, and ethnic community groups that provided services to about 165,000 eligible Illinois illegal immigrants who were successfully legalized and naturalized.

Considered to be one of the most sophisticated local-national lobbying programs in the organized Jewish community, it has taken twenty years to build the federation's Government Affairs Program and its tradition of significant leadership involvement. While skilled, excellent professionals are necessary, operating in the political arena cannot be successful without the ongoing involvement of a large number of volunteer leaders. Volunteer leaders "tell the story" in a way that professional lobbyists cannot, and no lobbyist can be effective without troops behind him or her. An example: On a trip to Washington, D.C., several years ago when Congress was in the throes of the Newt Gingrich "Contract with America" frenzy, a group from Chicago was visiting with a newly elected congressman from Illinois. As one volunteer leader explained, "I am a board member of one of the federation's agencies, and I contribute $50,000 a year to our local Jewish United Fund Campaign and each year I increase my gift. You guys are about to make my contribution irrelevant because of all the money for social programs you're talking about cutting. Without the government at the table, my contribution and those of my peers will become useless." The congressman was impressed; no donor to philanthropy had ever personally explained to him before the delicate fiscal relationship that exists between private and public funds.

The Chicago Federation's Government Affairs Program is successful because Jewish community volunteer and professional leaders and politicians perceive it as being both influential and effective. Politicians also see it as important because they understand that many Chicago Jewish community leaders participate as American citizens in the political process, rewarding and supporting those who support the interests of the Jewish community. In Illinois, no one who is or who is thinking about becoming a candidate for any significant public office at any level of government does so without making contact with the organized Jewish community. It is also true that Chicago has become known as a necessary place to visit for large numbers of candidates for congressional seats from other states. These contacts have to be carefully and properly structured so as to enable the federation to continue to operate appropriately within the laws and regulations governing it as a nonprofit. Having made that clear, these contacts represent important opportunities to build political relationships that will have great value at a later date.

The Washington Action Office of the United Jewish Communities

Established in 1975 by the Council of Jewish Federations, the Washington Action Office (WAO) was given a mandate to represent the domestic policy interests in social welfare and other human services, of CJF's member federations. It was also responsible for providing assistance to local federations in connection with their particular problems and interests on the federal level. In addition, it was hoped that a presence on the ground in Washington, D.C., would also greatly facilitate the acquisition of public funding for local Jewish community services. Over the years its small staff tried to meet those objectives by offering technical assistance to local communities; facilitating access to elected and appointed government officials; developing a series of handbooks on federal funding opportunities, grants and contracts; supporting energy conservation; and otherwise representing and protecting the social policy and appropriations interests of the community. Like its counterparts at the state level, the Washington office is often most effective when it works as part of a coalition of like-minded organizations.

Up until the early 1990s, when there was a change in leadership of the Washington Action Office and a dramatic expansion of its staff and its agenda, there was never more than a maximum of three full-time professionals on the staff. As a consequence, it is both remarkable and exemplary that, despite grossly inadequate resources, a number of major accomplishments took place during the decades before 1990:

- The WAO aggressively lobbied the U.S. Department of Housing and Urban Development to issue a ruling that the Jewish community's policy of requiring all residents of government supported housing operated by Jewish community agencies to eat only the kosher food that was served was appropriate. Not only did this ruling prevent all Jewish community housing for the elderly from becoming subject to legal challenges of discrimination, but it also permitted continuation of service to Jewish elderly in an environment that reflected their religious and cultural needs.

- In 1978, the WAO created the federal Voluntary Agency Matching Grant program for refugee resettlement. That program, which is now also used extensively by the Catholic, Episcopalian, and other communities to resettle refugees, was developed in the 1970s to meet the Jewish community's need for massive government support to help resettle the wave of Jewish refugees from the former Soviet Union (FSU). It was unique because for the first time the federal government not only provided significant new funds for domestic refugee resettlement, but it was a real partnership program in which the Jewish community and the federal government each provided an equal amount of funds up to $1,000 per person in families with employable adults. In 1999, due to the efforts of HIAS (Hebrew Immigrant Aid Society), the federal share increased significantly. The Washington office also played a major role in formulating the operating policies and regulations that governed the program. Administered by CJF (and by HIAS for the last several years), that single effort has produced an estimated $300 million in funding to the American Jewish community over the past twenty years in support of the community's domestic Jewish refugee resettlement effort. In Chicago, the program has generated more than $28.3 million in funding for the federation's Jewish refugee resettlement program since it began.

- The Washington office also played a primary role, together with other coalition partners, in securing the largest possible number of refugee admission numbers each year to meet the needs of Jews in the FSU, and worked to assure adequate appropriations levels and policies for overseas and domestic resettlement programs. As a result of the Jewish community's special interest in foreign affairs legislation and appropriations and the widespread network of relationships with elected officials and congressional staff and administration officials specializing in foreign affairs, the Washington office was often in a position to have a very important positive impact upon the outcome of the annual congressional process in this area.

- Tied closely to the annual fight for the maximum number of refugee admissions for people from the FSU is the Jackson-Vanik amendment that provided for more favorable trade relations between the United States and the then-USSR in return for guarantees of better treatment of religious minorities. The WAO played a pivotal role in the passage of that amendment. The periodic fight to maintain the amendment during the last decade, after the end of the Soviet Union, has been a major accomplishment because it formed the statutory foundation for the continuation of the refugee program from the FSU enabling Jews, Christians, Bahais, and Tartars to emigrate to the United States. The importance of the leadership of the WAO and HIAS in this endeavor, as well as the support of many other Jewish groups, cannot be underestimated.

- In 1983, the WAO convinced key members of Congress to establish the Emergency Food and Shelter Program to provide funds to local voluntary agencies to be used for food, housing the homeless, feeding the poor, paying for rent to prevent eviction, and paying for utility bills to prevent cold weather shut-offs. WAO staff designed the governing structure of the program so that it is administered nationally by the United Way of America, with a board of directors consisting of representatives of the major voluntary agencies, including Jewish federations, the Salvation Army, Lutheran Social Services, and Catholic Charities. The board members are named in the statutory language enacted by Congress, which requires that in every locality where the "FEMA" program, as it is called, operated, the local board be required to also consist of representatives of at least those voluntary entities. It was enacted with the explicit understanding that the program was to operate with a minimum of bureaucratic requirements, and speedily in order to get the money out on the street to deal with the emergencies people were facing in increasing numbers. The Federal Emergency Management Agency (FEMA) was selected as the auspice for the program because Mark Talisman, then director of the WAO, could not find any other federal agency with the word "emergency" in its name! The program has since been transferred to the U.S. Department of Housing and Urban Development (HUD), where it really does belong, but when the program was first enacted HUD was perceived by most to be a cumbersome, unresponsive, impermeable mega-bureaucracy. Much at HUD has since changed for the better. The significance of the program can be seen in terms of the additional funding it has provided to enable the Jewish community to better meet emergency food and shelter needs. In Chicago, for example, since its inception in 1983, the FEMA program has provided more than $1.6 million for expanded emergency food and shelter services provided by the Jewish federation through its agencies. Nationally, Jewish communities have benefited from having access to an estimated $12-15 million in FEMA funding since its inception.

- As one of his last acts, in December 2000, President Clinton signed into law legislation that now prevents HMOs from forcing elderly nursing home patients who require hospitalization to transfer upon their release to facilities selected by the HMO. The WAO played a major role in lobbying for the adoption of this law, which enables Jewish elderly to return to their Jewish nursing home where they can get kosher food and live in an environment that is designed to meet their cultural and religious needs.

These accomplishments make two things quite clear. First, there is no question about the wisdom of maintaining a presence in Washington. Second, from a financial perspective, the achievement of only a single one of the victories cited above more than justifies the financial expenditures in this area.

The United Jewish Communities' Washington Action Office has been very instrumental and helpful to the Jewish community in many crucial areas, but in recent years there is clearly one achievement that stands out. When the Congress enacted, and the president signed into law, the Personal Responsibility and Work Opportunity Reconciliation Act of 1996, the welfare reform statute included draconian provisions barring access to essential public benefits and services previously provided to all refugees and other immigrants legally residing in the United States. Eligibility for those benefits was eliminated. The bar included access to federal food stamps, SSI (cash assistance for the elderly and disabled), and other federal means-tested programs (defined to include TANF and Medicaid) for a five-year period after arrival. The new law also required nonprofit agencies to verify the immigration status of applicants for public services and benefits. Given the political environment in Congress and the fact that the White House supported the decision, few thought that there was any likelihood of revising that decision, despite the fact that within a short period of time there was widespread recognition across the United States that these provisions would produce great harm to many thousands of people.

A large coalition was formed in Washington that stretched across the country. Diana Aviv, director of the UJC's Washington office, took on major leadership responsibilities in that endeavor. To summarize in a few words the months of complex and artful work that she and others in the Jewish community did, does an injustice to the magnitude of the achievement. Had the law not been amended, it would have harmed the Jewish community and the tens of thousands of refugees and immigrants it has helped resettle during the past decade. In Chicago alone, it was estimated that the cost to the Jewish community to care for those who would be affected by the bar would have run into several millions of dollars annually, and those funds would have provided only a bare, minimum level of support. Had the Chicago Jewish community had to pay for the total cost of only essential services, such as housing, health care and food, it would have posed an impossible burden requiring radical restructuring of how the community's total resources are allocated.

Two years after its enactment, the administration and Congress restored SSI eligibility to qualified immigrants who were in the United States as of August 22, 1996; restored food stamp eligibility to elderly and disabled immigrants and to all legal immigrants younger than eighteen who were in the United States when the law was adopted; and after many months of debate, finally issued regulations defining "federally means-tested public benefits" very narrowly to include only the Temporary Assistance Program for Needy Families (TANF), Medicaid, SSI, food stamps, and the Child Health Insurance Program. Thus defined, only legal immigrants who arrived after the enactment date of the welfare reform bill are barred from eligibility for these services until citizenship is achieved, or for a minimum of five to six years. Nonprofits were exempted from the requirement of certifying the immigration status of public benefit program applicants. The period of time that refugees are eligible for SSI was expanded, as was the definition of "qualified aliens," and access was reinstated to a number of public benefit programs aimed at children (i.e., Head Start and the Maternal and Child Health Care program).[32]

In the late 1990s, when the Council of Jewish Federations, the United Israel Appeal, and the United Jewish Appeal merged to become the United Jewish Communities, the role of the Washington office was reconsidered. Under the new entity, the Washington office has been given greater responsibility for managing the Human Services and Social Policy (HSSP) interests of the organized Jewish community. Specifically, it is now responsible for coordinating planning and research for human service delivery, public policy and legislative activity, public affairs and community services and outreach, managing the annual resolutions process, planning Washington missions for leadership and others, and dealing with national agency relations. Operationally, planning for human services and lobbying have now been connected structurally.

The expansion of the Washington office staff in the 1990s enabled the Jewish community to engage in a much wider array of issues than had previously been possible. In addition to broadening the social welfare policy agenda, the additional capacity and the vision of the new leadership of the office resulted in several other important developments. Major investments were made in building a communications network with local federation communities: The flow of information on federal programs, policies, and issues was dramatically increased; a series of working groups and task forces on issues was created; and, perhaps most important, the WAO became the home for and the facilitator of regular contact between all the state lobbying office professionals. Included in that network are also a number of Jewish Community Relations Council professionals who have responsibility for advocacy efforts in their states. The annual Government Affairs Institute at the November 2000 General Assembly of the United Jewish Communities in Chicago attracted more than eighty participants, the largest number ever, and included a growing number of volunteer leaders.

The WAO convened a daylong consultation in December 2000 of thirty representatives from across the United States to identify the key issues that would shape the national legislative and policy agenda for the coming year. Prominent experts in health, tax policies affecting the nonprofit sector, and human services program and budget issues briefed the group. Among the issues under consideration for continuing or new attention are:

- Services for the elderly
- Social Security reform
- The Older Americans Act
- Nonprofit tax policy
- Attempts to limit lobbying by tax-exempt nonprofits
- Health care concerns
- Transportation for the disabled and elderly
- Title XX Social Services Block Grant
- Workforce issues
- Emergency food and shelter programs
- Support for caregivers
- Immigration and refugee policy
- Attacks on the tax-exempt status of nonprofit
- Low- and moderate-income housing
- Expansion of mental health services
- Mental health insurance coverage parity
- Charitable choice
- Domestic violence
- Low income energy assistance

The Agenda in 2001 and Beyond

As the new Congress and administration in Washington begin their first year, what will the social policy agenda look like? Perhaps the most far-reaching and little understood issue is "Charitable Choice." Under this program, the federal government would turn to religious institutions to make them providers of a major amount of the social welfare services needed by the poor. This is an issue of serious concern to the American Jewish community. Enacted in 1996 as part of federal welfare reform, it authorizes funding of social welfare services and programs through churches and synagogues. The election of George W. Bush as president assured this issue a central position on the federal social welfare agenda. As a strong believer in the idea, President Bush met with religious leaders immediately following his election to discuss implementing this initiative. Describing the way the Republican right supported Mr. Bush, *The Economist* had this to say:

> [T]he right's support of Mr. Bush has been based largely on conservatives' desire to throw Bill Clinton out of office as quickly as possible, and on their calculation that the best way to achieve that was to shut up. It is not based on any affinity with the president-elect, as it was with Mr. Reagan. With their aim achieved, the right's silence cannot be guaranteed. Already, one of its leaders, Tom DeLay, the majority whip in the House of Representatives, has claimed that Republican control of the presidency, the House and the Senate is the opportunity the party has been awaiting for decades to push through a truly conservative agenda.[33]

While this analysis suggests that President Bush's style is likely to provide a balance against the more extreme views of Representative Tom DeLay and others in his wing of the Republican Party, there can also be no doubt that the battle to once again dramatically change and diminish the scope of federal support for human services has begun.

"Charitable Choice" has been among the issues on the Jewish community's federal lobbying agenda, but prior to the presidential elections there was no action taken by the federal government to implement the program. Since January 2001, it has become a major priority for the Jewish community. The Jewish community's multiple messages in dealing with this issue reflect the complexity of the community's views about this issue. On the one hand, the provision of public funds to religious institutions is felt to be a direct threat to "the most fundamental understandings of church and state separation," according to Marc Stern of the American Jewish Congress. Coincidentally, he cites a disturbing example of an evangelical church consortium in Texas that uses the Bible as the text to provide job training for welfare recipients.

On the other hand, however, Marshall Breger makes the case that "Charitable Choice" is simply an extension of the current, widespread practice of the federal government contracting with secular and faith-based social service agencies. Breger points out that faith-based groups like the Catholic Charities and the Jewish community have been required to deny their sectarian character and create separate nonprofit entities to secure federal funds. "Charitable Choice," he maintains, will now give us a front door through which our community will be able to act on our precepts of *hesed, gemilut hasadim*, and *tikkun olam* directly through our religious institutions.[34] This "separation" has been the means to guarantee service recipients in these publicly funded programs that religious views would not be imposed upon them, and has also prevented the use of religious identity criteria from being used for both the employment of social service personnel, as well as the selection of clients to be served. The Bush administration is clearly aiming to create greater direct access to public funds for religious institutions. Many fear that funding religious institutions will lead to widespread employment discrimination in publicly funded programs, and the imposition of religious practices upon service recipients. The major, mainstream, faith-based, social service providers have scrupulously protected the rights of the individuals they serve and those they employ. Unfortunately, there have already been a number of documented examples where "Charitable Choice"-funded programs have both seriously violated client's rights and used public funds for explicitly religious purposes.

Marvin Olasky, who was born Jewish, is now a born-again Christian, conservative Republican, and was a major inner-circle member and adviser to George W. Bush during the presidential campaign. He has been credited with being the godfather of "compassionate conservatism," and is seen by some as a harbinger of the changing political identity among a segment of Jewish Americans. Among some centrist, politically moderate Jews, and among many in the right wing of the Orthodox Jewish community, his views are warmly received. His impact has been characterized by Bill Kristol, editor of *The Weekly Standard*, as having affected the conservative movement as if it had been hit by a thunderbolt. Olasky is a vocal, aggressive proponent of the move to place major responsibility for providing assistance to the needy in our country on faith-based and other private charities. He is reported to have "compared what some Republicans did to the poor to pulling the knife out of a person who had been mugged and then leaving him on the street to bleed. 'You can't just say, you're fine—get up,' he says. 'You have to spend a lot of time patching the guy up.'"[35] During the presidential campaign, George W. Bush proposed making available $8 billion in grants and tax credits to faith-based charities, churches, mosques, and synagogues that work with the poor, but many worry about the potential for inappropriate inclusion of denominational biases and religious practice into social services supported by the federal government. This, of course, is and ought to be of major concern to the American Jewish community.

As noted earlier, evidence has already surfaced that clearly indicates that the notion of "Charitable Choice" contains within it substantial threats to the separation of church and state, and thereby, to American democracy. Since the Bush administration formally introduced its proposals for "Charitable Choice," Marvin Olasky and Rev. Pat Robertson have become the most outspoken voices in the Christian conservative community expressing strong opposition to the plan. They are concerned that acceptance of government funds and the concomitant requirements and regulations imposed by government upon religious institutions will endanger their religious mission and functions.

There is, as well, the real possibility that those efforts will be used as an excuse to further reduce the amount of government resources available to aid the poor.[36] In the context of the more than $900 billion now spent annually by the voluntary sector, and the hundreds of billions allocated for human services by the federal government, $8 billion has been rightly called a paltry sum!

America's Second Harvest, the food bank umbrella organization, distributes $2.4 billion in donated food annually, and this sum does not include the value of the food generated locally by regional food banks and pantries. Compare the new administration's proposal to the fact that in fiscal year 2001, the federal food stamp program provided only $18 billion in aid to those who were eligible, a reduction of $7 billion from the $25 billion in food stamps distributed five years ago.[37] The danger is, however, that the inadequacy of the proposed level of support may only provide evidence to suggest that much greater sums should or might be diverted from other federal programs to adequately support this newly invigorated program.

There are also serious questions about the reality of the proposal. As one observer noted, "Churchgoers have day jobs. They can't do the government's work." In fact, "far from being untested, many of these troops of the faithful are already fully engaged. They have said yes to teaching Sunday school, buying bagels for the hospitality hour, and serving on the committee for a new roof. They are leading the men's prayer circle, chauffeuring the youth group on weekly field trips, singing in the choir, and coordinating the blood drive. And they have jobs, families, and secular volunteer obligations to boot. To suppose that they can also complete the task of feeding and housing the nation's poor appears, at best, unrealistic."[38] While the Clinton administration and the Jewish community's social welfare interests were sometimes severely at odds, there can be no misunderstanding that the American Jewish community needs to develop new strategies and tactics to address an entirely new political landscape. Many of the Jewish community's priorities are not likely to find support in the Bush administration in the way they did during the Clinton years.

Who/What Does the Jewish Social Welfare Lobby Represent?

Consider this: Jewish community leaders have decided to dedicate resources for lobbying in some forty-five Jewish communities, including all the states where all the large metropolitan cities are located and, therefore, the states where the overwhelming majority of the Jewish community can be found. The decision to lobby on domestic social policy issues represents a subset of the interests of the community and it is likely that the volunteer and professional leaders supporting that sector of communal activity is smaller than the body that is interested in Israel, church-state, or domestic Jewish security issues. So the question may properly be asked, from where does the political mandate of the Jewish social welfare lobby originate? One ought not assume that the political mandate of the organized Jewish community's lobbyists derives only from the interests of the federations. In fact, leaders of those institutions are very sensitive to the political pulse of the Jewish community. Experience and even some research has shown that although community leaders are often more liberal in their attitudes than their constituents, they rarely lead their organizations in a direction that is in opposition to a position held by a majority of community members.

A number of surveys show that between one-third and one-half of American Jewish adults of voting age identify their political position as centrist. How this translates into political behavior, however, is not so simple to discern. Murray Friedman, long a proponent of what he perceives as the move to the center and right of American Jewry, described some of the findings of the 1999 American Jewish Committee (AJC) annual survey this way: "As successive studies undertaken for the (AJC) have shown most Jews are pro-abortion and pro-gay rights, and most oppose government aid to parochial schools. But as these same surveys suggest, there are countervailing tendencies at work as well."[39] Friedman goes on to cite what he perceives to be dramatic shifts in American Jewish attitudes as reflected in the AJC 1999 attitudinal survey, including a lessening of support for special efforts for women, blacks, or disadvantaged groups; and little difference between Jews and other whites in attitudes about welfare and other government programs felt to be detrimental to people. He also said that while "approximately half now categorize themselves as either Republicans, independents, or unsure, suggesting that even the seemingly unshakable Jewish vote may be up for grabs," Jews continue to "heavily" vote for Democrats.[40]

In fact the appropriate description of the voting behavior of Jewish Americans should be that they continue to "overwhelmingly" vote for Democrats. The AJC survey data for the years 1997 (when the question was first asked) through 1999 clearly show that no more than 16 percent ever identified themselves as Republican, no less than 52 percent say they are Democrats, and no less than 30 percent say they are Independents.[41] Therefore, while it is certainly appropriate to note that some long-term changes in the political ideology of important segments of Jewish Americans are taking place, Friedman paints a more conservative picture of Jewish Americans than the AJC annual survey data and other surveys actually portray.

Most conclusively, perhaps, presidential election exit poll data reported by the Jewish Telegraphic Agency and the National Jewish Democratic Council show that 79 percent to 80 percent of Jewish Americans voted for Gore in the 2000 presidential election.[42] Of the approximately 30 percent of Jewish voters who call themselves Independents, only 1 percent voted for Nader, and only 19 percent voted for Bush.[43]

To obtain a clearer picture of the constituency represented by the Jewish social welfare lobby, let us examine some recent data from a number of surveys about the attitudes of various groups within the Jewish community, including leadership groups. The findings provide some interesting insights into the support behind communal lobbying behavior.

In a study conducted by Steven Cohen and Gerald Bubis that analyzed the attitudes of Jewish American leaders toward communal allocations, respondents ranked support for Jewish social and human services highest in importance, compared to both Jewish education and Israel and other overseas needs. When asked how difficult they felt it would be to replace funds in each of the three areas, respondents ranked social and human services as most vulnerable among the three areas.[44]

A national survey of 6,800 randomly selected Jewish federation donors in fourteen communities and more than 600 Jewish Community Relations Council leaders in twelve communities asked respondents to self-identify their political orientation. Thirty-three percent identified themselves as liberal, 54 percent as moderate, and 13 percent as conservative.[45]

Since 1997 the annual survey of Jewish Americans conducted by the American Jewish Committee asked respondents to identify their political affiliation. Some 52-54 percent reported they were Democrats, 29-35 percent Independents, and 12-15 percent Republicans. In 1999, survey participants reported that only 12 percent were Republicans, 52 percent identified themselves as Democrats, and 12 percent as Independents.[46]

An analysis of data from the 1990 National Jewish Population Study (NJPS) by Alan Fisher found that 12 percent of the respondents identify themselves as very liberal, 37 percent as liberal, 32 percent as middle of the road, 12 percent as conservative, and only 1 percent as very conservative. When examining the data on those who self-identified as liberal by denomination, the picture is even more interesting: 23 percent of observant Orthodox consider themselves liberal, as do 37 percent of the non-observant Orthodox, 35 percent of the Conservative and Reconstructionist (another 7 percent are very liberal), 44 percent of the Reform (another 8 percent are very liberal), and among the secular/just Jewish 27 percent are liberal and 43 percent are very liberal. The data also suggest that it is probable over the long term that further assimilation into American society, continuing intermarriage, and affluence will decrease the extent of liberalism among Jewish Americans. For the near-term, however, Jewish Americans will continue to be significantly more liberal than non-Jews.[47]

Steven Cohen conducted a survey of a national sample of 1,002 people early in 2000 as part of the Center for Jewish Community Studies project on "Jews and the American Public Square." The study compared the attitudes of Jews to non-Jews and a sample of Jewish leaders on social issues. Jews are clearly more liberal than their non-Jewish counterparts, and Jewish leaders are more liberal than Jews in general. When it comes to Jews' views about other liberal and conservative organizations, the results are predictable: Jews favor liberal groups more than non-Jews, and look upon conservative causes much less favorably than do non-Jews. Other major findings include the fact that Jews continue to strongly resist all attempts to weaken the wall of separation between church and state in public education, and the Jewish "public" in the sample feels even more strongly about this than do Jewish leaders.[48]

In another study of 1,005 Jewish respondents to a mail-back questionnaire in 1997, Steven Cohen found some countervailing information. Social justice activity, or the potential for personal involvement in such activities, had little appeal for people in the study sample. Only 45 percent said that being Jewish caused them to identify with the vulnerable or underdog, only 41 percent believe that Jews are more charitable than anyone else, and 75 percent said they felt as moved by the oppression of non-Jews as when Jews were oppressed.[49]

Bethamie Horowitz conducted focus groups, and then surveyed 1,504 American-born individuals between the ages of 22-52 residing in the New York metropolitan area for the UJA-Federation of New York in 1997. The purpose of the study was to assess the ways in which people defined their Jewish identity and engaged in Jewish activities. Fifty-five percent of the respondents (N=1,425) felt that making the world a better place was very important to the content of being Jewish, and 28 percent felt it was somewhat important. Thirty-nine percent replied that giving to charity was very important, while 37 percent said it was somewhat important to identifying one's self as Jewish.[50]

An important consequence of both the Jewish historical experience and the community's more liberal to moderate political identity is that Jews also tend to be more politically active. Despite recent increases in the numbers of Jews who are not registered and of those who are but may not vote, conservative estimates hold that about 80 percent of all adult Jews are registered to vote.[51] It is well known that as age declines, the percentage of those who are eligible to register, who in fact are registered, and who actually vote, declines. Thus, the community's disproportionately older makeup is a plus because it supports voting behavior. It is also common knowledge among those who seek elective office that the Jewish community can be counted upon to make contributions of time and money to help get those people it supports elected, and in a manner far beyond the community's proportion in the U.S. population. In one dramatic but not unusual example of this about ten days before the 2000 presidential election, in less than one week's time, a group of Jewish politically active women in Chicago organized a luncheon at a private home, arranged for Hadassah Lieberman to speak, and raised more than $120,000 in two hours for the Gore campaign. There also appears to be an increase in political activity among those aged twenty-five to thirty-five, as evidenced by the growth of political action committees in which younger cohorts of Jewish Americans are involved. Taken together, these data and the trends they reflect provide a basis for assuming continued broad political support in the Jewish community for the work of its social welfare lobbyists.

The Need for Training and Information for Effective Advocacy and Lobbying

When one considers the political interests of the Jewish community, and the financial implications of the fact that Jewish social service agencies use more than $1.2 billion annually in public funds to provide services to people, it is nothing short of astounding that the community has not developed the means to provide advocacy/lobbying skills training for its communal professionals and volunteer leaders.

It is still true that among many volunteer leaders and professionals there remains a psychological aversion to communal involvement in the political process, although it is legal, nonpartisan, and designed to serve the critical needs of the Jewish community. Earlier, we noted a continuing preference for the use of the word "advocacy" rather than the term "lobbying" among federation leadership. Undoubtedly, many communal leaders still believe, albeit incorrectly, that lobbying by Jewish federations and Jewish social service agencies is illegal. This may help to explain why a high level educational and training strategy has not been developed. Then, too, it is possible that the Jewish community has become accustomed to the notion that one just "picks up" advocacy skills, as it were, along the way. For decades federation leadership has also assumed that the same is true for the acquisition of core leadership skills needed by both volunteer leaders and professionals, so this arena likely is perceived no differently. Whatever the origins of this state of affairs, the time has come to develop a serious plan to establish a sophisticated program to equip future generations of volunteer and professional leaders with the skills required by the community.

First, it must be noted that within the boundaries established by federal law, lobbying by nonprofit organizations is perfectly legal. In 1976, the U.S. Congress enacted legislation that clearly established this right, and in 1990, the Internal Revenue Service (IRS) issued a new set of regulations that further clarified the right of public charities to participate in lobbying and to spend charitable funds in support of those efforts. In June 2000, the IRS issued a letter specifically clarifying the parameters of nonprofit lobbying, describing in easy-to-understand language the fact that lobbying by public charities is perfectly permissible under federal tax laws.[52] The emergence of the Internet as a tool of nonprofits in the lobbying and social policy development process has caught the attention of the IRS. A request from the IRS for public comments about the applicability of the current law governing tax-exempt organizations was issued in October 2000, together with a series of questions. The solicitation and collection of public comments and subsequent analysis led the IRS to issue a policy statement indicating that it has decided that the existing regulatory framework is sufficient to include this new communication medium.[53]

An excellent description of the range and types of allowable activities can be found in a guide written by Bob Smucker for the Independent Sector (IS), a well-known nonprofit advocacy organization.[54] The book also contains specific information on the skills and strategies one can employ to be an effective advocate. Nonprofits are prohibited from engaging in partisan behavior in support of candidates for elected office, and they may not distribute voting records of elected officials if such information is only circulated during election campaign periods.

Second, the resources needed to create effective, knowledge-based skills training programs are now widely available. Smucker's book, for example, also provides a thorough introduction to lobbying and the legislative process that could become the foundation for a curriculum development effort. Additionally, the IS has posted the entire book and two sets of slides describing the law and legal lobbying by nonprofits as well as a tutorial on how to lobby, on its Internet web site (www.independentsector.org). These efforts represent a significant investment, and they are part of a larger effort supported by IS which is designed to both protect and encourage lobbying by the nonprofit sector.

In 1984, Seton Hall University published a monograph by Philip Schrag and Mark Talisman (the former director of the Council of

Jewish Federations Washington Action Office for many years) documenting a simulation program developed to teach the federal legislative process.[55] Over the years techniques for achieving social change through communication strategies have become more sophisticated, especially as a result of improved social science technology and the widespread continuing growth of the Internet. Of particular relevance is the application of these new technologies in political campaigns and in the marketing of products to consumers. Applying these frameworks to the problem of improving public social policy advocacy presents an exciting opportunity, and in that regard several resources should be noted. Nearly thirty years ago Guy Benveniste published a book developed for use in graduate-level courses teaching effective management of policy development, policy analysis, and policy change in government. Included are sections on coalition building, team building, and techniques for development of effective strategies.[56]

Skills training in coalition building, a major strategy in social policy advocacy, has been honed to a fine art by Cherie Brown, whose original work was supported extensively by the American Jewish Committee's Irving Levine and the late David Roth who brilliantly led its Institute on Pluralism and Group Identity.[57] That work led to the establishment of the National Coalition Building Institute that conducts training programs throughout the United States, as well as in half a dozen countries worldwide. In 2000 the institute published a handbook for coalition activists.[58]

A useful model for developing the kinds of educational tools needed to teach and train the Jewish community in more effective lobbying can also be found in the project led by Gerald Bubis that began in 1992. It culminated with the 1997 publication by the Jerusalem Center for Public Affairs/Center for Jewish Community Studies of an extensive volume of background material, case studies, and curricula entitled, *Serving the Jewish Polity: The Application of Jewish Political Theory to Jewish Communal Practice.*[59] While that volume does not deal with the goals, issues, and problems the Jewish community seeks to resolve in its social welfare lobbying efforts, it does present a framework to which new background material, case studies, curricula, and bibliographies could easily be added. There are some very interesting texts available that are based upon the application of Jewish thought and law to social welfare issues. Topics include Jewish perspectives on the political process, Jews' responsibility for the repair of the world, and the application of Jewish thought to health care policy decisions. These materials can be used to build curricula and training experiences.[60]

Although current material from within the literature of Jewish communal service is limited, several Jewish communal professionals have written about examples of effective engagement in policy advocacy and nonprofit sector issues that are important to the community.[61] Development of a companion volume to the one by Bubis, et al. would serve the community well. If the Jewish community is going to be able to operate effectively in the social welfare lobbying sphere in the near term and over the long term, then it must generate the programs and the funds necessary to build the skills needed by volunteer and professional leaders who represent the community in halls of government. This goal cannot be achieved through a "quick fix," short-term investment, and it should begin soon.

Another short-term model that the community could adapt to begin such training is one created by the Donors Forum of Chicago. This regional association of foundations has developed a one-day seminar and handbook, *Advocacy 101: The Why, What & How of State and National Policy Advocacy.*[62] The program, which was led by leading practitioners of the art, including the state capital office director of the Jewish Federation of Metropolitan Chicago, has been offered several times to full-house audiences of social service agency leaders seeking to acquire the basic lobbying skills they do not have. The Donors Forum is now considering the creation of a more advanced, more intensive track to serve the high level of interest that is growing among Chicago area nonprofits and foundations.

Examples of new knowledge development includes the work of the Aspen Institute's Nonprofit Sector Research Fund that supported an important study by Susan Rees of the effectiveness of nonprofit advocacy efforts, including the value of the use of the Internet to achieve social policy changes. Among the many important findings reported, the study found that use of the Internet is no substitute for person-to-person contact with public officials and their staff, that making credible information about the problem available to policy makers continues to be important, and that direct advocacy is more effective than broad public education. The report also contains six case studies illustrating different effective strategies.[63] A major implication of the study is that lobbying effectiveness clearly continues to be tied to the degree to which there is a direct ability to influence decision makers in the public arena as a result of the existence of good one-on-one relationships.

A very useful exposition on the use of marketing in social change was written by Alan Andreasen, a marketing professor at the Georgetown University School of Business with a good deal of experience in working with nonprofits.[64] Other useful sources of information include case studies and research on human service organizational involvement in affecting the outcome of social policy regulatory proposals.[65] Training and development of future communal lobbying strategies must also take into account the radically changing environment of the nonprofit sector.[66] The mission and functions of the Jewish community's health and human services system will be affected as dramatically as the rest of the nonprofit sector, yet there still does not appear to be the kind of thinking, discourse, and strategic planning that is needed to function effectively and successfully in the twenty-first century.

Public officials and advocates often find themselves with few reliable sources of data or program evaluation and analysis that can be so useful to provide support for a policy position. Much has changed in this arena as well. Although data describing the social health of the nation are far from complete, efforts resulting from a long-standing project at Fordham University in New York to improve the availability of social indicators have now reached the point where reliable information is available annually.[67] The Center on Budget and Policy Priorities in Washington, D.C., is one of the most highly respected sources of nonpartisan analysis of federal health and human service policy and fiscal proposals in the United States. Many of their reports bear directly upon the populations served by Jewish community health and human services programs. Their analyses are routinely reported in the *Washington Post* and the *New York Times*.[68] Many other reliable sources of information also exist. Two influential research and policy centers that concentrate on problems and populations of interest to the community are the Chapin Hall Center for Children at the University of Chicago and the Urban Institute in Washington, D.C. State and federal government agencies responsible for health and human services are also excellent repositories of useful program data.

Unfortunately, the Jewish community has not invested any serious resources in recent years in the collection of data about the services provided by the organized Jewish community. Therefore, there is not a great deal of reliable data about the problems faced by the people who are served. It is possible, however, to document the experiences of clients. It is also possible to become more rigorous in efforts to document information about the numbers of people served as well as information about the effectiveness of the services provided, using well-known program evaluation methods. Alongside external data, these Jewish community data and case studies become the "human face" of the problem in order to influence policy makers. Paradoxically, years ago only sparse information was available about the extent of public funding in the system, but there was better information about how funds were spent for various types of services. Though the data were not totally reliable, at least they were collected regularly using the same basic framework for categorizing information.

The Jewish community cannot wait for the development of additional resources to begin to build a range of basic and advanced educational training programs, and to create the framework to gather the information about provided services that is required. It is only necessary to select the appropriate sponsors, develop an advisory committee of experts from within and outside the Jewish community, and then identify the auspice for such a program. One possible site could be the Nathan Perlmutter Institute for Jewish Advocacy at Brandeis University, but the scope of effort needed nationally should be reason enough to engage all the schools of Jewish communal service as well.

There already exists a cadre of Jewish elected and appointed officials and volunteer and professional leaders who are among the most sophisticated and effective lobbyists that work in the vineyards of city, state, and federal government. Among them is a core group who can become the faculty for training programs. For reasons of clear self-interest, and often because the timing could not be controlled, it was necessary to develop the capacity to get things done that the community deemed important without having the luxury of being able to plan for the future. Now, however, given the growth and importance of this sphere of activity to the community, that excuse is no longer acceptable.

Conclusion

The existence and effectiveness of the organized Jewish community's social welfare lobby are among the least known aspects of the work of the community. Few in the Jewish community understand the capacity of the Jewish social welfare lobby to achieve social policy goals on behalf of Jewish Americans. This perception gap is serious, and it needs to be addressed. J. J. Goldberg accurately portrays the significance of this community strength in his book *Jewish Power*:

> American Jewish power does not begin and end with Israel. Even more dramatic than foreign aid, perhaps, was the Jackson-Vanik amendment. Passed by Congress in 1974, it made U.S.–Soviet trade

relations conditional on the Soviets' treatment of their Jewish minority. The amendment remained on the books even after the Soviet Union collapsed in 1990, effectively giving the Jewish community a vote over America's commercial links with Moscow. Jewish power is felt, too, in a wide variety of domestic spheres: immigration and refugee policy, civil rights and affirmative action, abortion rights, church-state separation issues, and much more. Local Jewish communities from New York to Los Angeles have become major players on their own turf, helping to make the rules and call the shots on matters from health care to zoning.[69]

The Jewish social welfare lobby produces (and protects) the greatest proportion of those resources available to the Jewish community to serve the needs of the people it cares for. It is the source of much of the progressive and humane social policy work being done in human services in the local, state, and federal arenas. The Jewish social welfare lobby should be a source of pride as the Jewish community continues to carry its message of social justice to the world.

Notes

1. Arnold Eisen, *Rethinking Jewish Politics in America* (New York: Jewish Council on Public Affairs, 2000), 7.
2. Eisen, *Rethinking Jewish Politics*, 16.
3. Solomon Schechter, "Notes of Lectures on Jewish Philanthropy," *Studies in Judaism, Third Series* (Philadelphia, Pa.: Jewish Publication Society of America, 1924), 239.
4. Schechter, "Notes of Lectures," 239-40.
5. Schechter, "Notes of Lecturers," 253-56.
6. *Proceedings of the First National Conference of Jewish Charities in the United States, 1900* (Cincinnati, Ohio: Robert Clarke Company, 1900), 52-69, 137-41.
7. Lester M. Salamon, *America's Nonprofit Sector—A Primer* (New York: Foundation Center, 1999), 22.
8. "IRS Reports Nonprofits Are Growing Force in Economy," *National Newsbriefs*, February 1999.
9. There is no research that I am aware of to scientifically substantiate this assertion. I believe it to be true, however, based upon my personal knowledge of most of the professionals and many of the volunteer leaders from across the United States, with whom I have had the privilege of working on public policy matters over the past nearly two and half decades.

10. Martha K. Selig, *The Challenge of Public Funds to Voluntary Agencies—Report of the Subcommittee on the Use of Public Funds* (New York: National Conference of Jewish Communal Service, 1962).
11. Robert Morris and Michael Freund, eds., *Trends and Issues in Jewish Social Welfare in the United States, 1899-1958* (Philadelphia, Pa.: Jewish Publication Society, 1966).
12. Howard Adelstein and Charles Miller, *The Jewish Community Center's Role in Dealing with Jewish Communal Problems* (New York: National Jewish Welfare Board, ca. 1971).
13. Daniel J. Elazar, *Community and Polity—The Organizational Dynamics of American Jewry* (Philadelphia, Pa.: Jewish Publication Society, 1995), 301. Based upon intermittent discussions the author had with Elazar about this subject over the years, it is clear that he was acutely aware of the developments in the massive transfer of federal funding and policy responsibility to the states, and what their eventual impact upon the Jewish community would be. Even so, it is interesting that he continued to remain silent on the issue in 1995 when the book was revised, updated, and reissued. What makes this so puzzling is that, as will be described later on, by 1988 he became very interested in the issue of Jewish federation involvement in state government affairs matters. Further, in the mid-1990s, Elazar began to organize a major conference and a survey to assess this trend.
14. Council of Jewish Federations and Welfare Funds, "Government and Voluntary Responsibility: The Changing Relationship in Meeting Welfare Needs," *Sidney Hollander Colloquium Background Papers and Proceedings* (New York: Council of Jewish Federations and Welfare Funds, 1977).
15. Graenum Berger, ed., *The Turbulent Decades—Jewish Communal Services in America, 1958-1978* (New York: Conference of Jewish Communal Service, 1981).
16. Berger, *The Turbulent Decades,* 77.
17. Alan H. Gill, *An Index of Community Organization Articles Published 1924-1980* (New York: Council of Jewish Federations, May 1981).
18. Lawrence I. Sternberg, Gary A. Tobin, and Sylvia Barack Fishman, *Changing Jewish Life—Service Delivery and Planning in the 1990's* (Westport, Conn.: Greenwood Press, 1991).
19. Norman Linzer, David J. Schnall, and Jerome A. Chanes, *A Portrait of the American Jewish Community* (Westport, Conn.: Praeger, 1998).
20. Donald Feldstein, "The Jewish Federation: The First Hundred Years," in Linzer, *A Portrait of the American Jewish Community,* 65.
21. There is an effort presently underway at the new United Jewish Communities to more clearly document both the sources of revenue of member federations and their agencies, as well as the uses of those funds. Using information from the annual certified audits of federations and their agencies should, over time, produce a reliable annual picture of the role of

government funds and their relationship to other sources of income, such as federation allocations, agency fund-raising, and service user fees.

22. Martha K. Selig, "Implications of the Use of Public Funds in Jewish Communal Services," Graenum Berger, ed., *The Turbulent Decades*, 1274-88. The information was obtained from the annual survey of social services and funding conducted by the then Council of Jewish Federations and Welfare Funds.

23. Alvin Chenkin, *Government Support to Jewish Sponsored Agencies in Six Major Fields of Service, 1962-1973*, Background Paper Prepared for the Sidney Hollander Colloquium, April 24-25, 1976 (New York: Council of Jewish Federations and Welfare Funds, 1976).

24. *Government Funding for Human Services in the Jewish Community* (New York: Council of Jewish Federations, October 1995), 5-8.

25. Virginia Hodgkinson, *The Impact of Federal Budget Proposals upon the Activities of Charitable Organizations and the People They Serve—The 100 Nonprofit Organizations Study* (Washington, D.C.: Independent Sector, 1995), 3.

26. Daniel J. Elazar, "Strengthening the Ties between the American Jewish Community and the States," *Jerusalem Letter*, no. 364 (August 15, 1997).

27. Carl Schrag, "The American Jewish Community Turns to the States: The Springfield Office of the Jewish Federations of Illinois," *Jerusalem Letter*, no. 100 (February 21, 1988).

28. Source of UJA Campaign data: E-mail communication from Amy Goldstein, United Jewish Communities, Department of Financial Resource Development, November 28, 2000, and *1999 Resources of Caring* [unpublished UJC report]. Also see Jewish Telegraphic Agency, *Daily News Bulletin* (April 27, 2001), 2.

29. *1996-97 Distribution of Jewish Federation Funds* (New York: Council of Jewish Federations, May 1998).

30. The directors of the government affairs offices in the states included provided information in this table. Subsequent discussion of the activities of these state offices derives from the same sources. I am grateful to my colleagues for their willingness to respond in writing to my request for information about their efforts.

31. Daniel J. Elazar, "Strengthening the Ties," 4-8.

32. Michael Fix and Wendy Zimmerman, "The Legacies of Welfare Reform's Immigrant Restrictions," *Interpreter Releases*, 75, no. 44 (November 16, 1998), 1577-87.

33. "George Bush's Prospects: The Man Who, Finally, Will Be King," *The Economist* (December 16-22, 2000), 37.

34. Marc D. Stern, "Resist Temptation," *Hadassah Magazine* (March 2000), 12, 14; and Marshall J. Breger, "Don't Fight the Power of Faith," *Hadassah Magazine* (March 2000), 13, 15.

35. David Grann, "Where W. Got Compassion," *New York Times Magazine* (September 12, 1999), 62-65.

36. Albert R. Hunt, "Faith-Based Efforts: The Promise and Limitations," *Wall Street Journal* (August 12, 1999).
37. Nina Bernstein, "Charity Begins at the Rule Book," *New York Times* (December 24, 2000), 5.
38. Polly Morrice, "It Takes More than Faith to Save the Poor," *New York Times* (August 29, 1999), 15.
39. Murray Friedman, "Are American Jews Moving to the Right?" *Commentary* (April 2, 1999), 51.
40. Friedman, "Are American Jews Moving to the Right?"
41. Market Facts, Inc., *1999 Annual Survey of American Jewish Opinion* (New York: American Jewish Committee, 1999), 15.
42. Matthew E. Berger, "Elections 2000: The Key to the Presidency May Be Held by Florida Jews," *Jewish Telegraphic Agency* (November 9, 2000), 1.
43. "Study Sees Vote of Confidence for Clinton," *Forward* (December 15, 2000), 6.
44. Steven M. Cohen and Gerald B. Bubis, *"Post-Zionist" Philanthropists: Emerging Attitudes of American Jewish Leaders toward Communal Allocations* (Jerusalem: Jerusalem Center for Public Affairs, 1998), 7.
45. Earl Raab and Lawrence I. Sternberg, *National Jewish Community Public Affairs* (New York: Jewish Council for Public Affairs, 1998).
46. Market Facts, Inc., *1999 Annual Survey.*
47. Alan M. Fisher, "Political Liberalism and Involvement in Jewish Life," *American Jewry—Portrait and Prognosis* (West Orange, N.J.: Behrman House/Wilstein Institute of Jewish Policy Studies, 1997), 261-94.
48. Steven M. Cohen, *Attitudes of American Jews in Comparative Perspective* (Philadelphia, Pa.: Center for Jewish Community Studies, 2000), 18-41.
49. Steven M. Cohen, *Religious Stability and Ethnic Decline: Emerging Patterns of Jewish Identity in the United States* (New York: Florence H. Heller JCC Association Research Center, 1998), 29-30.
50. Bethamie Horowitz, *Connections and Journeys: Assessing Critical Opportunities for Enhancing Jewish Identity* (New York: Commission on Jewish Identity and Renewal, UJA-Federation of New York, 2000), 215.
51. Steven M. Cohen, *Patterns of Current Voter Registration among American Jews Today* (New York: Synagogue Council of America, June 1992).
52. Letter from Thomas J. Miller, manager, exempt organizations technical, Internal Revenue Service, Department of the Treasury, June 26, 2000, to Charity Lobbying in the Public Interest, a project of the Independent Sector.
53. "IRS Solicits Public Comment on EO Internet Issues," *The Nonprofit Counsel* (December 2000), 4-6.
54. Bob Smucker, *The Nonprofit Lobbying Guide,* 2nd ed. (Washington, D.C.: Independent Sector, 1999). See also Timothy Saasta, *Charity*

Lobbying: You Can Do It—Resource and Discussion Guide (Washington, D.C.: Charity Lobbying in the Public Interest/Independent Sector, 2000).

55. Philip G. Schrag, and Mark E. Talisman, "Teaching Legislative Process through an Intensive Simulation," *Seton Hall Legislative Journal*, vol. 8, no. 1 (Summer 1984).

56. Guy Benveniste, *The Politics of Expertise* (San Francisco: Boyd and Fraser, 1977).

57. Cherie R. Brown, *The Art of Coalition Building—A Guide for Community Leaders* (New York: American Jewish Committee, 1984). There are also many other excellent training manuals that have been written over the years, but one that was specially designed for nonprofits is particularly useful because it describes the process of coalition-building and advocacy in great detail. See National Assembly of National Voluntary Health and Social Welfare Organizations, *Working Together—Advocating for Change: A Manual for Voluntary Sector Organizations* (New York: National Assembly, 1982).

58. Cherie R. Brown, *Healing into Action* (Washington, D.C.: National Coalition Building Institute, 2000).

59. Gerald B. Bubis, Daniel J. Elazar, and Melvin L. Silberman, eds., *Serving the Jewish Polity: The Application of Jewish Political Theory to Jewish Communal Practice* (Philadelphia, Pa.: Jerusalem Center for Public Affairs/Center for Jewish Community Studies, 1997).

60. Jacob Neusner, *Tzedakah: Can Jewish Philanthropy Buy Jewish Survival?* (New York: Rossel Books, 1982); David Shatz, Chaim I. Waxman, and Nathan J. Diament, eds., *Tikkun Olam: Social Responsibility in Jewish Thought and Law* (Northvale, N.J.: Jason Aronson, 1997); Laurie Zoloth, *Health Care and the Ethics of Encounter: A Jewish Discussion of Social Justice* (Chapel Hill: University of North Carolina Press, 1999).

61. Anita Friedman, "The Great Welfare Debate of 1995: Ten Top Changes in Jewish Family Life and Their Social Policy Implications," *Journal of Jewish Communal Service*, 71, no. 4, (Summer 1995): 297-302; Jeffrey R. Solomon, "Beyond Jewish Communal Service: The Not-For-Profit Field at Risk," *Journal of Jewish Communal Service*, 71, no. 4 (Summer 1995): 303-08; and Sandra L. Garrett and Ellen Witman, "Policy and Politics: The Role of a Local Agency In Shaping National Public Policy," *Journal of Jewish Communal Service*, 75, no. 1 (Fall 1998): 66-75.

62. *Advocacy 101: The Why, What & How of State and National Policy Advocacy* (Chicago: Donors Forum of Chicago, 1999).

63. Susan Rees, *Effective Nonprofit Advocacy* (Nonprofit Sector Research Fund Working Paper Series) (Washington, D.C.: Aspen Institute, Autumn 1998). Also see Rees, "Strategic Choices for Nonprofit Advocates," *Nonprofit and Voluntary Sector Quarterly*, 28, no. 1 (March 1999): 65-73.

64. Alan R. Andreasen, *Marketing Social Change: Changing Behavior to Promote Health, Social Development and the Environment* (San Francisco: Jossey-Bass Publishers, 1995).

65. Richard Hoefer "Making a Difference: Human Service Interest Group Influence on Social Welfare Program Regulations," *Journal of Sociology and Social Welfare*, vol. XXVII, no. 3 (September 2000): 21-38.

66. Several excellent analyses include Wolfgang Bielfeld, "Metropolitan Nonprofit Sectors: Findings from NCCS Data," *Nonprofit and Voluntary Sector Quarterly*, vol. 29, no. 2 (June 2000): 297-314; Edward Skloot, "Evolution or Extinction: A Strategy for Nonprofits in the Marketplace," *Nonprofit and Voluntary Sector Quarterly,* vol. 29, no. 2 (June 2000): 315-24; and Pablo Eisenberg "The Nonprofit Sector in a Changing World," *Nonprofit and Voluntary Sector Quarterly*, vol. 29, no. 2 (June 2000): 325-30.

67. Marc Miringoff and Marque-Luisa Miringoff, *The Social Health of the Nation: How America is Really Doing* (New York: Oxford University Press, 1999).

68. Examples of recent reports from the Center on Budget and Policy Priorities in Washington, D.C., dealing with issues on the Jewish community's agenda include J. Horney, Isaac Shapiro, and Robert Greenstein, *How Should the Surplus be Used?* (September 2000); Isaac Shapiro, Robert Greenstein, and Wendell Primus, *An Analysis of New IRS Income Data* (September 4, 2000); L. Ku and M. Broaddus, *The Importance of Family-Based Insurance Expansions: New Research Findings About State Health Reforms* (September 5, 2000); L. Ku and S. Blaney, *Health Coverage for Legal Immigrant Children: New Census Data Highlight Importance of Restoring Medicaid and SCHIP Coverage* (October 10, 2000); *Poverty Rate Hits Lowest Level Since 1979 as Unemployment Reaches a 30-Year Low* (October 10, 2000).

69. J. J. Goldberg, *Jewish Power: Inside the American Jewish Establishment* (Reading, Mass.: Addison-Wesley, 1996), 5.

Part II

Religious Movements

5

The Conservative Movement and the Public Square

Gordon M. Freeman

Our God and God of our ancestors: We ask Your blessings for our country, for its government, for its leader and advisors, and for all who exercise just and rightful authority. Teach them insights of Your Torah, that they may administer all affairs of state fairly, that peace and security, happiness and prosperity, justice and freedom may forever abide in our midst. Creator of all flesh, bless all the inhabitants of our country with Your spirit. May citizens of all races and creeds forge a common bond in true harmony to banish all hatred and bigotry and to safeguard the ideals and free institutions which are the pride and glory of our country. May this land under Your Providence be an influence for good throughout the world, uniting all people in peace and freedom and helping them to fulfill the vision of Your prophet: "Nation shall not lift up sword against nation, neither shall they experience war any more," and let us say: Amen.[1]

This prayer, recited in every Conservative synagogue each Sabbath, reflects an ancient tradition that began with the prophet Jeremiah, who declared to his newly exiled countrymen that they must pray for the welfare of the government in which they lived.[2] This tradition was continued by the rabbis who taught that Jews must pray for the welfare of the government without which there would be dangerous chaos.[3] In fact, a prayer for the government is a feature of every type of prayer book of every land of the Jewish diaspora irrespective of the specific religious movement of the community. It is this tradition of praying for the government that epitomizes American Judaism and the public square.

At times the motivation for this prayer was that the government would not be inimical to its Jewish inhabitants. At other times it was a matter of hoping that the government would protect the Jewish community from hostile social and political forces. The primary concern of the community under such conditions was physical survival with a minimum of social, economic, and political disabilities that would prevent or harm Jewish existence.

With the creation of the nation-state in the eighteenth century, Jews living in Western democracies found themselves in a changing situation: the nation-state claimed primary public allegiance. Religion became, theoretically, a private matter. Every religious institution lost its ability to exact ultimate public authority from its adherents. Every citizen was regarded as an equal without regard to religious identity. Religion was a matter of conscience exercised in the privacy of one's own religious institution and in the home. In America, theory became practice: church and state were constitutionally separated. The Conservative movement was founded in the context of established Western democracies. It flourished in America. The above prayer functions to fulfill the ancient obligation to pray for the welfare of the government. It is not concerned with the attitude of the government toward its Jewish citizens. But it does advocate that Torah, the repository of Jewish values, be influential in the affairs of state to create a secure, just, and free society. It proclaims a vision for all citizens irrespective of religious or racial background: "forge a common bond in true harmony to banish all hatred and bigotry." Finally, this prayer envisions that America will influence the world to pursue the values of peace and freedom. The Conservative movement has an articulated policy toward issues of the public square. It seeks to integrate its understanding of Jewish values in the affairs of state so that policy decisions are influenced by those values. It seeks to accomplish this task by forging coalitions with various Jewish and non-Jewish communities. It hopes that the resulting society will go forth and influence other governments to accept the same values.

The Conservative Movement

The very nature of the Conservative movement determines its attitude toward the public square. This movement began with the establishment of the Jewish Theological Seminary of America by traditionalists who were reacting to the Reform movement. Its founders were Sephardi rabbis and traditional Ashkenazi rabbis who accepted critical academic study of Jewish texts. The Sephardim (Jews whose culture was formed in Spain) had a different attitude toward tradition than Ashkenazim (Jews whose culture was formed in Germany and spread eastward during the Middle Ages). They had experienced cultural integration in Spain before they were exiled in 1492. Their leaders served in prominent government positions, especially when Spain was dominated by Moslems. Before Christian domination, they were able to live in a fairly integrated society that was imbued by a common culture of philosophy, science, and the arts. Ashkenazi Jews did not experience the possibility of any acceptance by the dominant society until the eighteenth century. By the mid-nineteenth century, the political situation in Germany was such that many Jews left for America. At the same time, many German Jews were able to attend universities and were influenced by their academic experience, especially in terms of the critical study of traditional texts.

However, the vast majority of Ashkenazi Jews lived in Eastern Europe where they suffered severe political, social, and economic oppression and were not able to integrate into their respective societies until after World War I. They hardly ever had any university experience, living in radical social, if not physical, separation from the non-Jewish majority. Their rabbis were trained in traditional yeshivot without any critical study of Jewish texts or the influence of Western academic values.

The founders of the Jewish Theological Seminary were not inimical to the influences of Western learning and philosophy. Sabato Morais, the first president of the Seminary, was a traditionalist who felt at home in Western culture. Solomon Schechter, the second Seminary president, who was responsible for establishing the enduring institutions of the Conservative movement, was rooted in his native Romanian traditional Jewish culture while, at the same time, having served as a reader at Cambridge University in England, was fully at home in the Western scholarly tradition of critical study. They founded a seminary that required that its rabbinical students attain baccalaureate status in a university as one of the requirements of admission. While the Reform movement saw that the tradition had to change to meet the requirements of modern living and was willing to abandon what its leaders regarded as arcane rituals and liturgy, the Conservative movement began with the attitude that tradition needs to be conserved and that the tradition itself naturally evolved to meet new challenges. They sought Jewish life that integrated Jewish values with every aspect of life.

American Orthodoxy grew out of the milieu of the Eastern European Jewish experience, which had been radically separated from its non-Jewish environment. Integration was neither possible nor an ideal. Its traditional yeshiva education had not taken Western academic values or critical text study into account at all. In fact, it rejected critical study. The leaders of the Seminary did not want to create a separate movement.[4] They claimed to represent traditional Judaism in contrast to the reformers. However, they were far different from Orthodoxy, which also claimed to be traditional Judaism. While the other two movements formed and were established with specific values and attitudes, the Conservative movement attempted to accept Western standards of scholarship and critical thinking while at the same time preserving tradition. The outcome of this attempt was the creation of a movement based on a coalition of traditionalists and liberals. The central value of coalitions is consensus. In fact, as we shall see in this study, consensus-building has had both negative and positive consequences for the Conservative movement's involvement with public square issues.

Its rabbis have been socialized into secular values through their university training. While many subjects are covered in the Seminary, the primary emphasis has been on Talmud. This emphasis also has influenced rabbinic leadership in a consensus-building context while working in a coalition-type environment. Talmudic study emphasizes discussion and debate, and finding reconciliation between disparate points of view.

The typical Conservative synagogue is caught in the tension between traditionalists and innovators both attempting to maintain the sense of community where various points of view and attitudes toward tradition can be accommodated. The members of a Conservative synagogue range from traditionalists who eschew any change to liberals who welcome change. The rabbi attempts to deal with change in the context of Jewish law, feeling both the tensions of his/her own community and the requirements of the Rabbinical Assembly. The congregation feels the tension between its own local needs and the ritual and liturgical requirements of the United Synagogue of Conservative Judaism. While the range of acceptable behavior is very wide, it is still limited and largely determined by the movement's understanding of traditional obligations.

Taking a stand on any issues, especially those dealing with public policy, requires a consensus of the coalition based not only on local and regional concerns but also on the range of political, social, and religious attitudes of its membership. For example, at a Rabbinical Assembly convention in 2000[5] there was a debate on a resolution with regard to supporting a pro-choice policy on abortion on the part of the government. There was concern that this stand would be misconstrued, since the position of Jewish law, while providing for situations where abortions are allowable, does not accept the feminist view that women should have the sole right to make decisions about their pregnancies. There was concern that in supporting a pro-choice stand, the wrong message would be given to the Conservative constituency.

The Conservative movement itself will join coalitions outside of itself whenever possible and will rarely strike out on its own. For example, it has joined forces with other Jewish and non-Jewish environmental organizations. While using Jewish sources to encourage its people to be concerned with environmental issues, the movement has allied itself with others in the faith community who have a similar agenda. It continually seeks a community of support for public square issues.

In the last twenty years both the more traditional elements as well as their liberal counterparts have left Conservative Judaism to establish their own programs. For one side, change was not rapid enough, while for the other change was not acceptable. On the liberal side, there was impatience with the movement's determination that Jewish law, *halakhah*, would be the method through which any change would be evaluated. Hence, in the 1960s, the Reconstructionist movement began to train its own rabbis and coalesce as a separate movement. On the traditional side, there was concern that the movement had rejected the requirements of *halakhah* in dealing with issues that confronted it. The Union for Traditional Judaism was formed by Conservative rabbis and congregants who refused to accept women rabbis.

The partial breakdown of this loosely held coalition was clearly facilitated by pressures that sacrificed consensus to ideology. After that time the Conservative movement attempted to forge a clear ideology to respond to the constant criticism that it did not stand for anything but convenience. After tortuous negotiations within the various arms of the movement reflecting different points of view, a statement was finally produced: *Emet v'Emunah*.[6] This statement, while it failed to establish a distinctive ideology, was true to one of the basic values of Conservative Judaism, that is, consensus-building that is as inclusive as possible in order to encourage a sense of community.

This failure might be a reflection of the confusion of the American political center in attempting to find if it even has an ideology, caught between highly ideological traditional and liberal political positions. This center seems to be willing to accept ideological inconsistencies in order to emphasize values that might be the core of traditional or liberal ideologies. While the Conservative movement proclaims its commitment to Jewish tradition, at the same time, it understands that the tradition itself evolves; tradition is not static. Since its central value is community, Conservative Judaism tries to accommodate a variety of viewpoints under its own tent. Ideology is sacrificed in order to accomplish this task.

Nevertheless, Conservative Judaism is still a coalition that is concerned with consensus-building. The grounds of the coalition have shifted. Now the coalition is geographical as well as institutional. This new coalition is a major factor in the way the movement is involved with public square issues. The context of this new coalition within trends within American society at large is similar to the pull to the middle in American politics, away from the leftward trend of the Democratic Party in the 1960s and the rightward trend of the Republican Party in the 1980s and 1990s.

After the liberal and traditional wings spun off, there was a realization that, whatever the Conservative movement did or did not do, it would never be accepted by the Orthodox. This realization was a result of the growing unwillingness of Orthodoxy to cooperate in regard to Jewish identity issues and conversion as they impact on immigration policy in Israel. At the same time, the Reform movement's patrilineal stand was completely rejected by the Conservative movement. Even though from time to time there might be strategic advantages to cooperation with either group, for the most part the movement realizes that it must forge ahead on its own. Whereas there was certainly a timid approach to public square issues in the past to avoid offending either side, at present, the movement seems to have come into its own. Debate over issues is not concerned with what the traditionalists or liberals will think as much as over the concerns of the merit of the specific issue itself.

Over the decades there has been a tension building between East Coast Conservative Judaism and West Coast Conservative Judaism. While the East Coast is still dominant in terms of institutions and population, the West Coast has been slowly pulling away. First, the

University of Judaism in Los Angeles was established during the late 1940s, an institution that was regarded as a branch of the strong Jewish Theological Seminary. With the establishment of a rabbinical school as part of the University of Judaism, a complete break occurred with the Seminary, the central institution of Conservative Judaism in North America. This break is significant because it reflects a difference in attitude between the East and West coasts. East Coast Judaism tends to be wary of change and has an established leadership that has existed for generations. West Coast Judaism, like the West Coast in general, embraces innovation and change. There is very little establishment that has existed over time. Authority is easily challenged and certainly is not viewed as essentially intrinsic.

From its inception, the Jewish Theological Seminary was the premier institution that determined the destiny of the movement. The institutions of the movement were sponsored and developed by Seminary leadership who were regarded as having a strong influence over their programs and directions. That leadership had little experience with congregational life and held the values of study and scholarship for its rabbinical graduates over the concerns of the pulpit.

Probably because of the rapid growth of the United Synagogue, the congregational arm, as well as the Women's League and the Federation of Jewish Men's Clubs immediately after World War II, the Seminary's influence began to wane. No longer strong enough to control the movement, yet strong in relationship to the other institutions to become first among equals, an uneasy balance was maintained through constant testing and shifting of power back and forth.

After the creation of the rabbinical school in Los Angeles, in direct conflict with the Seminary, the only institution that had the power to maintain the coalition was the Rabbinical Assembly because of its quick action to find a way to accommodate rabbis of the new school. Previously, graduates of the Jewish Theological Seminary (as well as graduates of the Seminario Rabbinico in Argentina created by Seminary graduate Rabbi Marshal Meyer, the Beit Midrash in Jerusalem, and the Seminary in Budapest) were accepted as automatic members of the Rabbinical Assembly. Now the new rabbinical school had to negotiate with the Rabbinical Assembly so that its graduates could join its ranks and serve Conservative congregations.

These new pressures and tensions led to the need to continue with consensus-building to maintain the coalition, even though the definition of the coalition had changed. What is significant to the issue of the public square is that consensus-building is a very important political value. The challenge is that, despite differences and the struggle for power and influence that is the consequence of those differences, members of the coalition still feel a tie to each other and feel the need to maintain a sense of civility toward others in the coalition. Constant negotiation is the method of fulfilling the major value of maintaining the community.

Although the Conservative movement has continually been besieged by criticism for its middle-of-the-road attitudes, its tortuous road to any decision making, and its inability to define a clear ideology, its congregations and rabbis have been most successful in training its membership in the basic civic values that are required of public square participation: a sense of shared community that seeks to include every element possible through consensus-building, carefully using the tools of respectful negotiation to deal with change. Alexis de Tocqueville, in his *Democracy in America,* explained that it was these factors that had been fostered by religious communities that made democracy work, even though the separation between church and state was so radical. The Conservative movement is the least ideological of all the modern Jewish movements in America and has succeeded largely because of its ability to maintain its coalition through consensus-building skills. Most public square institutions in the Jewish community have drawn heavily for their professional and volunteer leadership from the ranks of Conservative Judaism, most likely because they are seen as not presenting an ideological challenge, on the one hand, and being able to maintain the communal sense of these institutions and organizations, on the other. So we come to a paradox: as we will see, while the institutions of Conservative Judaism have not developed as strong and comprehensive a public square program as its Reform and even Orthodox counterparts, they are still significant players in terms of being represented in the leadership of institutions that primarily are concerned with public policy issues.

Consensus-builders are either attracted to participation in the Conservative movement or the movement itself inherently trains people to be consensus-builders. The issues it chooses and the method it uses to develop and respond to these issues are the means by which the movement can proclaim its sense of integrity in the face of consensus-building.

The question that the critics of the Conservative movement continually pose is if it can continue to survive as a coalition, without a more distinctive persona. In response, the movement has stood for two consistent values providing it with its specific identity: a vigorous concern with community (*klal Yisrael*) and its willingness to apply Jewish law in determining new issues that arise. First, the issues chosen are not only strictly determined by their direct impact on Jewish survival. While there has been a concern regarding immigration, the safety and security of the State of Israel, and the fate of Jews living under oppressive regimes, there has been a wider interest in health care, environment and ecology, and abortion. These issues do not necessarily have a direct impact on Jewish survival; they speak to a larger concern for the public welfare.

There has been a tension within the movement regarding Israel's politics. Peace advocates coexist with those more skeptical of the possibility of achieving peace. However, recent events in Israel over the "Who is a Jew" issue, as well as support for the Conservative movement in Israel, has galvanized the various arms of the movement. Israel is viewed less and less as having a problem of survival with the peace process underway.

Because of the positive situation of Jewish populations around the world, advocacy in the public square with regard to survival issues has been less of an immediate concern. There has been a willingness to extend the teachings of Judaism as understood by the Conservative movement in policy proposal advocacy for issues facing the American public. While not among the main concerns of the movement, it has certainly weighed in, joining other coalitions when appropriate, providing material for its membership so that they can consider public square issues in terms of Jewish teachings and traditions. Below we will examine some of these public square issues, analyze the material created by the movement, and evaluate its delivery method to its constituency.

Prior to that, a description of the various institutions is appropriate. The United Synagogue for Conservative Judaism (USCJ) is an organization of affiliated congregations, organized into geographical regions.[7] The USCJ is governed by a volunteer board, but many of its professional staff, including the person holding its top position, are Conservative rabbis. The Women's League for Conservative Judaism (WLCJ) is the organization of sisterhoods existing in various Conservative congregations which may or may not be affiliated with the USCJ. It, too, is organized into regions. The Federation of Jewish Men's Clubs is the organization of men's clubs existing in Conservative congregations. Its current director is a Conservative rabbi. The Rabbinical Assembly (RA) is the organization of Conservative rabbis, most of whom are graduates of the Jewish Theological Seminary and the other rabbinical training institutions mentioned above. Rabbis who were not trained by these institutions need to apply for membership, which is not granted automatically.

Public Square Issues

The research for this chapter emanates from two sources: interviews and program material. Interviews were conducted with the following people: Rabbi Charles Simon, executive director of the Federation of Jewish Men's Clubs; Rabbi Joel Meyers, executive vice president of the Rabbinical Assembly; Rabbi Jan Kaufman, director of special projects for the Rabbinical Assembly; Rabbi Charles Feinberg, former chair of the RA Social Action Committee; Rabbi Richard Eisenberg, chair of the RA Social Action Committee; Rabbis Jack Moline, Dov Gartenberg, Lee Paskind, and Elliot Dorff, all of whom are involved in various aspects of the RA Social Action Committee; Dr. Ismar Schorsch, chancellor of the Jewish Theological Seminary; Dr. Anne Lapidus Lerner, former vice chancellor of the Jewish Theological Seminary; Professor Jack Wertheimer; Bernice Balter, executive director of the WLCJ; Renee Glazier, social action chair of the WLCJ; Sarrae Crane, project director for the United Synagogue for Conservative Judaism.

It is important to note that there is frequent formal and informal communication between the various institutions of the Conservative movement. Leaders meet at regular intervals to discuss issues of mutual concern. Information is shared at these meetings and, when appropriate, jointly sponsored programming is considered. For example, the RA sponsored a paper on poverty jointly issued with the USCJ. There seems to be very little conflict in terms of the issues chosen. In fact, agreement on public policy issues is overwhelming. However, each organization follows its own course of action, at times turning to others to seek partnership; at other times maintaining independence.

An example of how the organizations interact with each other on public policy issues is the concern that was consistently voiced by almost every person interviewed: the lack of a presence in the nation's capital, Washington, D.C. There were constant expressions of envy for the well-organized and appropriately funded Social Action Center of the Union of American Hebrew Congregations (the Reform movement). Also, the Union of Orthodox Congregations has an advocacy organization located in Washington, D.C. While there have been several instances when the Conservative movement has worked with the Social Action Center, this author was consistently told that the movement should have its own presence because of its unique understanding and method of dealing with public policy. Indeed, there has been pressure brought to bear on the RA and the

USCJ to create such a presence. In fall 2001, the USCJ opened an office in Washington, D.C., with a part-time director, but it is too soon to assess its impact on the movement.

For the decision makers, the expense for a full-time office is not justified in terms of the priorities of the movement. Social action is not at the top of the agenda for this movement, and this is definitely reflected in the budgets that are allocated for this purpose.

There was no clear answer as to how this proposed presence would operate or how it would affect the movement. The answers included: because the Reform and Orthodox movements are present, Conservative Judaism needs to have its own voice; by having a presence, it will concentrate Conservative efforts; that is, having it will ipso facto be an influence not only on the movement but on people in government involved with public policy issues.

It was suggested that the Reform movement is much more centralized than the Conservative movement in that the Union of American Hebrew Congregations takes the lead. Its rabbinic and seminary arms follow that lead. The major reason why the Reform movement has been so effective in public square issues is because its highly centralized organization is prepared for rapid response. While the respondents were aware of the contrasting organizational structures, they were jealous of organizational autonomy. Again, consensus was more important than the ideological pursuit of policy goals. It was clear that there was agreement as to the policy agenda; the question was which organization would the others allow to take the lead. While the interviewee expressed a respect for the work of the other organizations in terms of their public policy agenda, they voiced a commitment to the autonomy of each organization.

Because interorganizational coordination takes time and effort, a rapid-response ability in the fast-moving world of public policy is not possible for Conservative Judaism. So while there is a consensus on policy, organizational concerns prevent it from creating the type of structure that would make it more effective in this area. Also, it would seem by examining the organizational structure of each branch of the movement, that social action and public policy are not at the top of the agenda and are not expressed as major concerns.

Local congregations are involved in social action programming, whether it is information about current issues or participation in programs involving poverty and homelessness, immigrant rights, environment and ecology, and the support of local institutions that deal with a whole range of social issues. However, that involvement rarely involves public policy advocacy. There seems to be indifference with regard to participation in public policy agendas. Hence, there is no pressure from the local congregational level on the national organizations of the movement to devote more resources in these areas.

With the growth of Conservative Jewish day schools and the involvement of the movement in the day school movement, there has been a softening of the stand regarding school vouchers. Previously, the vast majority of Conservative rabbis were consistently against school vouchers. However, with the growth in days schools and the fact that many Conservative rabbis are sending their children to days schools (those under the aegis of the movement and those that are not), economic pressures in the increasingly expensive costs of supporting these schools has caused a gradual erosion of the anti-school voucher agenda. This concern has also caused a gradual but noticeable shift away from a firm church/state separation policy.

Another reason for this shift is that Conservative rabbis perceive that the church/state separation battle has already been won, so that a defensive posture is no longer necessary. There is no longer a need to maintain a doctrinaire approach; there is a willingness to deal with specific issues (such as school vouchers) on a more pragmatic level. This flexible attitude is consistent with a consensus-driven movement that is willing to choose the practical over the ideological in the area of public policy.

The Women's League for Conservative Judaism has been the most active branch of the movement in terms of public policy issues, not only in terms of providing consistent, informative, and high quality information to its membership but in providing the programmatic means for its regions and local sisterhoods to become involved in this area. It has demonstrated concern over Census 2000 and received a briefing from the Department of Commerce. It has sought out the Immigration and Naturalization Service in voicing its concerns over refugee and immigrant policy. It has met with members of Congress to support campaign finance reform, gun control, abortion rights, and women's health issues, as well as voicing its concern over the protection of the environment. As a non-governmental organization it sends a representative to the United Nations to monitor its proceedings and has lobbied Congress to pay U.S. back dues. The Women's League has taken stands in support of environmental issues and has been particularly involved with women's health, cosponsoring a conference on the subject at New York University, as well as advocating and supporting research.

As a national organization it solicits resolutions on various issues that are considered at its annual convention. Member sisterhoods are informed of the resolutions and have the opportunity to react to them. The Women's League has formed coalitions with the Jewish Council for Public Affairs, the World Jewish Congress, and participates in the national Conference of Presidents of Jewish Organizations as well as the Coalition on the Environment and Jewish Life (COEJL). Every other year it sponsors a conference in Washington, D.C., to give its membership the opportunity to participate in information and advocacy among policy makers and members of Congress. Its goal in its own work, as well as in its participation in various Jewish and non-Jewish coalitions, is to insure a Jewish tone in all public policy pursuits.

The Women's League sends out regular mailings to its membership devoted to social action issues. These mailings go to sisterhood presidents as well as branch (regional) officers. These mailings not only contain specific positions on various public policy issues but suggestions for the local sisterhood to pursue in terms of lobbying for legislation concerning resolutions that the Women's League has passed at its conventions.

Leadership of the Women's League has been self-critical in terms of its social action agenda. It feels that it is not as effective as the Reform movement, especially with its lack of a presence in Washington, D.C. It is prepared only to react to issues rather than to take a proactive position. At the same time, the leadership was concerned about maintaining its autonomy among the various Conservative organizations and was not willing to give up any power for a more centralized system. Also, most of the policy formation is accomplished on a national level. Where the local sisterhoods have been involved with community service programs, they have not been engaged, for the most part, in public policy.

In the last decade the Women's League has taken strong policy advocacy positions through its resolutions process, supporting comprehensive national health insurance (1990). It has taken a firm stand on gun control, with a 1976 resolution calling for the registration and licensing of all privately owned guns and the prohibition of the manufacture and importing of Saturday night specials. In 1988 it passed a resolution on refugee policy, calling for the enforcement of the antidiscrimination provisions of the Immigration Reform and Control Act of 1986, a policy of family reunification, and the swift and humane absorption and acculturation of new immigrants. In 1996 it called for a renewed commitment on the part of the United States to the United Nations and opposed what it viewed as an increasing tendency toward isolationism. This resolution called for sisterhoods to inform their membership of the importance of the United Nations as well as advising the membership to lobby members of Congress to support a strong United Nations and payment of the "debt which the United States legally owes."

Over the last decade, resolutions have covered the following public square issues:

Support for quality public education;
National urban policy to support public health, safety, day care centers, mass transportation, housing, recreation, and sanitation;
Ethics in government;
Support for the Refugee Act of 1980;
Prosecution of Nazi war criminals;
Maintaining church/state separation;
Social Security fiscal reliability;
Efforts to encourage voter registration;
Protecting women's right to a safe abortion;
Against congressional attempts to limit the jurisdiction of federal courts that would touch on limiting constitutional guarantees of individual and religious rights;
Equality for senior citizens;
Equal rights for women with regard to political, social, and economic concerns;
Protection for women from sexual harassment, violence, and wife abuse;
Support for nuclear arms control;
Disarmament as discussed in the United Nations;
Support for legislation with proper enforcement authority with regard to child abuse;
Against a proposed Constitutional Convention in 1984;
Against measures to deregulate broadcast media so as to guarantee the public's right to programs on issues of public importance; in support of the fairness doctrine providing equal opportunity for candidates for political office, and fairness in broadcasting to combat religious, racial, and ethnic discrimination;
Support measures against driving under the influence of drugs or alcohol;
Support for the homeless;
Condemnation of terrorism and support for international measures to combat it;
Against policies of apartheid;
Educational, communal, and legislative support for care givers;
Support for programs to feed the hungry;
Political campaign financing reform;
Opposition to any display of religious symbols on public property;
Support for people with AIDS including public funds for health measures to combat it;
Against censorship in schools and public libraries;

Support for governmental measures to support child care and the provision of child care for employees of private companies;
Support of government spending on social services and concern for cuts in social service budgets;
Support for legislation that provides health care for the elderly;
Concern for appropriate appointments to the federal court system;
Support for comprehensive national health care in the form of national health insurance;
Support for emerging democracies in Eastern Europe;
Support for national and international efforts to protect the global environment;
Support for national and international efforts to protect children against economic exploitation;
Support for women's health including support for research in various areas of women's health;
Support of gun control legislation, especially the Brady Act;
Concern for the maintenance of biodiversity;
Raising the quality of public discourse including programs to encourage "the teaching of Jewish values which stress mutual respect, civility, and the rejection of careless and profane speech";
Support for the reparation of Jewish property lost during World War II;
Support for continuation of foreign aid, promotion of global human rights; political and economic support for the world's democracies; help to economically develop poor nations;
Form a coalition with others concerned about genetic testing safety, provide genetic counseling, support medical research and funding and promote legislation that prevents discrimination based on genetic information;
Support of an International Criminal Court;
Protection of intellectual property;
Opposition to school vouchers (again in 1998).[8]

This list is comprehensive and does not include the Women's League measures in support of the State of Israel. Women's health care issues are emphasized. The Women's League has taken a clear pro-choice attitude toward abortion. The national office makes an effort to inform its branches and local sisterhoods about these efforts so that they will be implemented on a local level, whether through signing petitions or writing letters to legislators or educating its members about these various public policy issues. At times the resolutions are framed in terms of Jewish values and traditions, but they always emphasize the reason for the Women's League's interest in the specific issue.

As an academic institution, the Jewish Theological Seminary deals with public square issues through public forums, lectures, and colloquia for education and information. At times these forums are cosponsored by other institutions that share the same concerns. These forums always emphasize how the Jewish tradition is applicable and how Jewish law and values are fulfilled through a specific policy. Health care reform, the environment, and biomedical ethics have been the main concerns of the Seminary. Its goal is to not only provide for an exchange of ideas over policy proposals but also to apply the obligations derived from Jewish traditional sources. Future rabbis and teachers being trained by the Seminary are regarded as gate-keepers. Programs that deal with public policy will effect them as they go on to teach and lead local communities.

The Seminary has also utilized its annual High Holiday Message, which is printed in major newspapers throughout the United States during the time of the High Holidays, to apply Jewish teachings to various public square issues. In this way the Conservative movement can speak to the general community. Each year it sends a copy of this full-page message to rabbis and congregations, asking them to have the message placed in local newspapers. The point of this practice is to demonstrate that Jewish tradition can be successfully applied to the issues of the day. Ancient Jewish wisdom is relevant in dealing with ethical and moral issues. The Seminary's activist position is an assertion of moral leadership. Through these messages it proclaims that it wants to be in the forefront of the major issues of the day. This concern is not new to the Seminary. Under the leadership of Louis Finkelstein, the Conference on Science, Philosophy and Religion was established which featured a gathering of scholars in various disciplines to discuss contemporary issues. Today, the Seminary's Finkelstein Institute functions in a similar manner, placing Jewish thought in the center of modern issues.

Whenever possible, the Seminary finds partners within the Jewish world and outside of it in dealing with various issues. The Seminary is an active participant, for example, in the National Religious Partnership for the Environment, which is a coalition of Catholic, mainline Protestant, Evangelical, and Jewish groups. It is also a member of the COEJL, a Jewish coalition supporting measures and education to protect the environment.

The Rabbinical Assembly is the international organization of Conservative rabbis, most of whom are graduates of one of the five seminaries where they have been socialized into the Conservative movement and its institutions. This organization's involvement in public square issues centers on several programs: its annual Advocacy Day in Washington, D.C.; and its Social Action Committee, which not only informs the membership with regard to current issues but also formulates and publishes policy statements for the RA and resolutions discussed, debated, and passed at the annual convention.

The Social Action Committee began to plan and implement an annual Advocacy Day in Washington, D.C., for the purpose of inviting interested members of the RA to meet with legislators and policy people to exchange ideas and concerns. Some thirty to forty rabbis come as a group to deal with issues that have been a concern of the movement. The issues are determined by a perception of the consensus of the movement as well as through the resolutions that had been passed during annual conventions.

These issues include poverty, immigration, school violence and gun control, health care, and the environment. The concept of Advocacy Day is to inform legislators and policy people about what the Jewish tradition teaches about these issues and to speak to them from that tradition. The result has been a deeper appreciation on the part of the legislators and policy people of the Jewish tradition and the values that inform it. This interchange also provides a means for policy people and legislators to gain a different perspective of their work. The ancient Jewish tradition has dealt with these issues and understands that ethical and moral conflicts are usually the consequence of a clash of values. Jewish law (*halakhah*) grapples with the issues and determines which value prevails in any given situation. That method of dealing with public square issues is very compelling because it is not based on whim or fad or even popular will but on values rooted in wisdom. The people interviewed for this chapter constantly reiterated that Advocacy Day has succeeded in gaining the respectful ear of policy makers and legislators because the participants spoke from Jewish sources, which gave them a unique sense of authenticity.[9]

At the Centennial Convention in Philadelphia (March 2000), various resolutions that were proposed and debated exemplify the integration of Jewish sources applicable to contemporary issues. On a "Resolution on Proposed Congressional Tax Cuts," the introductory statement includes quotations from the Torah and rabbinic sources regarding communal responsibility in providing for the poor. The same is true on the "Resolution on the Comprehensive Test Ban Treaty." The concern expressed in the resolution on "Prayer at Public School Sporting Events" does not appeal to Jewish sources but supports the separation of church and state.

Whenever possible, the RA joins forces with other like-minded organizations in various coalitions which share its point of view. In the past it has included itself in the Religious Coalition for Reproductive Choice, coalitions helping to support disaster relief, and the Jewish environmental group COEJL. The Social Action Committee has represented the RA in a number of coalition-based organizations and has, as one of its goals, to supply the resources for the local rabbi to work within his or her community. The congregational rabbi is often swamped with conflicting concerns within the community and looks to the national organization for guidance with regard to policy and program. Also, the Social Action Committee has produced a series of pamphlets on various public square issues that are based on Jewish sources.[10] The local rabbi thus has available the sources of the tradition dealing with such issues as health care and poverty and can present a position to the congregation that is authentically based. When the rabbi goes out into the community to work with colleagues of other faiths, he or she can speak from Jewish sources on these issues.

The Social Action Committee sees itself as the lobbyists for the RA, providing education on public square issues for rabbis and volunteer leaders that is based on authentic Jewish sources, and a means to present the message of Judaism to the world at large; that is, to proclaim the commitment of Conservative Judaism to *tikkun olam*, repairing the world.

For the people interviewed for this study, the lack of a permanent presence in Washington, D.C., was a source of constant frustration. It was felt that without such a presence it would be difficult for the movement to have a focus for its concern with public square issues. There was a sense of mission expressed to influence national policy and to mobilize not only the Conservative movement but the nation to implement policies that reflect Jewish public values. Jewish tradition obligates its people to deal with the community and to enhance its quality. The Conservative movement needs to fulfill the mandate of the Jewish tradition to be engaged in communal issues and the public marketplace of ideas.

The list of concerns covered by annual resolutions at RA conventions is very similar to that of the Women's League and the United Synagogue for Conservative Judaism. For example, at the 2000 convention of the RA,[11] there was a resolution against the "Unborn Victims of Violence Act" proposed in the U.S. Senate that would prohibit abortion of a late-term pregnancy. The argumentation of this resolution was based on Jewish legal sources that do not regard the fetus as a separate entity from the mother and, therefore, its termination is not regarded as murder. There was heated debate over this resolution. Traditionalists were concerned that the RA would adopt a feminist, pro-abortion perspective, and stated that abortion is acceptable only when the life of the mother is at stake. The resolution finally passed when it came before the Administrative Committee, since there was not enough time for discussion during the convention. Its final passage was amended to remove a clause that supported a "woman's right to choose."

Another resolution that passed concerned proposed congressional tax cuts and, based on Jewish texts that mandate support of the poor, "supports all efforts to give priority to vital human needs programs, such as those which promote housing, health and education in assessing federal, state and local budget priorities."[12] This resolution opposed proposed tax cuts that would benefit "the wealthiest segments of our society."[13] This resolution was passed with little debate. Resolutions regarding support of a Comprehensive Test Ban Treaty[14] and against Prayer at Public School Sporting Events[15] were passed by the Rabbinical Assembly Executive Council, since there was not enough time at the convention to deal with them.

While some of these resolutions might not have had a direct connection with Jewish concerns, the Rabbinical Assembly as an international organization of rabbis felt compelled to be on record regarding these issues. Also, by making its will known, it would be able to join in coalition with other like-minded organizations, both Jewish and non-Jewish, thereby acquiring the ability to influence national policy.

The Rabbinical Assembly has been considering these kinds of resolutions of a public policy nature for decades, especially after World War II during the great growth of Conservative Judaism. From that time on there has been a growing awareness of the magnitude of the movement and its ability to gain the ear of public policy makers. Also, the movement was asked to join in various issue-based coalitions with other organizations since it influenced and represented a significant population.

The resolutions are discussed in the Resolutions Committee whose members represent a cross-section of the Rabbinical Assembly. There they are debated until balanced resolutions are formed. By the time they reach the convention, the resolutions, which are generated by the membership at large, have been tempered by that debate. The Resolutions Committee attempts to find consensus in writing the resolutions so that by the time they reach the convention, the policy represents the membership.

In general, comparing RA resolutions with those of the Women's League for Conservative Judaism and the United Synagogue for Conservative Judaism, there seems to be a consensus. These organizations do not take extreme views. Interestingly enough, without any consultation or formal discussion or negotiation regarding these issues between organizational bodies, there seems to be an implicit understanding of the will of the congregants. The issues that are covered by the resolutions are a good indication of the coherence of rabbis and congregants, as well as the various national organizations of Conservative Judaism.

Two public square issues that provide us a more in-depth look at the involvement of the RA are poverty and health care. The Rabbinic Letter on the Poor was prepared on behalf of the RA and later cosponsored by the USCJ. While it is a consensus-based document based on the RA-USCJ coalition, it came out of the Social Action Committee of the RA. It was written by Rabbi Elliot N. Dorff with material based on current government policies prepared by Rabbi Lee Paskind (with the assistance of Rabbi Debra Orenstein). Rabbi Paskind is also cochair of the Joint RA/USCJ Social Action Commission.

This document presents Jewish public policy with regard to poverty issues. It speaks from the sources and values of classic Jewish texts, outlining ancient Jewish programs to alleviate poverty. It then extrapolates ancient tradition to deal with contemporary issues. It advocates support of both governmental and private programs. The letter prescribes support for government/business coalitions to alleviate poverty, provide meaningful jobs, and support a communal safety net. Specific Jewish values are promoted: righteous giving (*tzedakah*), human acts of loving-kindness that reflect God's grace (*g'milut hasadim*), saving/preserving life (*pikuah nefesh*), and compassion (*rahamim*). The pamphlet includes an appendix of resolutions by branches of the Conservative movement that deal with welfare reform and related issues.

On health care issues there are two significant works: a pamphlet prepared as a resource for Rabbinical Assembly members for the High Holidays, and a publication entitled Allocation of Health Care Resources (1998). The second work is an issue of the quarterly journal published by the RA, *Conservative Judaism,* devoted to health care issues (Summer 1999). This work was published in cooperation with the *Union Seminary Quarterly Review,* which makes it another example of a coalition-based document. The articles included are written by both Jewish and Christian thinkers and academics. Members of the faculty of the Jewish Theological Seminary and the University of Judaism contributed articles. Articles by public policy advocates for health care reform are also included. What this document demonstrates is the willingness to express a clear point of view regarding the Conservative movement's concern regarding health care and to participate in a coalition to advocate for this purpose. The Allocation of Health Care Resources document presents resource material on behalf of the Rabbinical Assembly to guide its rabbis in presenting health care issues to their congregations during the High Holidays and for advocacy programming. The document demonstrates that the RA understands that there is a consensus with regard to these issues and encourages its members to bring them before their congregations.

Over the years there have been an increasing number of Conservative congregations involved with public square issues, due to the leadership of their rabbis who are advocating this agenda. Most of the involvement has been concerned with programming rather than policy advocacy. For example, congregations might be involved in various poverty programs, but they have not participated in the political groups advocating legislative solutions to alleviate poverty.

The reason for this apparent dichotomy between program and advocacy is that the synagogues themselves are coalitions. There is a fear of taking positions without a clear consensus. While synagogues might sponsor debates over the public square issues of the day, they do not feel compelled to advocate one position over another in any formal manner. Providing information so that the citizen-congregant can make his own informed decision seems to be the goal. The interviews constantly brought out contrasts with the Reform movement, which seems more disciplined in dealing with public square issues. One of the reasons that the Conservative movement is hardly ever proactive and constantly reactive is that it knows that the central institutions themselves are unable to clearly lead the way since they are all based on consensus. There is a deep fear of divisiveness that could break the fragile coalition of forces holding the movement together.

On the other hand, as noted above, the various bodies of the Conservative movement seem to be able to accurately read the attitude of its general membership. The basic concern of the entire movement is to demonstrate the relevancy of Jewish tradition and the ability to demonstrate how Jewish law and learning inform the issues of the day. The movement is attempting to state that Judaism is not only about ritual and liturgy but also instructs us about how to make choices as citizens. There is a concerted effort to insure that stances taken have integrity within Jewish sources, as seen above in the abortion debate and in the inclusion of citations from Jewish sources in preambles to various resolutions,

However, it is clear that the Conservative movement finds it safer to deal with narrow Jewish concerns, advocating for the State of Israel and protection of Jews living under oppression. The movement finds that it has a consensus to deal with continuity issues regarding the future of the Jewish people both here and abroad.

The United Synagogue for Conservative Judaism, the congregational branch of the movement, participates in a Joint Commission on Social Action with the Rabbinical Assembly. It also has its own social action program which is structured through two main methods: resolutions passed at its biennial conventions and its resolution implementation packets which present a program for each congregation to implement the resolutions on a local level. The goal of the implementation packets is to educate with regard to the issue at hand, as well as to provide a presentation of the applicable Jewish values. These packets demonstrate to the reader why the USCJ is concerned with this public policy issue; that is, it attempts to transform what would be regarded as a secular issue into one concerned with important Jewish values. Since the USCJ is not primarily a public policy agency, it does not have a full-time staff person devoted to public square issues. But as a religious agency it has strong opinions regarding how policy decisions are made, approaching the issues from a specifically Jewish perspective, which is the primary motive for entering the debate in the first place.

The USCJ has been concerned with the following issues (this list is not exhaustive): abortion/reproductive rights,[16] the environment,[17] domestic violence,[18] child welfare,[19] health care,[20] and poverty and economic justice.[21] It seeks to influence the public square issues by motivating its membership to participate in the political process and by joining coalitions with other Jewish and non-Jewish groups that share a similar outlook on the specific issues. For example, it is a member of the Religious Coalition for Reproductive Rights, which includes several liberal Christian groups as well as other Jewish groups. It participates in the Coalition on the Environment and Jewish Life (COEJL). It also participates in the Jewish Council for Public Affairs, a consortium of various Jewish religious and secular organizations concerned with public square issues.

The USCJ has joined the National Conference of Catholic Bishops in its opposition to capital punishment and pornography, as well as in support for national health care and welfare. It has joined the National Council of Churches in finding common ground to fulfill a shared goal to support the common good.[22]

The resolution implementation packets are good examples of how the USCJ tries to engage local congregations in public square issues. It sends these packets to the local congregations, but has no means to follow up or to see to it that the congregation indeed participates. Since there is little or no discipline from top down that can be exercised and because the movement is coalition-based, there is not even any strong motivation to get everyone to toe the "movement line." However, it can be said that, since the movement seeks consensus, there is probably wide agreement with regard to the issues. Whether the congregations actually are motivated to involve themselves with public policy cannot be determined.

The resolution implementation packets include several elements. First, there is a general discussion of the issue at hand and why there is a Jewish element to it. Next, a review of Jewish law and tradition regarding the issue is presented. Third, the official policy as determined by resolutions passed at the convention is then described. A review of the relevant American policy legislation is given, followed by programming ideas and a bibliography. The material succeeds in presenting the information in an easily readable form. A raging concern regarding pluralism in Israel has captured the attention of the Rabbinical Assembly and the United Synagogue of Conservative Judaism, who together have fought for this issue in both Israel and America. Reflecting an unequivocal consensus of the entire movement, and in cooperation with the Reform movement, this battle has been taken to the major policy and fund-raising organizations of American Jewry with great success. In the Jewish public square this issue has had a major impact in galvanizing the membership of both movements in unprecedented cooperation and a growing mutual respect for the achievements of each movement.

The attempt by the religious establishment in Israel to invalidate non-Orthodox movements has had tremendous consequences. First of all, the congregants of both movements understand what is at stake and enthusiastically endorse national policy. Second, pressure by local Jewish federations on national organizations has placed the pluralism issue in the forefront of concerns for the American Jewish public square. Third, there have been immediate consequences, with non-Orthodox movements receiving Jewish Agency funding in amounts not imagined in the past. Most important, the Conservative movement has had to make decisions regarding when to align itself with the Reform movement and when to stake out its own path. In that sense, the Conservative movement has been forced to define itself in a clearer manner as an *halakhic* movement (adhering to Jewish law), as distinct from the Reform movement.

None of the various branches of the movement have regarded public square issues as sufficiently important in their respective agendas to engage a full-time person to develop material and work on its implementation at the local level. Each branch has its own list of priorities. On top of the list is to expend efforts to serve the specific religious and educational needs of its membership. This agenda demonstrates an inward perspective. Public policy and social action issues primarily involve volunteer committees with some paid staff working in this area on a part-time basis.

Conclusion

Although the nature of this coalition-based movement has changed over the years from the traditional-liberal range of participants to one of organizations within the movement, the need for consensus prevails. It is not surprising that consensus-building is such a central value since Conservative Judaism is a centrist movement. Although it resists the attempt to be defined by what it is not or by Orthodoxy or Reform, it is not strongly unified by an explicitly stated ideology.

At one time the Jewish Theological Seminary of America was the central institution of the movement. It led and determined the agenda for the movement, and each branch lined up with this agenda. From the beginning, the concern about religious observance, developing appropriate materials for education and liturgy, and the training of rabbis, cantors, and teachers determined the agenda of Conservative Judaism. Public square issues have never been high on the agenda.

At the same time, it could be said that most of the leadership of various Jewish communal organizations involved with public square issues have been members of Conservative synagogues. That is also true of many of the people involved with public policy issues inside and outside of the government. We might be able to conclude that as a centrist, coalition-based movement, it attracts people who are able to succeed in consensus-building. Because these people are not ideologically threatening, they are more acceptable to the broad base of the larger Jewish community.

It can also be said that since the congregations themselves tend to seek consensus and compromise, attempting to be as inclusive as possible, they comprise a training ground for civility and political participation. The apparent paradox is that, although Conservative Judaism itself has not placed public square issues high on its agenda, its very character prepares its membership for involvement in the issues of the day, although that involvement is usually outside of the walls of the synagogue.

Moreover, despite the apparent concern for deeper involvement in public square issues that was expressed by almost all of the leadership interviewed for this study, there was an unwillingness for any of the various organizations to give up any autonomy in order to succeed in this task. The example that epitomized this concern was the near unanimous call for a presence in Washington, D.C., to create the kind of institutions that already represent the concerns of both the Union of American Hebrew Congregations (the Reform movement) and the Union of Orthodox Jewish Congregations. Yet the will to do so is not strong enough to overcome the need for institutional autonomy. None of the specific institutions feels that it has the resources at the present time to accomplish this task alone, but each finds it difficult to pool its resources with the other institutions in order to do so. In this case, the perceived need for autonomy takes precedence over cooperation, thus emphasizing the coalition nature of Conservative Judaism. Obviously, when it comes to public square issues the coalition has limits as to how much it will work with others to succeed in its goals. Another paradox is that, despite institutional autonomy, there is a wide agreement on attitudes toward specific public square issues. Reading the various policy statements, resolutions, and other documents of the Rabbinical Assembly, the Women's League for Conservative Judaism, and the United Synagogue for Conservative Judaism, one is struck by the virtual agreement throughout the movement concerning the key issues of the day.

Notes

1. *Siddur Sim Shalom*, 415.
2. Jeremiah 29:7.
3. Mishnah Avot 3:2.
4. Moshe Davis, *The Emergence of Conservative Judaism* (Philadelphia, Pa.: Jewish Publication Society of America, 1965), 17.
5. In Philadelphia, March 2000.
6. *Emet v'Emunah*, the United Synagogue of Conservative Judaism, New York.
7. There are, however, several congregations in the United States that are self-designated as Conservative, adhere to the standards of the movement, and have rabbinic leadership that is affiliated with the Rabbinical Assembly, but they do not formally affiliate with the USCJ for various reasons.
8. Resolutions, pamphlets published each year by the WLCJ.

9. A good example is the pamphlet published by the Rabbinical Assembly, "You Shall Strengthen Them: A Rabbinic Letter on the Poor," New York, 1999.

10. Philadelphia, March 2000.

11. RA Resolution no. 8, Philadelphia, March 2000.

12. RA Resolution no. 8.

13. RA Resolution no. 8.

14. RA Resolution no. 9.

15. RA Resolution no. 10.

16. *The Abortion Controversy: Jewish Religious Rights and Responsibilities*, United Synagogue Resolution Implementation Packet, October 1955.

17. *Judaism and the Environment*, United Synagogue of Conservative Judaism, undated.

18. *Judaism and Domestic Violence*, United Synagogue Resolution Implementation Packet, February 1995.

19. *Judaism and Child Welfare*, United Synagogue Background Paper, April 1994.

20. *Judaism and Health Care Reform*, United Synagogue Position Paper, April 1993.

21. *You Shall Strengthen Them: A Rabbinic Letter on the Poor*, issued by the Joint Social Action Commission of the Rabbinical Assembly and the United Synagogue of Conservative Judaism, April 1999.

22. Interview with Sarrae Crane of the USCJ, November 16, 1999.

6

Reform Judaism, Minority Rights, and the Separation of Church and State

Lance J. Sussman

For much of its history, the Reform movement in Judaism in the United States has been a strong advocate of the separation of church and state. Reform's views on separationism are rooted in the denationalization and emancipation of the Jewish community in Central Europe, a central conviction that American Jewish security is best served by maintaining a high "wall of separation," and close ties to American progressivism and liberalism in general.[1] Reform's advocacy of the separation of church and state is not only nuanced by the serpentine nature of the "wall of separation" in the United States but also by an awareness of the complex place of Judaism in the State of Israel and American Reform's active support of Progressive Judaism in the Jewish state. Thus, from a broad global-historical perspective, Reform Judaism has not been radically separationist, but rather has primarily concerned itself with the protection of minority religious rights, employing different political and legal strategies in the varied polities in which it has rooted itself during the last 200 years.[2]

The Reform movement also clearly distinguishes between what it views as a mandate to be openly involved in the larger political process in the United States and other countries, and the actual process of governance. Using the prophetic model of representing "truth to power," the Reform movement forcefully, if not ironically, uses its commitment to social justice to advocate for the continued separation of church and state in the United States.[3] In recent years, direct lobbying in Congress has been added to Reform's long-standing interest in religious liberty issues before the Supreme Court of the United States.

At various levels of leadership in the American Reform movement, there is an awareness of an essentially pragmatic approach to church-state relations whose goal is to protect and maximize the civil rights of minority religious traditions. Consciously breaking from earlier models provided by biblical and rabbinic Judaism, American Reform Judaism broadly argues for the separation of church and state for defense purposes. However, to date the Reform movement has not developed a systematic philosophy of church-state. The inherent pragmatism has also served to temper more radical separationist views within the movement and allows for exceptions like legislative prayers, military chaplains, invoking the name of God in the courts, the Pledge of Allegiance, and inclusion of the word "God" in the national motto.

In a 2000 web-based statement issued by the Religious Action Center (RAC) on "Jewish Values and School Prayer," the official political voice and lobby of the Reform movement in Washington, D.C., the Reform movement first equates its own views on the separation of church and state with those of the larger Jewish community. It then openly states that "neither biblical mandates nor rabbinic rulings completely explain the Jewish community's strong commitment to religious freedom and the separation of church and state." Rather, the statement continues, it is "historical experience which demonstrates that the Jewish people have suffered religious persecution when the state was controlled by a particular religion."[4] "Historical experience," as will be demonstrated, is often highly selective and malleable on the socially constructed anvils of ideology and memory.

The web document goes on to explain Reform Judaism's pragmatic approach to separationism in terms of a lachrymose view of pre-1776 Jewish history coupled with an endorsement of American exceptionalism.

The First Amendment made the United States the refuge of choice for Jews and others throughout the world when faced with persecution and oppression in countries without equivalent guarantees. American Jews have enjoyed the constitutionally guaranteed freedom to exercise religion and to organize communal lives under equal protection of the law. Therefore, the Jewish community has a deep stake in the preservation of the separation of church and state. As members of a religious minority whose history is so dominated by oppression, we are especially sensitive to any effort to weaken the safeguards of pluralism and minority expression and are keenly aware of the dangers of a partnership between government and religion.[5]

While it may be safe to assume that the "historical experience" of "persecution and oppression" is generic and includes everything from the destruction of the Second Temple to the Crusades and Inquisition, it is also probable that the actual experience of early Reformers directly contributed to Reform Judaism's inclination toward separationism. Ironically, perhaps the first major institutional representations of Reform Judaism, developed by Israel Jacobsohn in Westphalia during the brief reign of Jerome Bonaparte, received state sponsorship. Thereafter, throughout Germany the emerging Reform movement became fully engaged in an unhappy triangle with Orthodox Judaism and dozens of different governments in the former Holy Roman Empire. Numerous conflicts, including the famed Geiger-Tiktin Affair in Breslau, left many communities deeply and irrevocably split. In 1852, a radical Reform rabbi, David Einhorn, immigrated to America from Mecklenberg-Schwerin in the wake of an unsuccessful legal and political battle with local traditionalists in which the local archduke himself intervened on the side of Jewish religious orthodoxy.[6]

The legal and political situation in the United States in the nineteenth century was different from that in Germany. Both the American federal and state constitutions mandated various degrees of "freedom of religion," and although Protestantism dominated the religious landscape, no one church enjoyed the benefits of official establishment. Moreover, the Protestant pluralism that dominated American religious life after the Great Awakening was itself subject to a complex dynamic which pitted disestablishment against "free exercise," simultaneously limiting and validating the public use of religion in the United States.[7]

For the majority of American Jews during the middle decades of the nineteenth century, the threat of religious majoritarianism, structurally anticipated by James Madison and others in the early days of the nation and now manifest in the form of the so-called Christian America concept, was both visceral and legal. For most American Jews in the pre-Civil War era, the hope for social inclusion and political enfranchisement was clearly tied to an American model of separation which promised an "equality before the law" for Judaism in the United States. For Reform Jews, the struggle against religious majoritarianism, with an emphasis on the establishment clause of the First Amendment, emerged as an enduring principle of their movement during its infancy and remains so to the present day.[8]

In many ways the advocacy work of the leading American Jewish religious figure of the antebellum period, Isaac Leeser, an Orthodox hazzan at Mikveh Israel Congregation in Philadelphia and editor of the *Occident*, helped frame the basic American Jewish understanding of church-state relations in the decades prior to the Civil War. Leeser, who was also the most visible doctrinal opponent of Reform Judaism in America, had a long public record of advocating for Jewish rights in America. Reflecting the serpentine character of the "wall of separation," Leeser's view of the separation of the institutions of government and religion included important exceptions, such as support both for Jews seeking service as military chaplains in the Union army during the Civil War and for rabbis invited to offer invocations to open sessions of the U.S. Senate and House of Representatives. At least with respect to the chaplaincy, Leeser enjoyed the support of Isaac Mayer Wise, the leading Reform rabbi of the period, even though Wise did not fully support the North's war effort.[9]

Unlike many Reform leaders, however, Leeser also supported the creation of the Board of Delegates of American Israelites in 1859, the first national Jewish defense organization in the United States. Reform objections to the Board of Delegates, however, were not strictly based on beliefs about the apolitical character of religion. Indeed, many Reform leaders, most notably Isaac M. Wise, desisted from supporting the board because they did not want to play an inferior role in an organization dominated by Orthodox Jews.

Ironically, less than twenty years later, the Board of Delegates was absorbed by the newly founded Union of American Hebrew Congregations (UAHC), which reorganized it as a Washington-based standing committee on "Civil and Religious Rights" headed by Simon A. Wolf. Wolf, a well-known Jewish advocate in the nation's capital, maintained a broad agenda for the committee with a special emphasis on church-state issues.[10] The movement as a whole, including the Reform rabbinate, was not yet fully convinced that the Reform mission included overt political work. Instead, a general belief in progress and, to a lesser extent, a modified "gospel of wealth" became pervasive in Reform circles.

The most notable exception to Reform's broadly apolitical program during the Gilded Age was a collective interest in maintaining the "wall of separation" by combating recent attempts to "baptize" the Constitution and society at large. At its Third Council held in

Washington, D.C., in 1876, the UAHC passed a resolution commending the "Congress of Liberals . . . for their noble and energetic efforts . . . to secularize the State completely and to protest against all such laws of State or States, which are calculated to endanger the bulwarks of perfect freedom and justice." A committee was also appointed with the dual purpose of enabling Jews to keep the seventh day as their Sabbath without penalty and removing obstacles for Jews to do business on Sundays. At the Sixth UAHC Council in 1879, the "Sabbath Committee" was commended for its efforts and urged to "aid and assist, as far as it is in their power, in any legitimate effort to remove such Sunday laws . . . as encroachments upon the civil and religious rights of American citizens who, in accordance to the dictates of their conscience, observe the seventh day as a Sabbath."[11]

For the most part, however, nonrabbinic activism in the UAHC remained limited as the nineteenth century drew to a close, mirroring the general reticence among Reform rabbis to speak out on the great issues of the Reconstruction and early Gilded Age eras. Precedent for political advocacy work in the Reform rabbinate can principally be traced to the Civil War period activities of Rabbi David Einhorn, an outspoken abolitionist who first spoke out against slavery in Baltimore and subsequently in Philadelphia where he moved in 1861 to escape the wrath of pro-Confederate Marylanders.[12] Einhorn's influence was felt again in rabbinic circles six years later in 1885, when Rabbi Emil G. Hirsch, a Chicago-based son-in-law of Einhorn, successfully lobbied his colleagues to include a "social justice" plank as the final statement of the original Pittsburgh Platform, the defining document of classical Reform Judaism.[13]

With the establishment of the Central Conference of American Rabbis (CCAR) in 1885, the national restructuring of the Reform movement as an American denomination was complete. While the original goal of the Union of American Hebrew Congregations (UAHC), founded in 1873, was to unite much, if not all, of American Judaism under a single banner, the UAHC was quickly redefined as the umbrella organization for most Reform synagogues, including both moderate and more radical congregations. For its part, the Conference quickly moved to standardize the religious life of the movement and reestablish the priority of rabbinic leadership in Reform Judaism.

The issue of church-state relations was initially raised in the Central Conference of American Rabbis at its second annual convention in Baltimore in July 1891.[14] Rabbi David Philipson presented a paper based on Oscar S. Straus's *The Origin of the Repub-*

lican Form of Government in which he argued that both the idea of a democratic republic and the concept of the separation of church and state were biblical in origin. Wise, now president of the CCAR, had made a similar argument as early as 1854 in his first book, *History of the Israelitish Nation*.[15] While his views have long been rejected as ahistorical, the idea of separation remained central in the Reform community.

Philipson's paper was, in large part, a response to a renewal of the national debate over the idea of America as a "Christian Nation." The following year, in its decision in *Church of the Holy Trinity v. United States*, Supreme Court Justice David J. Brewer agreed that the United States was a Christian country and even published tracts to that effect.[16] For its part, the Conference passed a resolution protesting "all religious legislation as subversive of religious liberty" and a statement in support of nonsectarian public school education. On the other hand, a resolution protesting the closing of the Colombian World's Fair on Sundays failed to pass. The line between maintaining an antiestablishment position and appearing to be openly antireligious was not to be crossed. Thus, almost from the beginning of its involvement in the national debate over the separation of church and state in the United States, many leading Reform figures understood their movement could generally use the language of separation but would also have to accommodate some majority religious practice for practical purposes.[17]

More than a decade would pass before the Conference was moved to create a permanent mechanism to keep the wall of separation high and intact. Angered by the introduction of Sunday legislation in Washington, D.C., CCAR president Joseph Krauskopf called on the Conference to establish an ad hoc committee "against Sectarianism in Public Institutions" in 1904. Krauskopf asked Rabbi David Lefkowitz of Dayton, Ohio, to spearhead the effort. Lefkowitz, who later served as a CCAR president himself (1929-1931), worked quickly to establish ties with non-Jewish antiestablishment religious groups and drafted a report which helped focus the CCAR's attention on the issue of Bible readings in the public schools.[18] At first, resistance within the Conference to forming the committee was substantial, but with the appearance in 1905 of a booklet by Justice Brewer entitled "The United States—A Christian Nation," efforts to start a standing CCAR committee began to move forward. However, before the CCAR was able to act, the Brewer publication was forcefully attacked by an independent organization of southern rabbis. The Conference's ambivalence on the matter was now publicly exposed.[19]

Challenged both internally and externally, the CCAR upgraded Lefkowitz's investigatory group to a permanent committee on Church and State, the first Conference committee to go beyond purely religious or organizational work. Based on the model of the church-state committee, the CCAR subsequently formed a Social Justice Committee in 1910, which focused on labor strife between German and East European Jews. Eight years later, the Conference adopted a platform on "economic justice." A path had now been cleared for the expansion of Reform Judaism into a wider range of political and social issues with the close connection between general political activism and advocacy for separationism remaining a constant in the American Reform movement.[20]

However, it was matters of church and state that principally concerned the rabbis and their attention was focused most acutely on issues related to public schools. By the beginning of the 1910s, two school issues, ethical education and the role of religious instruction in public schools, were on the CCAR's national agenda. In 1911, the issue of nonreligious ethical education, in part based on models provided by Felix Adler, was debated by the CCAR. Julian Morgenstern, president of the Hebrew Union College, succeeded in having a motion adopted in support of secular ethical education. He told the Conference that "it would be a mistake for this Conference to go on record that because we are opposed to the teaching of religion in public schools, we will likewise oppose all positive ethical instruction."[21] Thereafter, in 1915 and 1916 the CCAR debated three different plans, including ethical instruction, uninterpreted Bible readings, and "release" plans.

Following World War I, the Conference returned to discussing "release plans" and adopted a motion in support of the "Gary Plan" in 1926, later ruled to be constitutional by the Supreme Court of the United States in 1952.[22] In urging a less radical approach to the separation of church and state, Morgenstern was joined by a past president of the Conference, Samuel Schulman, in the 1926 CCAR debate on church-state relations. Schulman openly warned his colleagues: "it is not a good thing for us to put ourselves always in the places of fighters against the religious forces of this nation who happen not to be Jews. Our business," Schulman concluded, "is to throw our influence on behalf of religion."[23] It is possible that growing Reform interest in interfaith affairs in the late 1920s represented a second strategy to promote religiosity in America without breaching the wall of separation.

Reform support for the Gary Plan was not long-lived. The reaction against accommodationism in the 1930s, however, was not only conditioned by a return to the older Reform strategy which primarily resisted the idea of a Christian America. During the Depression years, the American government began to invoke police powers in the regulation of the kosher food industry, pitting Orthodox Jews against Reform Jewish separationism. Moreover, the possibility of teaching Yiddish in the public schools was also raised, as was the compensatory teaching of Passover and Hanukkah during the school day.[24]

The long-standing Reform concern with establishment by the religious majority was now being redefined as a principled separationism which valued separation above free exercise even when free exercise involved public expressions of traditional Judaism. By contrast, other voices were being heard in the American Jewish community which maintained that free exercise could benefit Judaism in America without compromising the essential security of the American Jews as a religious minority. For Reform Jews, however, cultural accommodation and constitutional separation were inseparable, necessary partners in preserving the uneasy place Jews had secured for themselves in FDR's America.

Thus, the Central Conference also went on record in 1938 against the inclusion of religious information in the upcoming national census. "The issue in our world today," the church-state committee of the CCAR maintained, "is not church vs. state, but the defense of the democratic state and of religion against attacks by anti-democratic, irreligious forces hostile to both."[25] For American Reform Jews on the eve of World War II, a significant part of "the defense of the democratic state" was protecting minority rights by resisting any involvement of government in the internal affairs of the nation's many religious communities, starting with the complex business of a national census.

However, the rise of European fascism and concern over domestic anti-Semitism in the pre-World War II era do not fully explain the vast expansion and radicalization of Reform opinion in the immediate postwar era. Rather, a judicial basis for the expansion of Reform Jewish activism on issues related to freedom of religion was forged early in the 1940s in a series of decisions by the Supreme Court of the United States to hear First Amendment cases related to the separation of church and state. Indeed, the more the Supreme Court focused on issues concerning religious liberty in the Truman and Eisenhower years, the more the American Reform movement involved itself in the national debate on church-state relations.

The Court had acted slowly in this regard for decades following the passage of the Fourteenth Amendment to the Constitution in

1868. In its opinion, the key passage that "no state shall make or enforce any law which shall abridge the privileges or immunities of citizens of the United States" did not apply to the First Amendment's language on religious establishment and free exercise. In the 1920s, the Fourteenth Amendment was extended to freedom of speech in *Gitlow v. New York*, but it was not until 1940 in *Cantwell v. Connecticut* that the Hughes' Court applied "due process" to free exercise. Thereafter, the Court heard numerous cases on freedom of religion, stimulating numerous grassroots responses, including increased vigilance from Reform Jews through their national religious bodies.[26]

Reform activism in the area of church-state relations intensified in the 1950s in response to increased judicial activity in this area at the federal level, as well as part of a general trend toward greater public activism on the part of the Reform movement, particularly in the area of civil rights. American Jewish involvement in the civil rights movement was complex and connected, in part, with the Jewish community's struggle to guarantee and expand civil rights for itself. For most Reform Jews, the keystone to Jewish rights was the separation of church and state. Paradoxically, just as Reform Jews and their leaders struggled to find ways to tear down the wall of segregation, they also fought to maintain the wall of separation to insure freedom of religious expression for American Jews.

For most Reform Jews in America, the Vinson Court's attempt to find a middle ground between separation and establishment was unsatisfactory. On the one hand, the Court's decision in *McCollum v. Board of Education* (1948), in which the justices found religious instruction in public schools to be a violation of the establishment clause and therefore unconstitutional, was warmly welcomed by the Reform community. On the other hand, just four years later when the court ruled in favor of "release time" in *Zorach v. Clausen* (1952), Reform Jews were broadly unhappy with the decision despite the CCAR's embrace of the same stance a quarter of a century earlier.[27]

Justice William O. Douglas, writing for the majority in *Zorach*, wrote that, "we sponsor an attitude on the part of government that shows no partiality to any one group and that lets each flourish according to the zeal of its adherents and the appeal of its dogma." Douglas's shift in the direction of religious pluralism, free exercise, and legal accommodation was generally viewed with suspicion by American Reform Jews as a slippery slope to establishment.[28] Without question, for Cold War American Reform Jews, even government's inclusive neutrality toward all religions was an unacceptable interpretation of the Constitution.

Two Reform leaders, Rabbi Maurice Eisendrath, president of the UAHC, and Kivie Kaplan, a prominent Reform-affiliated civil rights activist and later president of the NAACP, combined to rally the movement to maintain its strict separationist ideology.[29] In 1959, the Union agreed to purchase the old Ecuadorian embassy in Washington, D.C., to establish a Religious Action Center, parallel to congressional lobbies created by numerous Christian denominations.[30]

The RAC's founding was challenged by Congregation Emanu-El of New York City, Washington Hebrew Congregation, as well as a host of southern temples concerned about the movement's role in the civil rights struggle. A dramatic challenge at the UAHC Biennial in 1961 failed, and the center was founded in the Northwest section of the nation's capital. The RAC, under the leadership of Rabbi Richard G. Hirsch, quickly emerged as a cutting edge of Reform Judaism and a champion of its struggle to maintain the wall of separation.[31]

For the most part, the Reform movement generally found itself in an advantageous situation during the Warren years, 1953 to 1969. While *Engel v. Vitale* (1962), which found prayer in public school unconstitutional, elicited a strong, negative response from leading Orthodox rabbis in the United States, Reform leaders widely applauded the decision. Similarly, the Court's decision the following year in *Abington School District v. Schempp* met with approbation in the Reform community.

For its part, the UAHC quickly took action to protest any accommodation by the Supreme Court during the 1960s to requests for lowering the wall of separation. Thus, at its national convention in 1965, the UAHC passed a sweeping resolution on the "Separation of Church and State," reversing sentiments heard in the CCAR a generation earlier by 180 degrees. The resolution was passed in response to a national debate "which has revolved about legislation to provide public aid to education, as well as the involvement of religious groups in the federal anti-poverty program." "While as citizens," the UAHC statement reads, "we accept and respect the laws of the land," the statement concludes, "we affirm our long-established position that the principle of separation of church and state is best both for church and state and is indispensable for the preservation of that spirit of religious liberty which is a unique blessing of American democracy."[32]

In this regard, it is interesting to note that at the height of the liberal Court's activities on church and state, the Reform movement even invoked an argument framed by James Madison and others that separation not only protected civil society from the inroads of religion but also it protected religion from the negative influences of government. For example, in his 1785 "Memorial and Remonstrance," Madison wrote that Christianity flourished "prior to its incorporation with Civil policy" until "fifteen centuries [of] the legal establishment of Christianity" resulted in the "pride and indolence of the Clergy, ignorance and servility in the laity, in both, superstition, bigotry and persecution."[33] For the most part, however, Reform advocates of separation stressed religious liberty, not the quality or purity of religious life.[34]

By the mid-1970s, Rabbi Richard Hirsch was succeeded by Rabbi David Saperstein, a lawyer and adjunct professor at the Georgetown University Law Center specializing in church-state law. Saperstein greatly expanded RAC's general scope of activities while maintaining a vigilant eye on church-state issues. Often combining with other liberal Jewish organizations and secular watchdog agencies, RAC became widely known for strong liberal religious advocacy work in Washington, D.C., under Saperstein's guidance. The indefatigable Saperstein earned a reputation for being the quintessential professional religious lobbyist in the nation's capital. More than any of his predecessors in the Reform movement, Saperstein became directly and widely involved in lobbying Congress on matters of church and state in addition to monitoring the activities of the Supreme Court.[35]

However, the political landscape in Washington was changing rapidly and RAC advocacy of liberal views on separationism was increasingly in the minority. Conservative appointments to the Supreme Court, the Reagan revolution, and Republican control of the House combined to create a very different agenda in Washington on domestic and foreign affairs alike. Moreover, within the larger Jewish community new voices calling for greater religious expression in the public square were being heard. Many Orthodox Jews even began to advocate for direct government financial support of parochial schools.

Initially, after Chief Justice Warren E. Burger was appointed by President Nixon in 1969, the Supreme Court generally maintained a "liberal" view of separation despite a controversial ruling on nativity displays in 1984. Subsequently, Burger was succeeded in 1986 by William H. Rehnquist, who, along with appointments to the court by presidents Reagan and Bush (senior), began to probe the wall of separation for legal breaches. In 1990, the court ruled in *Board of Education v. Mergens* that the Equal Access Act of 1986 did not violate the First Amendment. Under "equal access," schools that received federal funds and maintain a "limited open forum" must allow student groups based upon "religious, political, philosophical, or other content" to meet on school grounds. As a result, school-based Bible clubs began to proliferate. Remarkably and inexplicably, the use by the Court of "freedom of speech" to override the tenets of separationism was only meekly challenged by the Reform movement, although it clearly raised the possibility of majoritarian pressures on adherents of minority religious groups in the public schools.[36]

With the Court finding breaches in the wall and a conservative majority operating on Capitol Hill, Saperstein redirected much of his efforts at promoting a separationist viewpoint by shifting emphasis from the establishment to the free exercise clause in the First Amendment. Reacting against the Court's 1990 decision in *Employment Division v. Smith,* which reduced the level of constitutional scrutiny when a government "burdened" religious practice, Saperstein and RAC helped champion the 1993 Religious Freedom Restoration Act (RFRA). However, the Court ruled that the RFRA was unconstitutional in *Flores v. City of Boerne* in 1997. Outraged, Saperstein and other separationists helped introduce the Religious Liberty Protection Act (RLPA) of 1999 to broaden the legal meaning of free exercise. However, concern over the legal effects of the legislation on prisoner and gay rights led to its abandonment in the gridlocked Congress of the late 1990s following its initial passage in the House. The Reform movement now found itself increasingly trapped between a court and a Congress eager both to loosen the standards of establishment and prepared to reduce the meaning of free exercise in American constitutional law.[37]

However, the complex internal dynamics of the First Amendment and the long national legacy of separation in the United States combined to prevent a complete radical rereading of the Constitution at the end of the twentieth century. Thus, RAC found itself with the majority in Congress in defeating the Istook amendment in 1999 and helped block the legalization of student-led prayer in the public schools.[38] The Supreme Court also decided against allowing student-led prayers at public school sports activities in *Santa Fe Independent School District v. Doe* in 2000 and, by taking no action on a 2001 lower court ruling on the unconstitutionality of the display of the Ten Commandments, continued to uphold to a significant degree the long-term separationist legacy of the Court and American society at large.

While RAC's advocacy for separating church and state has been greatly complicated, both by the increasing constitutional sophistication and legislative activism of the American political right, often with Orthodox Jewish support, and the growing Reform interest in day schools, the Reform movement essentially remained loyal to the separationist model of church-state relations. However, at the same time, the Israeli Reform movement, increasingly engaged in legal battles to expand its base in Israel, also argued for "established" Jewish religious pluralism. By necessity, the Israeli Reform movement was compelled to shift away from Madisonian views of church and state, and instead took up a Jewish version of William Penn's, Patrick Henry's, and others' proposals for a Christian pluralism as the established mode of faith in America and its states. In short, Israeli Reform has been compelled to advocate the idea of equal Judaisms before the law in the Jewish state, as well as for state support of numerous other faiths, including Islam and a multitude of Christian faiths.[39]

The Israel Religious Action Center (IRAC), founded in 1987, receives significant support from American Reform backers. Faced with a radically different legal and constitutional situation, IRAC has had to take a more practical approach to issues involving the relationship of government and religion than its American counterpart. In one recent statement, IRAC maintained that "we believe that so long as there is State funding for religious facilities such as synagogues, Reform and Conservative congregations are entitled to their fair share of money."[40] In other words, although IRAC might prefer a true disestablishment of religion in Israel, it mostly is seeking a "fair share" for non-Orthodox Judaism for the time being. Like the RAC, IRAC often seeks partners with other liberal and pro-disestablishment organizations in Israel today.

In March 2000, the CCAR adopted a resolution entitled "Support for Religious Freedom in Israel," endorsing the adoption of a "Basic Law of Religious Freedom" in Israel which called for a pluralistic establishment of religion in the Jewish state.[41] Similarly, in its 1997 "Miami Platform" on Reform Judaism and Zionism, the CCAR called for "a Jewish state in which no religious interpretation of Judaism takes legal precedence over another" (Article V).[42] Two years later in Pittsburgh, when the CCAR adopted a new Statement of Principles, it called for an Israel where "full human and religious rights" are respected, but again did not invoke any principle of separation between government and organized religion.[43]

The influence of Israeli politics, polity, and piety on recent Reform Jewish thought has been striking. In 1999, Rabbi Dr. Moshe

Zemer, a leading Israeli Reform rabbi, published a wide-ranging collection of responsa entitled *Evolving Halakhah: A Progressive Approach to Traditional Jewish Law*.[44] In his book, Zemer argues that *halakhah*, or Jewish law, has always been pluralistic and that Reform Jews can best define themselves and their movement globally by existentially adopting an ethics-centered, rational, and critically defined *halakhah*. In the unlikely event that Reform Judaism becomes part of an "established religious pluralism" in Israel, Reform *halakhah* could theoretically and substantially be empowered by the Jewish state.

A similar approach to *halakhic* pluralism is growing among American Reform rabbis, who increasingly turn to law and not "principles" to define Reform Judaism. For example, Rabbi Dr. Mark Washofsky, a faculty member of Cincinnati's Hebrew Union College-Jewish Institute of Religion, systematizes a century of American Reform *halakhic* activity in his 2001 book, *Jewish Living: A Guide to Contemporary Reform Practice*. Building on the work of Solomon B. Freehof, Walter Jacob, Simeon J. Maslin, and others, Washofsky offers the most comprehensive "legal" summary of Reform Judaism in America in its history. While American Reform *halakhah* continues to remain advisorial and not authoritative, its growing role in the work of the Reform rabbinate parallels, to some extent, the expansion of government in North American polities in general, and thus creates possibilities for changes in the general interfacing of organized religion and state in the United States.[45]

Hints of tensions in current Reform thinking about how to define the separation of church and state in American law can be detected in the debate among Reform Jews about the place of day school education in their movement, as well as among the most outspoken separationists in the Reform movement on a whole variety of issues. For example, at the fifty-first General Assembly of the UAHC in Los Angeles in November 1971, a resolution was adopted on the "establishment of a national Reform Jewish Academy on the Secondary Level." The opening of "one school," the resolution reads, "will offer no threat to the public school system, nor breach the wall of separation between Church and State through reliance on public finances."[46]

Fourteen years later in 1985, the UAHC passed a second resolution stating that "the future educational needs of our children . . . demand that alternatives of quality public and Reform Jewish full-time education be among the legitimate educational options to our children." At the same time, the Union agreed that "it is incumbent upon the Jewish community to be deeply involved in the struggle to strengthen and reinvigorate our public schools."[47]

To that end, the movement has consistently argued against school vouchers. According to the Religious Action Center, "what we need instead is greater Jewish investment in Jewish educational institutions. Within our community, we have the resources," a RAC website maintains, "we simply need to refocus and redirect them."[48] In the long run, however, just as the Reform movement evolved from experimenting with one full-day program to backing the development of a system of Reform day schools, so it is possible that the financial challenge of maintaining progressive full-day schools may lead to enhance indirect government support of parochial education through business tax credits and other funding mechanisms that further challenge the legal structures of separation.

The problems inherent in separationism have even given several major leaders of the Reform movement pause in recent years. For example, Rabbi David Saperstein, director of RAC, and Al Vorspan, a former vice president of the UAHC and long-time social justice activist in the Reform movement, combined to write a full-length "textbook" in 1998 on *Jewish Dimensions of Social Justice: Tough Moral Choices of Our Time*.[49] In their nuanced discussion of "Religious Liberty: Will the Wall Come Tumbling Down?" (chapter 11), they present six "Real Dilemma(s)," including a report on the upstate New York hasidic village of Kiryas Joel, "Menorahs on Public Property" and a discussion about the possibilities of working with the religious right in common religiopolitical causes.

In their conclusion, Saperstein and Vorspan report that "Jewish influence and impact" in the area of the separation of church and state has been diminished because of splits over the value of separationism in the American Jewish community in recent years. "Some Jewish observers," they report, "say Jewish leadership has been too rigid. They say we have eroded our position as a faith group by lining up with atheist and secular groups in court tests and public controversy." Remarkably, instead of rejecting the criticisms and reaffirming the Reform "doctrine" on church and state, they end with a simple but bothersome question, "What do you think?"[50]

Most recently, the American Reform movement has attempted to resolve some of the tension between its historical use of separationism to protect minority rights and the need not to appear as antireligious in the eyes of the broader American public. For example, in June 2001, the president of the Union of American Hebrew Congregations announced formation of a "Tzedakah (charity) Collective." The fund would be used by the movement to collect tax rebates generated by the new Bush administration, which would then be allocated to underfunded federal programs in education, health care, and low-income housing. In essence, the "Tzedakkah Collective" is a self-imposed tax aimed at preserving liberal social service programs targeted for reduction by a conservative, Republican administration and Congress.[51]

Similarly, in addition to opposing President George W. Bush's "Faith-Based Initiative," which seeks to apply government funds to social welfare programs developed by religious organizations, Rabbi David Saperstein suggested alternatives to direct government funding of churches, synagogues, and mosques. Included on Saperstein's list were "technical assistance and training programs for staff of all groups; best practice sharing, targeted research on how to improve programs; reducing, or even eliminating fees for all small organizations, including churches and synagogues, [establishing] separately incorporated 501(c)(3) social service arms to assist the poor; [providing] more and better information to the public about available programs; and encouraging charitable contributions through appropriate tax relief."[52] Again, the goal was not radical separationism but pragmatism to maintain the "wall of separation" and find ways, some perilously close to being legal fictions themselves, to maximize government support of organized religion without direct government support of religious institutions.

While it is unlikely that the Reform movement will reverse its long-term support of the separation of church and state in the near future, it is clear that the liberal movement's responses to new constitutional challenges are becoming more complex. In the last few years, not only has a Reform rabbi challenged the constitutionality of erecting a Habad-sponsored Hanukkah menorah in public space in Cincinnati, Ohio, but another Reform rabbi was taken to court in Rhode Island for agreeing to offer a commencement prayer.[53] The old Reform belief in the safe haven of disestablishment is again in tension with the possibilities of pluralism under the guarantee of free exercise.

The serpentine character of the wall of separation, the place of public religion in American culture, the growth of Reform day schools, and the battle for Reform rights in Israel, a polity in which the institutions of government and religion are intertwined in innumerable ways, have all combined to make the challenge of Reform's traditional views on religious disestablishment more complicated than ever in the early years of the twenty-first century. Moreover, the cautionary words spoken by Rabbi Samuel Schulman seventy-five years ago that "it is not a good thing for us to put ourselves always in the places of fighters against the religious forces of this nation" may be echoing again in the ears of some of the Reform movement's more traditional religious leaders. The struggle to maintain constitutional separationism in a neo-conservative American environment and simultaneously promote "established" pluralism in the State of Israel suggests the Reform movement needs to look deeper into the complex interactions of religion and state.

While the vast majority of American Reform Jews continue to believe in the "naked public square," they also believe in a more traditionally clad Western Wall plaza in Jerusalem.[54] Ultimately, the tension between the "wall of separation" and the "Western Wall" in contemporary Reform Jewish thought and practice cannot be simply resolved by compartmentalizing the two legal and political realities represented by the United States and Israel. It just may be that the world Reform movement needs to articulate a political philosophy centered on minority rights consistent with its ever-evolving goals and practices and accordingly reassess the place of separationism in the history of Judaism's most liberal religious movement.

Notes

1. For a general analysis of American Reform Judaism and the separation of church and state, see Eugene Lipman, "The Conference Considers Relations between Church and State," in *Retrospect and Prospect: Essays in Commemoration of the Seventy-Fifth Anniversary of the Founding of the Central Conference of American Rabbis, 1889-1964,* Bertram W. Korn, ed. (New York: CCAR, 1965), 114-28. For an assessment of Reform and church-state relations before World War II, see Lance J. Sussman, "Rhetoric and Reality: The Central Conference of American Rabbis and the Church-State Debate, 1890-1940," in *In Celebration: An American Jewish Perspective on the Bicentennial of the United States Constitution*, Kerry M. Olitzky, ed. (Lanham, Md.: University Press of America, 1989), 72-100. For a general history of Reform Judaism, see Michael A. Meyer, *Response to Modernity: A History of the Reform Movement in Judaism* (New York: Oxford University Press, 1988).
2. Sussman, "Rhetoric and Reality," 95.
3. On American Reform Judaism and social justice, see Roland B. Gittelson, "The Conference Stance on Social Justice and Civil Rights," in Korn, *Retrospect and Prospect*, 81-113; and Leonard J. Mervis, "The Social Justice Movement and the American Reform Rabbi," *American Jewish Archives* (1955): 171-230.
4. "Issues: School Prayer," Religious Action Center of Reform Judaism, June 28, 2000, www.rac.org, 5.

5. "Issues: School Prayer," 5.

6. Meyer, *Response to Modernity*, 33, 110-14, and 245.

7. For an excellent introduction to nineteenth-century American religious history, see Nathan O. Hatch, *The Democratization of American Christianity* (New Haven, Conn.: Yale University Press, 1989).

8. For a general history of American Jews and the church-state debate in the nineteenth century, see Morton Borden, *Jews, Turks and Infidels* (Chapel Hill: University of North Carolina Press, 1984). More broadly, see Jonathan D. Sarna, "Christian America or Secular America? The Church-State Dilemma of American Jews," in *Jews in Unsecular America*, Richard J. Neuhaus, ed. (Grand Rapids, Mich.: W. B. Eerdmans and Center for the Study of the American Jewish Experience, New York, 1987), 8-18; David G. Dalin, ed., *American Jews and the Separationist Faith* (Washington, D.C.: Ethics and Public Policy Center, 1993); and Jonathan D. Sarna and David G. Dalin, *Religion and State in the American Experience* (Notre Dame, Ind.: University of Notre Dame Press, 1997).

9. For a biography of Isaac Leeser, see Lance J. Sussman, *Isaac Leeser and the Making of American Judaism* (Detroit, Mich.: Wayne State University Press, 1995).

10. On Simon Wolf, see Simon Wolf, *The American Jew as Patriot, Soldier and Citizen*, Louis Edward Levy, ed. (Philadelphia, 1895).

11. Typescript copies of "Commending the Congress of Liberals" and "Petition for Enactment of Sabbath Observance Laws" from the Third Council of the Union of American Hebrew Congregations (UAHC) held in Washington, D.C., in July 1876 were provided by the UAHC. Similarly, a typescript copy of "Instructing Committee on Civil and Religious Rights," UAHC 6th Council (July 1879), was made available to the author by the Union of American Hebrew Congregations.

12. A full-scale, critical biography of David Einhorn is a major desideratum. For insight into a relevant theme, see Gershon Greenberg, "The Significance of America in David Einhorn's Conception of History," *American Jewish Historical Quarterly,* 63 (1973): 160-84.

13. On Emil Hirsch, see Bernard Martin, "The Religious Philosophy of Emil G. Hirsch," *American Jewish Archives,* 4 (1952): 66-82. For biographical information on most of the major religious leaders of American Reform Judaism before 1975, see Kerry M. Olitzky, Lance J. Sussman, and Malcolm H. Stern, eds., *Reform Judaism in America: A Biographical Dictionary and Sourcebook* (Westport, Conn.: Greenwood Press, 1993).

14. *Central Conference of American Rabbis Yearbook (CCARY)* 3:42 and 45; and Sussman, "Rhetoric and Reality," 84-85.

15. Isaac M. Wise's and Oscar S. Straus's rereading of American political history as essentially biblical needs further investigation as it provides a theoretical framework, albeit ahistorical, for the widespread separationist faith among American Jews.

16. David B. Brewer (1837-1910) was born in Smyrna, Ottoman Empire (now Izmir, Turkey). His parents were missionaries. Justice Brewer served on the Supreme Court from 1889 to 1910 and openly advocated the

idea of a "Christian America." See Robert T. Handy, *A Christian America: Protestant Hopes and Historical Realities,* 2nd ed. (New York: Oxford University Press, 1984).

17. *CCARY* 3: 42, 45.

18. *CCARY* 14: 139-54.

19. A Southern Conference of Rabbis had also been organized prior to the founding of the CCAR. It may be possible that there are regional differences with respect to church-state relations both in and beyond the Reform movement in America.

20. The role of church-state concerns in stimulating social justice activism among American Reform Jews has not been noted previously in the literature of Reform Judaism. Indeed, in a recent anthology on the history of Reform, Michael A. Meyer and W. Gunther Plaut, eds., *The Reform Judaism Reader: North American Documents* (New York: UAHC Press, 2001), the church-state debate is only mentioned once in an introduction to documents on selected primary sources illustrating Reform's involvement in social justice.

21. *CCARY* 21: 108-09, 241, 253, 262.

22. Lipman, "Conference Considers," 118; and Sussman, "Rhetoric and Reality," 90.

23. *CCARY* 34: 82, 35: 65, 36: 39 and 87; 47: 62.

24. Sussman, "Rhetoric and Reality," 90-91.

25. Sussman, "Rhetoric and Reality," 91.

26. On the Fourteenth Amendment, see Michael Kent Curtis, *No State Shall Abridge: The Fourteenth Amendment and the Bill of Rights* (Durham, N.C.: Duke University Press, 1986). On the expansion of institutional religion in the post-World War II era, see Winthrop S. Hudson, *Religion in America,* 4th ed. (New York: Macmillan, 1987).

27. Lipman, "Conference Considers," 121-22; and Sussman, "Rhetoric and Reality," 92-95.

28. *Zorach v. Clausen,* 343 U.S. 306 (1952).

29. On Maurice N. Eisendrath, see Avi M. Schulman, "Visionary and Activist: A Biography of Maurice N. Eisendrath" (Rabbinical thesis, Hebrew Union College-Jewish Institute of Religion, Cincinnati, 1984). On Kivie Kaplan, see Norman Feingold and William Silverman, eds., *Kivie Kaplan: A Legend in His Own Time* (Chicago: Union of American Hebrew Congregations, 1976).

30. Meyer, *Response to Modernity,* 366.

31. On Hirsch, see Ammiel Hirsch, "Richard G. Hirsch," in *Reform Judaism in America,* 90-91.

32. UAHC 1965 Resolution on Separation of Church and State, typescript, provided by UAHC.

33. "James Madison's *Memorial and Remonstrance,* 1785," quoted in *A Documentary History of Religion in America: To the Civil War,* Edwin S. Gaustad, ed. (Grand Rapids, Mich.: W. B. Eerdmans, 1982), 1: 262-67.

34. See CCAR Committee on Church and State 1960 general policy statement, quoted in Lipman, "Conference Considers," 114-16.

35. Rabbi David Saperstein received his bachelor's degree from Cornell University, rabbinic ordination from HUC-JIR, and his J.D. from American University Law School.

36. "RAC Statement on Mergens Decision," typescript, 4 pages, provided by Religious Action Center.

37. "Statement of Rabbi David Saperstein, Director and Counsel, Religious Action Center, on The Religious Liberty Protection Act of 1999 (H.R. 1691)," May 12, 1999, www.uahc.org/reform/rac/oubs/protectionact.html, 5 pages. See also "Issues: Separation of Church and State," www.rac.org/issues/issueschst.html, June 28, 2000, 13 pages.

38. "Issues: School Prayer," www.rac.org/issues/issuessp.html, June 28, 2000, 6 pages.

39. "Who We Are," www.irac.org/we_e.html.

40. "Religion and State in Israel—Background Article," www.irac.org/article_e.asp?artid=14.

41. "Support for Religious Freedom in Israel: Resolution adopted at the 111th Convention of the Central Conference of American Rabbis" (March 2000).

42. "Reform Judaism and Zionism: A Centenary Platform—'The Miami Platform,'" accepted by the Central Conference of American Rabbis, June 24, 1997, Miami, Florida.

43. The text of Pittsburgh II is available at www.ccarnet.org. For an alternative view, see Robert M. Seltzer and Lance J. Sussman, "What Are the Basic Principles of Reform Judaism," in *Thinking Ahead: Toward the Next Generation of Judaism, Essays in Honor of Oskar Brecher*, Rabbi Judith S. Lewis, ed. (Binghamton, N.Y.: Keshet Press, 2000), 7-16.

44. Moshe Zemer, *Evolving Halakhah: A Progressive Approach to Traditional Jewish Law* (Woodstock, Vt.: Jewish Lights, 1999).

45. Mark Washofsky, *Jewish Living: A Guide to Contemporary Reform Practice* (New York: UAHC Press, 2001). To some extent, the 2001 CCAR convention debate in Monterey, California, on standards of conversion is being driven by the needs of the Israeli Reform rabbinate as well as by American factors.

46. "Establishment of a National Reform Jewish Academy on the Secondary Level," resolutions adopted by the UAHC, 51st General Assembly, November 1971, Los Angeles, California.

47. "Full Time Educational Options for Reform Jewish Children," 1985 resolution adopted by the Union of American Hebrew Congregations, typescript provided by UAHC.

48. "Issues: School Vouchers," www.rac.org/issues/issuevouch.html, June 29, 2000.

49. Albert Vorspan and David Saperstein, *Jewish Dimensions of Social Justice; Tough Moral Choices of Our Time* (New York: UAHC Press, 1998).

50. Vorspan and Saperstein, *Jewish Dimensions*, 302.

51. "RAC News: Reform Jews Urged to Give Tax Rebate Checks to Charity, Underfunded Federal Programs Targeted for Contributions," June 7, 2001.

52 "RAC News: Rabbi Saperstein Testifies before Congress in Oppostion to Charitable Choice," June 7, 2001.

53. Alan Fuchs, rabbi of the Wise Center, a Reform congregation in Cincinnati, Ohio, unsuccessfully litigated against a local Habad group to remove a menorah from a major public square in downtown Cincinnati in 1990. Two years later, Rabbi Leslie Y. Gutterman's invocation at a public school graduation in Providence, Rhode Island, was ruled unconstitutional by the Supreme Court in *Lee v. Weisman*. For a strong restatement of the "traditional" Reform view of church-state relations, see Rabbi Steven M. Fink, "Should We Still Seek Religious Equality?" 1996 Interfaith Theological Symposium, Davenport, Iowa, March 10, 1996, typescript, 33 pages.

54. The metaphor of the "naked public square" is suggested and developed most fully by Richard J. Neuhaus, *The Naked Public Square: Religion and Democracy in America* (Grand Rapids, Mich.: W. B. Eerdmans, 1984).

7

Mainstream Orthodoxy and the American Public Square

Lawrence Grossman

The historic nomination of Senator Joseph I. Lieberman, an observant Jew, as the Democratic Party candidate for vice president in 2000 drew considerable comment. Lieberman was touted as a potent asset for the Democratic ticket, combining a strongly liberal record on social and economic issues and civil rights, together with a reputation as a defender of traditional family values. He was open-minded about school vouchers, and he had attacked both the cultural influence of Hollywood and President Clinton's behavior in the Monica Lewinsky affair. Thus, he could well draw Independents and Republicans, particularly in the South and Midwest, to vote Democratic. Yet this very combination was confusing to many Americans, who found it hard to place him on the political map. In fact, a careful analysis of the evolution of the public-policy positions of the Jewish community that nurtured Lieberman, and with which he still identifies—the mainstream American Orthodoxy that emerged in the post-World War II generation—will go far to clarify the apparent political ambiguity of the Lieberman candidacy.

The Legacy of Avoidance

"Mainstream" Orthodoxy in the United States—more popularly known as "modern" or, since the early 1980s, "centrist" Orthodoxy—was heir to the traditional Jewish view that the public square was no place for Jews. Centuries of painful experience in premodern times had taught that a small, dependent minority, belonging to a despised religion, had to be very wary of involvement in public affairs that did not directly concern the welfare of the Jewish community. At most, the early leaders of traditional Judaism in America reasoned, the Jewish community might respectfully petition the government about violations of the legal equality accorded Jews under the American Constitution, and request intervention with foreign powers to quell anti-Semitic manifestations abroad. But the notion that Jews had any distinctive contribution to make to public policy, or even that the Jewish community might legitimately voice a collective interest in one set of policies over another, was absent. Thus, Isaac Leeser of Philadelphia (1806-1868), the first American Jewish leader to articulate a "modern" Jewish Orthodoxy, not only advised Jews not to take a position on the great political/moral crisis of his day—that over slavery and secession—but even thought Jews should not run for political office.[1]

The two mainstream Orthodox synagogue bodies that exist today, the Union of Orthodox Jewish Congregations of America, popularly known as the Orthodox Union (OU, org. 1898) and the National Council of Young Israel (org. 1912), were founded for the purpose of rejuvenating American Orthodoxy, with no expectation of involvement in the public square unless the rights and welfare of Orthodox Jews were directly at stake. Even the one seeming exception before World War II, the two groups' joining organized labor in advocating the five-day work week, was motivated by the religious problems facing Sabbath-observant Jews, not by any particular social vision.[2] For years the OU was content to be one of the institutional constituents of the American Jewish Committee (AJC, founded 1906), which was officially nondenominational but overwhelmingly Reform. AJC handled public policy for the OU until World War II, when AJC's coolness toward Zionism led to a walkout by the OU and other pro-Zionist groups. Young Israel began a similar arrangement with the pro-Zionist American Jewish Congress in the late 1940s that lasted into the 1960s. One longtime Orthodox professional felt that such Orthodox deference to the secular Jewish establishment was rooted in "a sense of social inferiority and a habituated posture of subordination to the non-Orthodox in collective Jewish external affairs."[3]

The handful of English-speaking, acculturated Orthodox rabbis active before World War II were equally uninvolved in the public square. Viewing their primary role as presenting an aesthetically pleasing version of the tradition to their rapidly Americanizing congregants, these rabbis devoted their energies to organization rather than to formulating Jewish public policy. As the best known of these men, Rabbi Joseph H. Lookstein of New York City, put it, "We didn't have time to write books, dear friends, because we were too busy building institutions."[4] Lookstein's more intellectually sophisticated colleague, Rabbi Leo Jung—educated at Cambridge and ordained by the Rabbiner-Seminar Fuer Das Orthodoxe Judentum (Hildesheimer Seminary) in Berlin—who did give sermons and write articles about the need to make traditional Judaism relevant to the modern world, also tended to focus on manners and decorum rather than public policy.[5]

The Liberal Impulse

It was not until after World War II that mainstream Orthodoxy began to take the broader American public square seriously. The initiative came from a new breed of Orthodox rabbis organized in the Rabbinical Council of America (RCA). The council evolved through two mergers, in 1935 and 1942, that brought together rabbinic alumni of Yeshiva University, those of the Hebrew Theological College in Chicago, and the rabbinical organization previously affiliated with the OU. The purpose of the RCA was to mobilize the young, English-speaking, Orthodox rabbinate as an institutional alternative to the Union of Orthodox Rabbis (Agudath Harabonim), which represented the European-born, Yiddish-speaking rabbis. The men of the RCA considered these older rabbis hopelessly out of touch with American reality and therefore partially responsible for the alienation of young Jews from Orthodoxy.[6]

The RCA, then, as a self-consciously "modern" Orthodox body, was intent on distinguishing itself from what it considered the old-fashioned and cloistered Orthodoxy that, by shunning the public square, had nothing to say to the modern world. Furthermore, for the RCA it was self-evident, right after the war, that social relevance meant left-of-center politics. Since the 1920s, in fact, all the branches of American Judaism, like many of the Christian denominations, had found it hard to compete with progressive politics for the allegiance of the young, and the Reform and Conservative denominations had, before and during the war, already staked out leftist public policy positions. Now the RCA hoped to counteract and perhaps even reverse the erosion of Orthodoxy by following their example, espousing the New Deal-Fair Deal programs popular among the liberals of that era, and even moving beyond them to positions that, a few years later, would be grounds for accusations of fellow-traveling, if not communism.

Prodded by the secular national Jewish organizations, organized labor, and even the Federal Council of Churches of Christ, all of which were committed to the liberal agenda, the RCA entered the public square with a vengeance. In a High Holiday message issued in September 1946, the RCA announced its support for "the right of laboring men to organize in unions, and advance their efforts toward greater security and a better standard of living," and for the "legal and human rights" of "the negro." The following April, the RCA convention approved resolutions drawn up by a "social justice commission" set up the year before (the Reform and Conservative movements created such commissions in the early 1930s, under the impact of the Great Depression). Thus, the RCA went on record with the declaration that "religious-minded people" were obliged to combat "any all-out attack on the positions of labor," including "*labor-baiting and red-labelling as a mask for an assault on the honest gains of the trade union movement.*" (The RCA would proceed to join the National Clergymen's Committee in opposing passage of the Taft-Hartley Act, which sought to weaken the power of labor unions.) To prevent discrimination in hiring, the RCA favored maintenance of the federal Fair Employment Practices Committee (FEPC) and the creation of similar bodies on the state level, and urged more funding for public health, all of which was justified on the basis of Jewish ethical values. The RCA also called for raising teachers' salaries, government construction of new homes, anti-inflation measures, and "the right of anyone accused of disloyalty to our government to face his accuser in a court of law and defend his good name." It denounced "lynchings, poll-taxes, 'white' primaries, [and] restrictive covenants in contracts." The RCA even made its voice heard on foreign policy, calling for "the ultimate liquidation of colonial empires," disarmament, and "the strengthening of international government."[7]

The *American Jewish Year Book,* reporting on the RCA's 1947 convention, fully recognized the revolutionary nature of the Orthodox rabbinate's entry into the public policy arena. This was, it noted "of some historic interest as a demonstration of the true 'modernism' of this self-styled 'modern Orthodoxy.'"[8]

The "modern" RCA would remain politically left-of-center through the 1950s, opposing manufacture of a hydrogen bomb, supporting wage and price controls, and denouncing the activities of Senator Joseph McCarthy—thereby eliciting unsolicited praise from the communist *Daily Worker* and the Jewish communist *Die Freiheit*. RCA's president reported to its 1952 convention that he had wanted to intercede on behalf of atomic spies Julius and Ethel Rosenberg, but was warned off by an FBI man who told him that such a move would link him, and the organization, to "communists or fellow travelers." As early as 1953, the RCA backed the racial desegregation of public schools, and five years later sought to make the bombing of schools and synagogues, as was then being carried out in the South, a federal crime.[9]

More surprising, in light of later events, was RCA adherence to the liberal separationist line on relations between church and state. The RCA, like the non-Orthodox and secular Jewish bodies, opposed both "released time" programs under which public schools let students out early for religious instruction upon parental request, and the celebration of religious holidays—of any religion—in the schools. At the same time, the RCA, like the other Jewish organizations, also sought to sever the connection between religion and government by combating the Sunday laws, on the books in many states, that discriminated against Sabbath observers by forcing them to close their businesses on Sunday, and thus stay closed two days a week. These mainstream Orthodox rabbis could be even more insistent on the "naked public square" than their non-Orthodox colleagues. In 1947, the RCA publicly dissociated itself from a statement of the Synagogue Council of America, the umbrella body encompassing all three Jewish denominations, a statement the RCA considered insufficiently separationist. The Synagogue Council held that public schools should not allow Bible readings except as part of a literature course, but the RCA felt that even a literature course could be used for religious indoctrination, and therefore such Bible readings should be opposed as well.[10]

The lawyers and businessmen who ran the OU—which in 1942 had accepted the RCA as its rabbinic authority—were hardly as outspoken in their politics as the rabbis, but emulated them in entering the public square after World War II and lining up on the left. In 1953, the OU joined the National Community Relations Council (NCRAC), the umbrella organization of national bodies and local Jewish community-relations councils that each year formulated a joint approach to issues of Jewish concern. Each NCRAC member organization had the right to abstain or dissent from the consensus and articulate its own position; in case of a dissent, the majority view could not be considered official NCRAC policy.[11] Despite being the only Orthodox body within NCRAC, the OU never once dissented from consensus positions through the 1950s, thus providing official Orthodox assent to the strongly liberal stand of non-Orthodox American Jewry, as enunciated in the NCRAC Joint Program Plan, on economic and social issues, civil rights and civil liberties, and the strict separation of church and state. In the early 1960s, the OU firmly supported an end to all nuclear arms tests, UN regulation of space exploration, and the U.S. Civil Rights Act of 1964. In 1966, the OU deplored the possibility of a "white backlash" against the civil rights gains of blacks, and in 1970 it argued that the solution to inner-city crime was the infusion of federal funds into the ghettos. The OU saw its distinctive role within NCRAC not as challenging the liberal Jewish consensus, but rather ensuring that the organized Jewish community safeguarded the rights of Orthodox Jews, for example, in fighting proposed "humane slaughter" legislation that threatened the practice of *shehitah*.[12]

The Young Israel movement lagged far behind the OU in the public policy arena, evincing no interest in devoting resources to it or in joining NCRAC. Nevertheless, the fact that Young Israel let the liberal-left AJCongress speak for it on public policy from the late 1940s through the early 1960s indicated that little distinguished the political views of Young Israel leaders from those of their counterparts at the OU. Even after it broke with AJCongress, Young Israel maintained an unequivocal stand in favor of civil rights: its official organ editorialized in 1962 against "the apparent indifference of Orthodox Jewry to the Negroes' struggle for equality," and in 1965, saluting "those who marched at Selma," it concluded that society must accept blacks as "free and equal."[13]

Applying the Tradition

Though mainstream Orthodoxy, through its major rabbinic and congregational organizations, emerged unambiguously liberal after World War II, none of its adherents sought seriously to justify such a political posture on the basis of Jewish sources. True enough, Judaism, Jewish values, and even Torah were sometimes invoked as sanction for these positions. But the absence of any sustained analysis of what the huge corpus of Jewish tradition had to say about socioeconomic matters suggests that the espousal of liberalism had little to do with the actual teachings of "Judaism" or "Torah." It emanated instead from mainstream, newly "modern" Orthodoxy's agreement with the non-Orthodox movements and with most secular Jews that Jewish well-being within the American democratic system was best served by the universalistic liberal agenda, which held out the prospect of maximum liberty for individuals, and the assumption that liberal positions were so self-evidently correct that the Jewish religion must surely agree with them.[14]

This superficial mode of relating Judaism to public policy became increasingly problematic as a more intellectually aware, college-educated, Orthodox constituency emerged in the 1950s and 1960s. Trained to use rigorous thought in the natural and social sciences, and exposed to sophisticated analysis of literature and comparative cultural patterns, the postwar Orthodox generation that created the Association of Orthodox Jewish Scientists (1948), the Young Israel campus kosher dining clubs (1957), and Yavneh, the highly intellectual association of Orthodox college students (1960), sorely felt the lack of any sustained application of classic Jewish tradition to contemporary social issues. Much was at stake: if, it was feared, the teachings of Orthodox Judaism consisted only of "religious" matters, and issues of the public square could not be addressed in terms of *halakhah* (classical Jewish law), the younger generation, for whom such issues were crucial, could very well defect.[15]

No one was more aware of the lag between the primitive state of Orthodox thought and the intellectual sophistication of the younger generation than Rabbi Joseph B. Soloveitchik (1903–1993), who emerged in the early 1950s as the unchallenged leader of mainstream Orthodoxy in the United States. The scion of an illustrious dynasty of Lithuanian Talmudic scholars and a brilliant practitioner of that field in his own right, Soloveitchik, who possessed a Ph.D. in philosophy from the University of Berlin, was also at home in a wide variety of secular disciplines, and, as a pulpit rabbi in Boston, had a keen understanding of American social reality. Senior Talmud professor at Yeshiva University's rabbinical school and chairman of the Halakhah Commission of the RCA, Soloveitchik was looked to by the mainstream Orthodox rabbinate and by many congregants as *the* authority on Jewish law and theology.[16]

In 1955, in an address to the rabbinic alumni of Yeshiva University, Soloveitchik publicly castigated the mainstream Orthodox rabbinate for the superficiality of its presentation of Jewish sources, and he reminded the rabbis that the children of their congregants—

college graduates, professionals, academics—were used to in-depth, sophisticated treatment of controversial issues. Approvingly citing the example of Harvard University Divinity School, which had recently announced the establishment of an institute on social ethics, Soloveitchik urged the rabbis to raise the level of their sermons and lectures to meet the religious and intellectual needs of their younger audiences.[17] In succeeding years Soloveitchik himself—without taking public positions on specific issues of the day—began to address the theological basis for Orthodox involvement in the broader social arena. This theme was prominent in his first two essays to be published in English, which appeared in *Tradition*, the RCA "journal of Orthodox Jewish thought," in the early 1960s. Both originated as lectures, and were clearly not meant for a limited audience of Talmudic scholars, but for educated, acculturated rabbis and congregants.

"Confrontation," which Soloveitchik delivered as a paper at the 1964 midwinter conference of the RCA, develops an Orthodox response to the movement, popular at that time, for Jewish-Christian dialogue. In the course of his analysis, Soloveitchik, as was his wont, argues in dialectical terms, setting up two ideal types of confrontation that Jews face. First, "we think of ourselves as human beings, sharing the destiny of Adam in his general encounter with nature," and, on this level, Jews must work together with all other peoples to improve the world. Second, Jews are "members of a covenantal community which has preserved its identity under most unfavorable conditions, confronted by another faith community," and, as such, cannot, in Soloveitchik's view, engage in dialogue over purely theological matters.[18]

While "Confrontation" is most often cited to prove its author's antipathy to interfaith dialogue, its enthusiastic endorsement of cooperation with non-Jews *as a religious duty* in the "general encounter with nature" is a clear departure from the traditional Orthodox view of the secular world as religiously meaningless, significant only for the utilitarian purposes of making a living and keeping anti-Semitism at bay. Furthermore, Soloveitchik specifies the nature of the religious imperative that joins Jews with all other people: "that we are all human beings, committed to the general welfare and progress of mankind, that we are interested in combating disease, in alleviating human suffering, in protecting man's rights, in helping the needy." "Yes," concludes Soloveitchik, "we are determined to participate in every civic, scientific, and political enterprise."[19]

The next year, Soloveitchik published "The Lonely Man of Faith," which originated as a series of lectures to family counselors and mental health professionals, and presents the existentialist side of Soloveitchik's worldview. It portrays the essential loneliness of the religious personality, "a stranger in modern society." Soloveitchik himself admits to this feeling of loneliness. In this essay, the dialectical tension is between the contrasting versions of Adam presented in the Book of Genesis's two accounts of the creation of the world. "Adam the first" (Gen. ch. 1), "majestic man," strives to create, to subdue nature through the use of his intellectual powers. This typology encapsulates the predominant drive of modern man. "Adam the second" (Gen. chs. 2-3), the "man of faith," seeks meaning, transcendence, awe, "an intimate relation with God." All men possess elements of both Adams, but, in the contemporary world of material progress and technological advances, it is only the man of religious faith who is haunted by the dualism, and suffers incurable loneliness because of it.[20]

Once again, as with "Confrontation," the contemporary reader of "Lonely Man of Faith" can easily miss the affirmative evaluation of extra-religious, "secular" life. The themes of existential conflict and tragic loneliness do predominate, but they should not crowd out Soloveitchik's clear assertion that "Adam the first" was created by God as "a dignified being":

> Human existence is a dignified one because it is a glorious, majestic, powerful experience. Hence, dignity is unobtainable as long as man has not reclaimed himself from co-existence with nature and has not risen from a non-reflective, degradingly helpless instinctive life to an intelligent, planned, and majestic one.[21]

Soloveitchik goes on to enumerate the *religiously mandated* accomplishments of "Adam the first": discovering cures for disease, improving means of transportation to make travel quicker and safer, creating things of beauty, and—crucial for activity in the public square—"he legislates for himself norms and laws because a dignified existence is an orderly one. Anarchy and dignity are mutually exclusive." Lest the emphasis on the existential loneliness of the man of faith obscure Soloveitchik's positive evaluation of "majestic man," he reiterates that the quest of "Adam the first . . . is a manifestation of obedience to rather than rebellion against God." The essay closes with a look at the biblical prophet Elisha, who begins as a prosperous farmer "reminiscent of a modern business executive"— "Adam the first"—and then receives the prophetic call and is initiated "into a new spiritual universe," that of "Adam the second." Yet even in his prophetic career, Soloveitchik notes, Elisha follows "the dialectical call": "he came back to society as a participant in state affairs, as an adviser of kings and a teacher of the majestic community."[22]

Soloveitchik, then, supplied Orthodox theological grounds for imputing religious value to secular activity, such as that which takes place in the public square, a view that set him apart from the rabbinic leaders of sectarian Orthodoxy who gave such activity instrumental value only. Interestingly, though having given a "kosher stamp" to the public square, Soloveitchik—who did occasionally express his personal opinions on the issues of the day—never publicly advocated any specific political or socioeconomic position on the basis of Jewish sources.[23] It was left to other mainstream Orthodox scholars to conceptualize the teachings of the tradition in terms that contemporary college-educated Jews could fathom, and apply them to the realities of the American public square. Indeed, the major work was done by a pair of Soloveitchik's relatives, who justified, on Orthodox Jewish grounds, the two great liberal causes of the New Frontier and the Great Society—antipoverty programs and civil rights.

Professor Isadore Twersky of Harvard University, an eminent expert on medieval Jewish thought, was the son of a Hassidic rabbi and son-in-law of Joseph B. Soloveitchik. In a December 1962 talk to Jewish social workers—members of the quintessentially liberal profession—Twersky discussed "Some Aspects of the Jewish Attitude toward the Welfare State." He spelled out the Jewish tradition's clear mandate to practice *tzedakah,* aid for the poor and downtrodden, and showed from *halakhic* and historical sources how the Jewish community, which he called "a modified welfare city-state," was charged with the responsibility, as "the executive branch," for seeing that the obligation was met. Twersky concluded that classical Judaism taught that "welfare activities which tend to mitigate financial difficulties, cannot be looked upon as corrosive of traditional values and obligations," a charge that was, of course, the primary complaint of those, primarily political conservatives, who opposed such government programs.[24] To be sure, the Jewish norms that Twersky cited had to do, in their original context, with the responsibility of the *Jewish community*—not the secular government—to its needy members, and it was Twersky who made the logical leap of applying them to the twentieth-century welfare state. Yet he was not guilty of deliberate distortion; he simply assumed that the Judaic precedents, when translated into the realities of his own time, led naturally to what most Jews considered self-evidently right: government aid for the poor.

A similar modern Orthodox scholarly consideration of the civil rights movement soon came from Rabbi Aaron Soloveitchik, the younger brother of Joseph B. Soloveitchik and himself recently appointed instructor of Talmud at Yeshiva University. Delivering the keynote address at the 1964 annual convention of the National Council of Young Israel on "Civil Rights in Terms of Halakha," Soloveitchik stressed that the biblical claim that all human beings were created in the image of God—which was, he said, the very basis of the concept of human rights—demanded that everyone, irrespective of race or color, was entitled to equal treatment. Yet it could not be denied that Orthodox Judaism mandated distinctions of status between people, and in this connection, the deep divide between Jews and non-Jews was surely relevant: if Jewish law discriminated against non-Jews, what basis was there for Orthodox opposition to racial discrimination? Soloveitchik, then, went into great detail to show that the Jew/non-Jew divide implied no inferiority of non-Jews at all—it simply placed special burdens on the Jew. Whether or not Soloveitchik's apologetics actually reflected the Jewish tradition's understanding of the meaning of Jews being the "chosen people," it enabled him to use, in good conscience, the "image of God" metaphor to argue that Orthodox Jews were obligated to support the civil rights movement.[25]

Cracks in the Liberal Edifice

As the years passed, the solidly liberal posture of mainstream Orthodox Judaism in the public square came under pressure in two separate waves, undergoing serious modification both times. The result is the "revised" liberalism that characterizes the mainstream Orthodox position today. The first challenge came in the early 1960s on church/state separation. The second, which began at the end of that decade and picked up steam in the 1970s, involved the assault of the counterculture on traditional values in the public square.

Church/State Dissent

As mainstream Orthodox liberalism gathered steam in the two decades after World War II, changing priorities in the Orthodox community gradually undermined its church/state-separation component. Hasidic rabbis as well as eminent heads of European yeshivas and their students, arriving in the United States as refugees from Nazism and communism, were intent on reproducing on these shores the intensive system of traditional Jewish learning that had been destroyed, and they had a profound impact on the preexisting mainstream Orthodox community. While it had previously been assumed that public school attendance supplemented by after-school Talmud Torah classes was perfectly compatible with Orthodoxy, by the 1950s the bar had been raised: parents were increasingly sending their children to Jewish day schools at least through the elementary grades, and many of these children—boys and girls—continued on in all-day Jewish high schools as well. By the 1960s it was becoming rare indeed for an Orthodox family to patronize the public schools, and Orthodox synagogues began closing down their supplementary Talmud Torahs for lack of students.

The new priority given to intensive Jewish education served as a bridge issue linking mainstream Orthodoxy with the new unacculturated Orthodox. The institutional manifestation of this bridge was Torah Umesorah (National Society for Hebrew Day Schools), founded in 1944 with the purpose of creating a nationwide network of day schools and training a cadre of dedicated teachers and principals for them. Though organizational policy was officially in the hands of the leading yeshiva heads—who would have preferred the separation of boys and girls and even the use of Yiddish as the language of instruction—many of the younger educators came from the ranks of mainstream Orthodoxy, and Torah Umesorah's leaders were prominent figures in Young Israel and the OU.[26]

What brought Jewish day schools into the American public square was the question of funding. As more families sought access to existing Jewish private schools, and as more communities planned new schools, it became evident that American Orthodoxy could not, by itself, bear the costs. With the exception of a few cities like Cleveland, requests for help from local Jewish federations failed to evoke much enthusiasm. The overwhelmingly non-Orthodox federation leaders tended to feel that if the Orthodox minority wanted day schools, it should not expect the majority—who saw them as ghettoizing and did not want them—to divert large sums from other priorities to fund them. Proponents of day-school funding managed to get the issue onto the agenda at the 1961 General Assembly of Jewish Federations and Welfare Funds, the umbrella agency for the federations, but when that body decided to stave off discussion by calling for an "intensive study" instead, it was clear to the Orthodox that no change in policy was in the offing.[27]

Rebuffed by the federations, day-school enthusiasts considered the pros and cons of following the example of the Catholic Church and seeking government aid. To the unacculturated rabbis and yeshiva heads, who viewed the American government in instrumental terms, as a somewhat more benevolent version of the European regimes they had known, the question was simple: did the potential infusion of income outweigh the risk of government meddling in Jewish education? The answer—heavily influenced by the advice of Agudath Israel of America, which was in the process of becoming the political arm of the sectarian Orthodox—was that there was much to gain and little to fear from government support. The principle of strict separation of church and state, which had become an essential element in the civil religion of acculturated American Jews, including the mainstream Orthodox, was foreign to these rabbis' experience, and, indeed, quite incomprehensible to them.[28]

For mainstream Orthodoxy, however, which was by now similarly committed to the day school and equally frustrated over the dearth of federation funding, the option of looking to government raised a painful conflict with separationist ideology. Dramatically personalizing the dilemma was the fact that attorney Leo Pfeffer of the American Jewish Congress, the leading Jewish spokesman for strict church/state separation, was himself an Orthodox Jew, a member of Young Israel, and the parent of children in day schools. The moment of decision came early in 1961 when newly elected president John F. Kennedy, fulfilling a campaign pledge, asked Congress to appropriate $5.6 billion for education, $3 billion of it for public elementary and secondary schools. The Catholic hierarchy immediately announced that it would oppose the legislation unless private and parochial education were included as well. Rabbi Morris Sherer, executive vice president of Agudath Israel, speaking for the sectarian Orthodox, took the Catholic side in testimony before a House of Representatives subcommittee.[29] The ball was now in the mainstream Orthodox court.

The rabbis of the RCA—always more enthusiastically liberal than the Orthodox synagogue bodies—reiterated their long-standing separationist position by voting down a proposal to reconsider their opposition to government aid. Rabbi Charles Weinberg, the president, announced the RCA's preference for "the democratic principle of self-taxation, which has made it possible for our community to flourish without the problems of government supervision or control."[30] But opinion was divided in Young Israel and the OU, and both organizations sponsored full-scale debates.

At a Young Israel meeting, Professor William Brickman of New York University, speaking in favor of seeking government aid, cited the long history of public support for religious schools in America as proof that such aid in no way endangered church/state separation. He further contended that the very notion that the public schools were non-sectarian was a myth, since they had always been suffused with Protestant Christianity. Rabbi Isaac Trainin countered that erosion of church/state separation could endanger the safety of Jews in America (a euphemism, in Jewish circles, for enhancing the power of the Catholic Church), and that federal funding would act as a disincentive for Jews to contribute to the day schools and furnish a new excuse for the federations not to give. A vote of delegates from Young Israel branches across the country was to follow. After a procedural vote to require a 60 percent majority to establish organizational policy, the delegates divided 26-25 in opposition to requesting government aid. The result was stalemate.[31]

For the OU, the stakes were much higher. Since it was a constituent member of NCRAC, any deviation from the separationist line would mean an unprecedented and lonely defiance of the Jewish communal consensus. The OU held its debate even before Kennedy's inauguration, at its convention in November 1960. Here, Leo Pfeffer argued the case against government aid, raising the specter of dangerous religious rivalries for public funds, and asserting that public schools might be endangered by the diversion of tax money to the private and parochial educational sector. William Brickman argued the other side, urging the OU to think of the benefit for Jewish education that would accrue from government funding rather than worry about "the position of the Catholics and the opposition of the Protestants." In the absence of a consensus, the delegates proceeded to invite thirteen national Jewish organizations and community councils to share their wisdom with the OU at an all-day conference the following April. But even then, ten hours of discussion did little to clarify the issue, as the secular organizations pressed the separationist line, while Agudath Israel and Torah Umesorah argued for government aid.[32]

At the NCRAC plenary in June 1961, the OU abstained from the otherwise unanimous position against aid to "church-related elementary and secondary schools," giving the reason that "it is in process of reviewing its position on the question." It abstained again in 1962, and at the OU's next biennial convention, in November 1962, it noted that the "multiplicity of views" in the organization necessitated further deliberations. The OU continued to abstain from the relevant NCRAC resolutions in 1963 and 1964.[33] But the OU gave clear signals that its old enthusiasm for strict separation was ebbing under the pressure of day-school budgets: Executive Director Samson Weiss warned—or better, threatened—the NCRAC plenum in 1963 "that if the Jewish community wished to avoid the problem of seeking tax funds, it should give serious consideration to making adequate Jewish communal funds available for the support of such schools."[34]

When Lyndon Johnson succeeded the assassinated president Kennedy, he devised a way to make federal funds available for private and parochial education—thereby picking up the Catholic support he needed for passage of the legislation—while at the same time not directly violating church/state separation. He did this through the "child benefit" formula: the federal money would go not to the school but to the child, who could then use it to pay educational costs at his or her school of choice, public or private. After Johnson's landslide victory in 1964, the Elementary and Secondary Education Act passed overwhelmingly in both houses of Congress, and Johnson signed it into law on April 11, 1965. The separationist national Jewish organizations viewed "child benefit" as little more than a subterfuge that would undermine the barrier between church and state, and NCRAC denounced it even after it was law. But the mainstream Orthodox bodies, which had been on the fence during the Kennedy administration when the bill had contained direct aid to schools, embraced it: *indirect* aid for private and religious education satisfied both their pragmatic need to help fund the day schools and their ideological commitment, as Americans, to church/state separation. Young Israel, the OU, and even the RCA joined the sectarian Orthodox groups in supporting the bill.[35] OU president Moses Feuerstein, describing the atmosphere at the NCRAC plenum discussion on the bill as "appropriate at a wake" and the mood there as "verging on the hysterical," urged NCRAC to shed its "Maginot mentality" about church/state separation and called the child-benefit formula "an act of political genius." The OU issued a long and ringing dissent from the NCRAC position—its first dissent ever—which endorsed the education bill and noted that, in light of its dissent: "there is no unified position which could be properly labeled the position of the American Jewish community."[36]

A joke began making the rounds that "Rabbi Johnson has *paskened* the *sha'alah*" (answered the *halakhic* question) of whether the Orthodox community should seek government aid for its day schools. It was surely no joke, however, that mainstream Orthodox involvement in the public square had entered a new era. While not rejecting the universalistic principles of liberalism espoused by the non-Orthodox, mainstream Orthodox bodies—the OU, Young Israel, and the RCA—were interpreting them, for the first time, "in terms of Jewish content and identification."[37] This moved them much closer than ever before to the sectarian Orthodox groups, particularly Agudath Israel, which itself, under Rabbi Sherer, had become more sophisticated in negotiating the American public square. In fact, a unified Orthodox front seemed to be coalescing, at least when it came to legal and legislative matters: toward the end of 1965, the three mainstream Orthodox groups joined with Agudath Israel in creating the National Jewish Commission on Law and Public Affairs (COLPA) to defend Orthodox interests.[38]

In succeeding years, as the consensus of NCRAC organizations continued to denounce government funding for nonpublic education, the OU, as the sole Orthodox member, repeated and amplified its dissents, even going beyond the child-benefit theory to espouse the Catholic Church's position in favor of direct subsidies for the secular component of day-school education.[39] The 1968 NCRAC plenum featured a debate between Leo Pfeffer, arguing against government aid, and Marvin Schick of the OU, who insisted that private schools deserved public support for their secular programs because they "in a way are public institutions, performing the most essential public function that needs to be performed in our society: the function of education."[40]

Persistent mainstream Orthodox advocacy in the public square had its effect on non-Orthodox Jewry. By 1970, the importance of day-school education was so well recognized that NJCRAC found itself compelled, for the first time, to couple its annual critique of government funding with a request to "Jewish community relations agencies" to "encourage adequate financial support of such schools by the Jewish community." While there was a noticeable upturn in federation support for day schools in the early 1970s, the recommendation was too little and too late to stem the Orthodox defection from liberal separationism. Indeed, a conference on the issue convened by the Synagogue Council of America in 1971 demonstrated that Jewish acceptance of some forms of government support for private schools was spreading beyond Orthodox circles.[41] In the 1980s and 1990s, mainstream Orthodox organizations would continue to advocate various forms of government help to nonpublic education, including tax credits, vouchers, and "school choice."[42]

School Prayer/Meditation

Meanwhile, the disaffection of mainstream Orthodoxy from the public square preferences of the separationists moved beyond the question of financing day schools, where the direct interests of Orthodoxy were at stake, to a realm where self-interest was absent. On June 25, 1962, the U.S. Supreme Court, in *Engel v. Vitale,* declared unconstitutional, as an "establishment of religion," the so-called regents prayer, the twenty-two-word nondenominational prayer that New York State authorized to be said every morning in its public schools. At first the mainstream Orthodox community—which had, by now, staked its future on its day schools, and was not directly affected—greeted the decision with equanimity. Indeed, the OU, as a member of both NCRAC and the Synagogue Council of America, and the RCA, as a member of the latter, had signed on to an amicus brief urging an end to the prayer. Young Israel, for its part, reacting to the decision, could not "see the value of a . . . prayer so innocuous as to invite the comment that it is addressed 'to whom it may concern.'"[43] The sectarian Orthodox, similarly unaffected since their children were not in the public schools, were generally silent, except for the Lubavitcher rebbe, who was alone in suggesting that all American children—of whatever faith or of none—needed to be reminded each day, in a nonsectarian way, that there was "a Supreme Authority, who is not only to be feared, but also loved."[44]

Outside the Jewish community, however, American public opinion was harshly critical of the ruling, with many Catholic and Protestant leaders charging that the invalidation of even nonsectarian prayer amounted to the judicial establishment of secularism in the public schools. Clearly shocked by the Christian reaction—especially a September 1 editorial in the Jesuit magazine *America* warning Jews that the prominence of AJCongress and Reform Jewish bodies in removing religion from the schools could lead to "heightened antisemitic feelings"—the mainstream Orthodox developed second thoughts. Yeshiva University hosted a debate between Will Maslow of the Anti-Defamation League, who defended the Court's action, and Rabbi Immanuel Jakobovits of the (Orthodox) Fifth Avenue Synagogue, who warned that blanket Jewish opposition to school prayer "added dangerous fuel to the flames of anti-Semitism" by linking Jews to "atheism and secularism." A wide variety of opinions on the case were aired in the Young Israel newspaper, including a scathing attack on the Supreme Court decision under the heading, "The Myth of Separation." The Young Israel movement itself expressed dismay at what it considered the American Jewish Congress's overly triumphalist publicity campaign claiming credit for the Supreme Court's invalidation of school prayer.[45]

The OU reconsidered the issue at its November 1962 convention. There, after considerable debate, the delegates did support the Supreme Court decision on the ground that nondenominational prayer could easily be perverted into denominational prayer. Nevertheless, the OU came out for granting students "the opportunity to set out on their day's task with a moment of devotion. . . . In this period of meditation, let every pupil think of the Almighty in terms of his faith and his parental religious heritage and thusly invoke His protection for himself, his family, his country, and all mankind." In 1971, when the NJCRAC consensus affirmed its opposition to such silent meditation, the OU issued a dissent.[46]

Of its two deviations from the liberal Jewish consensus on church and state in the 1960s, mainstream Orthodoxy's openness to the role of religion in the public schools—albeit in the truncated form of silent meditation—was even more significant, in the long run, than its successful efforts to attain federal aid for the day schools. As early as 1958, when the OU had not yet strayed from the Jewish consensus, its executive vice president, Samson Weiss, shocked the NCRAC plenum by questioning whether it was appropriate for Jewish communal leadership "to protect the atheistic or idolatrous point of view."[47] Precisely because there was little at stake tangibly for the Orthodox community in the dispute over a moment of silent meditation in public school—as more and more of its children were going to day schools—its rejection of the religion-free public square advocated by the non-Orthodox reflected a principled judgment that American society must not relegate religion to the private sphere alone. This was a position that would be sorely tested by the transformation of American values unleashed by the 1960s.

Defending Traditional Values

New public policy debates over challenges to traditional morality in the public square raised difficult dilemmas for mainstream Orthodoxy. Since Young Israel turned increasingly away from public policy concerns in the 1960s as part of its reorientation toward the Orthodox right,[48] it would fall to the RCA, and especially to the OU, to deal with these questions.[49]

As early as 1962, the OU had gone on record against "the rising tendency to disregard any standards of decency in the field of publication, motion pictures and television," and, while eschewing censorship, it had urged "all responsible forces within American society to join in combating this onslaught upon the moral health of this nation." Four years later the OU began to sense the impact of the new youth culture, criticizing "a rejection of all established authority without which society can neither function nor undergo meaningful changes," and calling for "a White House Conference on Moral Standards." In 1971 President Bernard Berzon of the RCA denounced the atmosphere on college campuses as "agnosticism, self-autonomy, sexual permissiveness, drugs, and experimentation with exotic ideologies."[50] Mainstream Orthodoxy's self-defined role as guardian of traditional morality within the Jewish community led to an open break with the Jewish consensus following the Supreme Court's 1973 decision legitimating the use of "community standards" in determining whether expression could be suppressed for "obscenity." While non-Orthodox groups criticized the ruling as opening the way toward local censorship of free expression, the RCA and the OU praised it, the latter officially dissenting from the NJCRAC consensus on the ground that "for a society suffering from the pollution of our moral environment by the twin social ills of obscenity and pornography, the force of law remains the only mechanism available for correcting those ills."[51]

Two especially thorny policy matters arose in the 1970s having to do with rising feminist consciousness: the proposed Equal Rights Amendment, which would enshrine in the U.S. Constitution the principle of gender equality, and abortion rights. Each in its own way potentially challenged the teachings and practices of Orthodox Judaism, forcing the mainstream Orthodox community to consider the wisdom of joining battle in the public square. There was no unanimity on strategy. On the one hand there were those who felt that "the safest course . . . would be to remain discreetly on the sidelines," since "pious Jews do not acquire their moral imperatives from state law," and any perception that the Orthodox wanted to legislate morality could trigger anti-Semitism from non-Jews and an anti-Orthodox backlash from liberal Jews. On the other hand, some held the view that, since the moral condition of society was crucial for the survival of the most basic Orthodox standards of family life—"from regulating the length of a sleeve up to the Seventh Commandment"—mainstream Orthodoxy had a clear stake in reversing "the current tide of permissiveness."[52] It was the second, assertive, view that won out.

Congressional passage of an Equal Rights Amendment to the Constitution early in 1972 and its submission to the states for ratification drew conflicting initial reactions from the Orthodox rabbinate. While the right-wing rabbinical groups denounced it out of hand as a potential threat to the practice of Orthodox Judaism—which did, after all, sanction gender distinctions—the RCA stated that the proposal, which did not mention religion, "poses no threat to the practice of Judaism in the United States."[53] In June, however, when NJCRAC endorsed the amendment, the OU dissented even while insisting that "it unequivocally champions equal rights for women." The dissent was grounded in three factors: the language could be construed to strike down laws giving special protections to women; institutions refusing to go coeducational might be denied funds; and—clearly most important—"this Amendment might place the power of government behind the immorality of dress and sexual mores that is already rampant in American society." In its dissent the following year, the OU added that the proposal was "antithetical to the distinctiveness and sanctity which Jewish law, tradition and heritage have invested in the lives of men and women and in the creation of healthy family life."[54] The OU continued to dissent year after year, stood alone against the NJCRAC consensus that sought to extend the ratification deadline set for 1979, and issued a similarly lonely protest against NJCRAC's call to its member organizations not to book meetings in states that had not ratified.[55] (Still not ratified by three-fourths of states at the end of the decade, the amendment dropped off the public agenda.)

Abortion and Homosexuality

Abortion rights constituted an even more emotional battleground between Orthodoxy and the rest of American Jewry since Jewish law prohibits even non-Jews from aborting their fetuses when the mother's life is not in danger, and thus can be interpreted as *requiring* involvement in the public square in opposition to abortion rights.[56] At first, however, mainstream Orthodoxy preferred to avoid open confrontation. In the early 1970s, when New York State liberalized its abortion laws, the RCA criticized it for contributing to "the general deterioration of moral values in our society," while making clear that the Orthodox rabbis were not trying to impose the norms of Jewish law on New Yorkers.[57] In 1973, when the U.S. Supreme Court announced its decision in *Roe v. Wade* that legalized the right to an abortion in the first twelve weeks of pregnancy, the RCA officially accepted the decision despite concerns that it would "create a climate for additional permissiveness." Three years later, however, the RCA was denouncing the ruling "as religiously reprehensible and socially destructive," and accusing Reform and secular Jews of falsifying Jewish tradition with their claim that Judaism backed a woman's right to choose.[58]

What accounted for the hardening of the RCA position was the virtually unanimous approval in the non-Orthodox community for an end to all restrictions on abortion, polarizing Jewish opinion and making impossible any middle ground. In 1974, NJCRAC opposed any amendment of the Constitution to reverse *Roe,* and the OU dissented with the unambiguous declaration that "an unborn fetus has the right to life." The next year, when NJCRAC added a rejection of "state laws or local ordinances" inconsistent with *Roe,* the OU countered that Jewish law only allowed abortion when there was "a serious threat to the life of the mother," and that where maternal health was at stake it was the role of "rabbinic authority" to review the medical data and make rulings. In 1978, the OU dissented from the NJCRAC consensus favoring public payment for abortion for poor women, on the ground that public policy should do nothing to encourage a practice "contradictory to clear *halakhic* opinion."[59] Like its dissents favoring government aid for nonpublic schools and calling for a less "wooden" application of church/state separation, the OU's dissent on abortion rights would become a standard annual feature of the NJCRAC plenum.[60]

Gay rights came on the public Jewish agenda in 1974, soon after the establishment—in the glare of publicity—of the first "gay synagogues." The OU denounced homosexuality as a "perversion" and considered it "inconceivable for any agency that is concerned with the preservation and promotion of Jewish values to condone, sanction, let alone advocate or foster homosexual relations." That same year, Rabbi Norman Lamm, soon to be named president of Yeshiva University, published the first serious analysis of the contemporary debate over homosexuality from an Orthodox perspective. Far more nuanced than the OU resolution, it argued for the preservation of the legal restrictions against homosexuals so as to register societal disapproval, but called for an end to their enforcement, thus eliminating discrimination against homosexuals in practice. It was not until twenty years later, in 1994, that NJCRAC first went on record in favor of gay rights. The OU, predictably, dissented. The language of the dissent, clearly influenced by Lamm, announced that while the OU opposed discrimination on the basis of sexual preference, it could not sign on to a resolution that might be interpreted as approving a form of sexual behavior prohibited by Jewish law.[61]

By 1974, the OU public affairs division was able to report that "differences of position on public issues between the Orthodox community and the others are no longer limited to church-state affairs. . . . Torah thinking, combined with greater communal and organizational strength, has moved the Orthodox Union to adopt different positions on some social issues."[62] But the OU's frustration—as NJCRAC's only Orthodox constituent—with ineffectual dissents from a secular Jewish communal consensus boiled over two years later, when the OU insisted on the publication, in the *Joint Program Plan,* of its fundamental critique of NJCRAC. According to the OU, any collective Jewish foray into the public square had to "place fundamental emphasis upon spiritual and moral values in contradistinction to the mere amelioration of material wants." Jewish social policy, it went on, should be predicated on "the biblical and prophetic social concerns that form the pinions of our American democratic society." Indeed, NJCRAC should "seek to uplift the moral fiber of our society in accordance with Torah ideals and principles." The OU inserted the same remarks in 1977, and then gave up.[63] (As it turned out, NJCRAC would not appeal to "the ethical precepts of our faith" until 1992, when alarm at the over-50 percent intermarriage rate uncovered by the Council of Jewish Federation's 1990 Jewish Population Survey led it to include a section on "Jewish Continuity" in the *Joint Program Plan,* and even then the significance of "Jewish tradition" per se was made subordinate to the practical need to provide "an important point of entry into the organized community for individuals who wish to engage in public affairs but from a Jewish perspective.")[64]

While maintaining its NJCRAC affiliation, the OU moved to build an autonomous presence in the public policy arena for its advocacy of Orthodox values and interests—traditional morality, aid to nonpublic school education, a flexible interpretation of the establishment clause of the First Amendment, the rights of Sabbath observers, and religion-driven support for Israel. In 1989 it established its own Institute for Public Affairs (IPA) which, a few years later, opened an office for government advocacy in Washington, thus emulating the right-wing Orthodox Agudath Israel, which had done so earlier.

The Persistence of Liberalism

The extent of mainstream Orthodox dissent from the Jewish communal consensus on church/state and "values" issues should not obscure Orthodoxy's ongoing agreement with that consensus on the positive role of government in ensuring social and economic justice for all Americans. Though, in the 1970s, it tended to side with those secular Jewish organizations (primarily the Anti-Defamation League) that were most antagonistic to preferential treatment for racial minorities in education and employment and to busing for the purpose of achieving school integration,[65] at no point did mainstream Orthodoxy develop a critique of activist government or of the regulatory state. In fact, in recent years the OU has even gone along with the stringent and detailed government controls on private business advocated by the strongly environmentalist JCPA, the successor organization to NJCRAC, and the OU joined the Coalition on the Environment and Jewish Life set up by the JCPA to advocate environmentalism.[66]

Thus for all of mainstream Orthodoxy's departures from liberal orthodoxy on the issues dear to its heart in the areas of church/state and moral values in the public square, its approach to policy is still guided by the arguments Isadore Twersky and Aaron Soloveitchik made in the early 1960s: that the religious teachings of Orthodox Judaism mandate state activity in securing socioeconomic justice and racial equality for all its citizens. While the neoconservatism of the 1980s drew Orthodox admiration on foreign policy grounds—its stanch stand against communism and its support for Israel—there has been no discernible Orthodox interest, either theoretical or practical, in reconsidering the role of the state in the lives of its citizens. The suggestive work of the Orthodox scholar Jon D. Levenson of Harvard University, indicating that the Hebrew Bible is extremely skeptical about government intervention in the economy, has been ignored by Orthodox public policy bodies.[67] Furthermore, Toward Tradition, the organization founded by modern Orthodox Rabbi Daniel Lapin to promote a Jewish conservative politics based on Jewish tradition, has attracted secular neoconservatives and some Hollywood figures but almost no Orthodox Jews.

Mainstream Orthodoxy's experience in the public square over the last half-century, then, is more or less embodied in the career of Senator Joseph I. Lieberman of Connecticut, the Democratic nominee for vice president in 2000. The product of a modern Orthodox upbringing in the late 1940s and 1950s, Lieberman espoused the liberal causes of the late twentieth century—social justice, government aid for the poor and underprivileged, racial justice—on moral/religious grounds. At the same time—at least until the political exigencies of a national campaign took their toll—he remained open to some forms of public aid for nonpublic schools, and he invoked traditional Jewish religious values in his frequent critiques of American popular culture. He seemed to constitute living proof, against the repeated assertions of right-wing Orthodoxy, that an Orthodox Jew could safely carry his values into the public square without jeopardizing his religion.

No doubt many mainstream Orthodox Jews, demoralized in recent years by attacks on their Orthodox legitimacy coming from the sectarian Orthodox right, reacted to Lieberman's selection the same way as did Norman Lamm, the embattled president of Yeshiva University, the flagship educational institution of modern Orthodoxy. Asked what he felt about the nomination, Lamm replied, "Vindication."

Notes

1. Bertram W. Korn, *American Jewry and the Civil War* (Philadelphia, Pa.: Jewish Publication Society, 1951), 24, 44; Hasia Diner, *A Time for Gathering: The Second Migration, 1820-1880* (Baltimore, Md.: Johns Hopkins University Press, 1992), 145, 147.

2. Saul Bernstein, *The Orthodox Union Story: A Centenary Portrayal* (Northvale, N.J.: Jason Aronson, 1997), 89.

3. Saul Bernstein, *Renaissance of the Torah Jew* (Hoboken, N.J.: Ktav, 1985), 194-95. Young Israel eventually broke with AJCongress over what it saw as the latter's neglect of Jewish interests in favor of universalistic causes. See *Young Israel Viewpoint,* July 20, August 24, 1962.

4. Quoted in Jenna Weissman Joselit, *New York's Jewish Jews: The Orthodox Community in the Interwar Years* (Bloomington: Indiana University Press, 1990), 149.

5. Joselit, *New York's Jewish Jews,* 68-71.

6. Louis Bernstein, *Challenge and Mission: The Emergence of the English Speaking Orthodox Rabbinate* (New York: Shengold, 1982), 9-15.

7. RCA press releases September 25, 1946, April 28 and 30, 1947, vertical files of the Blaustein Library, American Jewish Committee.

8. Joshua Trachtenberg, "Religion," *American Jewish Year Book,* XLIX (1947–1948), 145.

9. Bernstein, *Challenge and Mission,* 184-89, 202-03.

10. Bernstein, *Challenge and Mission,* 185, 187, 189-93.

11. In 1969 the organization added the word "Jewish" to its name, becoming the National Jewish Community Relations Advisory Council (NJCRAC).

12. Bernstein, *The Orthodox Union Story,* 266-78.

13. *Young Israel Viewpoint,* October 5, 1962, March 31, 1965.

14. On the prevalence of this ideology among Jews at the time, see Stuart Svonkin, *Jews against Prejudice: American Jews and the Fight for Civil Liberties* (New York: Columbia University Press, 1997).

15. See, for example, Yaakov Jacobs, "Strontium 90 and Orthodox Judaism," *Young Israel Viewpoint,* August 15, 1961.

16. The secondary literature on Soloveitchik tends to be highly partisan and polemical, and therefore unreliable, as demonstrated by Lawrence Kaplan in "Revisionism and the Rav," *Judaism* (Summer 1999): 290-311. Two sensitive treatments that catch the ambivalence of the man and the ambiguity of his legacy are David Singer and Moshe Sokol, "Joseph B. Soloveitchik: Lonely Man of Faith," *Modern Judaism* (October 1982): 227-72; and Norman Lamm, "A Eulogy for the Rav," *Tradition* (Fall 1993): 4-17.

17. "The Role of the Rabbi," unpublished address in Yiddish, delivered May 18, 1955, available on tape, Nordlicht collection #5123.

18. Joseph B. Soloveitchik, "Confrontation," *Tradition* (Spring-Summer 1964): 5-29, quotes on 17.

19. Soloveitchik, "Confrontation," 20-21, 27.

20. Joseph B. Soloveitchik, "The Lonely Man of Faith," *Tradition* (Summer 1965): 5-67; reprinted in book form (New York: Doubleday, 1992). Page citations are to the article.

21. Soloveitchik, "Lonely Man of Faith," 14.

22. Soloveitchik, "Lonely Man of Faith," 14-16, 67.

23. Soloveitchik was similarly loath to advocate firm stands on controversial policy issues within the Jewish community, and often even hesitated in deciding contested problems of Jewish law. Whether this trait was rooted in a temperamental reluctance to make decisions, was an educational strategy to train students to make their own judgments, or reflected an epistemological understanding that humans can grasp "truth" only partially and dialectically, is a matter of controversy. In addition to the articles mentioned in note 16 above, see Walter Wurzberger, "Rav Joseph B. Soloveitchik as Posek of Post-modern Orthodoxy," *Tradition* (Fall 1994): 5-20; and Shalom Carmy, "Polyphonic Diversity and Military Music," *Tradition* (Winter 2000): 6-32.

24. Isadore Twersky, "Some Aspects of the Jewish Attitude toward the Welfare State," *Tradition* (Spring 1963): 137-58.

25. *Young Israel Viewpoint,* May 11, 1964. Within a few years the logic of "image of God" liberal universalism would make Soloveitchik the only prominent Orthodox rabbi to oppose the morality of the Vietnam War, and to support, on what he deemed *halakhic* grounds, selective conscientious objection. See *Jewish Telegraphic Agency Daily News Bulletin,* September

11, 1968; and "For the Love of Torah," Elli Wohlgelernter's interview with Soloveitchik in *Jerusalem Post Magazine,* October 25, 2000.

26. Doniel Zvi Kramer, *The Day Schools and Torah Umesorah: The Seeding of Traditional Judaism in America* (New York: Yeshiva University Press, 1984).

27. *Young Israel Viewpoint,* December 4, 1961.

28. See the proceedings of the 1962 convention of the Union of Orthodox Rabbis in *Hapardes,* January 1963, 30-31 (Hebrew). The one exception to this generalization was Rabbi Menachem Mendel Schneerson, the Hassidic Lubavitcher rebbe, who had a sophisticated grasp of both American reality and the separationist position that he rejected.

29. *American Jewish Year Book,* LXIII (1962), 176-77.

30. *American Jewish Year Book,* LXIII (1962), 178.

31. *Young Israel Viewpoint,* August 15, 1961.

32. *American Jewish Year Book,* LXIII (1962), 205-07; Bernstein, *The Orthodox Union Story,* 203-04.

33. NCRAC, *Joint Program Plan,* 1961-1962, 12; 1962-1963, 7; 1963-1964, 14; 1964-1965, 8.

34. NCRAC, *Report of the Plenary Session,* 1963, 33.

35. *American Jewish Year Book* LXII (1966), 139-40; NCRAC, *Joint Program Plan,* 1965-1966, 14-16; *Young Israel Viewpoint,* January 31, February 28, 1965.

36. NCRAC, *Report of the Plenary Session,* 1965, 42-43; NCRAC, *Joint Program Plan,* 1965-1966, 16-17.

37. Bernstein, *Renaissance of the Torah Jew,* 267; Marvin Schick, "The New Style of American Orthodox Jewry," *Jewish Life* (January-February 1967): 36.

38. *American Jewish Year Book* LXII (1966), 129.

39. NCRAC, *Joint Program Plan* 1966-1967, 16; 1967-1968, 23; 1968-1969, 18; 1969-1970, 23. Also see Gregg Ivers, *To Build a Wall: American Jews and the Separation of Church and State* (Charlottesville: University of Virginia Press, 1995), 176-78.

40. NCRAC, *Proceedings,* 1968, 27.

41. NJCRAC, *Joint Program Plan,* 1970-1971, 15-16; Institute for Jewish Policy Planning and Research, Synagogue Council of America, *Jewish Education in a Secular Society: A Symposium on Public Aid to Non-public Education* (1971).

42. See the OU dissents from the NJCRAC consensus in the *Joint Program Plan* for these years, and also its refusal to join the NJCRAC legal brief against the constitutionality of the establishment of a special school district for Hassidic children in Kiryas Joel (New York), *Joint Program Plan* 1994-1995, 37-38.

43. *American Jewish Year Book,* LXIV (1963), 110; *Young Israel Viewpoint,* July 20, 1962.

44. Jonathan D. Sarna and David G. Dalin, eds., *Religion and State in the American Experience* (Notre Dame, Ind.: Notre Dame University Press, 1997), 216.

45. *Young Israel Viewpoint,* August 24, September 7, October 5 and 19, 1962.

46. Bernstein, *The Orthodox Union Story,* 207; NJCRAC, *Joint Program Plan,* 1971-1972, 26.

47. NCRAC, *Report of the Plenary Session,* 1958, 40.

48. Charles S. Liebman, "Orthodoxy in American Jewish Life," *American Jewish Year Book* LXVI (1965), 58-61.

49. Positions on moral issues taken by mainstream Orthodox bodies should not be confused with the actual behavior of mainstream Orthodox Jews, about which little is known. Samuel C. Heilman and Steven M. Cohen, in *Cosmopolitans and Parochials: Modern Orthodox Jews in America* (Chicago: University of Chicago Press, 1989), argue that the rank and file are considerably more liberal (libertine?) than their organizations, but the evidence is largely based on data from the Lincoln Square Synagogue in New York City, an atypical congregation.

50. Bernstein, *The Orthodox Union Story,* 271, 274; Berzon quoted in Jewish Telegraphic Agency, *Daily Bulletin,* May 4, 1971.

51. Jewish Telegraphic Agency, *Daily Bulletin,* June 28, 1973; NJCRAC, *Joint Program Plan,* 1974-1975, 42.

52. Stanley B. Wexler, "Should Orthodox Jews Fight for Legislating Morals? A Rabbi Says No!" Reuben E. Gross, "Should Orthodox Jews Fight for Legislating Morals? A Layman Says Yes!" *Jewish Life* (Summer 1977): 21-28.

53. Jewish Telegraphic Agency, *Daily Bulletin,* April 21, 1972.

54. NJCRAC, *Joint Program Plan,* 1972-1973, 42; 1973-1974, 30.

55. NJCRAC, *Joint Program Plan* 1974-1975, 34; 1975-1976, 37; 1976-1977, 21; 1977-1978, 32; 1978-1979, 39; 1979-1980, 45; 1980-1981, 50.

56. David M. Feldman, *Marital Relations, Birth Control, and Abortion in Jewish Law* (New York: Schocken, 1974), 259-62.

57. Jewish Telegraphic Agency, *Daily News Bulletin,* May 6, 1971, April 28, 1972.

58. *JTA Bulletin,* January 31, 1973, January 29, 1976.

59. NJCRAC, *Joint Program Plan,* 1974-1975, 42; 1975-1976, 42, 56; 1976-1977, 26; 1978-1979, 40.

60. NJCRAC, *Joint Program Plan,* 1982-1983, 37, 51-52; 1983-1984, 56, 62; 1984-1985, 33, 56; 1985-1986, 13, 39; 1986-1987, 36, 40; 1987-1988, 42, 55; 1988-1989, 46, 51; 1989-1990, 47, 58, 65; 1990-1991, 42, 65; 1991-1992, 48, 62; 1992-1993, 30, 58, 65; 1993-1994, 20, 51, 56; 1994-1995, 30, 42; 1995-1996, 27, 37, 43; 1996-1997, 30, 37; JCPA, *Agenda for Public Affairs,* 1997-1998, 23, 32; 1998-1999, 32, 38, 41.

61. Bernstein, *The Orthodox Union Story,* 280-81; Norman Lamm, "Judaism and the Modern Attitude to Homosexuality," *Encyclopedia Judaica*

Yearbook, 1974, 194-205; NJCRAC, *Joint Program Plan,* 1994-1995, 47, repeated each year since.

62. Union of Orthodox Jewish Congregations of America, *Program-Handbook, 76th Anniversary Biennial Convention* (unpaginated), "Report of the Public Affairs Division."

63. NJCRAC, *Joint Program Plan,* 1976-1977, 4; 1977-1978, 5.

64. NJCRAC, *Joint Program Plan,* 1992-1993, 3.

65. See, for example, the OU dissents in NJCRAC, *Joint Program Plan,* 1973-1974, 27; 1974-1975, 29, 32-33, 36; 1975-1976, 30, 56; 1977-1978, 33.

66. JCPA, *Agenda for Public Affairs,* 2000-2001, 62-73. Unlike its predecessor, the JCPA has no qualms about invoking Judaism, at least for environmentalist purposes, entitling this section "Jewish Values and the Environment."

67. Jon D. Levenson, "Poverty and the State in Biblical Thought," *Judaism* (Spring 1976): 230-41. Mainstream Orthodoxy in Great Britain has been more receptive to a Judaic argument for limited state intervention, as seen in Chief Rabbi Jonathan Sacks's "Markets and Morals," *First Things* (August-September, 2000): 23-28.

8

Haredim and the Public Square: The Nature of the Social Contract

Samuel C. Heilman

During the eighteenth and nineteenth centuries in Europe, the so-called Age of Enlightenment, the concept of the social contract, which asserted a new moral and civic compact between the individual and society, became popular. Social contract theory asserted that in their emergence from their primeval, irrational, and anarchic state of nature, human beings—governed by increasingly rational thinking—had formed a society (and a government) that was based on an agreement among them. In this agreement or "social contract," they emphasized civil order over the anarchy and absence of central authority in the state of nature, which Thomas Hobbes had memorably characterized as "solitary, poor, nasty, brutish and short," voluntarily abandoning purely selfish interests in favor of social obligations and what Rousseau called the *volonté générale* ("general will").[1]

At first, the Jews of Europe, viewed by the Christian majority and many of its leaders as a pariah nation, a group whom Voltaire, echoing a common view of the day in his *Dictionary of Philosophy,* called "the most abominable people in the world," were simply not considered to be parties to this social contract, nor was their consent or concern considered to be part of the general will.[2] Set apart from civil society by a legacy of religious hostility, residential segregation, social distance, political powerlessness, as well as theology, custom, law, language, and dress, these Jews, however, did not live in an anarchic state of nature. On the contrary, they had their own internal social compact in which traditional Judaism and Jewish culture were the dominant elements. This compact was built upon what the Jews believed was a covenant between them and God, the so-called *brit Avraham* and the Torah given at Sinai, augmented by a long and complex Jewish tradition. All this spelled out not only a special relationship of the Jews with their God but also how they were to relate to one another and those who did not share in the covenant. If Jewish life was poor, nasty, brutish, and short, it was, they believed, not because they did not have their own system of laws and order, but because the non-Jewish world that dominated over them had made it so. For generations, this arrangement—in which Jews had their own internal order—seemed to many of them the way life was always going to be. They suffered the scorn of the outside world, including even those who claimed to be enlightened, but maintained their own rich and complex civilization, which many of them considered a superior alternative to the rules of social order that non-Jewish civilization embraced.

When, however, as a result of political changes in Europe and the West, the boundaries of civil society were enlarged to include even the Jewish pariah, and the world outside their own opened up to them, those Jews for whom their own covenant suddenly felt too narrow and restrictive moved outside of its limits. Often as they bounded outward, these Jews discovered that the emergent Western civil society of the Age of Enlightenment would accept them only if they underwent what in Germany was called *verbesserung,* "improvement," and elsewhere was called "naturalization" or "enlightenment." In practice this meant, as many Jews soon found out, that the price of admission to being part of the general will and social contract was the excision of the totality of Jewish being from their personal lives or at the very least diminishing its role in their life to its margins. Naturalization and inclusion in the social contract, as far as they could achieve it, required the eradication of their "unnatural" Jewish identity and improvement required the abrogation of the Jewish covenant in favor of the general will, which was predominantly the will of non-Jews. This was the path taken by such Jews as Disraeli in England, Heine in Germany, and others like them who, while embracing the status of citizen in what they viewed as general society, essentially abandoned their Jewish identities and obligation to Jewish tradition, even if that meant a nominal conversion to the dominant Christianity of the day. In a statement that echoed the conviction that this path defined "improvement," the distinguished Orientalist Daniel Khwolson, who converted from Judaism, was quoted as saying, "I was *convinced* that it is better to be a Christian professor in Saint Petersburg than a Jewish *melamed* [school teacher] in the *shtetl* [Jewish village]."[3]

Other Jews were satisfied to re-form their Judaism so that it would be in harmony with contemporary civilization and its social contract. This meant making all practices and requirements that emphasized a separate Jewish corporate identity obsolete and finding instead a way to create a faith that allowed Jewish distinctions largely to disappear. Some groups were liberal in these reforms while others sought to be more conservative, trying to make changes that were somehow in tune with Jewish history. But for both approaches, in place of strictly Jewish culture, there arose Judeo-Christian society to which both Jews and Christians could belong alike. Of course, this did not mean that Christians emphasized Jewish elements in their religious identity.

Not all Jews viewed these paths as desirable. Those who came to be called "Orthodox," who embraced their Jewish identity along with the traditional commitments of Judaism, saw such a choice as a bad deal, for it meant exchanging what they considered the "eternal" and superior riches of their covenant for short-term advantages that they believed were inferior and culturally counterfeit.[4] As such they saw the social contract of "enlightened" European society, and ultimately of all Western civilization, as one which they had little or no stake in preserving. On the contrary, while they were ready to make instrumental use of its products for their own benefit, they denied its essential value. Even when most Jews had entered into the mainstreams of Western civil society and been assimilated into its increasingly secular humanist culture with its largely Christian roots, some Orthodox Jewish hold-outs watched from the sidelines, from within ghettoes that were now their cultural strongholds rather than their social prisons, and concluded that overall the effects of moving out into the public square of Western civil society were morally and culturally corrosive.[5] While they might make instrumental use of its goods and services—particularly its economic might, technology, and political freedoms—they would not fully enter into it. They would be *in* the larger society, pass through its public square, but they would not be part *of* it. At most, they would deal with controlling its influences upon them. Principally, however, they would maintain their allegiance to their own Jewish covenant above and beyond the general social contract. Those who remained rigorously at a distance and eschewed even the symbolic or partial stance of having a foot in each world were the Orthodox whom today we call "haredim." They numbered about 800,000 Jews worldwide in the year 2000, the majority of whom are in Israel and North America.[6]

The Haredi Way

For haredim this worldview has in practice led to an increasingly insular existence in which they live overwhelmingly among other Jews who share their ethos and values, shielding particularly those who would be most easily attracted by the counterfeit riches of civil society. However, because the contemporary world is forever enlarging its boundaries and because as well haredim remain instrumentally dependent on much that comes from this world, they cannot completely cut themselves off from it. Rather than creating a completely separate realm in which they live—as, for example, the Amish have tried to do (not very successfully)—the haredim have had to content themselves with living in an "enclave culture." "Torah man needs—besides Torah knowledge—a Torah tradition within which to live and grow," as one of them recently put it, explaining the desirability of creating such a territorial enclave.[7]

In the traditionalist haredi view the most vulnerable among them are women and especially children (from primary school age through adolescence and even into young adulthood).[8] Therefore, they must be kept secure within the enclave. Yet while females and the young were to be kept as far away as possible from the non-haredi public square, such insulation was no less a desideratum for adult males.

Because it is not absolutely set apart, however, the enclave must compete against the appeal of the neighboring community which may be powerful, attracting, enticing, and even seductive, encouraging desertion. In an open society like America's, where no corporate restrictions are sanctioned, and anyone can go where he or she wishes, the primary means that the enclave culture has for preventing its members from leaving is by fostering in them negative attitudes toward the other, the world and people outside the enclave. "In other words, the defining relations for the enclave are 'inside-outside'" relations between those in the enclave and those beyond its boundaries.[9] This may be accomplished by means of ideology, in which the inside is painted as superior and the outside as nefarious. Accordingly, haredim expend large measures of their energy and cultural capital on building protective institutions, reviving Jewish traditions, and a *kulturkampf* in which they struggle against the erosion of their way of life by denigrating and attacking the value or legitimacy of alternative ways of life. Thus, when some element of the outside seeps into their world, it is disparaged. It also helps to emphasize characteristics of those inside that make them different from, even stigmatized, by those on the outside. Finally, creating a series of obstacles to movement outward and away is helpful.

Haredim have used a variety of means to restrict their contact with what they consider the gentile provinces of the public square. They have tried to control access to the outside world by encouraging a limited range of permissible places to live, creating institutions that serve as cultural fortresses, and emphasizing behavior patterns that foster separation from those who do not share their worldview and beliefs. In most places where they live, they maintain their own press and, for significant numbers of them, this press is their primary or even their only source of authoritative news.[10] These days they even go so far as to try to control access to the electronic windows on the world that are the video and computer screen.[11] "I grew up watching television," an American haredi told me, "but when I got married I didn't bring one into the house."[12]

Even when the restrictions on Jews entering into the general social contract declined and when a pluralist society beckoned, particularly in the secular democracies that predominated in the places where Jews found themselves in the twentieth century, the haredim turned resolutely inward and away from it, considering those Jews who embraced the pleasures and rewards of Western civilization as having a dangerous love affair with a monster that would swallow and absorb them—*goyim nachas*, "the pleasures of the gentiles," as they called it.

Even the university, perhaps the crowning cultural achievement of that outside world, and the goal of generations of outward-bound and upwardly mobile Jews who saw in it a gateway to a broader understanding and appreciation of human civilization, became defined by haredim as an obstacle to faith and gateway to licentiousness, a place to be avoided like the plague. The yeshiva, with its delimited Torah and parochial learning, was the only place to go for study. "I went to law school," as David Zweibel, a haredi lawyer and official of Agudath Israel of America,[13] perhaps the premier haredi Orthodox institution in the United States, told me, "but my kids were satisfied with high school and then yeshiva."

Whether in the university or the attractive shopping mall or any part of the public square to which so many other Jews have been drawn for a cultural "great adventure," the haredi response is above all: "We will stay among our own; we don't want to assimilate because when you get too close to another culture, there's always a risk that you will be swallowed up by it." Indeed, they see rising intermarriage rates, dropping levels of Jewish affiliation and religious competence, and the adaptation of Jewish practices to norms and standards that were sought to be in harmony with Western (read: gentile) values as evidence that Jews who entered the precincts of Western civilization's public square were becoming *goyim*, gentiles.

Convinced that only haredim are the true heirs of the ancients and that all other Jews who do not share their beliefs and practices are not, they assert that they are the only authentic Jews (and should therefore be the only ones with the authority to define who is truly a Jew). They eschew pluralism and refuse to negotiate Judaism with their fellow Jews or those who do not share their values and worldviews. They not only embrace but also preach exclusivism, and they cynically mistrust ideological or behavioral tolerance as a form of cultural suicide. The public square, where once Jews were shunned or persecuted, now that it allows them entry is ironically perceived as a place no less dangerous. Where once the danger came from exclusiveness and intolerance by the host societies, now the perceived risk comes from their inclusiveness and tolerance. Where once Jews were endangered but a ghettoized Judaism was safe in its separation, now Jews are no longer endangered but Judaism is threatened to be culturally overwhelmed by its larger partner in the public square of Judeo-Christian society. The public square has, therefore, in great measure become useful as a *negative identifier*, a place that helps haredim to define who they are *not*. We are, the haredi Jews assert, the people who choose to be elsewhere.

Haredim have therefore created their own public squares governed by their own social contract and social order. In these, they bind themselves by a series of increasingly stringent and therefore insulating interpretations of Jewish law and conservative customs that make it difficult, if not impossible, for them to share in life with those who do not abide by these same rules of conduct. They even make insiders dress and groom themselves so as to look as if they come from another place. Here they celebrate their difference from those on the outside whom they characterize as ontologically inferior at best and insidious at worst. In this enclave, they have established a world apart. This is in Hebrew an *orach chayim*, a way of life.[14]

This *orach chayim* is a model *of* and a model *for* haredi life, synergistically demanding and constructing a series of involvements and expectations that keep haredim engaged in specifically Jewish activities—the more parochial the better. It has also demanded their engaging in the ongoing and sometimes aggressive culture war against anything they considered to be outside the covenant. Decisions of what was outside was to be determined by rabbis—the Agudah (like its Israeli counterpart) even created what they called "The Council of Torah Sages"[15]—religious virtuosi whose opinions and interpretations have become enshrined in the concept of "*da'as toyreh*," an understanding of the Torah's demands that allowed the rabbis to extrapolate them to all domains of life, including those not expressly covered in sacred texts. In the words of an Agudist publication, the dependence on *da'as toyreh* grew out of the "conviction that the Torah sages—precisely because they are immersed in and saturated with the word of G-d [sic]—are living, breathing embodiments of the Torah attitude toward every question, no matter how mundane."[16] In this attitude, if something was not explicitly Jewish (and Jewish meant "haredi"), then it must be gentile—or *goyish* as these Jews call it—and the *goyish* was ipso facto undesirable and to be avoided. In an inversion of the anti-Jewish attitudes that once were dominant in the general society, the haredim asserted that whatever was Jewish was good; whatever was *goyish* was bad.

This has led to American haredim not only rejecting the ideal of the melting pot but embracing, among other things, the ideal of separate but equal, a standard that of course has been repudiated in the United States where integration has been the goal for at least thirty years. In effect, the predilection that haredim have for living apart and yet still demanding no less a share in the goods and services available in the public square has fostered tensions between them and their neighbors.[17] In a sense it has exacerbated the feelings of emotional distance that already exist between them and those who do not share their world.

As for those so-called modern Orthodox who believed that they can be partners to both the social contract of secular Western society and the covenant of Torah, that they can be integrated into the larger culture while still maintaining their religious needs and values, that they could make the public square of secular society and culture responsive to and inclusive of their needs, they appear to the haredim, for whom the "notion of the smooth blend, of happily enjoying the 'best of both worlds'" remains "an insidious delusion remiss in truth and serious meaning," as hopelessly self-deceiving.[18]

For the haredim, no enclave is more important than the one they have created in and around their yeshivas. While originally institutions of advanced Jewish learning, chiefly emphasizing Talmud study, today's yeshiva communities are fortresses within which people, who might otherwise be moved to explore the world as they go out into the public square to make a living or pursue other goals, are restricted and protected from the insidious effects of outside culture and the invidious influence of secular society. Often they spend their time there not only in reviewing the sacred texts of Jewish tradition but also in being forewarned about and mutually reinforcing convictions that the evils of society are just beyond their doorstep.

In the yeshivas and other domains of their existence, haredim create what Emmanuel Sivan has called a "wall of virtue" made of activities and expressed by values through which members are assured that, by remaining apart from those on the other side of the wall, they are among the specially chosen and receive superior moral rewards.[19] Here they have "recouped and regrouped" from the losses that the first half of the twentieth century brought.[20] In return they share not only in the haredi social contract but also in the advantages that flow from it: advantages that include marriage, subsidies, charitable giving, high status, help and moral as well as social support in times of adversity, and a sense of belonging to an extended haredi family and community.[21]

The yeshiva must, of course, help provide them with an alternative way to live, and it does so both in terms of supplying meaning and in terms of securing economic support. Thus, haredim increasingly live *in* the yeshiva world and *off* the yeshiva world, receiving Torah training as well as stipends. There they are taught that to leave this fortress is anathema or at best a sell-out and sign of moral weakness. There they are informed that they are the elite, engaged in the only praiseworthy pursuit—"*Toyreh is di beste schoyreh*" as the Yiddish phrase goes, meaning Torah is the best merchandise to possess. Doing anything else is cultural betrayal, risky business, and a danger to the soul and heart. Even the community rabbi who has abandoned the yeshiva to serve in a paid position as a spiritual leader in the synagogue, and certainly anyone else who has left the yeshiva and entered the mainstreams of contemporary society with its claims on attention and involvement, has degraded status and endangered his Jewish identity. The yeshiva is the ideal place to stay so that will not happen. As for women, if they are not students of the yeshiva, then they can and should serve as supportive wives and mothers who enable their menfolk and children.

Ironically in Israel, where on the one hand a Jew would suffer no anti-Jewish prejudices or obvious obstacles to full participation in society, where the world outside the enclave cannot so easily be defined as "*goyish*," it is therefore paradoxically viewed as the most dangerous. For here, one who entered the public square would be confronted by an alternative working model of Jewish identity, and therefore the yeshiva has become a particularly important segregating institution for the enclave culture. Today, 60 percent of prime-aged males who live in the haredi enclaves of Israel are in yeshivas.[22] Moreover, they remain in these institutions until well into their forties. In the United States, where the society outside the gates can be more easily dismissed as non-Jewish and hence not offering an alternative Jewish identity, the numbers are somewhat lower (as are the available funds to subsidize such a life), but the imperative to remain in the yeshiva at the very least until past marriage remains strong and socially encouraged.

In both places, the wives and children of the students may be thought of as belonging to the yeshiva world. They are linked to it not only by virtue of their need to be physically near the institution and by the fact that they receive a subsidy or stipend that the yeshivas or kollels give to their members but also because they share in the special honor and status of the student head of household as well as the worldview of the yeshiva.[23] Increasingly, participation in yeshiva life thus provides individuals and families with what has been called a "signaling value," proof to others within the haredi world that one is truly an insider, engaged in the culture war against secular society. This is a strong signal that demonstrates that the students and their families are willing to sacrifice for their Judaism. By remaining in the yeshiva until well into their prime earning years and refusing the secular training or work experience that would make them self-sufficient, they not only signal but foster "a commitment that causes increased sacrifice" and insulation from contemporary society.[24] By living the haredi lifestyle, they embrace time-consuming practices and stringent interpretations of Judaism that further deprive them of time to pursue other ends, both economic and cultural. They often also have large families that they try to sustain with the yeshiva life, a particularly taxing choice to make that serves to demonstrate their willingness to endure economic burdens and social strains for the sake of their Judaism.

Because they have characterized the dangers of the outside as "an ever-lurking risk," the haredim manage to maintain a high degree of solidarity, both normative and behavioral, among themselves.[25] Who but the depraved or foolhardy would risk crossing beyond the wall of virtue? Moreover, if crossing the boundary links one with the discredited outsiders, why do so? The answer to this last question also provides insights into the nature of the connection between haredim and the public square.

Interaction with the Public Square

Clearly there are differences between those haredim who find themselves in Israel, a Jewish state where the right to define the nature of the public square is contested by Jews of various outlooks, and a place like the United States, where in the contesting claims to control and determine public life, Jews and Jewish values are minor players. In Israel, haredim can and do seek to play a part in shaping the character of life in the public square so that it is more in tune with their enclave culture, in limiting what they view as the erosion of Jewish tradition, and in demanding that the society and its governing legal authorities not only provide for their particularistic needs but also make them binding in many of the spheres of public life. To enhance this role, moreover, haredim may and increasingly do make use of their political power in a parliamentary system that has worked in their favor because of its dependence on small parties to tip the balance of power to one of the two major national blocs. Thus, for example, Israeli haredim these days claim a role in determining the nature of public education, what should be the laws that control moral behavior (including what may legitimately be viewed in public space), defining who may be called a Jew, and even what claims may be made on the public purse.

In the contemporary United States, with its democratic values and emerging ethos of ethnic pluralism, for which haredi Jews—no less so than other minorities—claim that they have an appreciation, the attitude, however, is different. "We have a *hakaras ha'tov* [a recognition of the goodness] of America," as one haredi put it, "but its culture is not our culture. If in [a multicultural] America we can be a culture apart within a patchwork quilt, that's the best any society could give us Jews." While some might argue, as one man did, that haredi Jews "have a great concern in making America a holier society," the far more prevalent attitude is that first and foremost these Jews had to make certain that what one man called "our family," by which he meant those who share internal Jewish ties and haredi values, was culturally "secure."

In large measure this latter, more dominant stance comes out of the fact that so many American haredim are either survivors or the children of survivors—survivors of the Holocaust and also of the waves of assimilation and religious reform that swept through the world of traditional Jewry—and that has led both to their idealizing of an imagined traditional Jewish society as well as to an abiding anxiety that it is on the verge of destruction, attitudes which frame their view of what Jewish life should be. From this perspective haredim perceive themselves as still suffering from an ongoing cultural crisis that emerged out of the double-barreled decimation of that Jewish world. Accordingly, their first priority remains to recoup and regroup, to restore "a flourishing Jewish civilization." But, of course, all survivors who idealize the past seek to restore it with an even greater power than it ever had in reality. Hence, this mentality reinforces the conviction that those engaged in restoration have never been (and probably will never be) able to do enough.

"We're still busy rebuilding, imbuing our children with our ideas and reaching out to people who are leaving," as one American haredi summed up this sentiment, concluding, "we have a long way to go until we recapture what was destroyed."[26] Faced with such a sense of mission, which the survivors rightly conclude requires a great many resources and much energy, leads easily to the self-serving conclusion by many in the haredi community that it is impossible to expect them simultaneously to give of their precious resources to the public square. The highest priority is "rebuilding from the ashes." This attitude has been reinforced by the fact that in its formative years what is perhaps the premier haredi institution, Agudath Israel of America, as well as those who identified or affiliated with it—such as, for example, Rabbi Aaron Kotler, a member of its Council of Torah Sages and head of the influential Beit Midrash Govoha Yeshiva in Lakewood, New Jersey—were largely defined by activities concerned with Jewish survival. The Agudah, for example, sponsored Va'ad Hatzalah, a rescue organization that worked assiduously and with some success to rescue Jews from Europe and afterward to help them resettle themselves and restore their way of life in America.[27] Many of the members of this organization and a significant number of the Orthodox were either Jews who left on the eve of the Nazi firestorm, survivors of the Shoah, or their children.

In addition, the fact that economically the haredim remain among the poorest of Jews and that they still have the highest relative costs for sustaining their Jewish way of life surely adds to this sense of crisis and the perceived need to turn attention to themselves first.[28] Because most Jewish philanthropy goes to other causes, and because in the United States the separation between religion and state makes it sometimes difficult for them to find governmental economic support for their educational system and community institutions, the largest drain on their resources, also adds to a sense that since America cannot concern itself with what they need most, they must not distract themselves with America's concerns.

Yet, in spite of this perceived situation of crisis and insularity as well as the "me-first" attitude of the community that sees itself as barely surviving and limits haredi contributions to the public square, there are at least three conditions that do lead to their becoming so engaged. Engagement may come about if they come to believe that by improving the character of life in the public square, they can somehow better protect the values and character of their enclave. They thus seek to affect the general society so that it will *provide a hospitable environment for their way of life.* In Israel, this requires a particularly activist stance because, as noted earlier, almost everything has the potential to suggest an alternative value system to the one haredim hold. That means fighting back against any actions that threaten to breach the wall of virtue. Thus, for example, in Israel advertising placards that present images that are viewed as immoral and which have been posted inside haredi neighborhoods have been the stimulus for violent outbursts in which these were removed. These sorts of actions stem from a sense of entitlement that encourages Israeli haredim to think of the public square as theirs to contest.

While similar sentiments about the moral significance of "immodest" posters in public are surely shared by American haredim, they would not attack images of scantily clad models on city bus stops in their neighborhoods with the same alacrity as their Israeli counterparts. Their approach, coming from a sense of their being a tolerated minority (the classic view of the Orthodox in the diaspora), would instead take the form of legal maneuvers, behind-the-scenes lobbying, or actions taken in the domains of public opinion. Thus, a haredi leader involved in such actions in New York described the actions taken by Agudath Israel of America on behalf of its constituency as follows: "We asked the courts to interpret the First Amendment so as to allow the city to place restrictions on the types of ads it will accept for city buses." Their reasons, as the haredim explained to the courts, were based on the fact that "our own children walk the streets and we want them protected" from what we consider morally offensive images. Yet it is not simply to protect their own children, they explained to the city powers. Rather, they claimed that they believed "that in general if the moral environment surrounding the city is healthier, less supportive or protective of a promiscuous life style, then that would in general improve the climate in which we live."[29]

Explaining this attitude homiletically, one American haredi rabbi recalled Abraham's biblical debate with God over the destruction of Sodom in which the first Jewish patriarch argued for this evil city's survival if at the very least ten righteous souls were to be found in it. Comparing the public square of secular society to Sodom, he declared: "If there *were* only ten pure souls in Sodom, I still wouldn't want to live there, to be one of them." Hence, if one lived in the Sodom of contemporary secular society, one had to make sure that there was more than a tiny minority of "pure souls."

As another haredi put it: "If the tenor of the society around us is hospitable to our way of thinking" and, by implication, to the haredi way of life, "then it is less likely to have a pernicious impact" and, accordingly, "it's useful for us to try to shape it." Yet, doing so, trying to improve the moral quality of life in the public square—when that public square is not a Jewish one—remains a second-level priority, to which the haredim can devote only a limited amount of what they view as their precious and limited resources. The haredim do not want to improve the public square for its own sake, "not because we want to make *them* better," as he went on to elucidate, but because making the surrounding society and culture hold to a way of life that seems "more moral" will "redound to *our* benefit."

Under the protective cover of the now popular principle that pluralism is American and minorities have a right to maintain their distinctive integrity, American haredim have been active in the legislative arena. Lobbying on behalf of causes that they consider crucial for maintaining their way of life and values, Orthodox Jews, often under the aegis of Agudath Israel of America, testified before Congress in 1961 on behalf of a bill that would support government aid to private schools. They, of course, universally viewed private education as the cornerstone of their continuity and key to their ability to maintain the integrity of their ways of life and enclave culture. The passage in 1965 of the Elementary and Secondary Education Act, which called for equal treatment of nonpublic school children in poverty areas, was one result. While this had concrete advantages for haredim who often qualified (according to the 1990 census, for example, 65 percent of the persons in Kiryas Joel and 55 percent of those in New Square, haredi, hasidic enclaves in suburban New York, were below the poverty line), this law assisted all poor Americans who chose private schools for their children. In the state of New York, haredim worked hard and ultimately successfully to press for the passage in 1974 of what became the Mandated Services Law, which requires the state to pay private schools for such state-required activities as testing and keeping attendance records (the law survived a constitutional challenge in the highest court). More recently, a June 2000 U.S. Supreme Court decision (*Mitchell v. Helms*), narrowly affirming the right of parochial schools to use public funds to subsidize the cost of computers and other instructional tools, was also one that the haredim publicly supported. Perhaps most important, they have managed to obtain legislative definitions and administrative rulings that guard and help maintain federal aid to yeshiva education, financial assistance that comes under some of the same programs that award money to colleges and universities. These funds have been lifeblood for many of these institutions and their students.

They have also over the years argued against recurring kindness to animals/anti-*shechita* (kosher slaughtering of meat and fowl) bills in Congress and various state legislatures. Lobbyists from Agudath Israel have worked assiduously to ban misleading uses of the word "kosher" in the public square and marketplace, leading to laws in New York, Maryland, California, and Ohio. They have worked to defeat moves that supported year-round daylight savings time bills—which they saw as threatening to the fulfillment of prayer ritual as well as Sabbath and holy day observances that are based upon the times of sunrise and sunset. They have helped win passage of a New York state law outlawing discrimination against Sabbath observers in private employment and even overturning a U.S. Department of Agriculture ban on the import of etrogs (a citron used for an essential ritual on the holiday of Sukkot) from Israel. In 1977, they succeeded in getting the New York governor to sign a bill banning fraudulent *mezuzot* and *tefillin*, making the state probably the source for the most reliable of such Jewish ritual objects in the world.

In perhaps one of the most far-reaching efforts to influence the public square, American haredim publicly lobbied for defeat of the Equal Rights Amendment to the Constitution. While the opposition derived from the haredi goal of maintaining the separation of men and women in their synagogues and schools, a practice they believe to be mandated by Jewish law and venerated custom, and their strongly felt desire to insure that women would maintain traditional family roles as wife and mother, their disfavor for the amendment was framed by arguments that sought to speak to the general concerns of the American public square. Thus, they argued that the amendment would add no new rights to women who were "already protected in employment, education, credit and public housing and the like by a multitude of laws, both federal and state." They asserted that the amendment's passage "will seriously threaten the stability of the family" because "husband and wife will be equally responsible for the financial support of the family—sometimes legally obligating a wife to provide half the family income." They insisted that the E.R.A. would "eliminate laws protective of women," offering the example that women might be forced by their employers to "travel to dangerous neighborhoods" that now were places where only men were sent. They affirmed that it would "threaten the ability of religious institutions to separate men and women" or even to "accent only one" of the sexes. Finally, they contended that the constitutional change would "accelerate the deterioration of society's moral fiber" by allowing women to serve in roles that were once exclusively male and vice versa.[30]

In order to insure that their constituents are provided for by the public sector, haredi institutions have at times had to redefine themselves as public service agencies, and as such have inserted their activity into the public square. During the 1970s, Agudath Israel of America in particular achieved notable success in this regard. Thus, in order to maintain the Orthodoxy of many of the newcomers from what was then the Soviet Union, they provided job counseling, training, and placement through their yeshivas and related community organizations. This led to the establishment of vocational training institutes and not incidentally to getting yeshivas and kollels to qualify for federally financed student loans, tuition grants, and work-study programs. These have served for almost thirty years as essential conduits for public funds insofar as they helped new immigrants and the impoverished. From the perspective of the public square, this would seem to be a contribution to the adaptation and establishment of the immigrant and the poor; from the haredi perspective this was yet another mechanism for enhancing and preserving their enclave culture and its members. So successful was this that even private agencies such as the Ford Foundation have supported haredi neighborhood associations (for example, in 1977 it gave a grant to the Southern Brooklyn Community Organization whose goal was to "stabilize" Borough Park and Flatbush, neighborhoods that are heavily Orthodox).

All these efforts and activities, while ostensibly evidence of the haredi engagement in the public square outside their enclave culture and of their participation in shaping its social contract, turn out upon closer scrutiny and analysis to be efforts to create an environment that will protect and preserve haredi culture and values. Only incidentally do they serve as a bridge into the life of that American public square.

There is a second reason that haredim may become engaged in trying to affect the character of life in the public square. This might be called "the battle to speak for the Jews." Here the dynamic that drives haredi involvement is an effort to make certain that the world outside the Jewish domains knows that not all voices that claim to speak for the Jews do indeed do so. In Israel, of course, this is a crucial matter for the secular state, the government, or the courts, and even polls that reflect the opinions of the majority of Jews (who are neither haredi nor any kind of Orthodox) may come to represent what is Jewish with an authority that is sweeping. In the United States, the haredim seek to present a countervoice that is not just different but somehow "Jewishly authentic" by virtue of its claim to be bonded to tradition. Since they have, throughout most of the history of the state, failed to persuade the majority that they are indeed authoritative and exclusively authentic, they have endeavored to coerce the state powers to cede to them institutional and legal hegemony over defining what is Jewish. They carry on this battle politically and even engage in street violence to accomplish their aims.

In the diaspora, however, and especially in America, the haredi effort is more limited. Here, where Jews are a minority—and often one whose views are not of particular interest to those who are the majority of cultures who make up the public square—the haredim simply try to make certain that the voices of those who are not strictly tied to traditional Judaism and its demands do not become the only ones to speak for the Jews. Moreover, because the Orthodox in general and the haredim in particular have eschewed inter- and intrareligious dialogue, this has forced them often to express themselves independently and at their own initiative in the public square. This they do in a variety of forums.

While there are a number of issues that could illustrate this, the matter of abortion will serve as a good canvas on which to paint a portrait. Although *halakhah*, Jewish law, is somewhat ambiguous on the status of a fetus, leaving some room to argue that abortion is not legally equivalent to murder and may, in cases where the life and health of the mother is endangered, be approved by even the most stringent of interpreters of the law, as a policy it is surely far from encouraged by the Orthodox.[31] In Israel, abortion, an increasingly common phenomenon, more often than not is the termination of a pregnancy of a Jewish woman. Opposition to its practice in the society at large, therefore, has been considered by many in the haredi community as a matter that affects the definition of what Jews may or may not do. Moreover, in their ongoing effort to force the Jewish state to be governed only by Jewish law, they could not abide a permissive attitude toward abortion. Accordingly, opposition to it is generally aimed at affecting an understanding in the society at large about what is properly Jewish.

While Israeli haredim do not believe that Israeli legislation permitting abortions carries any *halakhic* significance, they have been disturbed that Jews might come to mistakenly believe that Jewish law was, like the State of Israel, tolerant of abortion on demand.[32] Moreover, they have assumed that widely practiced abortions would morally erode not only the moral character of the society but of Judaism in Israel, leading in some subtle way to the subversion of their own religious life and virtue. They therefore direct their opposition to the public square so that those Jews who might not know what was "authentically Jewish" could be properly informed. This, they believe, necessitates changing the law, although exerting moral, social, and economic pressures upon those performing abortions and enlisting support for a ban among the population or, at the very least, for greater fertility, may have to do for the time being. Sephardic haredim, who inside Israel engage more actively in outreach to the nonobservant than do haredim of Ashkenazic background, have been in the forefront of this public opposition.

Thus, for example, during the 1980s, in the aftermath of the legislative loosening of restrictions on abortion in 1977, and when the number of abortions performed in Israel began to explode, the haredi opposition to abortion was led by Sephardic rabbis (who would, in the early part of the decade, form Shas—the Sephardic Torah Guardians Party).[33] One widely distributed poster at the time, headlined with the boldly printed words "Thou shalt not kill" and signed by Rabbi Ovadia Yosef, once Sephardic Chief Rabbi and spiritual head of Shas, called upon the "rabbis of Israel and the officials in synagogues everywhere to arouse the Israeli public to awareness of the seriousness of the prohibition [of abortion] and to work hard to encourage childbirth."[34] Over the next couple of years posters appeared urging social workers and particular hospitals to stop encouraging or performing abortions, while instructing citizens to withhold all donations and support to those institutions and groups that sanctioned abortion.[35]

The fact is that the furor among most Israeli haredim of Ashkenazic extraction over abortion has become generally muted since they have, by and large, not seen this as an issue that directly affects their own member families. Seeing the practice of abortion among other Israelis as an ineluctable feature of a promiscuous secular Israeli society, they have grown largely silent on the subject, allowing it to be simply another marker of the us-versus-them distinctions that make up their lives.

In the United States, however, the situation has developed somewhat differently. Unlike the case of their counterparts in Israel, haredim in the United States do not see their role as having to transform American society according to the *halakhah*.[36] Thus, if American non-Jews practice abortion on demand, no matter how abhorrent the practice may be to them as Jews, this should not concern the haredim—or so many of them reason, and hence they have dropped the matter from their priority agenda. Nevertheless, in the United States a person's stand on the abortion issue has for many citizens become perceived as a litmus test of whether one holds a liberal or conservative point of view or whether or not one is connected to the religious right.[37] Moreover, many American Jews, the majority of whom hold liberal points of view, also identify with the pro-choice supporters of a woman's right to an abortion on demand. These American realities have accordingly drawn at least some haredim into the abortion debate that has taken place in the American public square. They have done this, at least partially, for Jewish reasons. That is, like their Israeli counterparts, they want to make certain that Jews, uninformed of what haredim define as the Torah view, do not come to believe that somehow the pro-choice attitude, common among American Jews, represents an approved Jewish point of view or value. Hence, some have joined with anti-abortion forces in order to show that among the Orthodox there is "a different hierarchy of values," as one haredi anti-abortionist put it. Moreover, they also want to avoid the "perception in the public eye," among all Americans, that all Jews, and in particular those who see themselves as guardians of an "authentic" version of it, support such a permissive attitude toward abortion.

So while haredim in the United States do not aggressively lead the battle in the public square against abortion and for increased childbirth—as they tried to do for a while in Israel—at least some of them have entered the debate. Indeed, Agudath Israel of America, an organization that supports and seeks to express the haredi ethos, actually filed an amicus brief opposing a more liberal policy of abortion in the October 1998 U.S. Supreme Court case of *Webster et al. v. Reproductive Health Services et al.* That document was, as it states, "informed by classical Jewish tradition which teaches that all human life is sacred, and possessed of the firm view that laws which undermine the sanctity of human life send a message that is profoundly dangerous for all of society."[38]

Now why should the haredim care what others think is the authentic Jewish position or care about society beyond their own? If they are indeed insular, happy to remain bonded to their own covenant, taking their cues primarily from Jewish law and the norms within the walls of virtue surrounding their enclaves, why even bother to make certain their views of what is Jewish are understood by those outside? And why try to shape the surrounding society that is overwhelmingly made up of "goyim?"

For some, the reasons remain predominantly defensive and utilitarian. "We are concerned," as one haredi leader explained, "that [a negative image of Jews] might lead to anti-Semitism." Making certain that the public understands what haredi Judaism represents, this argument asserts, will help avoid such negative consequences. (Of course, it assumes as well that the haredi version of Judaism will be pleasing and appreciated rather than displeasing and arousing resentment—something that not all Jews might agree is the case.)

There is another explanation and it also accounts at least in part for haredi involvement in the public square in places other than the Jewish state. Neither defensive nor utilitarian, this engagement is an expression of what at least some haredim understand as "the divine mission of the Jews." That mandate is articulated in a verse in the Book of Isaiah (42:6): "I the Lord have called you in righteousness, and will hold your hand, and will keep you, and have you serve as a covenant for the people and a light unto the nations." This is understood to require the Jewish people to realize that their role in the world is not simply to illumine their own lives but also that of those nations with whom they come into contact. In other words, the Jewish mission is to be a living example, a Torah-prescribed injunction to contribute to civilization as a model *of* and a model *for* how to act in the world.

As an American haredi put it, "by standing firm in our belief system and by creating the type of families and systems that reflect our own religious worldview we are offering a model of people who take their religious faith seriously." That, as he put it, is an important contribution of haredi Jews to the public square in an America that often lacks such models. Without a doubt, behind the obvious triumphalism of this point of view there is also a conviction that there remains among the nations and peoples of the world—the gentiles—a kind of fascination with the Jews. That focus on the Jews can sometimes turn malevolent, as in the case of anti-Semitism, but at other times it also puts Jews in the position of acting as exemplars of human behavior. In particular, those like the haredim who see themselves as protectors and paragons of the tradition (one called them those "who are perceived as being the ground-zero of the Jewish people") can—even though they remain socially insular—serve as a kind of *ohr l'goyim,* "light unto the nations."[39]

These two perspectives—that concerns with the public square must be done for defensive purposes or alternatively for enlightening the nations—may be perceived in yet another matter of contemporary American interest recently before the U.S. Supreme Court. The case, *America v. Dale,* challenged the right of the Boy Scouts of America to ban one of its leaders who publicly presented himself as homosexual. On its face this would seem to be a matter that insular communities like haredi Jews would have no interest in at all. While their opposition to homosexuality is absolute, their youngsters do not normally participate in boy scouting and accordingly they might not be expected to care about what its policy is toward homosexuals. Indeed, the haredi-in-the-street probably does not care—probably does not even know that such a case was before the Court. Yet in this case, Agudath Israel of America once again filed a "friend of the court" brief (as it often does in cases perceived to have significance for them) in which it argued that forcing the Scouts to reinstate the discharged leader would open the door to infringing the right of "the free exercise of religion," because "if a non-religious body like the Boy Scouts of America is precluded by the anti-discrimination laws from establishing moral criteria for its leaders, religious groups would be similarly precluded."[40] The June 2000 U.S. Supreme Court ruling affirming that a state could not overrule the Scouts' ban on homosexuals serving as leaders was viewed by many haredim as a major victory.

Some might explain that this engagement in an American public moral debate is purely defensive. If the Boy Scouts can be forced to change their ideals and adjust their moral absolutes by the Supreme Court, who is to say that haredi Jews might not be thus challenged as well. Perchance they would be compelled to accept homosexuals. By helping to draw the line at the Boy Scouts, however, they can prevent what they view as a moral abomination from coming close to their domains.

Yet the brief also allowed the haredi leadership to present a Jewish position that they believed revealed a high moral ground and, hence, suggests that Jewish tradition, values, and law do not accept the legitimacy of homosexual behavior. Whether by doing this haredim may be seen as actively seeking to change the character of the society that surrounds them or are simply acting as a model, of course, brings us back to the question of how much responsibility the haredim believe they have for that society, the extent to which they believe they are included in the social contract, and the extent to which they believe that life in that surrounding society can impact on life in their enclave.

In Israel, as their numbers and political influence have grown, haredim have increasingly felt the society is theirs to shape and have become emboldened in affecting social legislation. In America and elsewhere in the diaspora, the impetus to be engaged in public debates and issues is dependent upon the extent to which such Jews believe they are part of the society. The advent of multiculturalism as well as the rise of fundamentalist religion in America has undoubtedly made haredim in principle able to feel more American than ever before in history. Those who are convinced that the contemporary American commitment to cultural pluralism includes them, that its traditional values are anchored in the Bible, especially its Old Testament, and that there are many in the public square who share their religious ethos, are thereby encouraged to take an active role in trying to shape the larger culture and society. It is out of that sentiment that at least some haredim are taking positions in the public square and adding their voices to public debate, even though a majority are probably still concerned only with their own world, believing that most of American society is beyond redemption and, hence, trying to repair it is largely hopeless—an attitude that radically distinguishes them from, say, Reform Judaism that has taken "*tikkun olam*," repairing the entire world, as a central principle of their Judaism. In a sense, then, the spectrum of those haredim runs from the majority who remain focused only on interior Jewish interests to those who, for utilitarian and defensive reasons, become engaged in the public square to finally those relative few who, accepting the reality of multiculturalism, seek to be a part of the larger society but do so convinced that they can offer moral leadership.

Confronted by those who might question their insularity—something that does not often occur precisely because they are a world apart—haredim have more and more argued that in their self-centeredness they are not that different from other subcultures who make up the mosaic that is the contemporary societies in which they generally have constructed their enclaves. They see ethnic communities all around them that are no less parochial, a standard of behavior that they now take as a given. In that sort of society they believe their behavior is in line with other unmeltable ethnics. "Do you vote in American elections because it is your civic duty or because you are trying to advance your own community's agenda?" as one haredi articulated the matter, concluding that, in effect, in today's America, at least, these are no longer mutually exclusive. Another, emphasizing the utilitarian explanation, concluded, "We vote because we want politicians to know that they have to pay attention to us." Those politicians, moreover, realize that haredim tend to pay attention to their own leadership, giving their leaders an authority and influence that reflects that of their followers.

Beyond this we-are-like-every-other-group argument, haredim maintain that insofar as members of their community are generally law-abiding and tax-paying citizens with overwhelmingly stable family lives and a low crime rate, they represent one of the more admirable and worthy sectors of the cultural mosaic in America. Of course, when haredim break the law, particularly in cases that draw a great deal of public attention, this undermines that claim. Then, it is far harder to see them as "good citizens," and instead their identity as aliens of some sort begins to loom large. Thus, for example, notorious instances in which haredim were found guilty of fraudulently taking government grants, convicted of sexual abuse, found guilty of drug-running or money-laundering, engaged in violent behavior in public, or even seem to be receiving society's benefits out of all proportion to their own reciprocal contributions, have all served not only to sully the public image of ultra-Orthodox Jewry but also call into question some of the essentials of their claims about their contributions as upstanding citizens and role models in the public square.[41] Accordingly, events like these have stimulated defensive postures not only from the accused but also from *all* quarters of the haredi world. The gist of these responses is that the malefactors were not representative or that the malfeasance can be explained, if not rationalized. At such times, there are also certain haredim who will take a more active stance of addressing the attention of the public square to make certain that the overall view of their way of life and values is not "distorted" by the actions of those whose behavior is reprobate.

Conclusion

"We are not out to change the world," as one haredi put it, referring to the relationship between his community and all those outside of it. "They have their covenant and we have ours." In Israel, of course, this is not quite correct since, as noted above, there is a conviction by the haredim that they, no less than the government or the army and maybe even more so, improve and protect the Jewish society by their moral superiority—a conviction far from shared by those outside their community. Elsewhere, however, where there is a greater sense of alienation from the surrounding society, the haredi objective remains to take care of themselves. If, however, in the course of the life that haredim have made for themselves, the world, the public square, becomes improved—"what's good for the Jews is good for the United States or even for the world," as one haredi expressed this principle—and even if this improvement comes about only indirectly, then the haredim believe that this should properly redound to their credit. "If we are what we're supposed to be," as one of the haredim already quoted put it, "we can change Sodom." In other words, the "righteous" who inhabit the Sodom of contemporary nonharedi society believe they have the right to see themselves as the instruments of its salvation, even when all they are doing is living up to their own covenantal obligation. Whether or not this attitude is shared by and acceptable to others in the public square is a question beyond the scope of this chapter. One suspects, however, that the answer would not be in line with haredi presumptions.

Notes

1. Thomas Hobbes, *Leviathan* (Oxford: James Thornton, 1881), 96; J. J. Rousseau, *A Treatise on the Social Contract* (New York: Penguin Classics, 1987).

2. F. M. Voltaire, *Dictionnaire Philosophique* (1764), translated by H. I. Woolf (1945) (New York: Penguin Classics, 1984).

3. Cited in Irving Howe, *World of Our Fathers* (New York: Simon & Schuster, 1976), 23.

4. See Hayim Greenberg, "Golus Jew," in I. Howe and H. Greenberg, *Voices from the Yiddish* (New York: Schocken Books, 1972).

5. See Samuel Heilman and Menachem Friedman, "Religious Fundamentalism and Religious Jews: The Case of the 'Haredim,'" in *Fundamentalisms Observed*, Martin Marty and Scott Appleby, eds. (Chicago: University of Chicago Press, 1992), 197-264.

6. For a fuller accounting of numbers, see Samuel Heilman, "Orthodox Jews—the City and the Suburb," *Studies in Contemporary Jewry*, vol. 15 (1999).

7. Yud Pnini, "The Unsmooth Blend—and Worse," *The Jewish Observer* (December 1999), 18. See also Emmanuel Sivan, "The Enclave Culture," in *Fundamentalisms Comprehended*, R. S. Appleby and M. Marty, eds. (Chicago: University of Chicago Press, 1995).

8. The association of women with children comes from their sharing a common status in traditional Jewish law. It is also a reflection of the established Jewish patriarchal social order that predominates in haredi society.

9. Sivan, "Enclave Culture," 17.

10. To be sure, there are certain haredi community newspapers published in Israel and New York that have an international readership, and even some wall posters from Jerusalem and Bnai Brak, Israel, are circulated internationally by mail.

11. The electronic windows remain among the most difficult to keep closed and opaque in our increasingly wired and media-conscious world. Even the haredim have been snared by the Internet and captured by the video.

12. Throughout this chapter, quoted comments from haredim come from field interviews this author conducted in late 1999 and early 2000. The identities of these speakers are not revealed unless the interviewee gave express permission.

13. Agudath Israel of America, part of the worldwide Agudah movement that began in 1912 in Poland, was officially founded in 1922 but began to grow in earnest after World War II when the great bulk of the Orthodox began to make the United States their home.

14. This is also the name of the Jewish codebook in which the laws and customs are to be found.

15. Many years later in the 1970s, their Sephardic haredi counterparts, the Shas Party, created a parallel "Council of Torah Wise Men."

16. *The Struggle and the Splendor* (New York: Agudath Israel of America, 1982), 22.

17. See, for example, Margot Hornblower, "Cultures Clash as Hasidic Jews Compete for Turf; Sect Uses Politics, Law to Overpower Hispanics," *Washington Post,* November 9, 1986, A1.

18. Pnini, "The Unsmooth Blend," 16.

19. Sivan, "The Enclave Culture," 17.

20. The language comes from *The Struggle and the Splendor*, vi.

21. See Eli Berman, "Subsidized Sacrifice: State Support of Religion in Israel," *Contemporary Jewry,* vol. 20 (2000); Laurence Iannaccone, "Sacrifice & Stigma: Reducing Free-Riding in Cults, Communes, and Other Collectives," *Journal of Political Economy* 100:2 (April 1992): 271-91.

22 . Berman, "Subsidized Sacrifice."

23. A kollel is generally a yeshiva for married men for whom Torah study is a vocation and who live not only for such study but also off of it.

24. Berman, "Subsidized Sacrifice."

25. Sivan, "The Enclave Culture," 19.

26. This attitude also infuses the Israeli haredi's worldview. There, however, the rebuilding power may include the entire Jewish society, not just the local one. In other words, the objectives are far grander in Israel.

27. See Yonason Rosenblum, *They Called Him Mike* (New York: Mesorah Publications, 1995), especially "Churban, Hatzalah, Restoration: The Work of Agudath Israel," 471-519. See also David Kranzler, *Thy Brother's Blood: The Orthodox Jewish Response during the Holocaust* (New York: Mesorah Publications, 1987).

28. See S. C. Heilman, "Orthodox Jews, the City and the Suburb," in *Studies in Contemporary Jewry XV* (1999): 32-33.

29. Chaim Dovid Zweibel, interview, February 2000.

30. For a copy of the lobbying letter from which these quotations were taken, see *The Struggle and the Splendor*, 142.

31. On the matter of the value of a fetus, compare: Leviticus 27:3, "And thy estimation shall be of the male from twenty years old even to sixty years old, even thy estimation shall be fifty shekels of silver, after the shekel of the sanctuary." Leviticus 27:4, "And if it shall be a female, then thy estimation shall be thirty shekels." Leviticus 27:5, "And if it shall be from five years old even to twenty years old, then thy estimation shall be of the male twenty shekels, and for the female ten shekels." Leviticus 27:6, "And if it shall be from a month old even to five years old, then thy estimation shall be of the male five shekels of silver, and for the female thy estimation shall be three shekels of silver."

Note that no value is given to individuals below one month of age. There is much that indicates that one was hardly considered anything more than a commodity before one was at least one month. Another pertinent passage is Exodus 21:22, "And if men strive together, and hurt a woman with child, so that her fruit depart, and yet no harm follow; he shall be surely fined, according as the woman's husband shall lay upon him; and he shall pay as the judges determine." For a fuller discussion, see J. Bleich, "Abortion in Contemporary Halakhic Literature," *Contemporary Halakhic Problems 325* (New York: Ktav, 1977), 354-56.

32. Actually, as Noga Morag-Levine reports, in Israel today abortion is quasi-legal. Until 1977 abortion in Israel was formally illegal but widely available. The revised law enacted in 1977 begins with a prohibition of abortion, but cites a list of circumstances (age of the mother, marital status, rape and incest, among others) under which specially appointed committees are authorized to approve the abortion. Although the committees differ in the strictness with which they interpret these exemptions, abortion is rarely difficult to obtain both because there are a number of liberal committees willing to turn a blind eye and because private abortions performed by doctors without committee consent are not prosecuted. Because of the availability of this option, official statistics present an incomplete picture of the number of abortions. A much fuller analysis of the law and politics surrounding the evolution of this issue in Israel is included in an article by Morag-Levine in *Israel Affairs,* vol. 5 (1999).

33. Since 1979, there have been about 150 abortions per 1,000 live births yearly. This is about one-half the rate in the United States. *Statistical Abstract of Israel, 1979-1996* (Jerusalem: Central Bureau of Statistics, 1980-1997).

34. Dated 5740, from the collection of Menachem Friedman.

35. See, for example, a poster signed by an organization called "Efrat, the Association for the Encouragement of Childbirth in the Jewish Nation," Friedman collection, Iyar 5742 (1982). See also Michael Gross,

"Autonomy and Paternalism in Communitarian Society" (discussion of the effects of the Israeli Patient Rights Act), *The Hastings Center Report*, vol. 29, i. 4 (July 1999), 13.

36. To be sure, they could do so by seeking to insure that the society abided by the seven Noahide commandments, a set of laws that the Torah established for all humanity except the Jews. Indeed, for a time the Lubavitcher Hasidim, in their messianic fervor, promoted such a program. They did so, however, not to improve American life but because they believed this would hasten the moment of Jewish redemption.

37. This is not to suggest here that this perception necessarily reflects the reality.

38. See brief No. 88-605, www.jlaw.com/Briefs/webster4.html.

39. This phrase from Isaiah 42:6 has become a kind of mission statement for those Jews who have tried to decipher their role vis-à-vis the world at large. The quotation comes from the author's interviews.

40. "U.S. Supreme Court Urged to Review Boy Scouts Ruling," *Coalition* (January 2000), 11.

41. See, for example: Alan Feuer, "Sentencing a Drug Courier, Judge Rebukes the Hasidim," *New York Times*, March 29, 2000, B3; Bill Egbert and Leo Standora, "Feds Charge Pill Plot, Money-Launder Plan," *New York Daily News*, January 6, 2000, 64; Marilyn Henry, "Brooklyn Rabbi Pleads Guilty to Laundering Drug Money," *Jerusalem Post*, December 24, 1997, 4; Bob Liff, "Feuding Satmar Hasidim Draw Cops into Dispute," *New York Daily News*, October 6, 1999, 1; Greg B. Smith, "Hasidim Fight Fed Fraud Charges," *New York Daily News*, June 1, 1997, 24; Maureen Fan, "Hasidim Beat Me, Man Says," *New York Daily News*, December 3, 1996, 1.

9

Reconstructionism and the Public Square: A Multicultural Approach to Judaism in America

David A. Teutsch

Unique among the major Jewish religious movements in America, Reconstructionism existed as a school of thought long before it emerged as a denominational grouping. Its founder, Rabbi Mordecai Kaplan (1881-1983), shaped the movement's ideology and practice through his prodigious writing and speaking as well as by the force of his personality. Thus, the effort to develop an understanding of Reconstructionist attitudes toward the public square must begin with Kaplan.

Educated at Columbia University and the Jewish Theological Seminary, Kaplan analyzed Jewish life using the tools of sociology and developed a theology from the perspective of a pragmatism concerned with the function of theology in human life. A student of John Dewey, William James, and Felix Adler, Kaplan believed that truth-claims are a reflection of the human experience that should be judged in part by their effect on people affirming them. For Kaplan, the test of theological truths is their moral value, their ability to be integrated into people's emotional and physical lives, and their coherence with related ideas, facts, and beliefs. Similarly, he believed that the morality of actions had to be determined in part by their individual and social outcomes.

Kaplan appreciated the freedom and democracy of America, and he incorporated these values into the Jewish value set upon which he based his work. He was among the leaders of the effort to establish the New York *kehillah*, which was to be a voluntary community-wide system of governance for New York Jewry. The *kehillah* in Eastern Europe was the governing body of the Jewish community. It created the institutions the community needed and enforced its laws. In its power to tax, legislate, and require compliance, it differed considerably from the New York *kehillah*, where membership was voluntary and efforts at enforcement therefore had no power. The New York *kehillah* received support because it had the potential to provide a united Jewish voice against anti-Semitism to the non-Jewish world. The fractious coalition that comprised the *kehillah* never could unite sufficiently to accomplish even this minimal purpose. Kaplan saw the *kehillah* as a vital venue for creating educational and cultural opportunities that would invigorate New York Jewish life. The *kehillah* was pluralistic, and Kaplan was committed to making it democratic because he believed that only a democratic body could generate sufficient moral power to unite the community.

While the New York *kehillah* existed from 1908 to 1922, it never lived up to Kaplan's expectations, and it ultimately failed for many reasons. Nevertheless, Kaplan never gave up hope for the vastly more ambitious project of creating a democratic governing body for world Jewry. This never came to be because of impediments that were already clear in the failure of the New York *kehillah*. Three of these impediments are particularly noteworthy: 1. Anyone who did not like its decisions refused to be bound by them. 2. Democracy was difficult to reconcile with unequal funding. 3. There was no agreement about priorities. These impediments would have been even more troubling on the scale of world Jewish governance. Thus, Kaplan's hopes for a large-scale governing body to embody a democratic and pluralistic Jewish community were doomed to failure.[1]

Kaplan was involved early on with the development of the 92nd Street YMHA in New York. This gave him a venue for developing his idea that Judaism is not only a religion but also an all-embracing culture. He hoped that the Y would create community through shared activity and that worship would then emerge as an integrated part of the community experience. Out of these shared experiences, Kaplan hoped, would emerge morally vigorous Jews. "Kaplan viewed religion as the effect of personal growth and moral behavior, not the cause."[2] He wanted this moral behavior to extend through all parts of Jews' lives and saw this as critical to Jews doing their part in America. As Kaplan put it, "The Jew to be a true American must be a better Jew. This means that he must belong to a Jewish community where the ideals, by means of which he is to help mold American life, are to be developed. To be a Jew means to participate in some form of Jewish community life where the standards of right and wrong are to be clearly formulated and accepted."[3] Kaplan often lectured at the Y, where he could express his views with a freedom that was not available to him from the pulpit until later in his career. In this context, he was able to flesh out the way in which he hoped American society could influence Judaism toward democracy and pluralism, while the Jewish community influenced America to greater social justice.

Since Kaplan came to understand Judaism as a civilization that evolved through its contacts with other civilizations, this recognition of mutual influence carried with it the notion that cultures can be improved by contact with one another. This claim carries the assumption that it is not in America's interest to simply be a melting pot. On the contrary, the greatness of America lies partly in its capacity to allow not only individuals their freedom and distinctiveness but groups as well. They are capable both of critiquing each other and of learning from one another. This is not an abstract philosophical process but a moral, social, and political one that varies from community to community based on history, inherited practices and beliefs, and contemporary conditions. Its outcomes often depend as much on emotion and imagery as on moral argument. The process reflects the degree of cultural vigor within the community, and its substance has a major role in determining the community's future. Any culture incapable of making a unique contribution to the larger society will cease to exist. As Kaplan expressed it much later, "Only a Judaism calculated to bring out all that is best in human nature, and to guide us Jews in applying that best to all our human interests, can command sufficient loyalty to insure its survival and advancement. America is a cultural melting pot. Cultural differences that do not contribute to the realization of universal human values are bound to vanish."[4]

This thinking contains the seeds of an important version of multiculturalism. One extreme version of multiculturalism holds that all cultures have unique worth and that those inside one culture are incapable of fully understanding another and are therefore incapable of making legitimate judgments about its value. The other extreme position holds that there is a best possible culture and that all other cultures should be judged by their degree of resemblance to it. Kaplan's model suggests that our cultures are capable of evolving toward higher values, that values must be seen in their technoscientific and sociopolitical context, and that a civilization can properly be judged in part by what values it holds and how effectively it lives by them. It also recognizes that an action that is moral in one cultural context will not necessarily be moral in another.

Kaplan recognized that the YMHA, with its emphasis primarily on social and athletic activities, would never provide the kind of spiritual and moral center for a community that he sought. He eventually became a trenchant critic of the Jewish community center movement for that reason. His concern is reflected in a 1939 editorial in *The Reconstructionist,* a journal where the ideas of the Reconstructionist movement were sharply articulated. "As for ghettoizing the Jews, let us reiterate that the community centers which add nothing distinctively Jewish to their programs are themselves ghettoizing the Jews. Activities which lend themselves to joint participation of Jews and non-Jews, and which are carried on separately, cut off that essential interaction of both groups so necessary to better understanding and mutual appreciation."[5]

Kaplan advocated the immersion of Jews in general American society and their simultaneous engagement in a Jewish community deeply engaged in religious and moral questions. While the Jewish community center movement did develop a much more elaborate cultural program than did such counterparts as the YWCAs and YMCAs, the centers did not evince interest in religious or moral questions, as they preferred to stay pluralistic and pancommunal.[6] Thus, Kaplan's quest for religious community found little satisfaction in the JCCs, and his search continued.

With a group of volunteer leaders he organized the Jewish Center on New York's Upper West Side in 1915. While the Jewish Center had athletic and social facilities, the focus of its life was much more on worship and study. *The Reconstructionist* would later proclaim that "the highest purpose of Jewish cooperation should be the furtherance of Jewish education and Jewish worship. Once the Jewish community definitely adopts this *highest* common denominator as its aim, its status in the American political set-up will be clearly defined. It will be the status not of a minority secular group, but of an ethical society."[7]

Still, Kaplan wanted the Jewish Center to have all the facilities and programs needed to create a genuine community, for he understood the community to be the only legitimate context for religion. This position naturally stems from a sociology in which the Jewish people generates Jewish culture and hence Jewish religion rather than Jewish peoplehood flowing from God's creation of Jewish religion at Sinai. This idea was articulated particularly well by Horace Kallen in his 1918 essay "Judaism in the Jewish Problem." "The place and function of Judaism in Jewish life is like the place and function of any religion in any national life. It is an item in that life; only an item, no matter how important, in a whole which is determined by the ethnic character of the people that live it, by their history, by their collective will and intent. These three factors define the total conditions of national life."[8]

If Judaism is an outcome of Jewish peoplehood, then Jewish community is the only authentic context for Jewish religion, which depends upon having a community for its full celebration. Furthermore, Jewish religion is an inseparable part of Jewish civilization, which Jewish communities necessarily embody. Thus, a vigorous Jewish community would be an antidote to the thinness of religious life that Kaplan saw around him.

The Jewish Center existed for several years before it occupied its building in 1918. By then, strains had already begun to appear between Kaplan and the other leaders of the Jewish Center. One of the tensions came from Kaplan's heterodox ideas, which were rapidly emerging in the formative years of the center. Another tension came from the social gospel that Kaplan preached at the center. He was a passionate supporter of women's suffrage, and he addressed that topic frequently. He also expressed concern about the rights of workers and the conditions under which they labored. He saw an improvement in the lives of workers as being a natural outgrowth of the moral uplift for which he hoped among the many employers who were members of his congregation. He attempted to emphasize "the need for Jews who exercise power in the dominion of industry and traffic to come together in the name of their faith . . . to see what they can do to ameliorate the evils and to improve the relations between employer and employee."[9]

To say the least, this was not a widely popular topic among his congregants. For Kaplan, however, the expression of these views was critical to the religious life of the Jewish community. He saw religion as significant only if it had an impact on social ethics. This, too, was an essential part of his agenda as an educator, an agenda that he exercised in many settings, including the Jewish Theological Seminary (JTS), which he created at Solomon Schechter's behest and served as dean for decades. For Kaplan, education was an undertaking that should engage people of all ages, not simply for the sake of acquiring knowledge but for absorbing values and learning the skills needed to sustain a vibrant Jewish community.

"The ideas, which set forth the meaning and purpose of community organization from the standpoint of Judaism as a whole and every individual Jew in particular, must be popularized and made integral to the Jewish consciousness through the process of education in all its stages. The idea of Jewish community must be made as much part of the Jewish school curriculum as Jewish ceremonies and observances, and all possible pedagogic devices must be employed to include it."[10] Thus, there is a long history to the Reconstructionist tradition of lifelong education aimed at intensifying engagement with the Jewish community and its values, and applying those values to all the spheres of daily life.

The Development of the Reconstructionist Movement

The tension between Kaplan and the leadership of the Jewish Center grew until Kaplan left in 1922 with a small band of followers and opened a new congregation, the Society for the Advancement of Judaism (SAJ), which was to be devoted to fulfilling his religious vision. The SAJ later came to be viewed as the first Reconstructionist synagogue, though that term only came into use after Kaplan published his most important book, *Judaism as a Civilization*, in 1934. This led to the launching of *The Reconstructionist* in 1935 and to the development of a more substantial presence for Reconstructionism as a school of thought shared by a large number of Kaplan disciples. Kaplan wanted Reconstructionism to remain a school of thought. His disciples argued for a more particularistic presence as well. This led first to the creation of the Jewish Reconstructionist Foundation in 1941 and eventually to the other institutions of a religious movement. But throughout its history, the movement has tried both to have the broad influence of a school of thought and the pungency and focus that come from being a distinctive movement.

The Reconstructionist became a major vehicle for addressing issues of public policy from a values-driven and largely politically progressive perspective. One magazine editorial, for example, spoke out against the mistreatment of Angelo Herndon (an African American whose unjust imprisonment was a liberal *cause célèbre* at the time) and the racism and fascism it represented.

> Why has the state of Georgia been so unreasonably brutal? Because Georgia's ruling class is unwilling to pay in taxes the cost of

adequate relief and they think they can terrorize the unemployed into acquiescence in their own misery by the ruthless suppression of their militant leadership. Because they are afraid that gifted leaders like Herndon can enlighten the exploited masses of the country to the true causes of their misery and that the mounting mass unrest may threaten their privilege and power. . . . The duty of all who would defend democracy therefore becomes clear. They must rally to the fight for the liberation of Herndon as an indispensable part of that larger fight against fascism in America.[11]

The Reconstructionist fight against fascism was not primarily motivated by concerns about anti-Semitism. It grew out of a deep-seated belief that democracy represents moral progress for all and that it should govern both the Jewish community and the rest of the world. Reconstructionists were committed to the effort "to raise democracy itself to the level of a religious principle."[12] Similarly, the concern for Herndon grew out of beliefs regarding the inalienable rights of all people. These Reconstructionists believed that there was a full confluence between their Jewish values and the best of American progressive politics, a view that they defended with vehemence in light of the dual loyalty accusations that were common at the time. Reconstructionists understood speaking out on social concerns as a religious act, and speaking out was intended to lead to political organizing and political change. For Reconstructionists, these too are religious acts. Concern for the welfare of our fellow citizens and for our country is elevated by our values to a matter of substantial spiritual concern. From the 1930s into the 1970s, Reconstructionists saw action to improve American society as being in the spiritual interest of the Jewish community.

American democracy, in affirming the dignity of the individual, recognizes the role of religiocultural groups in the development of human personality. Loyalty on the part of the Jews and members of other groups to their own religious civilizations is necessary for the full flowering of American democracy. It is needed to safeguard American democracy against the regimentation which issues in totalitarianism.[13]

Thus, a full melting pot was seen as bad for the preservation of American values, which are preserved by the ideological give-and-take between groups. Through today's lens, this suggests a basis for a political philosophy that supports a form of multiculturalism. "Real Americanism means not only a toleration of religious differences, but a toleration of ethnic and national differences as well. In fact real Americanism should mean an *active encouragement* of cultural diversity."[14]

One way that the interaction between America and the Jewish community would occur would be through education. For many years Reconstructionists were advocates for Jews attending public schools. But these schools were not envisioned as pure melting pots. Elements of the cultures that make up America, it was imagined, could be embedded in the curricula. Thus, it was suggested that "efforts should be made to make a specific Jewish contribution to the culture of America by having courses in the Hebrew language and literature and in the history of the Jewish people included as accredited subjects in the curricula of public high schools, colleges, and universities."[15] In 1950 this was a bold suggestion, but in the context of Reconstructionist ideology, a natural one.

The connection in Reconstructionist thought between the Jewish and American polities becomes clearer when the women's suffrage position Kaplan had taken is seen as having a religious parallel. That parallel is exemplified by his daughter Judith becoming the first bat mitzvah (a confirmation of adult responsibility parallel to bar mitzvah) in America and perhaps in the world at the SAJ in its first year of operation in 1922. For Reconstructionists there should be no gap between policies on American political issues and Jewish religious ones. Here the Reconstructionist theory differs sharply from that of the Conservative and Orthodox movements, which grant special decision-making powers to rabbis and special status to *halakhah*, Jewish law. They, therefore, end up with political positions that are often at odds with their religious ones. One current example is the Conservative Rabbinical Assembly resolution that supports the civil rights of gay men and lesbians at a time when the movement does not confer full equal religious rights.

The SAJ became a laboratory for finding ways to harmonize these issues. One critical liturgical decision involved the rejection of language that supports the doctrine that God chose the Jewish people. While such a claim is theologically problematic if one does not believe that God does that kind of active intervening in human affairs, Kaplan's motivation for making the liturgical change was ethical in nature. He understood that any group's claim that it is God's chosen creates an irrefutable triumphalism that must inevitably lead to a kind of intergroup strife that is incompatible with democracy and with the kind of dialogue that creates a stable and open society. All subsequent Reconstructionist prayer books have followed that liturgical decision, emphasizing the uniqueness of Jewish peoplehood and mission without claiming that God has provided Jews (or Reconstructionists for that matter) any unique access to God's will or to ultimate truth. This has become one of the criteria by which Reconstructionists have selected partners in dialogue because it is a critical part of affirming the value of pluralism.

The success of the SAJ as a laboratory did not lead Kaplan to talking about organic Jewish community in the small framework of the congregation. He continued to argue for the pancommunal model suggested by the New York *kehillah*. This has remained a theoretical feature of Reconstructionist thought, but it has gradually been deemphasized in light of the small likelihood of its achievement. While the need for a world Jewish parliament continued to figure in Kaplan's thinking, Kaplan also recognized the need for a new kind of partnership within the synagogue. "The needed Jewish life and thought can be achieved only as a cooperative undertaking to which both rabbis and laymen are prepared to give their best powers and most devoted interest."[16]

As his discussion of decision making in *The Future of the American Jew* (1948) makes clear, Kaplan did not develop a theoretical model for unequivocal democratic partnership between rabbi and congregation, even though he had instituted such a process at the SAJ. The Reconstructionist movement moved quite gradually to its emphasis on congregational community and to good governance there.

When, in 1955, several congregations banded together to form a Reconstructionist Federation, Reconstructionism began the critical shift away from being a school of thought to becoming a movement. Its 1961 introduction of the idea of *havurot*, mini-communities that meet for study, worship, celebration, social action, and/or socializing, is one indication of that shift. While the Conservative-trained and identified rabbis who provided much of the intellectual leadership of the movement in its early days were theologically Reconstructionist, they had been trained to lead by fiat in religious matters. Only after the Reconstructionist Rabbinical College came into existence in 1968 and started training rabbis in democratic decision making and in community-building did there become available rabbis who fully understood the organizational implications of Reconstructionist ideology. Many of these rabbis focused on the task of creating community in congregations as a central undertaking in generating authentic Jewish life. Efforts to create a warm and welcoming community atmosphere in congregations have become characteristic of the movement, as the movement itself has gradually shifted its attention from the utopian concern with democratizing the entire world Jewish community to democratizing the community life within its affiliated congregations and *havurot*.

Community-Building and Values-Based Decision Making

Involving congregational leaders in decision making was understood as crucial for creating commitment to the community's policies. This was hardly a new idea. Already in 1950 it had been noted in *The Reconstructionist* "that the regulative authority of communal institutions rests more upon the force of public opinion and social pressure than upon the police control of government or the parental control of family."[17] Democratic decision making assures the consent of the governed.

What makes the shift to democratic community important to the concerns of the public square is that developing modes for accomplishing democratic decision making became critical to the Reconstructionist enterprise. As a result, a values-based decision making methodology was developed. Its theoretical underpinnings had been developed over the preceding two decades by several movement thinkers, including Rabbis Rebecca Alpert, Jacob Staub, Sidney Schwarz, and David Teutsch.[18] The first time it was officially applied to a major movement decision was in the report of the movement's Commission on Homosexuality in 1990.[19] The Jewish Reconstructionist Federation and the Reconstructionist Rabbinical Association ratified that report, and subsequent movement documents reflect that method as well.[20] This method is also employed in the three-volume *Guide to Jewish Practice* currently being developed by the movement.

Because values-based decision making makes explicit the values relevant to any particular decision, the reasoning highlights the values that are added when a religious perspective is taken. In a discussion of health care, for example, Rebecca Alpert discusses Jews' concern, as caretakers of the world, for the well-being of all its creatures. Jews are also seen as bringing a reverence for life and seeing human beings as having infinite worth. "Judaism assumes a connection between health care and the supreme value of preserving life—the ultimate goal of the human caretaker. This reverence for life adds an important dimension to public policy discussions, which often are couched in the utilitarian language of cost-benefit analysis."[21] Such an outlook obviously affects how we look at the obligation of governments to provide health care to those who cannot otherwise afford it.

The importance of the values-based decision making methodology lies in its ability to articulate values separate from theological assumptions and beliefs so that moral discourse can take place effectively with people whose religious views differ considerably. The history and heritage of each community has much to do with its moral position. Definitions—such as whether a life begins at conception or at birth—play a critical role in policy conflicts, as do differing norms. Dialogue between communities depends upon discovering areas of agreement and conflict—as well as shared vocabulary. The language of values plays a critical role in providing that vocabulary, discovering areas of agreement, and exploring differences. Because values language has commonsense meaning, the fact that communities derive it from different faith traditions is not significant to the dialogue once agreement about definitions of value terms has been reached. This process also can help increase the shared agreement in American public life by providing a moral foundation for policy discourse. Insofar as religious groups are interested in influencing that discourse, values-based dialogue maximizes their influence while encouraging them not to depend for public purposes upon the religious origins of those values. This allows religious communities to be more particularistic about the policies they advocate while minimizing appeals to unbridgeable differences in religious heritage. In other words, maximizing the pungency of an individual faith community and forming areas of broad policy agreement across groups need not be purposes in tension with each other.

This approach harmonizes with the communitarian approaches of thinkers such as Michael Sandel and Amitai Etzioni.[22] Their interest in strengthening republican citizenship is generally shared by religious communities, which oppose the broad social breakdown to which communitarians also object. The multicultural approach of religious communities solves a critical problem in Etzioni's thinking by providing the intense communities of meaning with strong moral claims on their members that his argument requires, for religious communities can commit themselves to republican citizenship.

The values-based approach not only eases intra-Jewish dialogue and coalition building. It also creates the possibility of sophisticated moral discourse with people who have no initial sympathy for the positions Reconstructionists take on a particular issue. For groups struggling toward public policy decisions that are responsive to disparate points of view, finding values in common and values in conflict is a critical first step toward designing good policies. Perhaps more important, it creates a way of bringing together moral and political life that has the possibility of reinvigorating both through local and national dialogue. Thus, work done by the Reconstructionist movement in this area can serve as a model for American society.

Multiculturalism

As mentioned above, Kaplan's understanding of group relations anticipated what is now called multiculturalism. The Reconstructionist rejection of the theological doctrine of chosenness allows Reconstructionists to engage with representatives of other cultures without a theological triumphalism that interferes with the recognition that all cultures can make positive contributions to American society. It poses a positive model for group interaction in America based on the groups working together for the common good (which presumes there *is* a common good) and learning from each other in the process. This contrasts with the way multiculturalism often currently works in the United States, "where multiculturalism is typically addressed as an oppositional, minority-driven demand for 'recognition' and social advancement for racialised groups, and where the political intensity of the disputes over its usage in education and the 'culture wars' has made it all but unusable by its erstwhile proponents."[23]

Reconstructionists have argued that the moral vigor needed in a democratic, pluralistic society depends upon moral education that falls to religious and cultural groups. Thus, one measure of the worth of these groups in the United States lies in the degree of their ability and willingness to promote the fundamental principles upon which American culture rests. This establishes the importance of these groups and gives them an ability to critique and cooperate with each other. It would allow Americans "to teach cultural differences neither as objects of tolerance nor as problems to be solved, but as dialogical effects of the open-ended negotiation for which the democratic polity claims to provide."[24]

From the Reconstructionist perspective, the strength of the United States lies in its ability to maintain a national culture that supports that dialogue while providing the conditions that allow the participant groups to flourish, a point that Ira Eisenstein made in his 1941 book *The Ethics of Tolerance*.[25] This view provides insight into problems with the national cultures that have caused civil war in the Balkans and suggests the level of openness needed in the United States to fulfill American democratic ideals. It restricts—and perhaps even replaces—the ideology of the melting pot.

Why has this shift in American ideology become more important now? In part, because it has become clear that governmental and public educational institutions by themselves cannot create the moral vigor America needs. Perhaps more important, they cannot create the web of interpersonal connections found in subcommunities that are the locus for identity, moral education, and culture. Furthermore, in this era when meaning seeking has become more important for many Americans because their basic physical needs are met, the role of community, spirituality, and culture has become more central. Congregations and culturally based communities can play a critical role in sustaining American society. These provide an alternative to the materialistic hedonism of the mass media and consumerism. Reconstructionists would use Reconstructionist values to critique these aspects of mass culture and argue that hyphenated identities (e.g., Jewish-American, Arab-American) are the basis for a successful American culture because our common values (like democracy and liberty) are insufficient to create a national culture of sufficient richness.[26]

Individuals' identities rest upon their roles in their cultures and communities. Multiculturalism illuminates the individual's position as "gendered, raced, aged, classed, embodied and sexual."[27] There is no way to have a totally unidimensional identity. Thus, Reconstructionists suggest exploration of the complex sources of identity in the hope of increasing human dignity and the basis for shared meaning. Reconstructionists "believe that America should defend to the last the right to be different, so long as *unity* is not jeopardized; and we believe that the unity which America should achieve must be the kind which acknowledges the right to be different. . . . We believe those who are different (not Anglo-Saxon) have not only the right to share in the 'evolving culture and civilization,' but also to make for the survival of their distinctive ethnic and religious civilization, so that it will contribute not once but recurrently to the whole, and retain its right to live as an ancillary civilization."[28]

This version of multiculturalism does not require the government to take affirmative action to privilege religious or cultural minorities. It only requires the removal of government-controlled impediments to their success and encourages rhetoric and teaching that familiarizes Americans with the resources contained in such diversity, and at best, to move beyond tolerating that diversity in favor of celebrating it. We can agree to disagree about theology, about culture, and even about exclusivist claims of chosenness, and still work together vigorously to fulfill a communitarian vision for a revitalized America.

A Vision of Social Justice

The Reconstructionist movement has developed stances on a broad array of social issues. In the early days of the movement these were developed in *The Reconstructionist*. As the movement became established, these positions were often more democratically handled through resolutions ratified at conventions of the movement and later of the Reconstructionist Rabbinical Association as well.

The Reconstructionist position on issues has consistently grown out of the belief that "Judaism as a religious civilization affirms the dignity of the human soul" and that human life in its highest form takes place in community so that "Judaism calls for a social order that combines the maximum of individual liberty with the maximum of social cooperation."[29] The movement's 1950 Program for Jewish Life lays out principles that have changed little since then. It holds that the Reconstructionist vision requires a "just social order" that achieves a more equitable distribution of goods and power, eliminates all forms of discrimination, provides adequate health and social welfare programs, defends individual freedoms, and espouses world peace and human rights. Subsequent events strengthened the movement's involvement with environmental issues and issues of inclusion, but it remains possible to predict movement positions using the 1950 program.

The progressive origins of Reconstructionist thinking also explain its powerful opposition to fascism and totalitarianism, which long predated World War II. In a 1936 discussion of the meaning of Passover, a *Reconstructionist* editorial said,

> In fighting to preserve our democratic liberties against the tidal wave of fascism, it is not enough to argue that fascism means tyranny and that democracy affords the blessings of personal freedom. Our work must be extended to establishing the kind of social order where freedom can exist securely. An ideal system of legislation—social reforms that will protect the weak; the abolition of child labor; adequate unemployment insurance and old-age pensions, minimum wage and maximum profit scales . . . will all have to precede the establishment of a genuinely free society. For in the long run, there can be no freedom without justice.[30]

The progressive politics of the Reconstructionist movement were repeatedly seen in Jewish values terms. Daniel Nussbaum, for example, suggested that the two central value guidelines in thinking about government responsibilities are *tsedakah* (justice; the notion that having one's basic needs met is a human right) and *gemilut chesed* (acts of individual caring). He argues that it would be improper to leave the compulsory outcome of *tsedakah* up to the uncertainty of *gemilut chesed*.[31] Enlightened self-interest and moral demand were usually understood to be simultaneous. "The Jewish stake in removing the blot of white racialism from American life is clear. . . . Every totalitarian American movement, like the Ku Klux Klan, is bound to be directed against Negroes, Jews and Catholics. But as religious Jews we appeal to our fellow-Jews on higher grounds than Jewish self-interest. 'Ye shall remember that ye were slaves in the land of Egypt.'"[32] It was through that lens that anti-Semitism was viewed. It was grouped with other forms of prejudice, with democracy and social justice serving as their antidotes.

The Reconstructionist understanding of Judaism as evolving has allowed the movement to accept values from American culture into its own. Multiculturalism suggests that influence can be self-consciously mutual. Reconstructionists perceive this borrowing as strengthening Judaism and helping it to be more true to itself. "The reconstruction of Judaism to incorporate the best insights of twentieth century American democracy is necessary not only because of the historical accident that we live here, not only because Western democracy is the best available political option at this time, but because, in the American version of such ideals as democracy, freedom, equality, pluralism and justice, we should recognize a spiritual kinship, a contemporary manifestation of traditional Jewish teachings."[33]

The liberal ideology that characterized the formative years of Reconstructionism has gradually given way to a democratic communitarianism that emphasizes the importance of voluntaristic communities for creating moral vigor and passing on religious culture. That shift involves a recognition that social justice ideals will only be strived for in a country with subgroups dedicated to preserving the religious values that undergird them. Still, that view should not interfere with vigorous efforts for social justice. As Senator Carl Levin of Michigan, a long-time Reconstructionist, put it: "We need to demand from our lawmakers no less than what Rabbi Kaplan demanded of us: To use law to regulate the power we have for developing both individuals' potentialities for the good life and society's potential—for freedom, justice and peace. It is the right thing to do."[34]

Church and State

One area of ongoing concern for the movement has been religion and civil religion in the public schools. The Reconstructionist movement was always interested in keeping sectarian religious practices out of the public schools and therefore opposed school prayer and Christmas pageants. But the movement also recognized that inculcating virtues and American values is a critical educational function. An editorial in *The Reconstructionist* laid out part of its agenda for that part of education, suggesting that schools should teach "respect for the sanctity of human life, an awareness of man's limitations, an appreciation of his potentialities for good, a recognition of his propensity to evil, and an assumption of moral responsibility for the welfare of all his fellowmen."[35] Thus, the movement held that schools ought to teach religious values without teaching religious beliefs or practices. "From our perspective, our continued opposition to any attempt to impose Christian doctrine in the public schools by confusing it with American civil religion is a legitimate and necessary position taken in order to secure our rights as Americans who do not want to be subjected to religious coercion."[36]

Kaplan was a major supporter of the development of an American civil religion that could be employed in the schools and elsewhere in public life. He wanted schools to teach what he called "the religion of democracy."[37] He cowrote *The Faith of America* with Eugene Kohn and J. Paul Williams (republished by the Reconstructionist Press in 1963) to provide examples of rituals and liturgy for such occasions as Washington's Birthday, Independence Day, and Thanksgiving. This book illustrates the movement's effort to use such occasions to reinforce American values and ideals in school and interfaith settings. The effort to think through the strengthening of American civil religion has continued. One writer suggested that "Sacred American writings, often studied for purposes that are historical or recitative, might be studied in such a way as to be spiritually provocative and affirmative. This might take the form of beginning each school day with a brief reading and discussion of a suitable text from the literature of American democracy. Such study, pursued in the spirit of prayer, might help to convey the spiritual dimension felt to be lacking in our public schools."[38]

One area of public education that Reconstructionist thinking advocates strengthening is moral education—teaching virtues, values, and norms that reflect broad social agreement and help create effective citizens. Such virtues include honesty, courage, compassion, and commitment to improving society. This pragmatist approach is, if anything, more important to the multicultural theory currently advocated by Reconstructionists than it is to the melting-pot theory because establishing commonalities and shared commitments in a multicultural society is so critical. Civil religion should evolve around this common heritage and the American holidays that can reinforce it. It will interact in mutually reinforcing ways with the religious communities who support it.

The Reconstructionist movement was from its outset a powerful advocate of public education.[39] It urged all Jews to support the public schools. That direction was only officially reversed in the mid-1980s when a resolution supporting the use of Jewish day schools was passed by the Jewish Reconstructionist Federation (then known as the Federation of Reconstructionist Congregations and Havurot) convention in 1986. By then many Reconstructionist leaders were sending their own children to day schools. That reflected a recognition that, whereas the challenge for several preceding generations of Jews had been assimilating into America, the challenge for the current generation is to acculturate into Judaism. The shift in positions regarding day schools has led to a reconsideration of the movement's steadfast opposition to any governmental support for parochial or private schools. For the first time there have emerged Reconstructionist advocates of a school voucher system. In part this reflects the undesirably high cost of Jewish day-school education, which reduces the number of children who can attend day school. But it also carries a recognition that the public schools serving marginal populations have failed to teach the religion of democracy in the way that Reconstructionists advocate. The result is that children at risk are likely to grow up without a vigorous moral education that can be provided by parochial schools. This is a current policy debate within the movement.

Women's Rights, Inclusion, and Family Values

Given the fame of the Reconstructionist commitment to the religious rights of women,[40] it should be no surprise that the movement has taken equally strong stands in support of the Equal Rights Amendment and of women's reproductive rights. The movement had already stated its support for a woman's right to abortion in 1936.[41] In the same article it proclaimed, "*The Reconstructionist* endorses birth control. It sees in it nothing which is inherently irreligious, immoral and unnatural. On the contrary, insofar as birth control enables human beings to bring into the world richer personalities, it sees in birth control a means for attaining the goal of all moral effort—the spiritual enrichment of each individual."

Its stance on women is consistent with its overall position on human freedom and social justice. It expanded this commitment to avoiding judgments based on gender to the area of sexual orientation beginning in 1984, when the Reconstructionist Rabbinical College decided that sexual orientation would be irrelevant for admission to its rabbinical training program. In 1990 the joint movement commission advocated rabbinic officiation at gay commitment ceremonies and active engagement to eliminate impediments to legal marriage for gay men and lesbians, again seeking a parallel between religious and secular conduct. The Reconstructionist movement understands these positions as being consistent with its commitment to supporting the family as a basic social unit and sees the evolving nature of the family as an inevitable result of broader social change.

The movement worked toward egalitarianism from its outset, though the definition of egalitarianism shifted somewhat over the years. More recently it has moved beyond egalitarianism to the doctrine of inclusion not only in terms of the rights described above but also in working to provide equal access to people with handicaps and differing abilities. Kol Ehad, a task force of the Jewish Reconstructionist Federation, works to accomplish this end both within the congregations of the movement and in broader society.[42]

Israel and Zionism

The Reconstructionist movement identified as Zionist from its outset, but its Zionism was not of a politically neutral or unthinking sort. It wanted Israel to be a democratic state pursuing social justice for all its citizens regardless of religion, ethnicity, or color. The first issue of *The Reconstructionist* proclaimed, "We endorse every effort toward the establishment of a cooperative commonwealth in Palestine based upon social justice and social cooperation."[43] Thus it tended to side with Labor Zionists in debates with the Revisionists. It hoped for the implementation of the ideals embodied in the Israeli Declaration of Independence. From the outset of the "land for peace" proposal, the leadership of the movement favored it in the hope that it would create harmonious relationships in the region. Perhaps most strongly of all, Reconstructionists urged that Israel be a nontheocratic state and that it enter into a mutual and balanced dialogue with Jews around the world. These positions were repeated with great frequency in *The Reconstructionist*, but perhaps they reached their fullest statement in Kaplan's book *A New Zionism* (Herzl Press, 1959). These positions were controversial in the American Jewish community, where a fervent yet critical Zionism was slow to develop. What is most striking about them, however, is that the approach to American Jewish communities, to the general American polity, and to Israel carried with it the same recommendations, which grew out of values that Reconstructionists attempted to apply to every situation.

Communicating the Message

The single most powerful mode the Reconstructionist movement has used for public influence has been its publications. The best known of these is *The Reconstructionist*, which has changed formats several times but has come out regularly since 1935. After years under the control of the Jewish Reconstructionist Foundation and then the Federation, it is now published by the Reconstructionist Rabbinical College. The Federation now publishes the more popular *Reconstructionism Today*, which often features issues of social policy and model social action programs. Many of the books published by the Reconstructionist Press also engage issues of social justice at least in part. The movement and its leaders have also issued dozens of resolutions and statements addressing issues of social concern.

Public reinforcement of movement values through ritual and liturgy also helps to unify the community and teach new members. The first Reconstructionist liturgical publication, *The New Haggadah* (1941) emphasized the centrality of freedom and democracy to the human fulfillment envisioned by Judaism. In movement prayer books since then, both the editing of traditional prayers and the addition of new ones have emphasized the movement's values and social commitments across a broad array of issues. The values have been explicated more thoroughly through use of extensive commentary in the *Kol Haneshamah* series published beginning in 1989.

The written word was for decades the Reconstructionist movement's primary way of affecting American affairs, but it was certainly not the only one. Kaplan spoke all over North America, but more important, his disciples—hundreds of them his former rabbinical students at the Jewish Theological Seminary—carried his views to their pulpits. The movement was interested in their using their pulpits to address questions far beyond those of theology and ritual and encouraged them to address the social and political issues of their time. "Those who protest against pulpit discussion of economic problems seem to forget that Judaism teaches the divinity of man, his right to the fullness of life, and to protection against oppression. . . . Without claiming for rabbinical utterances on social problems any authority other than inheres in whatever truth they may convey, we insist that no arbitrary limit be placed on the freedom of speech of rabbis on those themes either in their individual or collective utterances."[44]

As noted above, the graduates of the Reconstructionist Rabbinical College quickly moved toward more democratic and community-oriented styles of leadership. Not only did they continue to use sermons and frontal education; they also began using more informal, experiential, and affective methods. Social justice projects found their way into religious school curricula and bar/bat mitzvah projects. These ranged from work in soup kitchens to letter-writing campaigns to fund-raising for social change projects.

The Reconstructionist spoke with approbation about those who marched for civil rights in the South,[45] and the magazine argued, as well, for appeals to Congress and state legislatures, as well as the use of investment and employment power to end discrimination.[46] "The Reconstructionist Federation will support every effort to encourage massive congressional action in readjusting social and economic inequalities. It pledges itself to engage the services only of those who practice fair employment. It calls upon its members to assist wherever possible the Black community's own efforts to provide Head Start, job opportunities and business investment."[47]

One of the ways that the Jewish Reconstructionist Federation accomplishes these purposes is through participation in the work of over a dozen umbrella organizations. Some of these are coalitions composed entirely of Jewish groups such as the Coalition on the Environment and Jewish Life, Joint Distribution Committee, and Conference of Presidents of Major Jewish Organizations. Other coalitions involve many religious groups but focus on narrow issues—for example, the Religious Coalition for Reproductive Rights, North American Coalition for Religious Pluralism in Israel, and the National Committee for Public Education and Religious Liberty. The JRF sends representatives to these groups and in some cases takes an active role in their work. The Federation has assigned a staff person the task of coordinating the movement's representation in coalitions.

The Federation has endorsed Mazon, a hunger project that requests a 3 percent contribution from the cost of banquets, parties, and celebrations. It works to publicize this endorsement and gain the support of congregational boards and members for Mazon.

Perhaps more important than what the Federation does is the action actually undertaken by its congregations and the members within them. Here the range of undertakings is striking. A few examples will have to suffice. Congregation Darchei Noam in Toronto obtained government-backed funding to create a cooperative apartment building two-thirds of which is subsidized; residents have diverse backgrounds, and some of the apartments are reserved for the disabled.[48] Kehillath Israel in Pacific Palisades, a prosperous Los Angeles suburb, entered into a partnership with a Black church in south central Los Angeles to provide jobs, tutoring, and other resources while creating a cultural exchange and building social relationships.[49] Mishkan Shalom in Philadelphia invested money from its building fund in community development banks. There are hundreds of such projects across the movement. To encourage these local initiatives, the Federation has created the Yad Mordechai Fund, which supports innovative social action undertakings in Reconstructionist congregations.

One of the other modes of interaction is interfaith dialogue. For a number of years, rabbinical students from the Reconstructionist Rabbinical College have been the largest Jewish contingent to participate in the Seminarians Interacting program of the National Conference (formerly NCCJ). The college also offers courses in Jewish-Christian dialogue and in "trialogue" that includes Muslims as well. A number of Reconstructionist congregations participate in local dialogue groups.

The college also provides training in this area for its students. Courses include topics such as the Rabbi as an Agent for Social Change; Money, Stewardship, and *Tsedakah*; Organizing for *Tikkun Olam*; and Community Relations. The college's student association has a social action committee that organizes projects in which students participate. One project launched several years ago was Mitzvah Day, when students could pick from a dozen different community volunteer undertakings. This became a model duplicated by many other organizations. Another group of students worked to urge government intervention to stop the slaughter in Bosnia. Their lobbying efforts and the demonstrations they organized were the most potent interventions on that issue in the American Jewish community. The college currently offers internships in a variety of organizations, some of which are in the public policy and social action arena. It is now in the process of designing for-credit volunteer activity in the social action field in the hope that supervised work of this type will strengthen graduates' commitment to activism and skill in bringing social change.

The Reconstructionist Rabbinical Association, like the Jewish Reconstructionist Federation, passes resolutions at its conventions both to guide its members and to increase its public influence. The vast majority of these resolutions deal with issues of social justice. It has also undertaken some small-scale projects of its own, such as the design and sale of a *tsedakah* box to encourage the collection of funds for charity. The Federation and Rabbinical Association together have had a Social Action Commission that coordinates efforts throughout the movement; it is currently in the process of reorganization.

Thus, there is considerable evidence of leadership commitment to action in support of the movement's social vision.

The Challenge Ahead

A young, if rapidly growing, movement, constricted in its programming by its lack of capital, the Reconstructionist movement has not yet invested in a formal public policy apparatus. Nevertheless, the professional leaders of the Reconstructionist Rabbinical College, Jewish Reconstructionist Federation, and Reconstructionist Rabbinical Association are committed to the values-based activism portrayed above. Many of the rabbis, rabbinical students, and congregational leaders of the movement share that commitment. Their future direction can perhaps be found in the history and ideas documented above, which provide an excellent approach to the renewal of Jewish involvement in strengthening a multicultural society. With WASPs no longer a majority in the United States, Latino and Asian groups expanding, and the number of Muslims growing rapidly, Reconstructionists are well positioned to articulate the basis for a pluralistic America where the common good remains the central concern.

Notes

* Nina Mandel did substantial research for this chapter. Melanie Schneider, Rabbis Richard Hirsh, and Jacob Staub, and Professor Alan Mittleman offered helpful comments on an earlier version of this chapter. I acknowledge their role with thanks.

1. See Arthur Goren, *New York Jews and the Quest for Community* (New York: Columbia University Press, 1970).
2. Mel Scult, *Judaism Faces the Twentieth Century* (Detroit, Mich.: Wayne State University Press, 1993), 132.
3. Quoted in Scult, *Judaism,* 133-34.
4. Mordecai Kaplan, *Future of the American Jew* (New York: Macmillan, 1948), 56-57.
6. *The Reconstructionist,* vol. 6 (May 5, 1939): 5.
7. Maurice Karpf, *Jewish Community Organization in the United States* (New York: Bloch Publishing, 1938), 97ff.
8. "The Highest Level of Cooperation," *The Reconstructionist,* I.14 (November 15, 1935): 5-6.
9. Horace Kallen, *Judaism at Bay* (New York: Bloch Publishing, 1932), 110.
10. Quoted in Scult, *Judaism,* 156.
11. "The Highest Level of Cooperation," 5.
12. "A Threat to Democracy," *The Reconstructionist,* I.16 (December 13, 1935): 6.
12. "Democracy in Search of a Philosophy," *The Reconstructionist,* VI.11 (October 4, 1940): 5.
13. "A Program for Jewish Life Today," *The Reconstructionist,* XVI.1 (February 24, 1950): 14.
14. Samuel Dinin, "Reflections on Jewish Community Organization in the United States," *The Reconstructionist,* IV.8 (June 3, 1938): 12.
15. Dinin, "Reflections," 18.
16. Mordecai Kaplan, "The American Rabbi in the Modern World," *The Reconstructionist,* VI.12 (October 16, 1940): 9.
17. Israel Rappoport, "'The Jewish Community' Is What It Does," *The Reconstructionist,* XVI.5 (April 21, 1950): 9.
18. See, for example, Sidney Schwarz, "Reconstructionism as Process," *The Reconstructionist,* XL.4 (June 1979): 14-18; Rebecca Alpert, "Ethical Decision Making: A Reconstructionist Framework, *The Reconstructionist,* L.7 (June 1985): 15-20; Rebecca Alpert and Jacob Staub, *Exploring Judaism: A Reconstructionist Approach* (New York: Reconstructionist Press, 1985), 29-36; David Teutsch, "Rethinking Jewish Sexual Ethics," *The Reconstructionist,* LIV.8 (July-August 1989): 6-11, 22.
19. The Jewish Reconstructionist Federation published the commission report along with an educational manual written by Rabbi Robert Gluck.

20. See, for example, the 1998 *Boundaries and Opportunities: The Role of Non-Jews in JRF Congregations: The Report of the JRF Task Force* and *Kol Ehad: FRCH Committee on Inclusion of People with Disabilities.*

21. Rebecca Alpert, "Jewish Tradition and the Right to Health Care," *The Reconstructionist,* XLIX.6 (April-May 1984): 19.

22. For example, see Michael Sandel, *Democracy's Discontent* (Cambridge, Mass.: Belknap Press, 1996); and Amitai Etzioni, *The Spirit of Community* (New York: Simon and Schuster, 1993).

23. David Bennett, ed., *Multicultural States: Rethinking Difference and Identity* (London: Routledge, 1998), 3.

24. Bennett, *Multicultural States,* 19.

25. Ira Eisenstein, *The Ethics of Tolerance* (New York: King's Crown Press, 1941).

26. See Stratton and Ang, "Multicultural Imagined Communities," in Bennett, ed., *Multicultural States,* 135-61.

27. Mary F. Rogers, *Multicultural Experiences, Multicultural Theories* (New York: McGraw Hill, 1996), 5.

28. "Common Ground," *The Reconstructionist,* VI.12 (October 16, 1940): 4.

29. "A Program for Jewish Life Today," 19.

30. "Freedom and Justice," *The Reconstructionist,* II.5 (April 17, 1936): 3-4.

31. Daniel Nussbaum, "Voluntarism and the Welfare State: A Reconstructionist Perspective," *Raayonot* (Winter 1983): 9-15.

32. "White Racialism in America," *The Reconstructionist,* IV.19 (January 27, 1939): 4.

33. Jacob J. Staub, "Living in Two Civilizations: Preliminary Notes towards a Reappraisal," *Raayonot* (Winter 1983): 24.

34. Carl Levin, "Lawmaking, Jewish-American Style," *The Reconstructionist,* XLIX.8 (July-August 1984): 8.

35. "The Supreme Court and Religion in America," *The Reconstructionist,* XXVIII.11 (October 5, 1962): 4.

36. Richard Hirsh, "Religion in Public Schools: A Reconstructionist Appraisal," *Raayonot* (Winter 1983): 16.

37. Mordecai Kaplan, "Religion in a Democracy," *Review of Religion* (January 1948): 520.

38. Hirsh, "Religion," 21.

39. See, for example, Seymour Cohen, "Religion in the Public School," *The Reconstructionist,* XVI.4 (April 7, 1950): 15-21.

40. See Ruth Brin, "Can a Woman Be a Jew?" *The Reconstructionist,* XXXIV.12 (October 25, 1968): 7-14.

41. "The Birth Control Controversy," *The Reconstructionist,* I.19 (January 24, 1936): 4-8.

42. The effort was launched in 1994. See the undated "Kol Ehad" report published by the Jewish Reconstructionist Federation.

43. "The Reconstructionist Position," *The Reconstructionist,* I.1 (January 11, 1935): 4.
44. "The Pulpit and Social Issues," *The Reconstructionist,* I.7 (April 5, 1935): 4.
45. Richard Rubenstein, "The Rabbis Visit Birmingham," *The Reconstructionist,* XXIX.8 (May 31, 1963): 5-11.
46. "We Too Have a Dream," *The Reconstructionist,* XXIX.11 (October 4, 1963): 3.
47. "Resolution on White Racism and Civil Disorder," *The Reconstructionist,* XXXIV.8, (May 31, 1968): 31.
48. See Valerie Hyman, "Moshav Noam Co-operative Housing: Social Action from a Reconstructionist Perspective," *Reconstructionism Today,* III.2 (Winter 1995-1996): 4-13.
49. Seven Carr Reuben, "A Black-Jewish Covenant in Los Angeles," *Reconstructionism Today* 2.1 (Summer 1994).

10

Jewish Renewal

Allan Arkush

A relatively fresh arrival on the American scene, Jewish Renewal is a movement that is still taking shape. In the words of one of its most prominent spokesmen, Arthur Waskow, it "is much less made up of specific institutions than it is a motion, a wave of energy."[1] In recent years this wave has carried thousands of people previously estranged from Judaism back to their ancestral religion. It has uprooted them from spiritually barren secular environments or, in many cases, from the exotic, non-Jewish religious surroundings in which they had sought spiritual sustenance, and deposited them in small but apparently growing synagogues, communities, and organizations of other, less familiar types. Loosely connected with one another in such frameworks as the Alliance for Jewish Renewal and the Network of Jewish Renewal Communities, these new groups are by no means hotbeds of political activity. More inclined to sponsor retreats than rallies, they seem to be focused primarily on fostering their members' as well as other people's achievement of higher levels of religious consciousness.[2] Not surprisingly, Bernard Susser and Charles S. Liebman, the authors of a highly insightful study of the latest trends in American Jewish life, have located them among the signs of a contemporary abandonment of the public square, a "privatization of Jewishness."[3] If we look closely at Jewish Renewal, however, we will see that it has always contained within itself the seeds of a more activist political orientation. Although they may not appear to be germinating at the moment, it is still conceivable that they will do so at some future date.

Jewish Renewal is anything but a rigidly structured, hierarchically organized movement. There is, however, one individual who has been since its inception its virtually unrivaled spiritual leader and guide: Zalman Schachter-Shalomi. Susser and Liebman have described him as a "highly colorful and inspirational personality . . . an ordained Orthodox Rabbi who long ago abandoned the rigors of traditional observance while preserving a neo-Hasidic atmosphere and an extravagantly exuberant guru style."[4]

In the eyes of a much more sympathetic observer, Rodger Kamenetz, he is "the architect of Jewish renewal in our time."[5] Our investigation of the politics of Jewish renewal will necessarily begin with an exploration of the rather limited evidence of political concerns found in Schachter-Shalomi's published works. From there we will proceed to an examination of the much more elaborate political teaching of Arthur Waskow, the man he has hailed as "the prophet in Jewish renewal," someone whose "readers will know in their hearts that the living God speaks through him."[6]

After considering Waskow, we will turn our attention to the political tendencies discernible in the writings of an increasingly visible group of Schachter-Shalomi's disciples and admirers. Jewish bookstores around the country now display similar-looking tomes by rabbis and teachers of Jewish Renewal such as David Cooper, Wayne Dosick, Tirzah Firestone, Shoni Labowitz, and Rami Shapiro. From a mere glance at the bucolic or celestial scenery depicted on the covers of most of these books it is clear that they are calls for spiritual reorientation, not political action. In virtually all of these works, to be sure, one can find some appreciative acknowledgement of the work of Arthur Waskow as well as some gestures in the direction of political activism. But, as we shall see, none of them echo Waskow's ardent advocacy of participation in the rough-and-tumble world of politics to help bring about *tikkun olam*. Their writings apparently warrant Susser and Leibman's conclusion that Jewish Renewal, at least for now, represents a "privatization of Judaism."

But the movement could change course. This, at least, is what Michael Lerner would like to see it do. The editor of *Tikkun*, the leading leftist Jewish journal in America, Lerner not only regards Schachter-Shalomi as his rebbe but also has recently been ordained by him as a rabbi.[7] In his magazine, in his book *Jewish Renewal*, and from other pulpits Lerner has been trying to steer the movement back into the waters of progressive politics. He may, perhaps, succeed. It seems more likely, however, that the zeitgeist will continue to blow in another direction and will thwart all such efforts.

Zalman Schachter-Shalomi

Rabbi Zalman Schachter-Shalomi was born in Poland in 1924 and raised in Vienna. The scion of a family of hasidic butchers, he studied in "Orthodox yeshivot and a secular high school and joined both socialist and religious Zionist groups." After escaping from Europe in the nick of time, a week before Passover 1940, he entered the Lubavitcher Yeshiva in Brooklyn, where he earned rabbinic ordination in 1947. He subsequently earned an M.A. in the psychology of religion at Boston University and a doctorate from Hebrew Union College. Under the Lubavitcher rebbe's direction, during the 1950s and early 1960s "he toured the college circuit" with singer and composer Rabbi Shlomo Carlebach. Eventually kicked out of Habad for praising "the sacramental potential of lysergic acid," Schachter-Shalomi ventured out to meet "a whole generation of Jewish seekers" on his own terms. In 1975 he moved to Philadelphia where he became a professor of religion at Temple University. There "he helped his followers integrate the feminism, ecological awareness, progressive politics, and egalitarianism of the havurah movement with a universalized hasidic mysticism." The movement he launched "called itself Jewish renewal." By the mid-1990s, "twenty-six Jewish renewal communities had sprouted in fifteen states, with seven more in Canada, England, Israel, Switzerland and Brazil."[8]

The teaching that gave rise to this movement may seem, at first glance, to be rooted primarily in traditional sources. "Jewish Renewal," writes Schachter-Shalomi in *Paradigm Shift*, "is based on the Kabbalah, Hasidism and other forms of Jewish mysticism." The immediately ensuing sentences make it clear, however, that the real basis of his own teaching lies not so much in the Jewish mystical tradition as in the "new paradigm" that "deals with what is coming down the revelation-redemption pipeline." Schachter-Shalomi refers here to new voices that necessitate the scrapping of "old reality maps" and their replacement by others "that are, if not identical, at least parallel to the intuitions and traditions of Jewish mysticism."[9] In other words, he takes his bearings primarily from some sort of extratextual, revelational experience, one that is not necessarily related to anything hitherto found in the Jewish mystical tradition.

The experience in question is, for Rabbi Schachter-Shalomi, not a merely personal but a generational one. All around him he senses a growing readiness to discard an older paradigm in favor of one that represents a higher degree of spiritual awareness. "The intellectual move of the new paradigm," he writes, "is not yet fully clear," but he nevertheless strives to put it into words.[10] He contrasts it with past paradigms, in which momentary flashes of understanding of the "Great Cosmic Allness" "were snatched from their eternal dimension and entombed in the world of relativity in the form of religious institution and symbolism. Revelations of cosmic commonality, when etched into stone, often became doctrines of exclusive particularism. It was the myth of a binary world, a world of either/or, of good or evil, of build up or tear down, of Us and them."[11]

At present, however, we are "entering an age of alternative, of elasticity, in which God is being liberated from stone engravings and doctrinal codes to become organic again, in turn freeing human consciousness to do the self-growing it was originally intended to do."[12]

"The paradigm shift" currently underway, it is important to recognize, "is not only a function of the history of the Jews. It has in a most palpable way become the shift for the entire planet."[13] But it is not necessary or advisable for all denizens of Earth to react to it in an undifferentiated manner. One should not downplay "the respective values of particular traditions. Everyone has something to offer, to share. This goes for peoples, genders, and traditions."[14]

The Jews, therefore, like everyone else, ought to adapt their own tradition to the new paradigm. This will require, among other things, a reassessment of the divine-human relationship. "We need to replace the active Father-passive Child, King-Subject, Judge-Defendant with something like mutual and interactive Friend-friend, Lover-lover, Partner-partner."[15] These new notions have radical implications with respect to the manner in which Jews ought to worship God and point to the need for a new understanding of their other duties as well. "Concerning Torah in the new paradigm, we must give up the notion of legislation and take on the notion of discovering the laws of nature. We need to discover what works for us instead of legislating what *should* work for us. This calls for an empirical study of *halakhah*, and pilot communities to test, in all self-awareness, the norms we would adopt in our discovery" of the divine will.[16]

Insofar as the norms pertaining to worship are concerned, the Jewish mystical tradition is a highly important (but by no means exclusive) source of practicable ideas.[17] But Jewish Renewal is concerned with much more than what Schachter-Shalomi playfully yet quite seriously labels "davenology." "The process of our renewal pervades everything: politics, economics, philosophy, physics, relationships, generations, and genders, Jew-Goy, Israeli-Palestinian, producer-consumer—all these and too many more to mention are being changed and metamorphosed."[18] Those who wish to adapt *halakhah* to contemporary political circumstances therefore face a vast undertaking. Schachter-Shalomi himself has provided only limited assistance in indicating how they ought to try to cope with it.

"I don't want to throw tradition away," he says, "but not everything in the Bible can be adopted whole as it is. Very often we have to ask, what was the intent that produced such a law and how do we best fulfill the intent now?"[19] Schachter-Shalomi's most original response to this question is his updated understanding of *kashrut*. "Sometime in the seventies," he writes, "I coined the term *eco-kosher*." He argued "that the one-way bottle is less kosher than the two-way bottle and that there is a real question from eco-kosher *halakhah* if the electricity from a Nuke is kosher." Guided by "an emerging reality map that sees Earth as a living *Gaia*," Schachter-Shalomi is able to contemplate many "further halakhic and ethical eco-*kashrut* questions."[20] But he has left the systematic resolution of these questions to others.

Schachter-Shalomi has gone no further in suggesting how *halakhah* can be utilized to deal with other questions, closer to the center of the contemporary political world. From some of his scattered remarks, however, it appears that if he were to make any such proposals they would be radical ones. At one point, for instance, he observes that "[r]eligious, political, economic, and mental strategies needed" in the current age "are different" from those of the past. "Property and land can no longer be dealt with as entities owned by conquest or acquisition." And we no longer live in a "time in which the individualistic person is the highest value." While it is necessary to grant the individual "the greatest scope for development," the "consciousness of larger social aggregates is now needed to network intelligence to act on many dimensions simultaneously, multitasking for our survival."[21] Although it is possible to credit the author of such statements with a commitment to the maintenance of liberal democracy, it is also possible to imagine that he possesses a vision of a better regime than the one under which we currently live.

Arthur Waskow

For a more complete elucidation of the political implications of Jewish Renewal we must turn from Schachter-Shalomi to a man whom he himself has designated, as we have already observed, as "the prophet in Jewish renewal. Born in Baltimore in 1933, the bearer of this sobriquet, Arthur Waskow, once worked in Washington as a legislative assistant for a U.S. congressman and was, during the 1960s, one of the founding fellows of the Institute for Policy Studies. An early opponent of the Vietnam War, he "co-authored 'A Call to Resist Illegitimate Authority' and was elected by the citizens of the District of Columbia to the 1968 Democratic National Convention." It was at this time that he underwent his Jewish reawakening.[22] Since 1969, he "has been one of the leading creators of theory, practice and institutions for Jewish renewal."[23]

Waskow speaks of Schachter-Shalomi as the man "who has helped me 'rename' and re-imagine" God.[24] Elsewhere he describes him as one "of the most important teachers of a newer generation, bridging in unconventional ways the chasm between materialism and mysticism."[25] None of this praise should mislead us, however, into regarding Waskow as merely a disciple of Shachter-Shalomi. Although his route to his own theology seems to have taken him over one of the bridges built by his mentor, he acknowledges his debt to many other teachers as well, including Martin Buber and Mordecai Kaplan.[26] He even suggests, at one point, that his own "life approach" can be characterized as "the fusion of Kabbalah with Reconstructionism."

What Waskow has taken from the Kabbalah is above all the idea of divine immanence. Nowadays, he maintains, "God is 'no longer' *out there*; God is not, in our era, most easily discerned as The Other. Instead God has fled *into* the world."[27] Following Schachter-Shalomi, Waskow dismisses as utterly antiquated the notion of God as a legislator. And like Mordecai Kaplan, he perceives Torah as man-made and in need of large-scale updating. His method of determining how much alteration is permissible is, however, all his own: "But is Torah *only* process, *only* historical development? Does anything and everything go? Abandoning Torah? Replacing

Torah? No. The irreducible minimum of Torah is that the Jewish people be struggling with Torah—with all or any of the teachings of the past."[28]

Struggling with Torah, or, as Waskow often puts it, wrestling with Torah is the means by which the Jews continually re-create Torah. But "if it is human beings," Waskow asks, "who we say are speaking 'Torah,' is it just a trick of language to call it Torah that they speak? Am I simply disguising secularism with some seductive language about God and Torah?"[29] Waskow attempts to prove that this is not the case by outlining in detail the precautions that interpreters of Torah must take to guard against missteps: "To make what we teach, learn, and do into Torah it is necessary to sound ourselves, to sound our depths—each of us, and between us. The Other that we seek is both each other, the tremor of communion that quivers between us when we are together listening for Torah, and in each of us that deeper spark of God—which also shakes us, makes us tremble, when the spark sputters and sizzles to leap across the gap."

In addition to maintaining this sort of alertness, it is necessary to engage in ritual practices as well, such as immersions in the mikveh, donning special garments, and sitting in a group around the texts that are to be interpreted.

> Then we draw on the written and oral traditions of Torah, on our secular knowledge of the world, and on our deepest feelings to create new Torah. We keep ourselves conscious of the political and social institutional wishes, interests, and conflicts among us; we try not to suppress them or eliminate them but to be clear about them, to learn from them, to see what these very tugs and conflicts teach us about the pulls and tugs of God in history.
>
> And finally we decide how to act, accepting disagreements in the spirit that both these actions and these other actions may be the expressions of the living God.[30]

Waskow here delineates a complex process of ritual activity, introspection, and deliberation, one that could surely prevent many of its practitioners from mistaking their individual whims for the dictates of Torah. This effort notwithstanding, there is still room to doubt whether what he has in mind is really something more than a disguised form of secularism. We will not make it our business, however, to judge whether Waskow's orientation is a genuinely religious one. What concern us are the results to which it seems to have led him.

As one can see from a comparison of his earlier with his more recent work, it has taken him down a path marked by interesting twists and turns. Ever since his self-transformation decades ago "from Jewish radical to radical Jew," Waskow has been trying to devise a Jewish politics that draws on both traditional sources and such wisdom as the modern world has to offer.[31] In *Godwrestling* (1978) he identified biblical practices, such as the jubilee year, which still have vigor and power. While acknowledging that modern society cannot simply reduplicate them, he called upon his contemporaries to wrestle with their "inner meanings," and to draw "analogous practices from them." At the same time, he wrote, they needed "to struggle with the intellectually and politically powerful set of ideas that has emerged in the modern world around the secular search for social justice." Waskow was referring at this time to Marxism, an ideology that he described as containing "profound, useful, and liberating ideas." "Somehow serious Christians and Jews must be able to learn from what is useful in Marxism while at the same time drawing on the truths in their own traditions that Marxism does not teach."[32]

The utility of Marxism, in Waskow's eyes, was not bound up with its call for class warfare but with its other virtues. While his hostility to the evil American "Empire" was, at this time, very pronounced, he never voiced support for its violent overthrow. What he envisioned instead was the gradual "shattering of the American super-state and the radical decentralization of power throughout the continent." He looked forward to the day when the United States would be replaced by Jewish as well as "other Commonwealths created according to real identities—some ethnic, some sexual, some regional, some economic."[33] These Jewish "Commonwealths" would be communities, regulating their affairs in accordance with a renovated *halakhah*, "more and more governing themselves, feeding themselves, teaching themselves according to their own perception of the Jewish path."[34] The people would determine the content of their new "Talmud"; "not an elite of rabbinic adepts but the whole community will be part of the discussions that work out our new life-practice."[35] Waskow yearned to see this process culminate in "the emergence of a democratic, ecstatic, libertarian, communitarian, socialist Judaism."[36]

This, at least, is what he longed for in the late 1970s and early 1980s. By the 1990s, however, "the prophet in Jewish renewal" had shed a great deal of his radicalism. In his most recent books, such as *Godwrestling Round 2* and *Down-to-Earth Judaism*, the overt hostility to the evil American empire is gone, along with the calls for a dialogue with Marxism. There is, to be sure, no evidence in these works of any new appreciation of the merits of the American polity. In *Godwrestling Round 2*, as in the earlier *Godwrestling*, of which it is a revised version, Waskow's American hero is the rebel Sam Adams, not James Madison.[37] There is no evidence, either, that Waskow has altogether soured on socialism. He continues to regard it as the aspiration of admirable visionaries, but he no longer views it as part of humankind's future.[38]

As we have already seen, Waskow's ruminations on the biblical jubilee year led him, in *Godwrestling*, from a focus on practical reforms to an emphasis on what Marxism had to teach. The parallel chapter in *Godwrestling Round 2* culminates in the strikingly unrevolutionary proposal of a neighborhood "jubilee festival." Such a holiday would serve as the occasion for Jews (as well as Christians) to address "the economic renewal of the city and its neighborhoods by inviting co-ops and worker-managed firms, innovative small businesses, etcetera, to explain their work." Among other things, it would focus on "the political empowerment of the neighborhood by gathering people to discuss in open town meetings some of the major issues of our society—energy, jobs, environment, prices, families."[39] It would not necessarily mark the beginning of the end of the American "empire."

Over the years, Jewish Renewal's prophet has evidently lost some of his fire and scaled down his vision. This is presumably the result of his having followed his own recommendation and remained attuned to "the political and social institutional wishes, interests, and conflicts among us." From these observable phenomena he seems to have learned that God is not pulling and tugging the world toward socialism, or that He is at least not doing so very quickly. But if Waskow has abandoned his grander dreams, he has not ceased to ponder the question of how Jewish communities (no longer called commonwealths) can apply the insights and values of the Torah to life in the modern state (no longer derided as a superstate). In *Down-to-Earth Judaism*, he lists the "four underlying issues that the Jewish community now needs to face and to provide answers for." He asks whether "any worldview can replace 'Jewish socialism' as an overall guide to Jewish practice about money and related matters?" He also asks, among other things, for "what purposes should Jews work together with other Jews on money questions, and for what purposes with the public at large?" Coherent answers to these and other such questions are necessary, according to Waskow, if the worldwide Jewish community is to "become renewed with elan and purpose."[40] Despite his decades of reflection on matters of this kind, he himself does not seem quite prepared to present the much-needed solutions.[41] But this is, perhaps, the job of a policy analyst, not a prophet.

Soul Judaism

Unlike Arthur Waskow, whose path to Jewish Renewal led through radical politics, the other leading spokespersons of the movement came to it after intense exposure to the utterly dissimilar world of Eastern religion. Some of them, such as Tirzah Firestone and David Cooper, were utterly immersed in it, alienated from Judaism and on the brink of being lost to it. Others, such as Shoni Labowitz, appear to have encountered and assimilated the wisdom of the East without losing their previous footing in the Jewish religion. Almost all of them identify Zalman Schachter-Shalomi as the person who assisted them, more than anyone else, in regaining their Judaism or in discovering it for the first time.[42] Through their association with Jewish Renewal, most of them also seem to have become familiar with Arthur Waskow and his political teachings, but this does not seem to have made a particularly deep impression on any of them. The stray notes of political radicalism audible in Schachter-Shalomi's teaching, and considerably amplified in Waskow's works, are largely muffled in the spiritual autobiographies and guides to living published in recent years by the other Jewish Renewal rabbis.

Although he can in no sense be taken to be the leader of this group, Wayne Dosick is the author of a volume whose title aptly describes the substance not only of his own book but the works of many of his colleagues as well: *Soul Judaism*. According to Dosick, Soul Judaism (or Neshamah Judaism) "will be defined by its core manifestation, the intimate spiritual soul-connection of each person with God, and by its forgers and shapers, precious individual souls."[43] It is principally concerned with the establishment of intimacy with the "new paradigm" deity through prayer, meditation, and other contemplative practices. The same is true of Shoni Labowitz's *Miraculous Living*, Tirzah Firestone's *With Roots in Heaven*, David Cooper's *God Is a Verb*, and Rami Shapiro's *Minyan*. The theological contents of these books are almost as indistinguishable as their subtitles are interchangeable.[44]

Their focus on communion with God does not prevent the Renewal authors from dwelling on the more mundane aspects of human life. They all stress the fact that Judaism is a this-worldly religion profoundly concerned with ethical behavior and social action, even if they are critical of the extent to which its American versions have tended to concentrate on such matters to the virtual exclusion of spirituality.[45] Their writings generally include some indications of how spiritually aware people ought to behave toward others. They understand such conduct to be not merely a good thing but a crucial factor in facilitating humanity's progress toward redemption. They do not show very much interest, however, in spelling out the ways in which people ought to act together in the political arena in order to achieve the same goal. What little they do have to say on this subject is rather sketchy and lacking in specificity and, at times, startlingly fanciful.

"Spirituality," according to Rami Shapiro, "is a conscious practice of living out the highest ethical ideals in the concreteness of everyday life."[46] He points to three ways of doing so: *tzedakah*, which he translates as "generosity," *gemilut chesed* or kindness, and eco-*kashrut*, that is, ethical consumption. "While *tzedakah* may apply," Shapiro writes, "to a wide variety of generous acts, giving of your time and possessions as well as your wealth, it is financial giving that is its primary focus." In addition to its obvious purpose of providing for the immediate needs of particular unfortunate individuals, *tzedakah* has a larger goal. It aims at "the creation of an economically just and compassionate society where everyone has an opportunity to sustain him- or herself and where help is available for those who cannot do so."[47] *Gemilut chesed*, "a wonderful practice," consists of "engaging in acts of kindness and treating everyone and everything with utmost respect."[48] This practice can be applied, as it has been by several members of Shapiro's congregation, to social projects. "One woman took upon herself the obligation of establishing a neighborhood CrimeWatch as an expression of helping others. Another formed a series of safe houses in her neighborhood where local children in need could come for help."[49]

Eco-*kashrut*, Zalman Schachter-Shalomi's familiar coinage, is the practical matter to which Shapiro devotes the most attention. He notes, among other things, how it leads to the "Principle against Spoiling Food," a principle that "led members of one Minyan retreat to negotiate with a local supermarket to rescue foodstuffs tossed into their Dumpsters at the close of each business day." This food was subsequently transported to a local community food bank and soup kitchen.[50] The members of this *minyan*, as well as the people engaged in the other practices Shapiro describes, are not just doing good; they are helping "to bring about *tikkun ha-olam*, perfecting the world through love and justice."[51]

David Cooper stresses the importance of *tzedakah, gemilut chesed*, and being eco-kosher.[52] Wayne Dosick has nothing to say about eco-*kashrut*, but he is completely in tune with the other two themes of Shapiro and Cooper. He urges his readers to participate in food collections for the poor on Yom Kippur and to contribute to Mazon: A Jewish Response to Hunger, which distributes money "to institutions and organizations throughout the country that feed hungry people and advocate and educate on their behalf."[53] His recommendations for the celebration of Hanukkah include an innovative plan of action for the holiday's eight days. He suggests that on each night one ought to take one's children to a homeless shelter, a blood bank, a retirement home, or the home of an elderly person to perform an act of *tzedakah* or lovingkindess.[54]

Shoni Labowitz holds that the "spiritually evolved being in mystical Judaism, as well as the bodhisattva in Buddhism, is dedicated to remaining in this world in order to serve humanity." The much-needed crown of light that the enlightened individual ought to carry into the streets of the world "can be ascertained only through unconditional love and selfless acts of kindness." "In selfless service," Labovitz writes, "you redeem the hidden sparks imprisoned in the *klippot* of the world."[55] An example of someone who has discovered this truth is her "friend Louis," who "learned that he was HIV-positive some years ago." After wallowing for a while in self-pity, he "redesigned his life." Louis "found his sense of purpose when he began working on political and social-action issues. He dedicated himself to campaigning for AIDS awareness and gay rights."[56]

Tirzah Firestone's account of her own passage, during the 1970s and 1980s, through a number of Eastern religious frameworks and back to Judaism reflects little involvement in the politics of the time. How unconcerned she was with such matters while trekking around the world in search of enlightenment can be seen, perhaps, from her description of the Israel she visited in 1973. She mentions how she left the country during that year "on the cusp of the Yom Kippur War, the air thick with prewar tension, everyone tight and growling."[57] But there was, of course, no prewar tension in Israel during the period leading up to the utterly unexpected Arab attack on the country (though there was undoubtedly a lot of growling). While this is the only passage in Firestone's book that evinces a great remoteness from politics, it is also one of the few passages that display any awareness at all of contemporary political developments.

By her own account, Firestone's return to Judaism has altered her overall perspective. "Instead of relating to our flawed, human world as separate from the divine," she writes, "I now know that life is best approached as an interpenetration of light and dark, a blend of spirit with matter and the timeless with time. Rather than pressuring ourselves to graduate from normal consciousness to ascend to another, higher plane of truth, our task is one of bringing heaven down to earth, to live life with an open heart, to walk the dark path while carrying an internal lantern."[58]

What this means in practice is something which Firestone does not elucidate in great detail. More than any of the other rabbis under consideration in this section, however, she has expressed her sense of indebtedness to Arthur Waskow. His provocative questions about eco-*kashrut* "resounded" in her, she informs us. He is, in her eyes, the "visionary" from whom she learned "that the path of Jewish spirituality was not only personal but political."[59] Yet the chapters of her autobiography dealing with her activities as a Jewish Renewal rabbi focus almost exclusively on their non-political aspects.

Near the end of *With Roots in Heaven*, Firestone reports on a retreat she organized, "with Zalman's blessing," of Jewish Renewal rabbis from around the country. This assemblage, we learn, was far from monolithic. Nevertheless, although their "politics widely diverged," the "group never once became polarized in its discussions." Even here, however, she divulges her own political position only in the most general terms. Acknowledging that Jewish "self-centeredness" may once have been somewhat appropriate, she maintains that

> this narrow approach must now be expanded to include what we know to be true about the interconnectedness of all life and the planet's plight. As Jews, we are taught never to endanger life, but to sustain it at all costs. But it is not the case that Jews are interconnected only with Jews or that Jews are responsible for the land of Israel and no other parcel of earth. If we fail to care for one another and the earth that sustains us all, regardless of our nationhood, we simply will not continue as a human species. This includes Jews.[60]

While these sentiments are easy enough to fathom, their precise implications with regard to the political arena are far from self-evident.

It is not only Firestone, of course, who neglects to provide her readers with a detailed political road map. None of the people grouped together here as proponents of "Soul Judaism" has chosen to supply one. Of all of them only Dosick endorses a specific type of mass action. "How," he asks, "will we, the few and not particularly politically powerful, bring an end to the gross inhumanity that threatens to destroy all that is precious?" He recalls that in the summer of 1987, "hundreds of thousands of men and women all over the world joined in a one-day convocation that they called the Harmonic Convergence. They held hands, sang songs and played musical instruments, prayed, invoked peaceful thoughts, and spoke of world peace and harmony. They joined their energy together to move the world closer toward decency and goodness."

At the time, all of this might have seemed laughable to skeptics, yet, Dosick observes, "within months of the Harmonic Convergence, strange and wonderful things began happening across the world. The Berlin Wall came down; communism fell in the Soviet Union and the satellite countries; blacks and whites began riding the bus together in South Africa; the shootings and bombings stopped in Northern Ireland; and ancient enemies in the Mideast sat down at the negotiating table."

"Mere coincidence?" Dosick inquires, and then acknowledges that this may be the case. "But perhaps the combined prayers and spiritual energy of hundreds of thousands of diverse and otherwise disconnected citizens of the world had a positive cosmic effect on the energy of the world. Prayer works. Sending focused energy into the universe works. Combined spiritual and energetic forces can alter momentary reality."[61]

Like Dosick, Shoni Labowitz identifies an instance of inspired political action, though she, for her part, does not broach the suggestion that it may have had any immediate efficacy. She describes an act undertaken by a "wise and spiritually seasoned person" who had succeeded in arriving at the state of formlessness in which it would be possible for the spirit of God to fill her at "just the right moment" with "the wisdom and understanding to act justly." At a diplomatic conference in the USSR during the Cold War, Labowitz's friend Florence Ross "stood up in front of the American and Russian delegations and told them 'to stop acting like little boys playing one-upmanship' and get on with the work of peace!"

This episode supplies the basis for a general lesson:
What does it mean to be formless? And how does that require strength and effect justice?

When you are formless, there is no form to which anyone or any thought can attach. When you are nonattached, you are walking the middle point in the road, between two directions. This enables you to view both directions and all thoughts with right mindfulness. Right mindfulness that witnesses without judging encourages right action. Right action flows from a clear mind, with clear intention. Nonjudgment observes without analyzing, accepts without criticizing, and acts with virtue through right action. Right action is always just." [62]

Aside from being innately just, right action will have positive consequences. "*Tikkun olam*, the transformation of the world, begins with you living the dreams that God is dreaming in you. When you deny your dreams, you deny God's dreams and leave a vacancy in the global vision of holiness. The Baal Shem Tov said that every person has a portion in bringing about an age of enlightenment and in constructing a collective Messiah. When you do your part individually, the global reality moves nearer to completion."[63]

In light of all of this, it is understandable enough why Labowitz's guide to miraculous living is essentially devoid of any substantive advice with regard to action in the political arena. What people really need to know, she believes, is not exactly what to do in the real world but how to render their souls receptive to the proper sort of inspiration. The right dispositions will ultimately produce the right actions.

It is not only Labowitz who sees things more or less in this way. David Cooper, too, highlights the link between elevated spiritual awareness and universal betterment. "Each time we do something that raises consciousness," he writes, "we lift sparks of holiness to new levels. This is called *tikkun ha-nefesh*, mending the soul, and *tikkun ha-olam*, mending the world, bringing it closer to its source." However different these two things may seem, "in reality they cannot be separated; we cannot raise sparks in ourselves without raising those in the world, and vice versa."[64] Similarly, Wayne Dosick states that "in order to heal the world, we have to bring full healing to our own souls. Then out of personal *tikkun* will come *tikkun olam*; out of deep inner peace will come world peace."[65]

Michael Lerner

This kind of talk about *tikkun olam* has the editor of *Tikkun* worried. In a 1998 editorial he outlined the danger he envisions:

> Some forms of spirituality focus inward and refuse to challenge the inherent materialism and selfishness of our economic and political institutions. For a significant section of the growing spiritual movement, political concerns are seen as antithetical to "inner work." Equanimity or peace of mind becomes the highest goal, and spiritual passion for *tikkun*, for building a world of love and caring in which every person on the planet is treated as equally precious and equally a manifestation of God-energy, is dismissed as something that will come later, after we've gotten our inner lives together (but that after never comes, because work on inner lives is necessarily and appropriately a life long venture).[66]

This criticism is undoubtedly directed at the Jewish Renewal writers we have just discussed. Lerner is much less interested, however, in engaging in any prolonged polemics against them than in identifying a better path than the one they have marked out. Jewish Renewal, he maintains, should be "an attempt to make us more fully alive to God's presence in the world, to build a life that is God-centered, and to provide us with a way of reclaiming the unique spirituality of Judaism, deeply embedded in political consciousness but not reducible to a particular political agenda or to a set of moral injunctions."[67]

Lerner's understanding of the relationship between Jewish Renewal and political activism obviously invites comparison with that of Arthur Waskow. He himself indicates both the appropriateness of such a comparison and the difficulties involved in undertaking it. In the preface to *Jewish Renewal* he lists Waskow among the people from whom he has derived "tremendous wisdom and inspiration (and sometimes very specific ideas in this book)." But he also warns us, in the same place, that he is not going to talk about these people in detail, apologizing "to them for all the times their ideas are incorporated without specific acknowledgement."

Like Waskow, Lerner owes a great deal to Zalman Schachter-Shalomi. He identifies him not only, as we have already noted, as his own rebbe, but also as "the originator of much contemporary Jewish-renewal theology" and "one of the inspired conveyors of a new revelation that will shape generations to come."[68] But Lerner, again like Waskow, is someone for whom many other Jewish theologians are of no less importance. In his eyes, the real "spiritual founder" of Jewish Renewal is not Schachter-Shalomi but Abraham Joshua Heschel, his teacher at the Jewish Theological Seminary during the 1960s. "So much of what I say in this book," Lerner observes in the prologue to *Jewish Renewal*, "derives from his insights that in some ways I see this whole book as a footnote and update to his thinking."[69] In fact, Lerner sounds more like Schachter-Shalomi when he talks about God; he sounds more like Heschel when he talks about the proper human response to God's call.

Peering down what Schachter-Shalomi calls the "revelation-redemption pipeline," Lerner sees that we are now "moving toward a conception of God that is based more on a conception of a Force that both includes all of Being as we know it, and surpasses all that we can ever know."[70] This deity is a deeply mysterious entity about which little can be known.[71] The most important thing that can be said about it, Lerner maintains, is that S/He is "the Force that allows" or "makes for "world repair" or "fundamental transformation."[72] When God "makes for transformation, however, it is not through direct action. God may be the "ultimate Force governing the world," yet this governance occurs not by means of supernatural intervention in human history but only through the exercise of "a spiritual pull within all Being to move beyond what it is to what it ought to be."[73] Or, as Lerner puts it elsewhere, God is like a voice calling us from the future. "To be in tune with that voice is to reject any idolization of that which is, to refuse to bow down to the gods of "reality," always to be moving toward that which we know and feel could and should be, even though it transcends that which seems "realistic," given the way things have been. To be called by this God is to be in touch with the God of Israel."[74]

People who establish such contact with God can begin to do what is required of them by heeding the Torah's "injunctions to love your neighbor as yourself, to love the stranger, to pursue justice."[75] In their reading of the Torah, however, they must learn to distinguish between the genuine divine voice calling for these things and the "the voice of pain and cruelty masquerading as the voice of God." This latter voice is, according to Lerner, an unfortunate echo of Israel's ancient experience of oppression. "Furious at their vulnerability and powerlessness, outraged at the immorality of those non-Jews who periodically murdered, raped, and pillaged them, some Jews adopted a Torah of cruelty that distorted the Torah of love and compassion."[76] It is only in this deformed Torah that one finds such things as the injunction to show no mercy to the Canaanite inhabitants of the Promised Land.[77]

Lerner perceives the authentic message contained in the Bible to be more than a call for moral action and social change. "It was from the Torah," he maintains, "that I learned a profound radicalism and a commitment to revolutionary transformation."[78] This commitment leads him to advocate a "Jewishly inspired politics of meaning." Such a politics would combine the reaffirmation of "the best aspects of democratic and liberal societies" with an insistence "on the priority of eliminating poverty, homelessness, hunger, ecological threats, and inadequate health care, shelter, education, physical security—for all the peoples of the world." It would also, among other things, "see mutual recognition, love, and spiritual sensitivity as the highest goals of life, and would seek to ensure that the very movement that fought for these transformations in the larger world would achieve these in their own practice."[79] Yet Lerner's politics of meaning would not set impossibly high goals for humankind. Informed by "the experience of the Jewish people, it would reject utopian criteria for how much individuals or the social movement could be expected to fully embody the values it holds."[80]

The politics of meaning is not supposed to be a solitary pursuit. It should "construct itself as a movement that seeks to embody its values."[81] The movement that Lerner envisions appears to have somewhat fewer quasi-traditional attributes than the one of which Waskow dreams. His description of it does not concentrate heavily on any elaborate, ritualistic manner of reformulating Torah. But he does see its fundamental task as the development of quintessentially Jewish responses to the same contemporary ethical and political issues that preoccupy Waskow. Indeed, at times he endorses the very same proposal. In *Jewish Renewal* he quotes Waskow's suggestion that "for the next several generations the Jewish people should shape itself into an intergenerational, international 'movement' with the goal of protecting the web of life on earth. We should shape our prayers, our celebrations, our spiritual practices, the rearing of our children, and our public policy with this purpose in mind." Waskow, says Lerner, "is right." Endorsing Zalman Schachter-Shalomi's concept of "eco-kosher," Lerner then declares that the "Jewish community should be at the center of ecological campaigns, and should make eco-kosher a *halakhic* requirement.[82]

Committed as he is to the creation of a movement, Lerner is nevertheless prepared to go it alone. During the early 1990s he did so rather famously. For a while, it seemed, the spouse of the president of the United States had become one of his acolytes.[83] Thanks to the attention she paid to him, "the politics of meaning" became a subject of discussion in circles far beyond the Jewish Renewal movement. After her interest flagged, however, Lerner's signature locution quickly vanished from the headlines of major newspapers. He himself is no longer to be found in Washington, whispering into the ears of the powerful, but has returned to San Francisco, where he serves as the leader of Beyt Tikkun, "a Jewish Renewal and Politics of Meaning oriented Synagogue."[84]

Political Concerns or "Inner Work"?

Most of the leaders of Jewish Renewal share the goal of re-imagining and connecting themselves to the "new paradigm" deity, a being whose resemblance to the God of Abraham, Isaac, and Jacob is, to say the least, open to question. This is a deity that exists, in some sense, but does not act, speak, or command. At most, He or He/She somehow "calls" to people. The content of this summons is something that it is up to its addressees to determine.

All of them, so far, have heard a similar call to participate in the repair of the world. Not all of them, however, have heard this message as loudly and clearly as have others. Products of the politics of the 1960s, like Arthur Waskow and Michael Lerner, still perceive it ringing in their ears. But most of the other Jewish Renewal teachers seem to be marching, or rather, dancing to the tune of a different drum (since they do not imagine there to be any drummer). While they usually continue to repeat some of the idealistic slogans of previous decades, they seem much less impelled to change the world than to ascend to another level of consciousness.

They do not pretend that there is anything distinctively Jewish about this state of awareness. Schachter-Shalomi and, indeed, all of the people following in his footsteps or along nearby paths conceive of themselves, quite correctly, as merely the Jewish representatives of much more widespread tendencies. The most illuminating context in which to view them is not, therefore, that of Jewish mysticism or Jewish political history but that of the broader, contemporary North American religious scene.[85]

Martin E. Marty, one of the most experienced and astute commentators on this scene, has described it as one in which religious energies are now devoted to "the personal, private, and autonomous at the expense of the communal, the public and the derivative."[86] If this is an accurate description of religious Americans in general, it fits especially well the groups categorized by Wade Clark Roof as "metaphysical believers and seekers." In his map of the American religious landscape, Roof includes within this amorphous subculture "Neo-pagans, Wiccans, goddess worshippers, Zen Buddhists, Theosophists" and many other groups typified by their concern with a kind of spirituality different from that found among "mainstream believers."[87] They are also characterized by rather unworldly and disinterested attitudes toward politics.

Roof does not include the leaders of Jewish Renewal among his metaphysical believers and seekers, but it is not hard to detect significant similarities between them. Like the people he describes, its spokespersons speak of energies and forces that "replace theistic concepts and belief in a personal God."[88] Also like the people described by Roof, the leaders of Jewish Renewal "like thinking of themselves as a spiritual vanguard, as innovators of a new movement that in the long run they believe will have global consequences." In Roof's sketch of the political stance of these "metaphysical believers and seekers," one can detect the family resemblance: "Of all the religious subcultures, they are the most optimistic about a new world in the making. When asked about this new world to emerge, respondents usually affirm a simple degree of optimism, without much clarity as to how this will come about except through the power of mental constructions."[89]

As Michael Lerner knows quite well, such people do not constitute the best raw material for building a profoundly radical movement of revolutionary transformation. But he has not given up on them, even if he is not as hopeful as Arthur Waskow. "Sniffing in the wind," Waskow now senses "energy simmering, occasionally coming to a boil, for a new generation of progressive Jewish activists."[90] Are his perceptions correct? Will Waskow, Lerner, and their allies succeed in resuscitating Jewish Renewal's more activist tendencies? Or will the movement continue down the road toward a privatized form of Judaism, as Bernard Susser and Charles Liebman have projected? In seeking an answer to these questions, one cannot confine oneself to the writings of the individuals examined here. These works outline some rather divergent, if not necessarily conflicting, sets of ideas, but they cannot tell us which ideas will prove most attractive in the long run to the kinds of people who are drawn to Jewish Renewal circles. Nor, on the other hand, could a sociological analysis of the rank-and-file membership of the Jewish Renewal movement establish with certainty the direction in which these people are going to move. Everything depends on the dynamic interaction of leaders and followers under circumstances that cannot be completely foreseen. Quietism might reign, radical activism might revive, or new alternatives might yet arise. Jewish Renewal might even become affiliated, for instance, with a conservative Jewish politics. Unlikely as such a development might seem, there is at least one Renewal rabbi who seems to be headed in this direction. Mordecai Finley, the co-rabbi of a Renewal synagogue in the Los Angeles area, is described by Roger Kamenetz as having "conservative political views." Perhaps this "fiercely intellectual" young man represents the wave of the future.[91]

It is admittedly difficult to believe that this is the case. But it is even more difficult to imagine that the aging survivors of the radical politics of the 1960s will succeed in transmitting their time-worn enthusiasms to the current generation of Jewish spiritual seekers. There is, at least, nothing readily visible on the horizon that suggests a widespread readiness on their part to absorb anything like Michael Lerner's "profound radicalism" and "commitment to revolutionary transformation." They may all decide to keep eco-kosher, but they do not seem to be poised either to shake the world or to reshape it. For those who are concerned about the future conduct of American Jews in the public square, therefore, it is probably not necessary to watch the Jewish Renewal movement very closely.

Notes

1. Arthur Waskow, *Down-to-Earth Judaism: Food, Money, Sex and the Rest of Life* (New York: William and Morrow, 1997), 3.

2. For an up-to-date description of the movement, see *Jerusalem Report*, August 2, 1999, 38-39.

3. See Bernard Susser and Charles S. Liebman, *Choosing Survival: Strategies for a Jewish Future* (Oxford: Oxford University Press, 1999), 68-89.

4. Susser and Liebman, *Choosing Survival*, 40.

5. Rodger Kamenetz, *Stalking Elijah: Adventures with Today's Jewish Mystical Masters* (New York: HarperCollins, 1997), 6.

6. See the back jacket of *Down-to-Earth Judaism*.

7. Michael Lerner, *Jewish Renewal: A Path to Healing and Transformation* (New York: Putnam's, 1994), xvi.

8. Kamenetz, *Stalking Elijah*, 18-21.

9. Zalman Schacter-Shalomi, *Paradigm Shift* (Northvale, N.J.: Jason Aronson, 1993), xx.

10. Schachter-Shalomi, *Paradigm Shift*, 292.

11. Schachter-Shalomi, *Paradigm Shift*, 303.

12. Schachter-Shalomi, *Paradigm Shift*, 303.

13. Schachter-Shalomi, *Paradigm Shift*, 279.

14. Schachter-Shalomi, *Paradigm Shift*, 305.

15. Schachter-Shalomi, *Paradigm Shift*, 266.

16. Schachter-Shalomi, *Paradigm Shift*, 267-68.
17. See, for instance, Schachter-Shalomi, *Paradigm Shift*, 161-232.
18. Schachter-Shalomi, *Paradigm Shift*, 281.
19. Schachter-Shalomi, *Paradigm Shift*, 147.
20. Schachter-Shalomi, *Paradigm Shift*, 269-70.
21. Schachter-Shalomi, *Paradigm Shift*, 294.
22. See the beginning of Arthur Waskow, *Godwrestling* (New York: Schocken, 1978), for a detailed description of this experience.
23. Arthur Waskow, *Godwrestling Round 2* (Woodstock, Vt.: Jewish Lights, 1996), 338.
24. Waskow, *Down-to-Earth Judaism*, 385.
25. Waskow, *These Holy Sparks: The Rebirth of the Jewish People* (New York: Harper & Row, 1983), 172.
26. Waskow, *Down-to-Earth Judaism*, 385.
27. Waskow, *These Holy Sparks*, 176.
28. Waskow, *These Holy Sparks*, 183.
29. Waskow, *These Holy Sparks*, 184.
30. Waskow, *These Holy Sparks*, 185.
31. For a description of this process, see Arthur Waskow, *The Bush Is Burning! Radical Judaism Faces the Pharoahs of the Modern Superstate* (New York: Macmillan, 1971), chap. I.
32. Waskow, *Godwrestling*, 126.
33. Waskow, *The Bush Is Burning*, 138.
34. Waskow, *The Bush Is Burning*, 140.
35. Waskow, *These Holy Sparks*, 141.
36. Waskow, *The Bush Is Burning*, 138.
37. Waskow, *Godwrestling*, 114-15, *Godwrestling Round 2*, 248. The earlier version appreciatively alludes to Nat Turner and Eugene Debs, who are omitted in the revised edition.
38. Waskow, *Down-to-Earth Judaism*, 194-204.
39. Waskow, *Godwrestling Round 2*, 258.
40. Waskow, *Down-to-Earth Judaism*, 210-11.
41. Waskow's very latest ruminations on these matters can be found at the website of the Shalom Center he now directs (www.shalomctr.org). There he lists "Ten Questions for Tikkun Olam of the Future." "I have been mulling over and trying to crystallize some new ways of looking at *tikkun olam*—Jewish action to heal the world—that I think I have learned in the past year. I have many more questions than answers, and even my 'answers' I feel are tentative." Among his questions are the following: "3) Do we see 'oppression' chiefly as economic-political, or also as spiritual/cultural; . . . 6) Can there be a progressive Judaism for affluent Jewish communities?; . . . 8) Should we organize a moshav/co-housing community committed to a progressive/renewal/activist Jewish life-path?; and . . . 10) How/where do we discuss these issues, relating our real lives to theory and practice?"

Waskow's discussion of the tenth question is the briefest and possibly the most revealing: How do we get together to discuss these questions in terms of the realities of our lives, not vague generalizations and airy theory? By Email? By physical gatherings? If the latter, how do we plan such a gathering? Could it be regional? Transnational?"

42. Many of them, however, mention the singer Shlomo Carlebach in the same breath.

43. Wayne Dasick, *Soul Judaism: Dancing with God into a New Era* (Woodstock, Vt.: Jewish Lights, 1997), 13.

44. Compare Dosick's title and subtitle with Shoni Labowitz, *Miraculous Living: A Guided Journey in Kabbalah through the Ten Gates of the Tree of Life* (New York: Simon & Schuster, 1996); Tirzah Firestone, *With Roots in Heaven: One Woman's Passionate Journey into the Heart of Her Faith* (New York: Penguin, 1998); David Cooper, *God Is a Verb: Kabbalah and the Practice of Mystical Judaism* (New York: Penguin Putnam, 1997); and Rami Shapiro, *Minyan: Ten Principles for Living a Life of Integrity* (New York: Random House, 1997). The current positions of their authors are also quite similar. Dosick is the spiritual guide of the Elijah Minyan in San Diego, California. Labowitz is the co-rabbi of Temple Adath Or in Fort Lauderdale, Florida. Firestone is the rabbi of the Jewish Renewal Community of Boulder, Colorado. Cooper codirects the Heart of Stillness Hermitage in the mountains near Boulder. Shapiro is the rabbi and storyteller of Temple Beth Or in Miami, Florida.

45. A complaint voiced by Dosick, *Soul Judaism*, 3; and Shapiro, *Minyan*, 64.

46. Shapiro, *Minyan*, 54.

47. Shapiro, *Minyan*, 119.

48. Shapiro, *Minyan*, 134, 136.

49. Shapiro, *Minyan*, 136.

50. Shapiro, *Minyan*, 154.

51. Shapiro, *Minyan*, 69.

52. Cooper, *God Is a Verb*, 14, 191-201.

53. Dasick, *Soul Judaism*, 127.

54. Dasick, *Soul Judaism*, 134-5.

55. Labowitz, *Miraculous Living*, 132-33.

56. Labowitz, *Miraculous Living*, 122-23.

57. Firestone, *With Roots in Heaven*, 12.

58. Firestone, *With Roots in Heaven*, 143.

59. Firestone, *With Roots in Heaven*, 233-34.

60. Firestone, *With Roots in Heaven*, 330-33.

61. Dasick, *Soul Judaism*, 147-58.

62. Labowitz, *Miraculous Living*, 156-57.

63. Labowitz, *Miraculous Living*, 304.

64. Cooper, *God is a Verb*, 179.

65. Dasick, *Soul Judaism*, 234.

66. Michael Lerner, "Spirituality in America," *Tikkun*, November/December 1998, 33.
67. Lerner, *Jewish Renewal*, 283.
68. Lerner, *Jewish Renewal*, xvi.
69. Lerner, *Jewish Renewal*, 17-18. Lerner describes his exposure to Heschel in the context of an account of his passage from a secular but Jewishly committed background through the institutions of Conservative Judaism to radical Jewish politics and Jewish Renewal.
70. Lerner, *Jewish Renewal*, 36.
71. Lerner, *Jewish Renewal*, 408-22.
72. Lerner, *Jewish Renewal*, viii, 38.
73. Lerner, *Jewish Renewal*, 65.
74. Lerner, *Jewish Renewal*, 36.
75. Lerner, *Jewish Renewal*, 132.
76. Lerner, *Jewish Renewal*, 92.
77. Lerner, *Jewish Renewal*, 91-92.
78. Lerner, *Jewish Renewal*, 12.
79. Lerner, *Jewish Renewal*, 268-70.
80. Lerner, *Jewish Renewal*, 268-70.
81. Lerner, *Jewish Renewal*, 269.
82. Lerner, *Jewish Renewal*, 336.
83. See the *New York Times Magazine*, July 27, 1993, for a portrait of Lerner at the height of his influence and celebrity.
84. "Beyt Tikkun is a spiritually alive community dedicated to the Jewish principles of *tikkun olam*—the obligation to be involved in healing and transforming the world. We are part of a growing Jewish renewal movement that seeks to reclaim Judaism from materialism, conformism, and spiritual deadness. We seek to build spirituality that is real. Yet we insist that no matter how deep our inner experience, we are not living a 'spiritually realized life' when we ignore the pain and suffering of others, either on the individual or the planetary level. We are deeply rooted in the Jewish tradition, but also emphasize our connectedness to all other human beings on the planet and the Unity of All Being as central reality and as a guide to ecological sanity." More information on Beyt Tikkun is available on the web page (www.tikkun.org/bt) from which this paragraph was drawn.
85. Although it has a few outposts in Europe and Israel, Jewish Renewal is almost an exclusively American phenomenon. Little has been written about the movement outside the United States. In his recent book *The New Religious Jews: Recent Developments among Observant Jews in Israel* (Jerusalem: Keter Publishing House, 2000) [Hebrew], Yair Sheleg includes a chapter entitled "The New Spiritual Religiosity." Two pages of this chapter (255-56) are devoted to Renewal-type congregations in Israel, which are marked by their extensive use of the music of Shlomo Carlebach. The preponderant majority of their members are of American origin.

86. Martin E. Marty, "Where the Energies Go," in *Annals of the American Academy of Political and Social Science* 527 (May 1993).

87. Wade Clark Roof, *Spiritual Marketplace: Baby Boomers and the Remaking of American Religion* (Princeton, N.J.: Princeton University Press, 1999), 203. See also Roger Housden's *Sacred America: The Emerging Spirit of the People* (New York: Simon & Schuster, 1999). Neither the Jewish nor the non-Jewish spiritual seekers interviewed and discussed in these books sound like the harbingers of a new political movement.

88. Roof, *Spiritual Marketplace*, 210.

89. Roof, *Spiritual Marketplace*, 208.

90. Arthur Waskow, "Ten Questions on Tikkun Olam of the Future," Answer to Question 1, www.shalomctr.org.

91. *Stalking Elijah*, 92, 97.

Afterword

Alan Mittleman

This volume has considered the multiple ways in which Jewish communal agencies and religious movements have engaged the public square. It has explored the history, evolution, internal tensions, and present condition of different institutional actors. Throughout the study several dominant themes have come into view.

First, each group has had to change with the times. The original purpose of each group has changed with the correlative change in historical circumstances. Each group has had to face the challenge of reinventing itself, of adapting its message and its methods to changed social conditions. The agencies and denominations have had to convince their Jewish constituents that they are still relevant and have a clearly defined role to play as effective representatives of Jewish interests.

Second, each group has had to grapple with what constitutes the "Jewish interest." Although these actors constitute this concept in differing ways, all work within a field that stretches between the universal and the particular, between a narrow-gauged interest politics and a utopian vision of a common good.

Third, and related to this tension, all, explicitly or implicitly, articulate an argument about what they offer to American civil society. They propose, if only tacitly, a "public philosophy" or "public theology" that justifies and rationalizes their participation in the public square. Every group, to one degree or another, tries to relate itself to a Jewish past. Some reach back into what they imagine to constitute the "Jewish political tradition," as described by Daniel

Elazar. Others, solidly based in the American progressive tradition, nonetheless argue that that tradition has an affinity with Judaism. They wager that the two are one.

Fourth, every group must lay a claim to legitimate leadership. Against the implicit anarchic challenge of "Who appointed so and so king of the Jews?" Jewish organizations must constantly nurture the presumption of their legitimacy. Leadership in a voluntary polity must constantly renew itself. Fifth, each group has had to wrestle with how best to allocate its public affairs resources. Should they be directed toward the center of power, Washington, D.C., or toward the periphery? What are the relative advantages of lobbying versus public education?

Finally, each group must cope with a problem that afflicts American civil society as such, namely, the problem of declining institutional loyalty. If, as stated at the outset, we live in an age of "porous" institutions, which people occasionally use rather than join, membership-based organizations must constantly work at replacing their aging bases. Sociological studies point to an erosion of interest and loyalty among Jews toward nonsynagogal institutions. Jewish organizations are perceived to be remote and disconnected from the Judaism of many contemporary American Jews. While synagogues themselves remain relatively healthy, supralocal synagogue movements and communal agencies may decline. This will decrease the social capital of the Jewish community. The uncertain status of civic engagement among followers of the Jewish Renewal movement expresses this trend. In its relative disposition of the private and public, this movement may well be a bellwether for the direction of Jewish involvement in the American public square.

Index

"The ABCs of Scapegoating," 37
Abington Township School District v. Schempp, 47, 270
abortions, and Israeli legislation, 327
Abraham, 322
Abram, Morris, 50, 58, 61, 123, 149
Ad Hoc Committee on International Affairs, 71
Adenauer, Konrad, 50
Adler, Cyrus, 27
Adler, Felix, 267
Adorno, Theodor, 36
Advocacy 101: The Why, What and How of State and National Policy Advocacy, 224
Advocacy Day, 250-51
affirmative action, 19
AFL-CIO, 205
African American, x, 143-44, 342; community, 79; leaders, pro-Palestinian, 144; press, 118
Age of Enlightenment, 311-12
Agudath Israel (of America), 295-96, 298, 304, 315, 317, 321-25, 328, 330
AIDS, 205, 248, 374
AJCommittee. *See* American Jewish Committee
AJCongress. *See* American Jewish Congress

Al Qaeda, 174-75
Al-Aksa mosque, 161
Alliance for Jewish Renewal, 363
Allocation of Health Care Resources, 254-55
Allport, Dr. Gordon W., 37
Alpert, Rabbi Rebecca, 346
America(n), ix, 4, 6, 8, 14-15, 17-20, 27-29, 31-32, 37, 43, 47, 51, 54, 62, 69, 75-76, 79-80, 83, 97-98, 104, 106, 116, 118-19, 131, 142-44, 146, 162, 164, 172-73, 186, 227, 236-37, 240, 263-64, 266, 268-69, 274, 284, 289, 295-96, 299, 304, 314, 320-21, 326, 329, 331-32, 337-39, 343-44, 347-49, 351, 353, 358, 364, 370-71; Catholic leaders, 139; churchmen, 53; citizenship, xiv; constitution, 272, 284; constitutional law, 272; democracy, ix, 28, 54, 72, 216, 270, 343, 351; democratic ideals, 348; democratic society, 85; federal and state constitution, 263; Jewish condition in, 30; Jewish politics in, 28; Jewish rights in, 264; law, 274; media, 34; national interests, 121; NGOs, 170; political right, 273; progressive tradition, 390; Protestant, xiii; race

relations in, 96; religious landscape, 381; society, 21, 35-36, 52, 84, 104, 118, 128, 166, 219, 240, 272, 301, 328, 343, 348-49; support for Israel, 56; values, 15, 300, 343; Zionist movement, 106
America First, 17
America v. Dale, 330
America's Second Harvest, 216
America-Israel Dialogue, 55, 57
America-Israel Friendship League, 145
American Arab Institute, 140
American Civil Liberties Union, 74
American Committee on Jerusalem and American Muslims, 149
American Council for Judaism, 35, 109, 111
American Emergency Committee for Zionist Affairs, 109
American Federation of Labor, 144
American Friends of Likud, 119
American Friends of the Middle East (AFME), 142
American Friends Service Committee (AFSC), 34, 137-38
American Israel Public Affairs Committee (AIPAC), 17, 104, 112-15, 118, 120, 122-24, 128-29, 132, 134, 136-37, 141, 145, 149, 153-54, 156, 158-60, 164, 167; Policy Conference, 154
American Jewish Committee, xii, 6, 13-17, 19-29, 32-36, 38-42, 44-45, 47-57, 59-61, 68, 83-85, 95, 105, 107-11, 126, 138, 145, 164, 167, 218-19, 223, 284, 358
American Jewish community, communities. *See* Jewish community, communities
American Jewish Conference of Soviet Jewry, 48. *See* also National Conference for Soviet Jewry
American Jewish Conference, 40-41, 108, 110
American Jewish Congress, xii-xiii, 6, 15-23, 25-27, 29-30, 33-36, 38-39, 41-42, 44, 46-47, 50, 54-61, 68, 73, 83-84, 86, 108, 110, 126-127, 130, 132, 138, 145, 149, 151, 215, 284, 288, 295, 299-300
American Jewish Council for Soviet Jewry (AJCSJ), 85
American Jewish Yearbook, 49, 286
American Jewry. *See* Jewry
American Jews. *See* Jews
American Muslim Council (AMC), 142
American Professors for Peace in the Middle East (APPME), 150
American Zionist Council of Public Affairs (AZCPA), 113
American Zionist Emergency Council, 109
American Zionist movement, 107-8, 110
Americanism, 36, 46, 105-6, 343
American-Israel relationship, 77-78
American-Israeli Cooperative Enterprise, 166
Americanization, 46
American-Jewish integration, 83
Americans, x, xiii, 19, 34, 36, 61, 76, 98, 133, 145-46, 166, 283, 297, 305, 323, 348-49, 352, 381
Americans for a Safe Israel (AFSI), 159-60
Americans for Peace Now (APN), 119, 154, 158
Amir, Yigal, 157
Amish, 314
Amitay, Morris, 129, 137
Ammerman, Nancy, x
Amnesty International, 133

Index

Andreasen, Alan, 224
Anglican Church, 4
Anti-Defamation League (ADL), xiii, 5, 15-17, 19-20, 22-23, 25-27, 30-32, 35-45, 47, 49-52, 54-55, 58-61, 68, 71, 73, 83-86, 95, 108, 118, 138, 145, 149-50, 164, 167, 169, 299, 305; "ADL Hatefilter," 59; Speakers Bureau, 44; website, 59
anti-Jewish, 318; bias, 43; drive, 32; hostility, 47; policies, 33-34
anti-Semites, professional, 54
anti-Semitic, 170; articles, 32; attitudes, 45, 51, 75, 79; backlash, 36; books, 44; charges, 33; policies, Moscow's, 28; propaganda, 30; trends, 44; views, 37
anti-Semitism, 36, 81, 83, 98, 108, 116, 118, 130, 268, 290, 299, 301, 329, 338, 343, 351; black, 45
anti-war movement, 44
apartheid, 143
Arab(s), 69, 79, 107, 112, 124-27, 141-42, 145-46, 161, 173; allies, America's, 175; armies, 117; boycott of Israel, 20, 42, 73, 148, 205; propaganda, 150; propagandists, 116; states, 115, 123, 145-46, 171; violence, 147; world, 104, 115, 125, 128, 138, 140, 143, 150-51, 163, 170, 172, 174
Arab-American, 145, 349; advocacy, 140; community, 129; groups, 137, 140; organizations, 144
Arab-American Anti-Discrimination Committee (ADC), 140, 142
Arab and Islamic nations, 170
Arab-Israeli conflict, 133, 150
Arab-Israeli reconciliation, 171

Arab League, 148
Arab and Muslim American(s), 149-50
Arafat, Yasser, 79, 122, 124, 143, 152-53, 157, 160-63, 170, 173
Argentina, 49, 97
Armenia, 164
Aronson, Arnold, 17, 84
Ashkenazi rabbis, 237
Ashkenazic, 327
Ashkenazim, 237
Asia, 2
Asian Americans, 79
Asian group, 151, 358
askamot, or constitutions, 3
Aspen Institute's Nonprofit Sector Research Fund, 224
Assad, Bashar, 160
Assad, President, 160
assimilation, 14, 56, 76, 87, 156, 174
Associated Jewish Charities (Chicago), 184
association(s), voluntary, ix-xii
Association of Orthodox Jewish Scientists, 289
Auschwitz, 80
The Authoritarian Personality, 36
autonomy, 2
Avital, Colette, 157
Aviv, Diana, 212
AWACS, 128-29, 136, 139, 145
Azerbaijan, 164

B'nai B'rith, 5, 26-27, 30, 33-34, 58, 68, 71-72, 83, 106, 108, 110, 119
B'nai Zion House, 157
Baal Shem Tov, 377
Balfour, Arthur, 107
Balfour Declaration, 107-8
Balkinization, 80
Balter, Bernice, 244
bar/bat mitzva projects, 356
Barak, (Prime Minister) Ehud, 150, 159-63,
Barak-Clinton proposals, 173

Basel Congress, 105
Basel, Switzerland, 104-5
Baum, Phil, 59, 61, 130
Bayer, Abraham, 85
Bayme, Stephen, 57
Begin, Menachem, 124, 126-28, 139, 152
Beirut, 129-30, 146
Beit Midrash Gevoha Yeshiva (Lakewood, N.J.), 321
Beit Midrash (Jerusalem), 241
Belfer (Arthur and Rochelle) Center on American Pluralism, 51
Ben and Jerry's ice cream, 150
Ben-Gurion, David, 54, 112, 114, 116, 167-68
Benveniste, Guy, 223
Berger, Graenum, 188-89
Berger, Rabbi Elmer, 109
Berlin, 48
Bernardin, Joseph Cardinal, 80-81
Bernstein, Philip, 185
Berzon, President Bernard, 301
Bettelheim, Bruno, 36
Beyt Tikkun, 381
Bible, 1, 331, 367, 379; clubs, 272; readings, 266-67, 287
biblical political tradition, 8
"Big Three," 20, 23, 41
bigotry, 58, 108; anti-Jewish, 69
Biltmore platform, 109-10
Bin-Laden, Osama, 174-75
Birthright Israel, 169
Bitburg controversy, 20, 49-50
black(s), 18, 31, 75, 79, 96, 218, 288, 357; community, 75, 356; nationalism, 44; -Jewish confrontations, 144; -Jewish relations, 45, 75
Blaustein, Jacob, 54, 58
Blix, Rolf, 157
Board of Delegates (of American Israelites), 264
Board of Deputies of American Israelites, 5
Board of Deputies of British Jews, 3, 6

Board of Education v. Mergens, 271
Bolshevik Revolution, 29
Bonaparte, Jerome, 263
Bosnia, 49, 142
Bowling Alone, ix
Boy Scouts of America, 330
Brady Act, 249
Brandeis, Louis, 27-29, 106, 108
Breger, Marshall, 215
Breira (Choice), 125
Brewer, Supreme Court Justice David J., 266
Brickman, Professor William, 296
brit Avraham, 312
Britain, 3, 115
British Mandate, 125
British North America, 3
British society, and Jews, 4
Brown v. Board of Education, 36
Brown, General George, 73
Buber, Martin, 368
Bubis, Gerald, 219, 223-24
Buenos Aires, 49
Burger, Chief Justice Warren E., 271
Bush administration, 152, 163, 175, 215-17
Bush administration, new, 276
Bush, George H. W., 86, 112, 128, 134-36, 271
Bush, President George W., 155, 157, 162-63, 174-75, 214-16, 218, 276
Business Roundtable, 149
Butz, Arthur, 74

Callen, Horace, 106
Camp David, 127-28, 152
Camp David summit (July 2000), 104, 124, 160-61, 173
Canaanite inhabitants, 379
Canada, 6, 115
Canadian Jewish Congress, 6
Cantwell v. Connecticut, 269
Capitol Hill, 87, 115, 153-54, 159, 164, 272

Cardin, Shoshana, 136
Carlebach, Rabbi Shlomo, 365
Carter, President Jimmy, 128, 148-49
Catholics, 137, 186, 351
Catholic Charities, 210, 215
Catholic Church, 14, 52, 138, 295-96, 298
Catholic-Jewish, 53
Catholic-Jewish Scholars Dialogue, 80
Catholic support, 297
Catholic traditions, 53
CBS Radio, 55
Census 2000, 246
Centennial Convention, 251
Center for Jewish Community Studies, 194, 196, 219, 223
Center on Budget and Policy Priorities, 225
Central Conference of American Rabbis (CCAR), 105, 109, 265-69, 273
Central Europe, 261
Central Intelligence Agency, 142
Central-Verein Deutscher Staatsburger Jüdischen Glaubens (CV), 34
Chancellor, John, 148
Chanes, Jerome, 68
charitable appeals, 5
charitable choice, xiii, 25, 214-16
Chernin, Albert, 85, 128
Chicago, 71-82, 85-86, 88, 91-92, 95-96, 142, 194, 198, 200, 204-5, 207, 211-12, 221, 224
Chicago, Archdiocese of, 80
Chicago Board of Rabbis, 80
Chicago CRC, 99
Chicago Conference on Soviet Jewry, 73
Chief Rabbinate, 167
Child Health Insurance Program, 212
Christian(s), 137, 183, 371; allies, Israel's, 130; America, 263, 268; born-again, 215; charitable endeavors, 182; clergy, 34, 50, 52; conservative community, 216; denominations, 237, 285-86; education, 53; evangelicals, 53, 160; faiths, 273; groups, 141; majority, 311; religious community, 137; right, 139; teachings, 52; writers, 182
Christian Friends Bulletin, 52
Christian Front, 17
Christianity, 271, 312; Protestant, 296
Christians' Israel Public Action Campaign (CIPAC), 160
church and state, church/state, church-state, separation (of), 15-16, 18-20, 24, 40-41, 46-47, 72, 75-76, 84, 90-91, 94, 139, 165, 215-17, 220, 236, 242, 246, 248, 251, 262-65, 267-71, 273-75, 287-88, 293, 295-97, 303, 305, 321, 352
Church of the Holy Trinity v. United States, 266
Churches for Middle East Peace (CMEP), 138
Citizen's Council for a Democratic Germany, 48
citizenship in the Jewish polity, xiv
civic agenda, Jewish, 15, 46
civic culture, 62; American, 15, 20; Jewish, 15-16, 19-20, 23
civic decline, xv
civic education, 58
civic engagement, 14
civic principles, 62
civil liberties, 39, 46, 70, 74, 83, 85, 91, 94, 98
civil religion, 353; American, 352
civil rights, 15-16, 18-20, 27, 35, 39-40, 43-44, 61, 69-70, 74-75, 83, 85-87, 98, 143, 165, 227, 262, 269-70, 283, 288, 292-93,

344, 356; Jewish participation in, 44; movement, 69; organizations, 50
civil society, ix, xii-xv, 312, 314; American, ix-x, xii, 389-90; apocalypse of, x; religious groups in, x; Western, 313
Civil War, 5, 263-65
Clark, Kenneth, 36
Clifford, Clark, 112
Clinton administration, 154, 156, 158, 217
Clinton, President, 13, 112, 131, 155, 158-62, 166, 211, 214, 283
CNN, 147
Coalition of Ethiopian Education, 169
Coalition on the Environment and Jewish Life (COEJL), 247, 250, 252, 256, 305
Coalition on Human Services, 202
Cohen, Naomi, 46
Cohen, Steven M., xi, 166, 219-20
Cold War, 48, 76, 116, 146
Cole, Leonard, 97
Collin, Frank, 74
Columbia University, 39, 41
Comay, Shalom, 61
Commentary, 60, 93
Commission on Women's Equality, 57
Committee on American Islamic Relations (CAIR), 142
Committee on Individual Liberty, 74
Committee on Public Issues, 187
Committee on Scope, Structure, Planning and Membership, 72
Common Council for American Unity, 18
Common Quest, 51
communal agencies, xii
communal agenda, xi, 182
communal consensus, 125
communism, 39, 48

Communists, 48
communities, religious, x
Community and Polity, 188
community relations, 13-14, 16, 21-22, 24, 26, 50, 58-59, 62, 68-71, 75-77, 79, 81-85, 87-88, 91-92, 97-100, 357
community relations agencies, 298
community relations councils (committees) (CRCs), xiii, 26, 36, 40, 73, 77, 82-83, 98, 110, 113, 120, 133, 135, 141-42, 145, 149, 151, 153, 156, 161, 167, 172
community service programs, 247
Comprehensive Test Ban Treaty, 253
Conference of Presidents of Major American Jewish Organizations (Presidents Conference), 72, 104, 108, 110, 114, 119-20, 122-23, 126-27, 129, 134-36, 142, 153-54, 160, 162-64, 167, 247, 356
Conference on Science, Philosophy and Religion, 250
Congregation Darchei Noam (Toronto), 357
Congregation Emanu-El (New York City), 270
Congress Weekly, 39
Congress, congresses (U.S.), 46, 113, 121, 128, 135-36, 138, 148, 154-56, 164-65, 171, 174-75, 201, 206-7, 210-12, 214, 222, 226, 262, 271-72, 276, 297, 323; African American members of, 144; anti-*shechita* bills, 324; Democratic members, 134; Members of, 103-4, 111, 113, 121, 137-38, 141-42, 145-46, 154, 164, 171-72, 246-48
Conservative (movement in Judaism), xiv, 106, 167-68, 219, 235-40, 242-45, 247, 250, 252,

254-55, 257, 286, 344; congregations, 241, 255, 273; denominations, 286; Jewish day schools, 246; Judaism, 106, 239-42, 245, 252-54, 258-59; rabbis, 243, 246, 250; synagogues, 258
Conservative Judaism, 254
Constitution (U.S.), 128, 270, 301-3; First Amendment, 16, 31, 262, 264, 268-69, 272, 304, 322; Fourteenth Amendment, 268-69
Cooper, David, 364, 372, 374, 377
Council for the National Interest, 142
Council of Jewish Federations (CJF), 7, 40, 68, 76, 83, 87, 95, 109-10, 118, 161, 166, 183-85, 188-89, 191-92, 208, 212, 222-23, 304; General Assembly, 84-85
Council of Torah Sages, 317, 321
covenantal community, 290
Crane, Sarrae, 244
crèche, 75
Crime Watch, 373
Cromwell, Oliver, 2
Crown Heights riots, 44
Czechoslovakia, 115

da'as toyreh, 317
Daily Worker, 287
"davenology," 367
Dawidowicz, Lucy, 27
Day Care Action Council, 202
day-school education, 298
de Tocqueville, Alexis, ix, 242
Dearborn Foundation, 142
Dearborn Independent, 32, 40
Declaration of Independence, 354
defense agency, agencies, 21, 23, 30, 32, 34, 41, 46-47, 49, 53-54, 83, 110, 118-19, 122, 128-29, 132, 142, 149, 167; organizations, 68, 72, 83
DeLay, Tom, 214

Demjanjuk, John, 49
democracies, secular, 315
democracy, 35, 61, 96, 175, 338, 343, 350, 355; in Germany, 34; liberal, 368; religion of, 352; Western, 351
Democracy in America, 242
Democrat(s), 141, 187, 218-19
Democratic (Party), 107, 110, 116, 129, 140-41, 200, 202, 240, 283; administration, 155; national convention, 110
Department of Commerce, 246
Department of Public Aid, 205
Department of Scientific Research 36
Depression, 33
Der Judenstaat, 105
"dialogue" groups, 53, 55
dialogue, intra-Jewish, 347
diaspora, 1-2, 167-68, 322
Dictionary of Philosophy, 311
Die Freiheit, 287
Dine, Tom, 124
discrimination, 37, 39, 42-43, 69, 83
Disney Corporation, 150
Disraeli, B., 312
Dole, Senator Robert, 13, 154
Dome of the Rock, 161
"Donated Funds Initiative," 202
Donors Forum of Chicago, 224
Dorff, Rabbi Elliot, 244, 254
Dosick, Wayne, 364, 372, 376-77
Douglas, Justice William O., 269
Down-to-Earth Judaism, 370-71
"dual loyalty," 54
Dulles, Secretary of State John Foster, 114-15
Durban, South Africa, 170
d'var Torah, 76
The Dynamics of Prejudice, 36

Eastern Europe, 237, 249; ethnic groups, 79; *kehillah* in, 338
Eastern religion, 372
Eban, Abba, 113-15

eco-*kashrut*, eco-kosher, 367, 373-75, 380
economic justice, 16
economic opportunity, 15
The Economist, 214
Education Budget Program Initiatives, 202, 210
education, public, 16
educational training programs, 226
egalitarianism, 354
Egypt, 73, 115, 125, 173, 175
Eilat, 115
Einhorn, Reform Rabbi David, 263, 265
Eisen, Arnold, xi, 181-82
Eisenberg, Rabbi Richard, 244
Eisendrath, Rabbi Maurice, 270
Eisenhower (President), 113-15
Eisenstein, Ira, 348
Elazar, Daniel J., xi-xii, 67, 188, 194, 380-90
Electronic Intifada, 173
Elementary and Secondary Education Act, 297, 323
Elisha, 291
e-mail, e-mails, 172-73; advocacy, 172
Emergency Council, 111, 113
Emergency Food and Shelter Board, 205
Emet v'Emunah, 239
Emet, 162
emigration, 76-77
Employment Division v. Smith, 272
Engel v. Vitale, 46-47, 270, 299
England, 2-3; Jewish communities in, 3
English-speaking countries, 2, 6; Jews, 8; societies, 2; world, 1-3
Epcot Center, 150
Epstein, Benjamin, 54, 58
Equal Access Act, 271
Equal Rights Amendment (E.R.A.), 301-2, 324-25, 353

Eretz Israel, Eretz Yisrael, 105, 126, 139
The Ethics of Tolerance, 348
Ethiopia(n), 139, 165, 169
etrogs, import of, 324
Etzioni, Amitai, 347
Europe, 2-3, 48, 311-12, 321; anti-Semitism in, 29; Jewish communities in, 1; Jewish conditions in, 27; Nazism in, 108
European Union, 170
Evangelical community, 79
evangelical grassroots, 139
Evangelicals, white, xi
Everson v. Board of Education, 46
Export Administration Act, 149
Export-Import Bank loan, 113

Fact Finding and Research Departments, 52
Fair Employment Practices Committee (FEPC), 286
Faith-Based Initiative, 276
faith communities, 81
The Faith of America, 352
Far East, 171
Farrakhan, Louis, 75, 79
fascism, 342-43, 350; European, 268
Fatah, 170
Federal Council of Churches of Christ, 286
Federal Election Committee, 137
Federal Emergency Management Agency (FEMA), 205, 210-11
federal government, xiii, 214-16, 226
federal law, 222
federal programs, 206, 276
federalism, 188
federation(s), xii-xiii, 4-8, 41, 67-68, 71-72, 74, 77, 80, 82, 86, 91-92, 95, 98-99, 165, 167-69, 183-90, 192, 194-207, 210-11, 217, 219, 221, 257, 294-96, 298, 355, 357; dollars, 26; leadership, 7

Federation of American Zionists (FAZ), 105, 108
Federation of Jewish Men's Clubs, 241, 243-44
Federation of Reconstructionist Congregations, 353
Federations of Jewish Charities, 5
Fein, Leonard, 92
Feinberg, Rabbi Charles, 244
Feuerstsin, Moses, 297
Fifth Avenue Synagogue, 299
Findley, Representative Paul, 136
Finkelstein Institute, 250
Finkelstein, Louis, 250
Finley, Mordecai, 383
First National Conference of Jewish Charities, 183
Fisher, Alan, 219
Fisher, Max, 115
Flores V. City of Boevne, 272
Ford Foundation, 325
Ford, Henry, 28, 32, 40; Ford's anti-Semitic campaign, 43
Ford, President (Gerald), 136, 148-49
Forrestal, Secretary of Defense James V., 111
Forster, Arnold, 30-31
Forward, 91-92
Foxman Abe (Abraham), 50, 58, 61, 118
France, 115-16
Frank, Leo, 30
Frankfurt school, 36
Free World, 115
Freedom Pamphlet, 37
Freehof, Solomon B., 274
Friedman, Howard, 61
Friedman, Murray, 85, 218
Friedman, Tom, 162
"Frontline," 45
fund-raising, 23, 42, 72, 129, 139; techniques, 7
The Future of the American Jew, 345

Gallup Organization, 51

Gartenberg, Rabbi Dov, 244
Gary Plan, 267
gay synagogues, 303
Gaza Strip, 125-26, 131, 133, 140, 150, 159, 161
Geiger-Tiktin Affair, 263
gemilut chesed, gemilut hasadim, 215, 254, 351, 373-74
General Assembly, 183, 198, 213, 294
General Assembly of Jewish Funds and Welfare Funds, 294
General Jewish Council, 40, 83
Genesis, Book of, 291
George, Frances Cardinal, 81
Georgetown University School of Business, 224
Gephardt, Representative Richard, 142
German democracy, 48; government, 33; reeducation, 48; soldiers, 49
German-American Bund, 17
German-Jewish understanding, 48
Germany, 34, 36, 263; post-Hitler, 48
Gilded Age, 264-65
Gillan, Sister Ann, 13
Gingrich, Newt, 154, 207
Gitlow v. New York, 269
God Is a Verb, 372
Godwrestling, 370-71
Golan Heights, 118, 125, 150, 160, 171
Gold, Bert, 45, 57, 60
Goldberg, Arthur, 115
Goldberg, J. J., 36, 92, 226
Goldmann, Dr. Nahum, 114
Goldstein, Israel, 30
Goldstein, Sol, 74-75
Gordis, David, 60
Gore (Al), 218, 220
Government Affairs Institute, 213
Government Affairs Offices, 82
Government Affairs Program, 199-203, 207
Graham, Billy, 50

grassroots activism, 141, 155, 165, 170, 174; advocacy, 172
Great Awakening, 263
Great Britain, 3
Great Depression, 286
Great Society, 292
group identity, 51, 69
Guide to Jewish Practice, 346
Gulf Cooperation Council, 149
Gush Emunim, 126
Gutstadt, Richard, 58

Haass, Richard, 135
Habad, 276
Hadassah, 108, 119, 150
halakhah, 119, 168, 182, 239, 251, 274, 289, 326-28, 344, 366-67, 370
halakhic movement, 257; opinion, 303; pluralism, 274; sources, 292
Hamas, 142, 175
Hanukkah, 268, 276, 374
haredi(m), xiv, 311, 314-33; social contract, 318
Harkheimer, Max, 36
Harmonic Convergence, 376
Harris, David, 60
Harvard University Divinity School, 290
hasidic mysticism, 365
Hasidic rabbis, 293
Hasidism, 365
hate crimes, 79, 97; groups, 78; legislation, 31
havurah movement, 365
havurot, 345, 353
Head Start, 212, 356
Hebrew, 81-82, 316; Bible, 305; language, 344
Hebrew Immigrant Aid Society (HIAS), 209-10
Hebrew Theological College, 285
Hebrew Union College-Jewish Institute of Religion (Cincinnati), 267, 274

Hebrew University in Jerusalem, 166
Hebron agreements, 158
Heine, 312
Hellman, Richard, 160
Hellman, Yehuda, 114
Henry, Patrick, 273
Herndon, Angelo, 342-43
Hertzberg, Arthur, 30
Herzl, Theodor, 105, 112
Heschel, Abraham Joshua, 69, 378-79
hesed, 215
Hewitt, Don, 148
Hezbollah, 175
Hier, Rabbi Marvin, 26
High Holidays, 250, 254-55, 286
Higher Education Act (HEA), 150
Hildesheimer Seminary, 285
Hillel, 171
Hills, Carla, 140
Hirsch, Rabbi Emil G., 265
Hirsch, Rabbi Richard G., 270-71
Histadrut, 144
Hitler, 6, 25, 33-34, 74, 109, 175
HMO(s), 211
Hobbes, Thomas, 311
holiday observances, 18
Holocaust (Shoah), 19-20, 25-26, 45, 59, 69-70, 74-75, 77-79, 81, 90, 96-97, 104, 109-10, 117, 119, 198, 206, 320-21; denial of, 44, 74; teaching of, 75
The Holocaust, 74
Holy Roman Empire, 263
Home Instruction Program for Pre-School Mothers (HIPPY), 166
Horowitz, Bethamie, 220
House of Representatives, 163, 200
Howard University, 51
HUD, 193
Hull, Secretary of State Cordell, 33

human rights, 19, 49; Palestinian, 140; violations, 133, 138
Human Rights Watch, 133
Human Services and Social Policy (HSSP), 212
Human Services Budget, 203

Illinois House of Representatives, 202
Illinois General Assembly, 200-201, 203
Immigration and Naturalization Service, 246
Immigration Reform and Control Act, 247
Independence Day, U.S., 352
Independent(s), 218-19, 283
Independent Sector (IS), 185, 197, 222
An Index of Community Organization Articles Published 1924-1980, 189
Indyk, Martin, 154
Institute on American Jewish-Israeli Relations, 55
Institute on Pluralism and Group Identity, 57, 223
Institute for Public Affairs (IPA), 304
institutional culture, 19
Instituto Judio Argentino de Cultura e Inforacion, 49
interest group politics, 62
interfaith, 49, 52, 72; coalitions, 47; dialogue, 357; mission to Israel, 81
intergroup, 62, 80-81; hostility, 36; relations, 20, 37, 50-52, 70, 81, 84-85
intermarriage, xi, 3, 14, 76, 156, 174, 304; and Jewish assimilation, 172
international conspiracy, 79
International Criminal Court, 249
international relief campaigns, 60
international terrorist activity, 78
Internet, 96, 172-73, 222, 24

interreligious affairs, 16, 52; agenda, 20, 53; cooperation, 43; event, 53; relations, 19, 90
interwar, 43
intifada, 56, 104, 131-33, 140-41, 147, 152, 161, 167, 170, 174
Intifada.com, 173
Iran, 156, 163, 171
Iraq, 115, 133-34, 152, 156-57, 163, 171
Iron Curtain, 77
IRS, 222
Is Curly Jewish?, 16
Isaiah, Book of, 329
Islam, 273
Islamic extremists, 174; fundamentalism, 72, 174; world, 175
Islamic Jihad, 175
isolationism, 247
Israel, Israeli(s), xi, xiii, 13, 15, 19-20, 25-27, 34-35, 44, 50, 53-56, 58, 60-61, 69-73, 75, 77-78, 81-82, 84-86, 89-90, 97, 103-5, 108, 110-71, 173-75, 182, 184, 201, 217, 226, 243, 249, 256-57, 261, 273, 277, 304-5, 314, 318-20, 322, 324, 326-28, 331, 354-55, 365, 374, 379; advocacy, 103-4, 108, 110, 114, 118-20, 130-31, 152, 155, 162, 164-68, 170, 172, 174; agenda, 53, 56; American identification with, 174; and American Jewry, 126-27; American public opinion against, 162; American support for, 125, 146, 148, 173; anti-Israel, 55, 73, 75, 116, 122, 134, 137, 140, 142-43, 147-48, 150-51, 161-63, 171, 173, 175; and Arab neighbors, 55, 79, 173; black community's relationship with, 143; boycott of, 115; -diaspora relations, 14, 54, 134; -Egypt negotiations, 132; government(s), 103, 113, 121-22, 125, 127-28, 132, 135,

152-53, 158-59, 161, 167-70, 172; immigration, 135, 240; Independence Day, 73, 77, 81, 157; -Lebanon border, 130; loan guarantees for, 86; lynching, 161-62; missions, 117; officials, 55-56; peace policies, 7, 87, 122, 126-28, 130, 135, 153-54, 175; political allegiance to, 54; "post-Zionist," 167; pro-, 73, 90, 104, 113, 136-37, 141, 143-44, 150, 152, 161-62; rabbis of, 327; Reform rights in, 276; religious pluralism in, 168; settlement policy, 75, 126; *shaliach* (emissary), 171; society, 166, 169; soldiers, 140, 147; sovereignty, 124; trips, 55; U.S. aid to, 72; and world Jewry, 16; and Zionism, 354
Israel Ministry of Labor and Social Affairs, 166
Israel Policy Forum (IPF), 154, 158
Israel Religious Action Center (IRAC), 273
Israel Studies Association, 150
Israel Task Force, 86, 118
Israeli-Palestinian, 367; agreement, 158, 163; negotiations, 154; warfare, 162
Istook amendment, 272
Ivers, Gregg, 47, 84

Jabalya Palestinian refugee camp, 141
Jackson, Reverend Jesse, 75, 141, 143
Jackson-Vanik legislation, 136, 209, 226
Jacob, Walter, 274
Jacobs, Paul, 16-17
Jacobsohn, Israel, 263
Jacobson, Eddie, 111-12
Jacoby, Jonathan, 154
Jakobovits, Rabbi Immanuel, 299

Jeremiah, prophet, 235
Jerusalem Center for Public Affairs (JCPA), 194, 223
Jerusalem, 114, 118, 121-22, 124, 127, 150, 154-55, 157, 160-62, 163, 169, 173, 241, 277; Arab areas inside, 160; Old City, 117, 161
Jew(s), xi, xv, 1-6, 8, 13-19, 24, 27-36, 38-39, 43-44, 46-48, 50, 52-55, 57, 61, 69-70, 72-73, 97, 100, 103, 105-7, 109-10, 112, 116-17, 119-22, 125, 127, 129-33, 136, 143-145, 147, 149, 152-54, 157-61, 164-69, 172-75, 181-82, 184, 186-87, 191-92, 197, 199, 210, 215, 218-21, 226, 284-85, 290, 292-93, 295-96, 299, 312-16, 320-21, 325-230, 338-40, 342-44, 346, 351, 353, 355, 366, 369, 371, 375, 379, 383, 390; and the American Public Square, 219; Ashkenazi, 237; Central European, 6; discrimination against, 37, 39, 73; in distress, 7; Eastern Europe, 6, 29, 107, 238, 267; of England, 2; Ethiopian, 169; European, xii, 28, 32, 34, 38, 59, 311; German, 6, 267; haredi, 320; in Hungary, 29; Iranian, 164; Israeli, 72, 126, 167-69; liberal, 301; non-, 121, 219-20, 293, 301-2, 340, 379; in North Africa and the Middle East, 54; Orthodox, xiii, 305-6, 312; Rumanian, 29; Russian, 28; secular, 289, 303
Jews in the Soviet Satellites, 48
Jews in the Soviet Union, 48
Jewish activism, national, xiii, 156, 158, 164
Jewish advocacy, 118, 121, 129, 133, 145, 153, 173
Jewish affairs, world, 54
Jewish agency, agencies, 24, 164, 167, 187, 191-93, 198

Jewish Agency for Israel (JAFI), 169, 257
Jewish agenda, 85, 87, 167; and gay rights, 303
Jewish attitudes, 218
Jewish-American, 349
Jewish bodies, secular, 287
Jewish bourgeoisie, 28
Jewish Center, 340-42
Jewish charity, charities, 182-84
Jewish Children's Bureau, 204
Jewish-Christian dialogue, 290, 357; relations, 52
Jewish civic culture, 40; principles, 57
Jewish civilization, 321
Jewish coalitions, 247
Jewish "Commonwealths," 370
Jewish communal (community) agencies, 85, 190, 192, 389; affairs, 98; competition, 25; funds, 297; interests, 82; life, 31, 76, 86; self-interest, 94; service(s), 183, 185, 187, 190, 192, 194, 224, 226; sphere, xiii; world, 20
Jewish Communal Affairs Department, 24
Jewish Communal Service Department, 56
Jewish community, communities, xii, 2-3, 5-8, 14-16, 22, 24-28, 34-35, 39, 41-42, 44-45, 48, 52, 60, 62, 67, 69, 74-85, 87, 90-99, 103-6, 108, 111, 114, 116-18, 121-23, 125-26, 128-32, 134-36, 138-41, 144-46, 148-49, 151-52, 154, 156-58, 163-66, 168-69, 172, 174, 181-89, 192-201, 203-4, 206-12, 214-18, 220-21, 223-27, 236, 258, 261-62, 268-69, 275, 283-84, 292, 297-99, 301, 305, 338-45, 355, 358, 371, 380, 390; Chicago, 71; European, 48; German, 33; New York, 91

Jewish Community Center (JCC), 187-88, 190-91, 340
Jewish community relations, 13-14, 16, 18-19, 21, 23, 43, 68, 83
Jewish Community Relations Council (JCRC), 6, 53, 67-68, 71, 75-80, 82-83, 85-86, 90, 95-96, 99, 184, 196, 212, 219, 287; Chicago, 70-71, 77-78, 93; Philadelphia, 47; San Francisco, 142
Jewish consensus, 300-1, 304; liberal, 288
Jewish conspiracy, international, 32-33
Jewish continuity, xi, 56, 61, 76, 82, 155, 304
Jewish Council for Public Affairs (JCPA), xiii, 6, 41, 68, 83, 88-98, 110, 118, 120, 122, 128-32, 134, 142, 149, 153-54, 157, 167, 181, 223, 247, 256; Agenda for Public Affairs, 89; Joint Program Plan, 130; Plenum, 135; Task Force on Israel, 134
Jewish covenant, 313
Jewish culture, 312-13
Jewish day schools, 94, 294, 353
Jewish defense organizations, xii
Jewish denominations, 287
Jewish diaspora, 89, 168, 236
Jewish Dimensions of Social Justice: Tough Moral Choices of Our Time, 275
Jewish donors, 170
Jewish education, 14, 170, 172, 296, 340
Jewish environmental group, 252
Jewish establishment, secular, 284
Jewish external affairs, 285
Jewish Federation, 42, 202
Jewish Federation of Metropolitan Chicago, 91, 184, 198, 200-1, 203, 206, 224

Jewish groups, 56, 116, 141, 143, 148, 152, 155, 250, 256
Jewish healthcare foundations, 192
Jewish history, 2, 7, 313
Jewish homeland, 109
Jewish identity, xi, 92, 169, 312, 318-19
Jewish immigration, 5
Jewish Information, Office of, 38
Jewish ingathering, 139
Jewish Institute for National Security Affairs (JINSA), 145, 160
Jewish institutions, xii, 8, 31, 43, 50
Jewish interests, xii, 8, 27-28, 41, 85
Jewish and interfaith solidarity, 161
Jewish Labor Commission, 83
Jewish Labor Committee (JLC), 6, 17, 68, 140, 144
Jewish law, 168, 239, 243, 250-51, 255, 257, 274, 293, 302-304, 316, 324, 326-27, 329, 337, 344; and theology, 289
Jewish leadership, 4, 104, 118
Jewish learning, advanced, 317; traditional 294
Jewish life, 8, 24, 38, 40, 60, 108, 238, 312, 321, 341, 345; American, 57, 363; New York, 338
Jewish Literacy, 57
Jewish lives, safeguarding, 70
Jewish Living: A Guide to Contemporary Reform Practice, 274
Jewish lobby, 55, 194
Jewish minority, Soviets' treatment of, 227
Jewish model(s), 8
Jewish mystical tradition, 365-66
Jewish mysticism, 365, 381
Jewish national home, 7
Jewish nationalism, 28, 30, 104, 109

Jewish organizational affairs, 91
Jewish organizations, 113, 122, 130, 142, 148, 158, 174, 390; American, 137; national and local, 138; secular, 305; separationist national, 297
Jewish Palestine, 125
Jewish peace corps, 169
Jewish people, 32, 38, 55, 144, 183, 329-30, 340, 344, 369, 380
Jewish peoplehood, 35, 82, 106
Jewish philanthropy, 4, 182, 189, 321
Jewish policy considerations, 20
Jewish political influence, 14
Jewish political right, 24
Jewish political tradition, 389
Jewish politics, 29
Jewish polity, xi-xiii, 344
Jewish population, 3-4, 118
Jewish Population Survey, 304
Jewish Power: Inside the American-Jewish Establishment, 92, 226
Jewish power, Israel-based, 164
Jewish principles, 69
Jewish prostitutes, 3
Jewish-Protestant dialogues, 138
Jewish public affairs, 84
Jewish public policy, 254
Jewish public realm, xiii
Jewish Reconstructionist Federation, 353-54
Jewish Reconstructionist Foundation (JRF), 342, 355
Jewish religion, 289
Jewish religious movements, 389; values, 306
Jewish Renewal, 364, 378, 380
Jewish Renewal movement, xiv, 56, 363-66, 368, 371, 373, 378, 380-83, 390
Jewish Republicans, 115
Jewish rescue, 92
Jewish rights, 29-30, 69, 269
"Jewish Roll-Call," 44

Jewish roots, 70
Jewish security, 15, 25, 46, 68-69, 72, 217
Jewish settlers, 159
Jewish social service agencies, 221
Jewish social welfare, 194, 227
Jewish social workers, 292
Jewish socialism, 371
Jewish society, 332
Jewish solidarity, xi
Jewish sources, 292
Jewish state, 54, 71, 105, 112, 124, 143, 146, 173, 249, 261, 273-74, 320, 329
Jewish statehood, 35, 41, 110-11, 119; U.S. support for, 112
Jewish students, 171
Jewish survival, 70, 321
Jewish Telegraphic Agency, 218
Jewish Theological Seminary (of America) (JTS), 93, 106, 237-38, 241, 244, 249-50, 254, 258, 341, 356, 378
Jewish thought, medieval, 292
Jewish tradition, 70, 186, 250-51, 255, 257, 274, 289, 292-93, 303-5, 312, 314, 318, 328
Jewish United Fund, 71
Jewish United Fund Campaign, 207
Jewish United Fund (Chicago), 196
Jewish unity, 3, 40
Jewish values, 69, 72, 143, 184, 186, 238, 288, 303, 320, 343
"Jewish Values and School Prayer," 262
Jewish voluntarism, xi
Jewish vote, 218
Jewish War Veterans, 6
Jewish way of life, 321
Jewish Week, 97
Jewish Welfare Federations, 5
Jewish Welfare Fund of Metropolitan Chicago, 71
Jewish women, 57

Jewish working class, 28
Jewish world, 20, 96, 250, 321; parliament, 345
Jewish worship, 340
Jewishness, 191
Jewry, Jewries, xi, 6; American, 6, 9, 14, 16, 26-27, 29-30, 32, 35, 38-40, 43, 48, 54-55, 61-62, 72, 92, 98, 109-10, 115, 117, 129, 135, 155, 159, 166-68, 218, 288, 302; Argentinian, 165; Boston, 4; diaspora, 2, 86; distressed, xi; European, 6, 25, 105; German, 34; New York, 338; Russian, 15; Soviet, 13, 26, 53, 70, 72-73, 75, 77, 82, 84, 87, 89, 91, 139, 172; Syrian, 55; traditional, 320; ultra-Orthodox, 332; world, 26, 35, 62, 162, 338
Johnson, Lyndon, 54, 115-16, 297
Joint Commission on Social Action, 256
Joint Consultative Council, 40
Joint Defense Appeal, 41
Joint Distribution Committee (JDC), 169, 356
Joint Program Plan for Community Relations, 89
Jordan, 114, 124, 156, 173; Jordanian, 152
Jordan River irrigation project, 114, 132
Jordan Valley, 126
Joseph, Burt, 149
Josephson, Marvin, 137
Journal of Jewish Communal Service, 85
"jubilee festival," 371
Judaism, 1, 3, 27, 36, 43, 52-53, 107, 166-68, 236, 238, 243, 252, 255, 261, 263, 265, 268, 273, 277, 284-85, 288-89, 292-93, 303, 312-13, 316, 319, 326-27, 329, 331, 337, 339, 341-42, 346, 350, 353, 355, 370, 372-74; biblical and rab-

binic, 262; Judaism, convert to, 168; Judaism, mystical, 374; Judaism, non-Orthodox, 273; Judaism, soul (Neshamah Judaism), 372, 376; Judaism, traditional, 268
Judaism as a Civilization, 342
Judea and Samaria, 139
Judeo-Christian society, 313, 316; values, 17-18
judicial activism, 19, 40; intervention, 62
Jung, Rabbi Leo, 285
Justice Department, Office of Special Investigations, 74, 78
Juvenile Justice Task Force, 202

Kabbalah, 365, 368
Kallen, Horace, 341
Kamenetz, Rodger, 364, 383
Kaplan, Kivie, 270
Kaplan, Rabbi Mordecai, 106, 337-42, 344-45, 348, 351-52, 355-56, 368
kashrut, 3, 367
Kaufman, Rabbi Jan, 244
Kaye, Danny, 74
kehillah, 3, 7, 77; New York, 4, 338, 345
Kehillath Israel, 357
Kenen, I. L., 113-15, 118, 129
Kennedy (President), 116, 295-97; administration, 297
Khartoum Resolution, 125
Khwolson, Daniel, 313
King, Martin Luther, Jr., 143
Kiryas Joel, 275, 323
Kissinger, Henry, 136
klal Yisrael, 242
Klein, Morton, 153
klippot, 374
Klutznik, Philip, 71-72, 82
Knesset, 55, 168
Kohl, Chancellor Helmut, 49
Kohn, Eugene, 352
Kol Ehad, 354
Kol Haneshamah, 355

Kosovo, 97
Kotler, Rabbi Aaron, 321
Krauskopf, Joseph, 266
Kristol, Bill, 215
Ku Klux Klan, 28, 31, 38, 351
kulturkampf, 314
Kuwait, 133, 152

Labor (party), 121, 123, 125-26, 132, 168
labor movement, 6, 111, 144
Labor Zionist Alliance, 119
Labor Zionists, 354
Labowitz, Shoni, 364, 372, 374, 376-77
Lamm, Rabbi Norman, 303, 306
Land of Israel. *See* Eretz Israel
Lapin, Rabbi Daniel, 305
Latin America, 48
Latino Americans, 79, 358
Lauder, Ronald, 163
Law of Return, 168
Lazin, Frederick, 33
Leadership Conference on Civil Rights, 84, 170
leadership mission, 145; volunteer, 16
Learning Company of Massachusetts, 59
Lebanon, 55, 75, 86, 128, 130, 152, 156, 159, 171; campaign, 130; southern, 129; War, 129, 146-47, 161
Lee, Mordechai, 82
Leesen, Isaac, 264, 284
Lefkowitz, Rabbi David, 266-67
left, Israeli and American Jewish, 157
Lelyveld, Arthur, 30
Lerner Lapidus, Dr. Anne, 244
Lerner, Michael, 364-65, 377, 379-83
Levenson, Jon D., 305
Levin, Senator Carl, 351
Levine, Irving, 223
Lewis, Leon, 58
liberal groups, 34

liberalism, 85, 289, 297, 305
liberalism, mainstream Orthodox, 293
Liberty, U.S.S., 140
Libya, 71
Lieberman, Hadassah, 221
Lieberman, Senator Joseph I., 283, 305-6
Liebman, Charles S., 166, 363-64, 382
Lifton, Robert, 42
Likud (party), 121, 123, 125-27, 132, 139, 147-48, 153, 159, 168
Lipsky, Attorney Louis, 108, 113
Lipstadt, Deborah, 49
Lithuanian talmudic scholars, 289
Livingston, Sigmund, 27, 30
loan guarantee(s), 135-36, 139, 145
lobbying, 390
"The Lonely Man of Faith," 290-91
Lookstein, Rabbi Joseph H., 285
Los Angeles, 227
Lubavitcher rebbe, 299
Lubavitcher Yeshiva, 365
Lurie, Walter A., 83-84
Lutheran Social Services, 210
Lutherans, 186

MacIver, Robert (R. M.), 41, 58, 71, 83, 85, 87
Mack, Judge Julian, 106
Madison, James, 263, 271
Madrid (peace conference), 117, 133, 152
Mandated Services Law, 323
Mandatory Palestine, Jewish population in, 148
Mann, Ted, 127, 154
al-Marayati, Salam, 142
Marcuse, Herbert, 36
Marrilac House, 202
Marshall, Louis, 27, 29, 32, 58, 105, 112

Marshall, Secretary of State George C., 111
Marty, Martin E., 381
Marxism, 370-71
Maslin, Simeon J., 274
Maslow, Will, 42, 59, 299
Maternal and Child Health Care Program, 212
Mazon: A Jewish Response to Hunger, 359, 374
McCarthy, Senator Joseph, 287
McCollum v. Board of Education, 46, 269
McVeigh trial, 51
Meany, George, 115
Medding, Peter, 28
Medicare, 196-97, 205, 211-12
Meir, Golda, 54
melamed (school teacher), 313
melting pot, 18, 80, 317, 343-44, 348, 353
The Merchant of Venice, 31
Messiah, 377
Methodists, xiii
Meyer, Rabbi Joel, 244
Meyer, Rabbi Marshal, 241
Middle East, 55, 72-73, 103, 113, 116-17, 121, 130, 133, 138, 140, 142-46, 148, 150-52, 154, 163, 170-75, 376; conflict(s), 138, 161; American military bases, 116; American policy in, 128, 172
Middle East Affairs Department, 118
Middle East Peace Commitments Act (MEPCA), 175
Middle East Review, 150
Middle East Studies Association (MESA), 150
Mikveh Israel Congregation, 264
militia activities, 51; groups, 61
Miller, Irving, 30
"Million Man March," 44
Minkoff, Isaiah, 84
Minyan, 372-73

Miraculous Living, 372
Mishkan Shalom, 357
Mitchell report, 164
Mitchell v. Helms, 323
Mitchell, George, 163
Mitzvah Day, 357
Mizrachi Organization of America, 106
Moline, Rabbi Jack, 244
Moment Magazine, 13-14, 126
Morais, Sabato, 237
Morgenstern, Julian, 267
Moscow, 48, 156, 227
Moses, Al (Alfred), 13, 42, 61, 149
Muslim(s) (Moslems), 79, 237, 357-58; fundamentalism, 51; groups, 142
Muslim Public Affairs Council (MPAC), 142
multiculturalism, 343, 348-49
Museum of Tolerance, 26

NAACP, 270
Nader (Ralph), 218
Nasser, 115
Nat PAC, 137
Nathan Perlmutter Institute for Jewish Advocacy, 226
Nation of Islam, 75
National Association of Arab Americans (NAAA), 140, 142
National Association of Jewish State Legislators, 194
National Clergymen's Committee, 286
National Coalition Building Institute, 223
National Committee for Public Education and Religious Liberty, 356
National Conference on Soviet Jewry, 48, 85, 87
National Conference of Catholic Bishops, 256
National Conference of Christians and Jews (NCCJ), 18, 357

National Conference of Jewish Communal Service, 187
National Council of Churches, 138, 256
National Council of Jewish Women (NCJW), 119, 166
National Council of Young Israel, 284
National Geographic, 55
National Jewish Commission on Law and Order (COLPA), 298
National (Jewish) Community Relations Advisory Council(s) (NJCRAC; NCRAC), 40-41, 68, 71, 83-89, 110, 118, 198, 287-28, 296-99, 300-1, 303-5; Joint Program Plan, 288, 304
National Jewish Democratic Council, 218
National Jewish Population Study (NJPS), xi, 219
National Jewish Population Survey, 155
National Jewish Welfare Board, 187
National Peace Process Advocacy Day, 154
National Public Radio (NPR), 147
National Religious Partnership for the Environment, 250
national religious circles, 126
National Solidarity Day for Soviet Jewry, 72
national unity government, 163
Nazi(s), 50, 74; anti-, 40; era, 50; march (Skokie), 44; neo-, 48, 73-74; period, 48; war criminals, 49, 248
Nazism, 108, 294; American supporters, 27
Negroes, 351
neoconservatism, 277, 305
Netanyahu, Benjamin (Prime Minister), 124, 157-59
Network of Jewish Renewal Communities, 363
New Deal-Fair Deal, 286

New Frontier, 292
The New Haggadah, 355
New Jewish Agenda, 125
"New Left," 44
New Square, 323
"new world order," 78
New York, 71, 85, 88, 91-92, 95, 106, 109, 123, 151, 157, 174, 189, 192, 195, 220, 225, 227; and black-Jewish relations, 45; and fair educational practices, 38
New York Federation, 95
New York Jewish Week, 92
New York State, 299; Anti-Trust Act, 4; Regents' Prayer, 46
New York Times, 49, 57, 160, 162, 225
New York University, 246
A New Zionism, 355
Niles, David K., 111
Nixon, Richard, 113, 116-17, 123-24, 136, 271
nonprofit agencies, 186
nonpublic schools, public aid for, 306
North Africa, 113, 171
North America, 314
North American Coalition for Religious Pluralism in Israel, 356
Nostra Aetate, 53
Novick, Peter, 69, 81
Nuremberg Laws, 34
Nussbaum, Daniel, 350
Nussbaum, Max, 38

Occident, 264
ohr l'goyim (light unto the nations), 330
Oklahoma City bombing, 61
Olasky, Marvin, 215-16
Old Testament, 331
Older American(s) Act, 193, 204, 213
Operation Peace for Galilee, 129
Opinion Research Center, University of Denver, 37

orach chayim (a way of life), 316
Orenstein, Rabbi Debra, 254
Organski, A. F. K., 137
The Origin of the Republican Form of Government, 265-66
Orthodox(y) (movement in Judaism), 167-68, 215, 219, 240, 242, 245, 258, 263, 268, 271, 273, 283-86, 288-290, 292-95, 297-99, 301, 303, 305, 313, 321-23, 325-26, 328, 344; advocacy, 298; communions, 138; community, 105, 126, 293, 297, 299-301, 304; constituency, 289; Jewish thought, 290; leaders, 106; liberal, 305; mainstream, 283-85, 288, 292-94, 298, 300-1, 305; modern, 284-85, 287, 289, 305-6, 317; rabbinate, 285-87, 289, 302; right, 300, 306; values, 304
Orthodox Union (OU), 93, 284-85, 287-88, 294-301, 303-5
OSI, 49
Oslo Accords, 86, 117, 124, 138, 142, 152-59, 163, 174; collapse of, 78. *See also* peace process
Overseas Needs Assessment and Distribution (ONAD), 169, 300, 302, 305, 325

PAC(s) (political action committees), 136-37; Jewish, 137; pro-Israel, 167
Palestine, 30, 107, 109-10, 125, 144, 354; British control over, 112; economic development in, 108; Jewish commonwealth in, 109; Jewish community in, 108; Jewish immigration into, 111; Jewish nation in, 107; Jewish settlement in, 105; national home for the Jewish people in, 107
Palestine Development Council, 108

Palestinian(s), 124, 130-131, 138-41, 143, 147, 152-53, 156, 158-63, 170-171, 173-74; Authority, 153, 161, 175; independence, 141; -Israeli negotiations, 163; and Israelis, 56; issue, 133, 175; people, 152, 170; population, 125-26; pro-, 138; refugees, 160; rejectionist camp, 79; self-determination, 140; sovereignty, 139; state, 124, 132, 175; track, 160; violence, 104, 161, 170, 174
Paradigm Shift, 365
Paris Peace Conference, 30, 107
parochial schools, 46, 323
Partnership 2000, 169
Paskind, Rabbi Lee, 244, 254
Passover, 268
peace conference, international, 123
"Peace for Galilee" campaign, 55
peace process, 77-78, 86-87, 91, 103-4, 112, 125-26, 152-53, 155-56, 158-59, 164; Israel and Egypt, 73
Pekelis, Alexander, 38-39, 61
Pelavin, Michael, 135
Penn, William, 273
Pennsylvania, western 174
Pentagon, 175
peoplehood, 28
Percy, Senator Charles, 73, 137
Peres, Shimon, 123, 153-54, 157-58, 163
Perlmutter, Nathan, 58
Persian Gulf, 171; crisis, 133; states, 151; War, 104, 156
Personal Responsibility and Work Opportunity Reconciliation Act of 1996, 211
Petegorsky, David, 38-39, 59-60
Pfeffer, Leo, 46-47, 59-60, 84, 295-96, 298
Philadelphia, 29, 251

philanthropy, 7
Philipson, Rabbi David, 265-66
Pierpoint, Robert, 55
pikuah nefesh (saving/preserving life), 254
Pledge of Allegiance, 262
PLO, 45, 75, 122, 124, 129-30, 132, 138, 143, 146-47, 152, 170
pluralism, 51, 56, 60, 80, 269, 273, 323, 345; Christian, 273; in Israel, xiv
Po'alai Zion, 106
Poland, Jews in, 29
Poles, relations with, 79
politics of consensus, 20
polity, church, 8
Pollard, Jonathan, 130-31
Pompidou, President Georges, 71
A Portrait of the American Jewish Community, 189
Powell, General Colin, 163
prayer, in the public schools, 46-47, 272; at public school sporting events, 251, 253; nondenominational, 299-300; public and silent, 18
prejudice, 36-38, 45, 60; anti-Jewish, 53; German, 48
Prejudice, 37
Presbyterian Church (USA), 138
Presbyterians, xiii
Prinz, Joachim, 30
privatization, 7
pro-choice, 328
Program for Jewish Life (1950), 350
Progressive Judaism, 261
Progressive movement, 5
Project Interchange, 145
Promised Land, 379
prophetic model, 261
prophetic tradition, 69
Protestant(s), xiv, 4, 34, 52, 111, 138-39, 263, 296; communities, 138; evangelical and fun-

damentalist, 137; liberal, 137; mainline, 138; pluralism, 263; traditions, 53
Protestant Film Commission, 37
Protocols of the Elders of Zion, 32
public affairs, 99, 119
Public Affairs Committee (Chicago), 71-75, 82
Public Broadcasting System (PBS), 147
public education, 248, 390
public funding for religious day schools, 76
public policy, xiv, 20, 91, 94
public relations, 56
public schools, 94, 274-75, 287; Bible readings in, 47; nonsectarian, 266
public sector, 14
public sphere, xiv, 20, 69, 71, 74, 81-83, 86, 91, 98-99, 103, 131, 167, 237, 243, 284-85, 304-6, 311, 313, 315-16, 318, 320-22, 324, 329, 346, 363
public square, 100, 103, 105, 145, 172, 174, 244, 248, 250-52, 254-59, 283, 285-87, 292, 294, 297-300, 302, 304, 316, 320, 323-26, 328-32, 337, 383, 389-90; and haredim, 319; and Reconstructionism, 337; religion-free, 300
Putnam, Robert, ix-x

Quaker, 138
quota(s), 28, 32, 37, 39

Raab, Earl, 83-84, 87
Rabbinic Letter on the Poor, 254
Rabbinical Assembly (RA), 238-39, 241, 243-44, 250-57, 259, 344; Executive Council, 253; Resolutions Committee, 253
Rabbinical Council of America (RCA), 285-87, 289-90, 295, 297-98, 300-3; Halakhah Commission of, 289; Social Action Committee, 244
Rabin, Prime Minister Yitzhak, 77, 131, 136, 152-54, 156-57, 159
Rabinovich, Israeli Ambassador Itamar, 13, 157
Rabin-Peres years, 158, 160
race, 51, 95
racism, 58, 60, 118, 151, 342
rahamim (compassion), 254
Ramallah, 162
Ramer, Bruce, 61
Randolph, A. Philip, 143
Reagan, President Ronald, 49, 116, 122-23, 139, 214; administration, 184, 198-99; revolution, 271
The Reconstructionist, 340, 342, 346, 350, 352-56
Reconstruction era, 265
Reconstructionism, 337, 342, 345, 351, 368
Reconstructionism Today, 355
Reconstructionist (movement), 106, 167, 219, 239, 340, 343-45, 347-55, 357-58; synagogue, first, 342; thought, 345, 352; tradition, 342
Reconstructionist Federation, 345
Reconstructionist Press, 352, 355
Reconstructionist Rabbinical Association, 346, 350, 358
Reconstructionist Rabbinical College, 345, 354-58
Rees, Susan, 224
Reform (movement in Judaism), xiv, 105, 109, 144, 155, 160, 167-68, 219, 237-38, 240, 242, 244-45, 247, 255, 257-59, 261-67, 270-77, 284, 286, 299, 303, 331; activism, 268-69; circles, 264; community, 266, 269; congregations, 273; day schools, 274-75; Jewish thought, 273, 277; Israeli, 273;

rabbinate, 106, 109, 274; strategy, 268; summer camps, 160
Reform Jewish Academy, 274
Reform Judaism, Social Action Commission, 126
Reformers, 263
Refugee Act, 248
Refugee Facts, 34
Rehnquist, William H., 271
religion and state. *See* church and state
Religious Action Center (RAC), 262, 270-73, 275
Religious Coalition for Reproductive Choice (Rights), 251-52, 256, 356
Religious Freedom Restoration Act (RFRA), 79, 272
religious groups, xxi, 72; use of public facilities, 18
religious intolerance, 18
religious liberty, 270
Religious Liberty Protection Act (RLPA), 272
religious revival, 75
religious right, 328
religious symbols on public property, 18
religious tolerance, 15
Republican(s), 13, 153-54, 159, 187, 200, 202, 214-16, 218-19, 271, 276, 283
Republican Party, 109, 214, 240; national convention, 110
Reuther, Walter, 115
Revisionists, 354
Robertson, Rev. Pat, 216
Roe v. Wade, 302-3
Rogers Plan, 124
Roof, Wade Clark, 381-82
Roosevelt, Eleanor, 115
Rosenberg, Julius and Ethel, 287
Rosenman, Judge Samuel I., 111
Rosenthal, Hannah, 97
Rosenwald, Lessing, 109
Ross, Dennis, 154, 162
Roth, David, 223

Rothschild, Lord, 107
Rousseau, 311
Rubin, Lawrence (Larry), 90, 96-97
Rubinstein, Elyakim, 162
Rudin, Rabbi A. James, 50, 53
Russia(n), 29, 48, 156; anti-Semitic, 77; American Jewish policy toward, 48; immigrants, 135; -U.S. trade treaty, 28
Rustin, Bayard, 143

Sabbath (Shabbat), 3, 81, 235, 265, 324; observers, 287, 304
Sabra and Shatila, 130, 146
Sadat, Anwar, 73, 127-28, 173
Saddam Hussein, 133, 152, 156
Salvation Army, 210
Sandel, Michael, 347
Santa Fe Independent School District v. Doe, 272
Saperstein, Rabbi David, 144, 271-72, 275-76
Saudi Arabia, 128, 133, 136, 139, 145, 149, 151, 175
scapegoating, 37
Schachter-Shalomi, Zalman, 364-66, 368, 372-73, 375, 378-81
Schechter, Solomon, 106, 182-83, 237
Schick, Marvin, 298
Schiff, Jacob, 27-28, 58, 105
Schindler, Rabbi Alexander, 126-27
Schrag, Philip, 222
Schulman, Rabbi Samuel, 267, 276
Schulweis, Rabbi Harold, 59
Schwarz, Rabbi Sidney, 346
Second Temple, 263
Second Vatican Council, 53
secularism, 369
Security Council, 151
Selig, Martha, 187
Seminarians Interacting program, 357
Seminario Rabbinico, 241

Index

Senate, 28, 129, 137
Senate Foreign Relations Committee, 137
Sephardi rabbis, 237, 327
Sephardim, 3, 237
Serving the Jewish Polity: The Application of Jewish Political Theory to Jewish Communal Practice, 223
settlements, 86, 125-27, 135, 138, 160
Shamir, Prime Minister, 123, 132, 134-36, 152
Shanks, Hershel, 13
Shapiro, Rami, 364, 372-74
Sharansky, Natan, 160, 162
Sharon, Ariel (Prime Minister), 114, 132, 161-63, 175
Shas (Sephardic Torah Guardians party), 160, 327
shehitah (ritual slaughter), 288
Sherer, Rabbi Morris, 295, 298
shtadlan, 27, 29, 118
shtetl (Jewish village), 313
Shultz, Secretary of State, 122
Siegman, Rabbi Henry, 55-56, 59, 126
Silver, Dr. Abba Hillel, 109-10, 115
Silverman, Ira, 60
Simon Wiesenthal Center, 26
Simon, Rabbi Charles, 244
Sinai (Peninsula), 115-16, 118
Sinai Health Systems, 206
Sinai, 127, 341
Sivan, Emmanuel, 318
Six-Day War, 7, 43, 69-70, 72, 84, 96, 104, 110-11, 117-19, 125-26, 129, 137, 140, 143-44, 167
Skirball Institute on American Values, 51
Skokie, 74-75
Slawson, John, 36, 54, 59-60
Smith, Benjamin, 79
Smucker, Bob, 222
social action, 155, 358
Social Action Center, 244

Social Action Commission, 358
Social Action Committee, 250, 252, 254
social action groups, 72
social activism, 15, 182
social behavior, 62
social change, 58
social contract (theory), 311-13, 317
social issues, 139
social justice, 15-16, 70, 82, 87, 90, 265
Social Justice Committee, 267
social justice projects, 356
social progressive movement, 15
Social Security reform, 213
social welfare, 92, 98, 181, 185, 187, 217-18; lobby, 226
socialism, 371
socialist and labor factions, 29
Society for the Advancement of Judaism (SAJ), 342, 344-45
Soloveitchik, Rabbi Joseph B., 289-93, 305
South Africa, 131, 143
Southern Brooklyn Community Organization, 325
Soviet bloc, 115
Soviet expansionism, 116
Soviet Union, 48, 75-77, 87, 104, 112, 115-16, 135, 168, 210, 227, 325, 376; FSU (former Soviet Union), 209-10; human rights in, 136
Spanish and Portuguese, 3
Squadron, Howard, 59
SSI, 211-12
State Department, 33, 48, 107, 111-12, 121, 142
State Legalization Impact Assistance Grant, 206
Staub, Rabbi Jacob, 346
stereotypes, 31; anti-Jewish, 45
Stern, Marc, 46, 215
Stern, Walter, 149
Straits of Tiran, 116
Straus, Oscar (S.), 27-28, 58, 265

Studies in Prejudice, 36
Suez Campaign, 114-15
Suez crisis, 135
Sunday burials, 205
Sunday laws, 265-66, 287
Supreme Court, 17, 47, 94, 262, 267-68, 270-72, 299-302, 323, 328, 330
Survey Committee, 34
Survey Research Center, 52
survivors group, 75
Susser, Bernard, 363, 382
Synagogue Council of America, 53, 287, 298-99
Syria, 72, 114, 125, 156, 159-60, 165, 171; and Jewish citizens, 55
Syrian(s), 152, 159
Szold, Henrietta, 106, 108

t'shuvah, 82
Taba, talks at, 161
Taft, President, 28, 32
Taft-Hartley Act, 286
Talisman, Mark, 210, 222
Talmud, 238, 317, 370
Talmud Torah(s), 294
Tanenbaum, Rabbi Marc, 53
TANF (Temporary Assistance Program for Needy Families), 211-12
Task Force on Homelessness, 205
Task Force on Hunger, 205
Tel Aviv, 154, 157
Temple Mount, 161
Temple University, 365
Ten Commandments, display of, 272
Tenet, George, 164
territorial compromise, 125, 139
terrorism, 49, 97, 124, 170, 174-75
Teutsch, Rabbi David, 346
Thanksgiving, 352
Third Council, 264
Third World, 143-44
Thompson, Jim, 202

Tikkun, 364, 378
tikkun ha-nefesh, 377
tikkun olam, 82, 181, 186, 196, 215, 252, 331, 357, 364, 374, 377
tikkun, personal, 377
Title XX Social Services, 193, 202, 213
torah as man-made, 368
Torah, 236, 251, 288-89, 368-69, 371, 379-80; covenant of, 317; ideals, 304; view, 328
Torah Umesorah (National Society for Hebrew Day Schools), 294, 296
Toward Tradition, 305
Tradition, 290
Trainin, Rabbi Isaac, 296
Trends and Issues in Jewish Social Welfare in the United States, 1899-1958, 187
tribalism, domestic, 80
Truman administration, 112
Truman, President Harry S, 111, 115
The Turbulent Decades—Jewish Communal Services in America 1958-1978, 188
Twersky, Professor Isadore, 292, 305
twinning relationships, 77
tzedakah, 181, 183, 254, 292, 350, 357, 373-74
"Tzedakah (charity) Collective," 275-76

U.S. aid package, 159; arms sales, 115; Army manual, 31; foreign aid program, 139; foreign policy, 103; law, 122; national interests, 173; policy, 103-4, 121, 130, 174; policy makers, 138; presidential race (2000), 161
U.S. Civil Rights Act (1964), 288
U.S. Conference of Catholic Bishops, 138-39

U.S. Department of Agriculture, 324
U.S. Department of Health and Human Services, 166
U.S. Department of Housing and Urban Development (HUD), 208, 210
U.S. House of Representatives, 264
U.S.-Israel alliance, 173; partnership, 112; relationship(s), 165, 173
U.S.-Middle East Policy, 89
U.S.-Soviet trade relations, 226
U.S. Trade Representative, 140
UJA-Federation of New York, 91, 169, 220
Ukrainian community, 77
UN, 48, 112-13, 124, 134, 143, 151, 156-57, 170, 247-48
UN Monitoring, Verification and Inspection Commission, 156-57
UN Partition Plan, 111-12
UN Security Council, 115
UN Security Council Resolutions 242 and 338, 122
UN World Conference on Women, 57
Unborn Victims of Violence Act, 252
Understanding Jewish History, 57
Union for Traditional Judaism, 239
Union of American Hebrew Congregations (UAHC), 5, 86, 92, 105, 109, 132, 244-45, 259, 264-65, 270, 274-75; General Assembly, 274
Union of Orthodox Jewish Congregations of America (UOJCA), 119, 244, 259, 284
Union of Orthodox Rabbis (Agudath Harabonim), 285
Union Seminary Quarterly Review, 254
United Autoworkers, 145

United Israel Appeal, 161
United Jewish Agency, 109
United Jewish Appeal (UJA), 6, 95, 117, 161, 169, 183, 195, 200, 212
United Jewish Charities, 5
United Jewish Communities (UJC), 95, 97, 161, 169, 183-84, 194, 198-99, 208, 211-13
United Kingdom, 2, 4
United States, xii, 2-8, 15, 27, 32, 35, 39, 42, 44, 48, 52-56, 61, 74, 79, 105, 111-17, 119, 122-24, 128, 130, 133-36, 138, 140, 142, 144-47, 150-54, 156-58, 160, 162-66, 170-75, 184-85, 187-88, 190, 196, 206, 209-13, 220, 223, 225, 247-48, 250, 261-64, 266-70, 272, 274, 277, 284, 289, 294, 317, 319-21, 326, 328, 333, 348, 358, 370, 380. *See also* U.S.; America
"The United States—A Christian Nation," 266
United Synagogue for Conservative Judaism (USCJ), 238, 241, 243-45, 252-54, 256-57, 259
United Way of America, 202, 210
United Way of Metropolitan Chicago, 202
United Ways of Illinois, 202
Universal Pictures, 31
University of Judaism, 241, 254
University of Wisconsin, 44
UNSCOM, 156
USSR, 72, 209, 376. *See* also Soviet Union

Va'ad Hatzalah, 321
values-based dialogue, 347
Vatican, 53, 81, 139
victimization, psychology of, 80
Vietnam War, 54, 57, 368
Vigilance Committee, 30
Voluntary Agency Matching Grant, 208
Vorspan, Al, 275

voucher(s) (school), 76, 93-94, 246, 249, 275, 283, 298, 353

Wallace, Mike, 148
war criminals, 74
Warren years, 270
Washington Action Office, 166, 194, 199, 208, 210-11, 213, 223
Washington, D.C., 8, 13-14, 54-55, 82, 86-88, 113, 118, 121, 127, 129, 135, 137-38, 141, 143, 149, 154, 164-65, 167, 173-74, 184, 194, 197-99, 201, 204, 207-9, 211-14, 225, 244-45, 247, 250, 252, 259, 262, 264-66, 270-71, 304, 380, 390; Arab embassies in, 111
Washington Hebrew Congregation, 270
Washington Post, 225
Washington's Birthday, 352
Washofsky, Rabbi Dr. Mark, 274
Waskow, Arthur, 363-64, 368-72, 375, 378, 380-82
WASPs, 358
Watson, Thomas, 30
weapons of mass destruction, 156
Webster et al. v. Reproductive Health Services et al., 328
Weekly Standard, 215
Weinberg, Rabbi Charles, 295
Weinberger, Caspar, 130
Weiss, Samson, 297, 300
Weizmann, Dr. Chaim, 108-9, 112
welfare services, xiii
Western European and Others Group (WEOG), 151
Wertheimer, Jack, 24, 93-94, 244
West Bank, 125-26, 131, 133, 139-40, 149-50, 152, 158-61
Western civilization, 313, 315
Western democracies, 236
Western Europe, 143, 149, 171
Western interests, 116
Western society, secular, 317
Western values, 316

Western Wall plaza, 277
White ethnic behavior, 51
White House, 49-50, 111-12, 121, 129, 135, 142, 152, 157, 164, 211
White House Conference on Moral Standards, 301
White House Office on Faith-Based and Community Initiatives, x
White Paper, British, 109, 111
Who is a Jew?, 55, 243
Williams, J. Paul, 352
Wilson, President Woodrow, 31-32, 106-7
Wise, Isaac Mayer, 264, 266
Wise, Rabbi Stephen, 27-28, 30, 38-39, 58-61, 106-7, 111
With Roots in Heaven, 372, 382
WNET, 147
WNYC, 147
Wolf, Simon A., 264
women, equal rights for, 248; status of, 56; welfare of, 57
Women's Division, 57
Women's League for Conservative Judaism (WLCJ), 241, 243-44, 246-47, 249, 252-53, 259
World Conference against Racism, Racial Discrimination, Xenophobia, and Related Intolerance (WCAR), 170
World Jewish Congress, 53, 114, 247
World Trade Center, 175
World War I, 5, 31, 41, 46, 59, 106, 110, 237, 267
World War II, 35, 41, 43, 47, 59, 104, 109-10, 150, 175, 241, 249, 253, 268, 285, 287-88, 293, 350; post-, 18, 25, 69, 83, 110-11, 283-84
World Zionist Organization (WZO), 105, 108
Wuthnow, Robert, x-xi
Wye River agreement, 158-59, 171

Yad Mordechai Fund, 357
Yamit, 127
Yanowitz, Bennett, 165
Yavneh, 289
Yemen, 165
yeshiva education, 238; federal aid to, 324
Yeshiva University, 285, 289, 293, 299, 303, 306
yeshiva world, 318-19
yeshivas, European, 293
Yiddish, 268, 294, 318
Yishuv, 108
Yisrael B'Aliyah party, 160
YMCA of Metropolitan Chicago, 202
YMHA, 340
Yom Ha'Atzmaut, 81
Yom Kippur, 374
Yom Kippur War, 72, 84, 110-11, 117-18, 129, 146, 148, 167, 374
Yosef, Rabbi Ovadia, 327
Young Israel, 284, 288-89, 294-300; National Council, 293
Young, Andrew, 45, 75, 143
Yugoslavia, former, 142

YWCA, 340

Zemer, Rabbi Dr. Moshe, 273-74
Zionism, 15, 27, 38, 103, 105-6, 108-9, 111, 141, 144, 151, 173, 284, 354-55; American, 108; European, 109
"Zionism equals racism," 170
Zionist advocacy, 118; agenda, 26, 30; anti-, 107, 112; aspirations, 107; camp, 28-29; cause, 106; commitment, 60; Congress, 104-5; establishment, 108-9; groups, 56, 72, 109-10, 365; idea, 119; ideology, 38; Labor, 106; movement, 104-7, 128; non-, 14, 25, 54, 60, 107, 109-10, 113; post-, 167; pro-, 106, 111, 284; societies, 106;
Zionist Organization of America (ZOA), 108-9, 114, 153, 158
Zionist(s), American, 108-9; European, 108
Zogby, Jim, 140-41
Zorach v. Clausen, 269
Zweibel, David, 315

About the Contributors

Allan Arkush is associate professor of Judaic studies and history at Binghamton University. He is the author of *Moses Mendelssohn and the Enlightenment* and coeditor of *Perspectives on Jewish Thought and Mysticism*. His articles on modern Jewish thought and history have appeared in *Jewish Social Studies, Modern Judaism, AJS Review*, and other periodicals.

Joel M. Carp is senior vice president of the Jewish United Fund/Jewish Federation of Metropolitan Chicago, where he is responsible for community services, grants development and government programs. He is the author of more than two dozen published papers dealing with social policy and social welfare, poverty in the Jewish community, refugee resettlement, mental health and social work services, and voluntarism. He has a Masters of Social Work from the Wurzweiler School of Social Work, Yeshiva University, and is a member of the Academy of Certified Social Workers.

Daniel J. Elazar (1934-1999) was a leading political scientist and specialist in the study of the Jewish political tradition, Israel, and the world Jewish community. He was founder and president of the Jerusalem Center for Public Affairs, professor of political science at Temple University in Philadelphia, and Senator N.M. Paterson Professor in intergovernmental relations at Bar-Ilan University in Israel. He was the author or editor of more than sixty books, including a four-volume study of the *Covenant Tradition in Politics*, as well as *Community and Polity, The Jewish Polity*, and *People and Polity*, a trilogy on Jewish political and community organization from earliest times to the present. He also founded and edited the scholarly journal *Jewish Political Studies Review*.

Gordon M. Freeman, an associate of the Jerusalem Center for Public Affairs, has served as the rabbi of Congregation B'nai Shalom, Walnut Creek, California, since 1968. He holds a Ph.D. in political science from the University of California, Berkeley, and writes on Jewish political themes. A member of the editorial board of the *Jewish Political Studies Review,* he is currently an officer of the Rabbinical Assembly.

Lawrence Grossman is editor of the *American Jewish Year Book* and associate director of research for the American Jewish Committee.

Samuel Heilman holds the Harold Proshansky Professorship in Jewish studies and sociology at the City University of New York. His books include *Cosmopolitans and Parochials: Modern Orthodox Jews in America* (coauthored with Steven M. Cohen), *Defenders of the Faith: Inside Ultra-Orthodox Jewry, Portrait of American Jewry: The Last Half of the 20th Century,* and *When a Jew Dies.*

Michael C. Kotzin is executive vice president of the Jewish Federation of Metropolitan Chicago, a position he has held since 1999. Dr. Kotzin served on the faculty of the Department of English at Tel Aviv University from 1968 until 1979, when he began his current career as a Jewish communal professional, and he has written extensively on communal issues and world affairs.

Martin J. Raffel is associate executive director of the Jewish Council for Public Affairs (JCPA). At the JCPA since 1987, he has been responsible for staffing the agency's Task Force on Israel and Other International Concerns. Prior to that he worked in Philadelphia for the American Jewish Committee and the American Jewish Congress.

Lance J. Sussman was associate professor of American Jewish history at Binghamton University and is currently rabbi at Keneset Israel (Reform) in Elkins Park, Pennsylvania. He is the author of *Isaac Leeser and the Making of American Judaism,* editor of *Reform Judaism in America: A Biographical Dictionary and Source Book,* and associate editor of the forthcoming *Encyclopedia of the State of New York.*